Helping Skills

Helping Skills

Facilitating Exploration, Insight, and Action

Second Edition

Clara E. Hill

American Psychological Association

Washington, DC

First Printing February 2004
Second Printing June 2004

Published by
American Psychological Association
750 First Street, NE
Washington, DC 20002
www.apa.org

To order
APA Order Department
P.O. Box 92984
Washington, DC 20090-2984
Tel: (800) 374-2721; Direct: (202) 336-5510
Fax: (202) 336-5502; TDD/TTY: (202) 336-6123
Online: www.apa.org/books/
E-mail: order@apa.org

In the U.K., Europe, Africa, and the Middle East, copies may be ordered from
American Psychological Association
3 Henrietta Street
Covent Garden, London
WC2E 8LU England

Typeset in Meridien by Stephen McDougal, Mechanicsville, MD

Printer: United Book Press, Inc., Baltimore MD
Cover Designer: Minker Design, Bethesda, MD
Technical/Production Editor: Casey Ann Reever
Cover art: Paul Gaugin, *Breton Girls Dancing, Pont-Aven*, Collection of Mr. and Mrs. Paul Mellon, Image © 2003 Board of Trustees, National Gallery of Art, Washington, DC, 1888, oil on canvas.

The opinions and statements published are the responsibility of the author, and such opinions and statements do not necessarily represent the policies of the American Psychological Association.

Library of Congress Cataloging-in-Publication Data

Hill, Clara E., 1948–
    Helping skills : facilitating exploration, insight, and action / Clara E. Hill.— 2nd ed.
        p. cm.
Includes bibliographical references and index.
    ISBN 1-59147-104-4 (hardcover : alk. paper)
    1. Counseling—Textbooks. 2. Helping behavior—Textbooks. I. Title.
    BF637.C6H46 2004
    158'.3—dc22   2003026067

British Library Cataloguing-in-Publication Data
A CIP record is available from the British Library.

Printed in the United States of America

To my husband, Jim Gormally, my fellow traveler in the process of learning helping skills; to my children, Kevin and Katie, who have tested my helping skills; and to my students, who have taught me how to teach helping skills.

Contents

Part I. Overview

1

11

Part III. Insight Stage

12

13

Part IV. Action Stage

Labs

Preface

M y interest in training helpers has developed from teaching helping skills classes to undergraduate and graduate students for about 30 years. When I first taught these courses, I felt frustrated trying to find the right textbook that would embody my philosophy of helping and address the needs of my students. Few, if any, helping skills texts integrate the importance of affect, cognition, and behavior in the process of change. Some texts concentrate on feelings while disregarding the role of challenge and action in facilitating critical life changes, whereas others highlight insight at the expense of affective exploration and behavioral change. Several popular texts focus solely on a problem-solving approach, which neglects the critical role of affect in helping clients express, understand, and alter the dissatisfactions in their lives. Other books do not provide the crucial theoretical and empirical foundation for the helping skills. To address these limitations, I used the knowledge garnered from my experiences as a student, teacher, counselor, supervisor, and researcher to write a book that teaches helpers to assist clients in exploring their feelings and thoughts, gaining new insights about their problems, and moving toward positive behavioral changes.

This text introduces an integrated model that is grounded in practice, theory, and research. Grounding the model in practice and theory is important to take advantage of the work of accomplished clinicians and theoreticians who have articulated a rich theoretical knowledge base. Rogers, Freud, Erikson, Mahler, Skinner, Ellis, Beck, and others have provided brilliant insights into the nature of human beings, the mechanisms of change in counseling and therapy, and the techniques for assisting individuals to achieve their potential and accomplish their goals. The three-stage model is grounded in the contributions of these sage theorists, and readers are introduced to the salient aspects of their work.

Grounding the model in research is also important. Research educates helpers about the effective (and ineffective) use of helping skills. My confidence in promoting the helping skills is strengthened by the knowledge that these skills have been tested empirically and found to be useful to clients. Of course, research on helping skills is still in its infancy, so there is much that we do not know. I hope that by providing a clear model of the helping process, more people will take on the task of doing empirical research testing the model (see also the companion text, Hill, 2001, on empirical foundations).

The model involves three stages: exploration, insight, and action. The exploration stage is based on client-centered theory (e.g., Rogers, 1942, 1951, 1957, 1959). The foundation for the insight stage is psychoanalytic and interpersonal theories (e.g., Freud, 1940/1949; Teyber, 2000; Yalom, 1980). Behavioral (e.g., Goldfried & Davison, 1994; Kazdin, 2001; D. L. Watson & Tharp, 2002) and cognitive (J. S. Beck, 1995) theories form the foundation for the action stage. The three major theories are integrated in this model because all have proven to be effective in helping clients (see Wampold, 2001).

I conceptualize the helping process as comprising moment-by-moment interactional sequences. Using a tested theory of the interactions between helpers and clients (Hill, 1992), I postulate that at any moment in the helping process, helpers develop intentions for how they want to help clients. These intentions are based on what they know about clients and what they hope to accomplish with clients at a given time. With these intentions in mind, helpers select verbal and nonverbal skills with which to intervene. In turn, clients react to the interventions in ways that influence how they then choose to behave with helpers. Thus, helping involves not only the overt behaviors but also the cognitive processes of helpers (i.e., intentions) and clients (i.e., reactions). Awareness of intentions assists helpers in selecting effective interventions. In addition, attention to the clients' reactions to the interventions can aid helpers in planning future interventions.

Finally, I sought to write a book that both supports students' development as helpers and provides challenges to facilitate the development of helping skills. Becoming an effective helper is an exciting and challenging process. For some, this undertaking can be life changing. Many students are fascinated by the process of becoming helpers, and they pose thoughtful questions as they struggle to learn the skills and develop confidence in their ability to assist others. Because the focus of this book is on helpers (not clients), I pose many questions that relate to the helpers' development and concomitant feelings and thoughts.

It is necessary to clarify the focus of this book by indicating what this text does not provide. This book is not intended to provide information about counseling children, families, or clients who have serious emotional or psychological difficulties. Although the helping skills taught in this book are crucial and form the foundation for work with all these groups, helpers will need much more extensive and specialized training before they will be qualified to work with these groups.

Furthermore, I do not address the diagnosis of psychological problems or identify characteristics of psychopathology, which are two important topics that require extensive additional training. I encourage helpers to pursue further training in assessment and psychopathology after developing a working knowledge of basic helping skills. I believe that all helpers, even those working with healthy populations, should be able to recognize serious psychological disorders. This level of knowledge allows helpers to make appropriate referrals and to work only with clients they have been trained to assist.

In addition, this book touches briefly on the myriad cross-cultural issues related to helping. I believe that the influence of culture is pervasive and is reflected in the helping process through the client's and helper's worldviews and the interaction between them. Clients need to be viewed in the context of the multitude of influences that have an impact on their lives (e.g., family and friends, support systems, racial and cultural background, work experiences, life transitions, socioeconomic status). I strongly encourage helpers to educate themselves about multicultural theory and research (e.g., Atkinson, Morten, & Sue, 1993; Helms & Cook, 1999; Pedersen, Draguns, Lonner, & Trimble, 2002; Ponterotto, Casas, Suzuki, & Alexander, 2001; Sue & Sue, 1999).

I have several goals for those who read this book and complete the exercises. Readers should be able to articulate the principles of the integrated three-stage model of helping as well as the theoretical and research foundations underlying this model. They should demonstrate an understanding of the interactional sequences of helping, including the intentions that helpers have for interventions with clients, the helping skills that are commensurate with these intentions, the possible reactions and behaviors demonstrated by clients, and the means by which helpers evaluate the interventions used. In addition, readers should gain a better understanding of themselves relative to becoming helpers, including their thoughts about helping as well as their strengths and areas for continued growth. Finally, I hope to instill enthusiasm for the process of learning to help others—an enterprise that is certain to provide countless challenges and rewards throughout a lifetime.

The second edition of this book differs from the first edition in several ways. First, most of the reviews of the research have been deleted from this book and put in a companion text (Hill, 2001), so that the research can be covered more thoroughly. I strongly suggest that readers use both texts concurrently, so that they can learn the skills and also learn the empirical foundation for the skills. Second, the chapter on challenges has been changed to make it clearer and easier to learn. Third, the structure of the action stage has been changed markedly. Rather than conceptualizing the action stage as a set of discrete skills, I now talk about it as a set of steps. This revision allowed me to incorporate more of the current thinking about action in a coherent way that is easier to teach. Fourth, I have included more references to culture throughout the book. Because there is so much more awareness now of the influence of culture on the helping process, I wanted to draw attention to these issues throughout the book. Although there is still not enough research to specifically identify how culture influences each of the individual skills, I make some guesses about its influence in all the chapters. Fifth, I have shifted the chapter on open questions so it is now before restatement. Given that most people already know how to use open questions to some extent, it makes it easier to start by focusing on a skill with which they have some strength. Sixth, I have focused more on the helper as a coach who helps clients arrive at insight in the insight stage rather than as the dispenser of challenges and interpretations. Seventh, I have clarified the use of self-disclosure in the three different stages. Self-disclosure is an interesting skill because it mimics several other skills (e.g., helpers can disclose to encourage clients to get into feelings, to gain insight, or to suggest strategies for action), so it was important to clarify its uses in the different stages. Eighth, I have included more information in the final chapter about how helping skills are used within the context of therapy, specifically focusing on session management and dealing with difficult clients.

I have also created a Web site (www.apa.org/books/resources/hill) to accompany this edition of the book. It provides additional resources, such as sample test questions and syllabi for instructors and, for students, additional practice exercises and downloadable electronic versions of the scales and research material that I refer to throughout the text.

Finally, I have included several measures on the Web site that people can use to assess the influence of training. Specifically, Hill and Kellems (2002) developed several measures (Helping Skills Measure, Relationship Scale, Session Evaluation Scale) that can be completed by helpers and clients after sessions to assess whether helpers are able to implement the skills they have learned in an actual session with a client (see Web Form I). Lent, Hill, and Hoffman (2003) developed a measure of self-efficacy to assess helpers' feelings of confidence in their helping abilities (see Web Form K). Williams, Hurley, O'Brien, and DeGregorio (2003) have developed a measure that can be used to help assess trainee self-awareness and strategies for managing stress during sessions (Web Form J). I hope that much more empirical work will be done on the effects of training in helping skills before the next edition of this book.

Acknowledgments

am very grateful for the many people who have read selected chapters or all of this book and have provided valuable feedback on one or both editions: Margaret Barott, Elizabeth Doschek, Lisa Flores, Suzanne Friedman, Melissa Goates, Julie Goldberg, Jim Gormally, Allison Grolnick, Beth Haverkamp, Jeff Hayes, Kelly Hennessey, Debby Herbenick, Pamela Highlen, Merris Hollingworth, Ian Kellems, Sarah Knox, Misty Kolchakian, Jim Lichtenberg, Rayna Markin, John Norcross, Sheetal Patel, David Petersen, Missy Roffman, Eric Spiegel, Jessica Stahl, Nicole Taylor, Linda Tipton, Terry Tracey, Heather Walton, and Elizabeth Nutt Williams. I profited considerably from the editorial feedback, guidance, and encouragement of Beth Beisel, Amy Clarke, Phuong Huynh, Linda McCarter, Casey Reever, and Susan Reynolds, all from the American Psychological Association books program.

I am most indebted to the many students in both my undergraduate course in helping skills and graduate course in theories and strategies of counseling over the last several years. They have taught me a tremendous amount about how to teach helping skills by their willingness to challenge my ideas, their thoughtful perspectives on the process of becoming helpers, and by providing examples for the text. I tried out all the chapters and the lab exercises on several classes before including them in the book. Finally, and with much gratitude, I recognize and acknowledge my therapist, professors, and supervisors, who served as wonderful models for how to use helping skills and provided much encouragement throughout my process of becoming a helper. I particularly want to acknowledge Bill Anthony (who studied with Robert Carkhuff), from whom I first learned helping skills many years ago in graduate school. I clearly recall the heady times of coming to believe that I could help clients if I applied the helping skills.

I

Overview

Introduction to Helping

Nothing in life is achieved without effort, daring to take risks, and often some suffering.

—Erich Fromm

ngeli was a stellar student and athlete. She was president of her high school class and had been accepted into an elite eastern university. By any standard, she was an exceptional and talented individual with much promise. However, after arriving at college, Angeli began to exhibit sadness and inactivity. Much to the dismay of her family, teachers, and friends, she lost interest in interacting with others, studying for her classes, and attending track practice. Angeli's track coach encouraged her to meet with a helper, who helped Angeli explore her feelings and gain understanding of the issues underlying her sadness and inactivity. Angeli felt supported by, cared for, and challenged by her helper. The helping relationship enabled her to express, understand, struggle with, and overcome the feelings of inadequacy, loneliness, and loss that emerged when she left home for college.

As you read about Angeli and think about what it would be like to be her helper, you may have contradictory thoughts and feelings. You may feel confident that you could help someone like Angeli because you have listened to and advised friends and family members about their problems. But you may also feel anxiety about knowing how to help her explore her feelings and gain understanding.

If you are interested in learning more about the skills that would help you work with someone like Angeli, you have come to the right place. The first purpose of this book is to provide you with a theoretical framework that you can use to approach the helping process. The second purpose is to teach you specific skills to use in sessions with clients to help them explore, gain insight, and make changes in their lives. A third purpose is to get you started in the process of coming to think of yourself as a helper.

In this chapter, I provide an introduction to the helping process, define helping, and review facilitative and problematic aspects of helping. I then talk about what makes people seek out professional helpers, which leads naturally to a discussion about the effectiveness of helping. Next, I provide an introduction to the idea of becoming a helper, specifically exploring the healthy and unhealthy motivators for helping other people. Finally, I describe the organization of the book and discuss how it can best be used.

Welcome aboard! I hope you enjoy learning helping skills as much as I have.

What Is Helping?

Throughout this book, I use the terms *helper* to describe the individual providing assistance and *client* to indicate the person receiving support. *Helping* can be defined as one person assisting another in exploring feelings, gaining insight, and making changes in his or her life. Helpers and clients work together to achieve these outcomes, with helpers guiding the process and clients deciding what, when, and how they want to change. Helping is often an effective means for clients to obtain relief from emotional pain, discover a direction for their lives, and receive feedback that can facilitate change. Furthermore, the process of helping enables clients to experience healthy relationships, work toward personal growth, address existential concerns, and learn valuable skills.

Helping skills encompass both verbal and nonverbal forms of communication. These interventions include attending and listening behaviors, closed and open questions, restatements, reflections of feelings, approval and reassurance, silence, challenges, interpretations, self-disclosures, immediacy, information, and direct guidance. These skills have been shown by researchers to be effective in developing helping relationships with clients and assisting clients in improving their lives. Before focusing on the development of these skills, however, I articulate the similarities and differences among helping, counseling, and psychotherapy and then describe some facilitative and problematic aspects of helping.

HELPING VERSUS COUNSELING
VERSUS PSYCHOTHERAPY

Helping is a broad and generic term that includes the assistance provided by a variety of individuals such as friends, physicians, nurses, counselors, psychotherapists, and human service providers. Before one can consider oneself to be a counselor or therapist, more extensive training, practice, and supervision are needed than you will receive in this helping skills course. Beginning helpers can, of course, aspire to become counselors and therapists.

A final note relates to the differences between counseling and psychotherapy. At times, the two are differentiated by length of treatment (counseling may have fewer sessions than therapy); clientele (counseling is more often used with relatively "healthy" individuals who have issues with adjustment, whereas therapy serves those with more serious pathology); qualifications of the provider (counselors may have masters' or doctoral degrees, whereas therapists tend to be doctoral-level practitioners); and types of problems presented in sessions (counseling may deal with development and life transition issues, whereas therapy may address more serious psychological disturbances). However, this book is written from the perspective that counseling and psychotherapy are very similar, that helping skills form the foundation for both counseling and therapy, and that most individuals can benefit from learning basic helping skills.

FACILITATIVE ASPECTS OF HELPING

There are a number of ways in which helping can be facilitative. For people in emotional pain, effective helping can provide support and relief. For example, Jillian and Jesse came to couples counseling because Jillian had been involved in a sexual relationship with a colleague at work. Both Jillian and Jesse were extremely hurt and felt very angry with each other. Positive changes in their relationship came after months of working on communication skills, receiving assistance in exploring feelings, understanding the factors related to the affair, and learning how to work proactively to improve their relationship. After several sessions, Jillian and Jesse were able to communicate their feelings more openly, grieve the loss of trust in their relationship, and move toward rebuilding their lives as a cohesive and caring couple.

Helping can also assist individuals in making decisions about the direction of their lives. Sometimes, clients seek help with determining future plans. The most effective helpers have the ability to assist individuals in determining goals that are consistent with their dreams, values, and abilities. For example, Mai Lin came to counseling because she was uncertain about whether she should move far away from her family and end her relationship with her live-in boyfriend. She described her current situation and asked the helper to tell her what the best path for her would be. After dealing with her anger and frustration at the helper for not providing the answers, Mai Lin was able to explore her unwillingness to take responsibility for the direction of her life and her reluctance to address the questions that plagued her. She contemplated her fear of taking action and of making wrong decisions and connected this with feelings of helplessness she had experienced as a child of a battered woman. Further exploration of thoughts, feelings, and behaviors provided her with the desire to make small decisions (with the support and encouragement of her helper). Soon, Mai Lin was able to progress to more challenging decisions (e.g., ending her romantic relationship; moving across the country alone to explore her independence and to understand herself better).

An additional facilitative aspect of helping involves helpers providing feedback about how clients appear to others, information that others might hesitate to provide. For example, a client who is having difficulty maintaining relationships may be able to hear (from the helper) that he appears dependent and needy in sessions and may want to examine whether these behaviors are present in other relationships. Although helpers should phrase their comments in a gentle manner, honest feedback can be extremely helpful in motivating individuals to change.

Helping also can enable clients to experience healthy, nondamaging relationships with other people. Sometimes, the helping process is described as *reparenting* in that a caring relationship with a helper alleviates some of the hurtful and unhealthy interactions experienced with important figures early in life. For example, Kondja came to helping because she felt depressed and lacked direction in her life. She believed that her mother did not want her as a child, and she cried when she saw mothers and daughters who were connected and loving with one another. Kondja had been in a series of relationships in which she felt ignored, alone, uncared for, and discounted. During the helping process, Kondja experienced the helper as unconditionally accepting, actively listening, and genuinely caring. The development of a supportive relationship with a helper assisted Kondja in healing past wounds, drinking less alcohol to numb her feelings, and developing healthy relationships in which she valued herself enough to ensure that her needs were met.

Moreover, clients can learn skills needed to live more effectively and reach their potential. These skills might include learning how to communicate with others; practicing ways to resolve conflicts; becoming more assertive; identifying decision-making strategies; or changing unhealthy habits (e.g., rarely exercising; having unprotected, anonymous sex). Often, these skills can alleviate the powerlessness that individuals feel when they are unable to communicate their emotions directly and can assist clients in engaging more fully in their lives.

In addition, helping can assist individuals in dealing with existential concerns (i.e., who am I, where am I going, and what do I want out of life). As Socrates said, "The unexamined life is not worth living." Helping can promote proactive involvement in life when these questions are asked, reflected on, and answered. Max was referred for helping because of failing grades, poor peer relationships, and generalized sadness. After several sessions, Max began to address critical questions regarding how he might live his life, the fears he often confronts within himself, and the salience of his relationships with others. Helping provided him with an opportunity to look within himself, discover what felt important, and then make decisions about how to change his unhealthy behaviors.

Finally, effective helping teaches clients to function on their own. Similar to the way children grow up and leave their parents, clients also need to leave their helpers. Perhaps some of you have tried to teach others the art of in-line skating: You hold them up, and they hang on while they make their first attempt at skating. In time, they begin to skate by themselves. The steps that they make on their own are rewarding not only for the beginning skater, but also for the teacher. The same is true with helping: Providing the initial support and teaching the skills are most effective when individuals internalize the messages and take off on their own.

PROBLEMATIC ASPECTS OF HELPING

Although helping is usually beneficial, there are a few potentially problematic aspects. Sometimes helping can provide just enough relief to enable people to stay in maladaptive situations or relationships. For example, battered women's shelters provide needed safety and security to abused women and their children. However, shelter workers have observed that occasionally they provide just enough assistance to enable women to return to the abusive situation. When the workers in one shelter confronted this "enabling" in themselves and discussed these behaviors with the residents, some of the battered women were able to identify their pattern of seeking shelter during the abusive periods and returning home in the honeymoon period. Without this insight, helping could have enabled some of the women to continue in a potentially deadly cycle.

Another potential problem is that helping can create dependency if clients rely too much on their helpers for support and feel unable to explore feelings or make changes in their lives without assistance from the helper. For example, Kathleen might decline a spontaneous invitation to join her new partner's family on Cape Cod for a week because her helper is on vacation and unavailable for consultation. Helpers sometimes facilitate dependency by providing clients with "the answers" to their problems (e.g., if her helper told Kathleen not to go to Cape Cod). Effective helpers understand that providing the answers does not typically help others; rather, most clients need to participate actively in a process where they uncover new insights and discover which actions feel best for themselves. This strategy works because only clients fully know the situations, experience the associated feelings, and have the best answers to the presenting problems. In addition, advising others may be problematic when the solution that is provided does not fit with their needs. Many of us have made suggestions to family members or friends about how to handle difficult situations, only to find that our advice was not exactly what they wanted to hear. For example, a helper told a close friend to stay away from the boyfriend who broke up with her because he was not good enough for her. After they got back together, the friend resented the helper's critical words about her sweetheart. Although challenging, empowering clients to make their own decisions is critically important. In addition, helpers' personal issues sometimes place them at risk for encouraging dependency in those they assist. For helpers who are lonely and isolated, their clients' dependency may fulfill personal needs that are not being met elsewhere. Helpers who have not developed a network of social support and personal relationships may be at special risk for encouraging their clients to rely extensively on them.

Another problematic aspect of helping emerges when helpers try to impose personal or societal values onto their clients (McWhirter, 1994). For example, some helping professionals have attempted to alter the sexual orientation of people who are lesbian, gay, or bisexual (Haldeman, 2002). Other helpers advised parents to raise their children in a certain religion because the helper believed that problems in families result from children not having a strong religious foundation. One of the challenges of being a helper involves recognizing how personal values influence our work with clients. An individual's values undeniably have an influence on the helping process; thus, becoming an effective helper entails learning more about yourself and your values to ensure that they do not affect the helping process negatively. For example, an older male client working with a feminist female helper stated that women should not work outside the home because they take jobs away from qualified men who have families to raise. In this case, the helper's and client's values differed, yet challenging the client about his belief system did not seem to be an effective means of developing a therapeutic relationship. Fortunately, the helper was able to separate her values from those of the client and was able to reflect an underlying message of concern about his fears about his job stability.

When Do People Seek Help From Others?

Two factors seem to be necessary for people to seek help (Gross & McMullen, 1983). First, they must become aware that they are in pain or are facing a difficult situation, perceive their feelings or situation as problematic, and believe that help could assist them in alleviating their distress. Second, the pain must be greater than the perceived barriers to seeking help. Sometimes the barriers involve practical considerations, such as the time or money required to obtain help; but often, the obstacles are emotional and can include fears about deeply exploring problems or concerns about the opinions of others regarding people who seek therapy.

For example, Conchita came to her first helping session because she was experiencing multiple stressors: Her mother had committed suicide three years earlier, her sister had been diagnosed with depression, she was failing all of her courses (previously she had been an "A" student), her first serious boyfriend had broken up with her, and she was pregnant. For some time, Conchita had felt that she should handle her problems by herself because she feared what others might think of her if they knew that she needed to see a helper. Moreover, she was on a limited budget and was reluctant to pay for helping. However, Conchita had begun to feel that she could no longer cope with her problems by herself. Her brother had gone to a helper and felt better, so she thought that going to a helper might work for her. Thus, Conchita sought help because she believed that the potential benefits (e.g., emotional support and assistance with coping) outweighed the costs associated with helping (e.g., financial expense and perceived stigma).

Many people, however, hesitate to seek professional help (Gross & McMullen, 1983). They feel embarrassed or ashamed about asking for assistance or believe that seeking help constitutes emotional weakness or inadequacy (Shapiro, 1984). Many Americans, for example, believe that individuals should rely solely on themselves and that all problems should be solved individually. Given these beliefs, it is not surprising that researchers have found that people seek help first from friends and family members and only last from professionals (Tinsley, de St. Aubin, & Brown, 1982; Webster & Fretz, 1978).

Some people are concerned about talking with others because they feel that no one could possibly understand their situation (e.g., Thomas thought that no one could understand his experience growing up in a religious cult). Others fear a punitive response or a value judgment regarding their thoughts, feelings, or actions (e.g., Candace felt that she would be judged for having had two abortions). Furthermore, individuals may be concerned that they will be labeled *mentally ill* and thus be subject to the many negative stereotypes and stigma associated with this label (Sue, Sue, & Sue, 1994). Some clients may be hesitant to seek therapy because they rely on their insurance companies to pay for therapy: They may be concerned that the stigma associated with receiving therapy could have negative ramifications for obtaining insurance or employment in the future.

Clearly, many people experience distress about seeking professional help. Individuals in considerable pain who admit their need for psychological assistance have made significant progress toward obtaining the help they need. Support from friends and family can provide the encouragement these individuals need to contact trained helpers (Gourash, 1978). For example, Joe was reluctant to seek help after his wife of 40 years died. His friends and children encouraged him to attend a support group for adults who had lost their partner. Although initially reluctant, Joe was so upset about his loss that he agreed to participate in the group sessions if his daughters would accompany him. The support his family and friends provided enabled Joe to access the help that he needed.

Helpers need to work to change negative attitudes about seeking professional psychological assistance in our society. We helpers can begin by seeking help ourselves and encouraging others to seek help when needed. We can also work to initiate and support legislation for additional mental health benefits. Finally, we can work to educate the public by spreading information about mental health treatments through the media.

Is Helping Effective?

This section is focused on research about the effectiveness of psychotherapy. In 1952, Eysenck compiled the results of 24 studies that investigated the outcome of therapy interventions in an attempt to answer the question, "Does psychotherapy work?" Although this early compilation of studies questioned the efficacy of psychotherapy, later investigators with more sophisticated research designs have overwhelmingly concluded that counseling and therapy are helpful and that most clients improved by the end of therapy at a greater rate than those in need who did not receive therapeutic interventions (Smith, Glass, & Miller, 1980). Specifically, Smith et al. found that the average client who received therapy was psychologically healthier than 80% of untreated individuals.

Why the discrepancy between Eysenck's work and the investigation of subsequent researchers? Reviewers have criticized Eysenck's (1952) conclusions because they were based on a faulty research methodology. Specifically, Eysenck used different guidelines for evaluating the outcome of the control and treatment groups, applying more stringent criteria for determining improvement in the treatment groups. For example, at the beginning of the study, clients in the treatment groups had more serious psychological disturbances than those in the control groups. One would expect the healthiest individuals to demonstrate the highest level of functioning at the end of the study because they had the fewest problems at the start of the study. Moreover, people in the control groups did, in fact, receive treatment because they were often the recipients of helping behaviors from friends, family members, clergy, and medical personnel.

Once researchers established conclusively that psychotherapy in general is indeed helpful (see Wampold, 2001), they began to ask about the relative effectiveness of different types of therapy. To date, hundreds of studies have been conducted comparing different types of therapy (e.g., client-centered, psychodynamic, cognitive–behavioral, experiential). Wampold et al. (1997) performed a meta-analysis of psychotherapy outcome studies and concluded that no one type of therapy is more effective than another. The findings from this area of research have been humorously summarized using the Dodo bird verdict from *Alice in Wonderland*: "Everyone has won and all must have prizes" (Carroll, 1865/1962, p. 412).

Another interesting line of research has examined how many psychotherapy sessions are needed to reduce psychological distress and return the client to normal psychological functioning (e.g., Grissom, Lyons, & Lutz, 2002; Howard, Lueger, Maling, & Martinovich, 1993; Kopta, Howard, Lowry, & Beutler, 1994). In their reviews of a large number of studies, these researchers proposed three progressive sequential phases of the psychotherapeutic recovery process. In the first phase of remoralization, clients change rapidly in terms of feeling subjectively better. In the second, slower phase, there is a remediation of symptoms such as depression and anxiety. In the third and slowest phase, there is rehabilitation of troublesome, maladaptive behaviors that interfere with life functioning in areas such as family and work. Clients with minimal distress improve fairly quickly, whereas clients with chronic characterological problems (i.e., innate, severe, ongoing, and difficult-to-treat disorders) require the greatest number of sessions to return to normal functioning.

In summary, therapy has been shown to be an effective means of helping people cope with emotional pain and interpersonal problems (Strupp, 1996). Furthermore, researchers have identified myriad factors that relate to positive outcome in therapy and have described the difficulty in studying factors related to client change (Hill & Lambert, 2003). Additional research is clearly needed, though, to help us understand more about psychotherapy.

On Becoming a Helper

Helping seems to be a natural tendency in many people who have an innate desire to assist others. For many of us, our natural inclination toward helping must be complemented by learning and practicing helping skills until they become an integral part of who we are. Helpers who have integrated helping skills tend to have several characteristics in common: They listen carefully and empathically, are nonjudgmental, encourage exploration of thoughts and feelings, assist others in gaining new perspectives on problems, and motivate others to take actions to improve their lives. Furthermore, effective helpers work from a clearly articulated theoretical foundation and remain knowledgeable about recent research findings related to helping interventions.

Many people can become more effective helpers if they are motivated to learn helping skills and practice these new behaviors (even when those behaviors initially feel awkward and forced). Many effective helpers have stories about their initial attempts at assisting others. For example, when one person first started studying helping behaviors, her father was undergoing heart surgery. She spoke to him every day and asked him how he was feeling. After weeks of this, he asked her if she really wanted to know how he was feeling. "Finally!" she thought, "he'll share his innermost feelings with me." Her father said he was feeling that he liked her a lot more before she began studying helping skills. Many of your friends and family may have similar reactions as you begin to learn helping skills. This may initially be discouraging, but it may help to know that most effective helpers practice these behaviors for many years before comfortably integrating them into their interactions with clients. In fact, many helpers discover that during the process of becoming a helper, their helping skills and confidence seem to deteriorate before they improve. This may occur because beginning helpers often learn how difficult it is to use helping skills in an integrated and comfortable manner. The process of becoming a helper might begin profitably with helpers trying to understand what motivates them to want to help others.

HEALTHY MOTIVATIONS

Many individuals aspire to help others for healthy reasons. Some are altruistic and want to make a difference in people's lives. For example, helpers might want to provide support to those in need by volunteering to work in a shelter for homeless women or by becoming a buddy to a gerontology patient confined to a nursing home. People who are motivated to use helping skills in situations like these provide others with supportive relationships in which clients feel listened to, cared for, and understood. Some helpers also choose to make a difference in children's lives by mentoring or tutoring young students, using the foundation of helping skills to develop encouraging relationships. Others hope to make life less painful for those in troubled situations. For example, helpers can provide an important function by assisting teens who think they might be gay or lesbian and fear retribution from family and friends.

Individuals may also recognize a special talent in themselves for listening and supporting others. Perhaps you are the person that friends and family talk with when they are hurt or upset. Others may have role models (e.g., parents, aunts or uncles, cousins) who have dedicated their lives to the service of others. Some people view helping as consistent with their cultural values and thus seek careers that enable them to assist others.

Furthermore, some people aspire to be helpers because they experienced therapy as helpful when they were struggling with painful issues. For example, Kendra was 12 years old when she lost her mother and had to assume the role of mother to her five siblings. She received therapy to help her cope with her loss and her new responsibilities. Kendra now aspires to help children who have experienced loss in their lives. Another example involves rape survivors who become crisis counselors after receiving supportive counseling that helped them resolve disturbing issues related to the rape.

For many individuals, the helping environment is attractive because it allows them to work with people who are striving toward actualization of their potential. Helpers who work in group practice settings may have the opportunity to interact with smart, capable colleagues who value personal growth and helping others. Many helpers receive support from their colleagues to actively examine their own issues and improve themselves to ensure their continued success in the helping role. Furthermore, helpers are often excited by their contribution to the process of change in clients' lives and are energized by their clients' hard work and striving toward personal growth.

Finally, people may enter helping fields to work for social change. Helping affords a unique opportunity to make a difference in the lives of individuals and to sometimes influence social policies. Helpers who work with adolescents in at-risk environments may provide them with skills, hope, and encouragement to overcome obstacles and graduate from high school and college. Other helpers may draft legislation or testify on behalf of policies that fight discrimination (e.g., sexual harassment) or encourage funding for social services (e.g., child care). Contributions to social change also occur through research that helpers undertake to evaluate the effectiveness of helping interventions (e.g., studying the efficacy of training undergraduate students to be effective helpers for battered women who have entered the criminal justice system).

UNHEALTHY MOTIVATIONS

Unfortunately, helpers can sometimes be motivated to work with people for less healthy reasons (Bugental, 1965). Typically, these reasons are not known consciously but still influence the person.

Individuals sometimes envision themselves as saviors for the less fortunate or as wise distributors of knowledge and advice. These people want to go into the helping profession as a mission. However, such motivations can be dangerous. When helpers need to make clients change to build their own self-esteem, they cannot allow clients to make their own choices.

Furthermore, some people may want to help others because they are needy themselves and view helping as a way to develop relationships. These people might have difficulty with intimacy and so seek a safe way of getting close to others.

Others may use helping as a way to feel better about what they have by comparing themselves with those who are less fortunate. For some people, helping others enables them to feel superior to those whom they are helping.

Finally, most of us have heard the jokes about how all psychology students go into the major to figure themselves out. Indeed, many people seem to enter helping fields to work through unresolved personal issues or to change situations that they found unchangeable in their past (e.g., an unhappy childhood).

Most of us probably aspire to help others for a combination of healthy and unhealthy reasons. The key is to understand our motivations and to monitor them in the helping process. I recommend that helpers seek therapy to learn more about themselves and their motivation for becoming helpers and to resolve personal problems. Helpers also should have some form of supervision available to them when they are learning, and later practicing, helping skills. I believe that the more aware helpers are of themselves and their personal issues, the less they allow unconscious influences to disrupt the process of helping.

Organization of This Book

The remaining chapters in part I describe the three-stage approach to helping, the theoretical rationale for this helping model, and an overview of ethics.

Parts II, III, and IV detail the skills necessary to assist clients in progressing through the exploration, insight, and action stages. In each section, an overview chapter highlights the theoretical foundation and the goals of the stage, with discussion questions at the end of the chapter to facilitate the helper in thinking about the stage. The skills chapters follow the overview chapters and include sections describing the definition of and the rationale for each skill and the helper intentions and client reactions associated with the skill. Helpers are taught how to determine the effects of the skill on clients, as well as to be aware of problems that helpers may encounter when learning and using the skill. A case example of how the skill can be used effectively is provided, and the skills chapters conclude with helpful hints for implementing the skill. Readers are encouraged to become actively involved by answering the discussion questions and by participating in practice exercises and lab experiences formulated to assist them in learning and performing the skills. At the end of each stage, a chapter addresses the integration of the skills taught for that stage. I also describe common problems that helpers face, as well as provide ideas for how helpers can manage these difficulties. In addition, an extended clinical example is included to illustrate the skills used in the stage.

Finally, the last chapter reviews techniques related to managing helping sessions and addresses issues related to integrating the helping skills in the three stages. It closes with an example of how the skills are interwoven in a helping session and with concluding comments about your journey to becoming an effective helper.

Please note that a lot of examples are used throughout the book. Some of these examples are based on real people; some are fictitious, created to make a certain point. Names have been changed to protect the identities of those involved when the examples are based on actual situations.

Experiential Component of the Book

Reading about helping skills is important, but reading alone does not make you an effective helper. Acquiring extensive knowledge about helping, although important, is only the first step in your journey toward helping others. The best way for you to learn the skills is first to read and study the text and then to apply what you have learned by answering questions about the material and by participating in practice helping exercises and lab experiences. The following sections describe the ways in which you can use this book to maximize your growth as a helper.

PRACTICE EXERCISES

At the end of each skills chapter, there are practice exercises which provide readers with the opportunity to think about and formulate responses to hypothetical client situations before practicing the skills in the lab setting. You can practice by writing down your intervention for each client situation and then comparing your answers with my suggestions for possible responses. There are additional exercises on this book's companion Web site www.apa.org/books/resources/hill.

WHAT DO YOU THINK?

In addition to the practice exercises, several questions are provided at the end of each chapter to stimulate your thinking about the text material. I suggest that you contemplate each question and discuss your responses with your classmates. Professors may elect to assign these questions as homework or include them in examinations.

LAB EXPERIENCES

Throughout this book, I provide lab exercises for beginning helpers to practice helping skills in dyads or small groups. These experiences are a critical component of learning to become an effective helper. Practice is necessary to go beyond understanding the skills to integrate the skills into one's repertoire as a helper. During labs, helpers are asked to practice the skills with peers who act as clients presenting real or role-played problems. Observers take careful notes and attend to the helper's ability to deliver a particular skill, so that they can provide feedback to the helper. Thus, everyone has an opportunity to experience the roles of helper, client, and observer for each skill. At the end of each lab, readers are asked to complete the "personal reflections" section in which they contemplate questions of importance to their development as skilled helpers and discuss their responses with their classmates.

The way I structure my helping skills class is to have one class each week devoted to lecture and discussion of the theory and research related to the individual skill. A second session is devoted to practicing in small groups. Students who have successfully completed the helping skills course serve as lab leaders to facilitate the lab experiences and provide feedback to the beginning helpers. Instructors may view my syllabi on on this book's companion Web site www.apa.org/books/resources/hill.

The success of the lab experiences depends partly on the participants' willingness to reveal information about personal topics. I hope that participants will discuss personal topics rather than fabricate problems for two reasons. First, helpers have difficulty learning what is effective when students are not responding genuinely. Second, students often are unable to provide useful feedback to helpers about what is helpful and how the interventions feel if they are not discussing real problems. When role-playing, students are often more involved in trying to think of how the person they are pretending to be might feel or behave than immersing themselves in the immediate experience.

As clients, however, students should only disclose about easy, safe topics. They should never disclose about deep topics, even if they are comfortable disclosing because their classmates will not be comfortable trying to help them and it takes the focus too much off the helper learning helping skills to the helper trying to help the client.

At times, students might start talking about an issue they think is safe but then become uncomfortable, either because of the depth of the topic or because they do not feel comfortable with the helper. I stress that students always have the right (without jeopardy or prejudice) to indicate that they choose not to explore a particular issue further.

If students are not willing to disclose personal information, they can role play problems if they can play them realistically. In such cases, they should not reveal whether the problem is role-played or real—in this way no one ever knows whether the person is actually disclosing or whether the problem is role-played, thus preserving confidentiality.

Exhibit 1.1 provides topics that students in our courses have discussed. Again, students should present only about safe topics. Although I indicate that a topic may be "safe" for many people, it may not be comfortable for an individual student, so each person must think about what they want to discuss. Students may want to refer to this list throughout the semester when a topic is needed for the lab exercises.

Although practice sessions might seem somewhat artificial, the information shared is personal and should be treated in a confidential manner. Helpers should not disclose information shared in practice sessions without the permission of the client. Specifically, helpers should only discuss the material presented in helping sessions with their supervisors and classmates, and then only when it relates to developing their helping skills. When one respects clients, they respond by sharing personal information and delving deeply into their thoughts and feelings. Confidentiality of shared information provides a foundation for respectful interactions with others (see extended discussion in chap. 4).

The focus of the lab experiences is on the helper and teaching the helping skills. However, students often report that it is beneficial to talk about their concerns when they participate in the client role and that the experience of being clients provided them with firsthand exposure to how it feels to receive the various helping skills. Moreover, students often develop empathy with their clients after having experienced what is involved in being a client. Being a participant in counseling allows students to experience "the other side" of helping and to gain respect for the courage clients exhibit when they share their concerns with their helpers. Moreover, beginning helpers often report that watching their counselors provide helping skills can teach them about effective (and ineffective) helping techniques.

EXHIBIT 1.1

Topics That Are Appropriate to Talk About in the Labs

Ideal Topics
 Academic issues (e.g., studying, test anxiety)
 Career; future plans
 Choosing a major or graduate program
 Pets
 Problems at work
 Public speaking anxiety
 Roommate issues
 Romantic relationships
 Feelings about technology
 Happy childhood memories
 Hobbies and extracurricular activities
 Problems with health

Relatively Safe Topics
 Minor family issues
 Autonomy–independence struggles
 Minor relationship concerns
 High school experiences
 Personal views on alcohol and drugs
 Existential concerns (e.g., Who am I? What is the meaning
 of life? death?)
 Financial difficulties
 Problems with physical appearance
 Moral dilemmas

Topics That Could Be Too Disclosing
 Alcohol abuse
 Fears about going crazy
 Traumas (e.g., sexual or physical abuse, rape, victimization,
 child abuse, serious medical condition)
 Serious problems in romantic relationships
 Shameful feelings
 Serious family disputes

A final issue to discuss in this section involves the recognition that problems can occur when practicing helping skills with classmates who are friends or acquaintances. During helping sessions with friends, helpers can pretend that they know nothing about them and respond only to what clients actually reveal during helping sessions. Although it is challenging to discount relevant information, students in my classes have found the lab exercises easier to perform if they consider only information provided in the practice helping session. For example, Nancy was practicing her helping skills with her friend, Katrina. Katrina was bemoaning the fact that her partner had not called her in two weeks. Although Nancy knew the reasons Katrina's partner had not called (Katrina had dated someone else the previous weekend), she focused only on Katrina's expressed feelings related to not having contact with her partner.

PROVIDING FEEDBACK TO YOUR PEERS

Providing feedback is an essential component of training. Helpers need to learn what they do well and what skills are most helpful to the clients. It is equally important that they know what skills are not effective, so that they can improve as helpers.

Helpers appreciate positive feedback because learning helping skills is challenging, and they appreciate encouragement when they are on the right track. However, they also need and want feedback that helps them change and improve their helping skills. It is enjoyable to have people tell us that we are doing a terrific job as helpers, but we also need people to point out our errors and provide concrete recommendations for how we might improve our skills. Students often feel cheated if they consistently receive only positive feedback yet also may feel wounded if they receive only critical comments.

Claiborn, Goodyear, and Horner (2002) recommended providing positive feedback first and only then providing one piece of constructive feedback (e.g., "You used good attending and listening skills, but you asked too many questions, making it hard for the client to know which one to respond to"). It is less overwhelming and more feasible to focus on making one change in a given lab experience. Feedback should be stated in behavioral terms (e.g., "You were looking away a lot and playing with your hair") rather than in broad and nonspecific terms (e.g., "You did not connect with the client") to give the helper specific ideas for how to change.

The best sources of feedback are the clients who have experienced the helper's interventions firsthand. The next best sources of feedback are the observers who have watched the practice sessions and imagined how the interventions might feel if they were the client. It is beneficial for helpers to hear that different people had different responses to the same intervention, thus emphasizing that there is no one right way to intervene.

Finally, being a client in practice helping sessions should not be used as a substitute for seeking counseling or therapy. Students experiencing personal distress should seek help from a trained and qualified counselor or therapist. University counseling centers often provide counseling services for students at little or no cost and offer an excellent opportunity to learn more about themselves and address salient issues. Hence, I want to encourage people to seek counseling and psychotherapy when needed. I firmly believe that helpers should work through their problems so their issues do not exert a negative influence on the helping process. I also encourage helpers to experience the benefits that result from a careful exploration of their thoughts and feelings.

Is This Book Right for You?

The material presented in this book can be applied to countless helping situations involving both professional and lay helpers. Perhaps the most obvious audience for this book is students who are training to become mental health professionals. Individuals who plan to provide psychological services to others benefit from learning the helping skills because they serve as the foundation for most psychological interventions. Specifically, students enrolled in counseling classes at the undergraduate, master's, and doctoral level could use this text to learn helping skills that can be applied to their work with clients. For example, students in counseling psychology, clinical psychology, social work, and psychiatry may be interested in this book. Of course, counselors who plan to work with specific types of clients (e.g., alcohol and drug counselors, rehabilitation counselors, and marriage and family counselors) will need to learn additional, more specialized knowledge to work effectively with their clients.

The helping skills taught in this book are also applicable to people who assist clients in helping professions other than psychology. For example, volunteers and staff members in nonprofit agencies often are required to practice effective helping skills. Hot line volunteers benefit from applying basic helping skills to communicate empathy and understanding to the clients with diverse problems whom they encounter over the phone. Crisis workers assisting battered women and their children use basic helping skills to ensure the safety of their clients. Hospice workers can learn how to respond empathically to individuals struggling with despair, loss, loneliness, and pain. Furthermore, hospice workers often use basic helping skills when interacting with patients' family members and close friends. Being able to listen empathically and reflect feelings appropriately can assist patients' significant others in resolving issues related to illness and death.

Another application of helping skills in professional interactions involves other health professionals. Recently, a physician inquired whether the university provided basic helping skills courses. She explained that about 60% of her clients presented with emotional concerns as well as physical complaints. She felt that her medical training did not prepare her to deal effectively with the personal problems presented by her patients. Many medical professionals and health service providers could enhance their effectiveness by using helping skills. Doctors, dentists, and nurses could learn to respond effectively to clients who fear invasive procedures or want additional information about sick loved ones. In fact, researchers have found that breast cancer patients who interacted with a surgeon trained either to use basic helping skills or to chat with them on the night before surgery evidenced less anxiety and depression one year after their operation (Burton, Parker, & Wollner, 1991). Furthermore, there is probably no time when effective helping skills are needed more by medical professionals than when they must notify a patient's significant others of a death. The use of the skills taught in this book could enable helpers to respond empathically toward the families and significant others in these situations. Finally, volunteers in medical settings encounter many instances in which the use of helping skills is warranted (e.g., when worried families are frustrated with waiting to hear about the results of surgery or when visiting with a patient who has been unable to leave the hospital for weeks).

In addition, training in helping skills could assist nuns, priests, rabbis, ministers, and lay clergy in working with individuals who question their faith, celebrate important events, or struggle with loss and grief. Many people turn to religious leaders in times of crisis, so training in basic helping skills could prepare these leaders for responding empathically at critical moments in people's lives.

Professionals pursuing business and law careers that involve working with others also could benefit from learning to communicate effectively. Many people would rather do business with, and make referrals to, an accountant who listens patiently and understands their fears related to paying taxes. Helping skills also can be useful to attorneys when confronting hostile couples filing for divorce or when helping personal injury clients make decisions about whether to accept a settlement. The ability to listen effectively and understand nonverbal behavior could assist lawyers in uncovering important material in depositions to further positive outcomes for their clients. The importance of helping skills in the legal profession is demonstrated by the inclusion of a basic counseling skills course in the curriculum of some law schools.

A less obvious (but equally important) reason for learning helping skills involves improving relationships with friends, significant others, and family members. After learning the attending and listening skills, students often report that they now realize how often they have not really listened to the people they love. Although difficult, using listening skills while a significant other is complaining about one of your irritating behaviors could help in resolving the issue. Improvements in listening often result in more open and healthy communication with significant others.

Helping skills can also be used to assist friends and family members who are struggling with important choices or painful issues. At times, friends may ask for help when they experience significant losses (e.g., the ending of a relationship, the death of a family member). Family members may request assistance when they encounter an important decision (e.g., which job to pursue, whether to relocate for a romantic relationship). In addition, helping skills are used when people experience a crisis in their significant relationships (e.g., close friends strongly disagree about an important topic; two members of a couple feel differently about having children). Although using some of the basic helping skills in relationships is appropriate (e.g., listening carefully to the feelings of others), I caution students against becoming too involved in the helper role with friends and family members because it is not usually possible to be objective. Furthermore, relationships may be less satisfying and less mutual when one person is always the helper and the other is always the client. It is usually best for the other person to seek therapeutic help from a professional who is not personally involved (see also chap. 4 about the ethical issues involved in dual relationships) and for you to remain as the interested, loyal friend who provides emotional support.

Some of my students have suggested that all professors be required to learn basic helping skills. Imagine if every teacher was trained to be an effective helper! Although they still might not believe outlandish excuses for late assignments, professors might be able to respond more positively to questions posed or personal struggles faced by students.

Research on Helping Skills

The first edition of this book provided a brief review of the research for each skill and proposed research ideas for each of the three stages. For this edition, I decided not to do that (other than briefly in chap. 3) because I could not do justice to the extensive research. Instead, I put together a book of readings of the best empirical studies on the skills (Hill, 2001). I strongly recommend that instructors use this book as a companion text so that students become familiar with the empirical basis for the helping skills.

Concluding Comments

You are about to embark on an exciting and challenging journey toward becoming an effective helper. Although learning helping skills takes time, knowledge, and a lot of practice, the rewards for integrating helping skills in your personal and professional repertoire are plentiful. I hope to help you reach your destination of learning helping skills by focusing on the development of these skills while providing a theoretical and research foundation for helping behaviors, as well as providing exercises to practice these skills. Unfortunately, understanding the information is not sufficient to make you an effective helper. Effective helping requires practice, and even experienced helpers often return to the basics to review and refresh skills. I hope this book assists you in learning helping skills and exploring your potential for, and interest in, becoming an effective helper. Bon voyage!

WHAT DO YOU THINK?

▪ Think of a time when you felt helped by someone. What did that person do that was helpful to you?
▪ Now remember a time when you needed help and the person you turned to was not at all helpful. What did she or he do to make this experience unhelpful?
▪ Describe how society perceives those who seek professional help. How could you help decrease the stigma attached to help seeking?
▪ Write a brief job description for a helper. Include personal characteristics, required training, and job responsibilities. Now, evaluate yourself in comparison with the description that you developed.
▪ What would it take for you to seek professional help? Address the benefits and costs you associate with seeking assistance.
▪ Discuss the healthy and unhealthy reasons that motivate you to learn helping skills.
▪ Identify several current situations in your life where helping skills could be used.
▪ In your opinion, what are the top three characteristics of an effective helper?

Theoretical Foundation of the Three-Stage Model of Helping | 2

To be where we are, and to become what we are capable of becoming, is the only end in life.

—*Robert Louis Stevenson*

M onci was introduced to several different theoretical orientations and read the research that shows no outcome differences among the various orientations. She was confused about which approach to use. When she learned that she could integrate all the approaches, she felt relieved because she really did not want to choose a single approach. The three-stage model felt very comfortable for her and fit with her personal philosophy.

The helping process involves taking clients "down and into" understanding themselves more and then "up and out" into the world, better able to cope with problems (Carkhuff, 1969; Carkhuff & Anthony, 1979). To accomplish this, helpers act as collaborators and facilitators. Although they have no special knowledge or wisdom about how clients ought to live their lives, helpers can be empathic and use specific helping skills to guide clients in exploring their feelings and values, understanding their problems, making choices, and implementing changes in thoughts, affect, and behaviors.

The three-stage model for helping (exploration, insight, action) is a framework for using helping skills to lead clients through the process of exploring concerns, coming to greater understanding of problems, and making changes in their lives. It is based on my clinical and teaching and research experiences, and it is influenced by client-centered, psychoanalytic, and cognitive and behavioral theories. In this chapter, I lay the foundation for this model by describing my assumptions about human nature; providing a brief overview of the three stages (which are expanded on in subsequent chapters); and discussing two key components of the model: empathic collaboration and cultural factors.

Assumptions Underlying the Three-Stage Model

Assumptions about human nature form the philosophical foundation for any model, so it is important to explicate my assumptions before presenting the model. I discuss these assumptions only briefly, though, because my focus is on describing the helping model rather than creating a theory of personality development.

I believe that people are born with varied potential in the psychological, intellectual, physical, and interpersonal domains. Thus, some people are genetically more intelligent, attractive, physically strong, active, verbally articulate, and mechanically adept than other people. Temperamental differences among infants at birth (e.g., some children are active, whereas others are phlegmatic) carry over to adulthood. These potentials unfold as children develop, and there is a strong biological pull toward growing and developing one's potential. I do not believe that people are either inherently good (as Carl Rogers postulated) or inherently governed by instinctual urges (as Sigmund Freud postulated) at birth. Instead, as stated above, I believe that people have certain biological predispositions at birth and have a tendency toward fulfilling these potentials. How they are developed depends largely on the environment, to which I turn next.

The environment can enhance or thwart the innate movement toward survival and development. Healthy environments provide basic biological needs (e.g., food and shelter) and emotional needs (e.g., relationships characterized by acceptance, love, support, encouragement, recognition, and appropriate challenges). When infants and children are provided with a "good enough" environment that meets their basic needs, their potential unfolds naturally. No environment is perfect, but the environment needs to be at least adequate to allow children to prosper. In contrast, when negative things happen in the person's environment, his or her development is thwarted. A person growing up in the midst of war and terrorist attacks has a different view of life than a person growing up during peace. Either too much gratification or too much deprivation stunts children's growth, but an adequate amount of support allows children to develop naturally to fulfill their potential. So resiliency, or the ability to adapt, is both biologically and environmentally determined.

Early experiences, particularly in terms of attachment and self-esteem, are crucial in laying the foundation for personality. Infants need to be nurtured by caretakers to have a firm foundation for interpersonal relationships and self-esteem. If these attachment needs are not met, children become anxious or avoidant of human contact (Bowlby, 1969, 1988). People continue to change and adapt throughout their lives, within the limits of their biological predispositions and early experiences. Thus, although a foundation is laid, there is still a wide range within which people can grow and develop. They cannot transform their personalities completely, but they can come to accept who they are and make the most of their potential.

People develop defenses to cope with anxiety, particularly during childhood when they tend to have less control over their personal destinies (e.g., a child might learn to withdraw to defend against dominating parents). A moderate level of defenses is adaptive because all of us need strategies to cope with life. These defenses become problematic, however, when the individual cannot discriminate when it is appropriate to use defenses. For example, if a child who was abused avoids all adults, she or he cannot form benevolent relationships with caring protectors.

Although people are influenced by genetics, past learning, and external circumstances, I believe that they have some degree of control over their lives and choice about how they behave. Within our limits, we make choices and alter the course of our life. For example, although friendliness is influenced by personality (e.g., introversion vs. extroversion) and previous experiences with meeting people, a person still has some range of choices about how she or he acts with others in a new situation. Thus, determinism is balanced by free will.

Free will is enhanced if individuals gain insight into their background, needs, and desires. Understanding enables one to have more control over one's fate. One can never have complete control over fate but can have some influence through awareness and conscious effort.

I also propose that emotions, cognitions, and behaviors are all key components of personality. All are intertwined and operate in combination with one another—mind and body cannot be separated. How people think influences how they feel and behave (e.g., if a person thinks that others are out to get him, he or she will feel afraid when another person approaches). How people feel has an impact on how they think and behave (e.g., if a person feels happy, she or he is likely to seek out other people and think that they will like her or him). Finally, how people behave affects how they think about themselves and how they feel (e.g., if a person studies hard and gets good grades, he or she is likely to feel efficacious). Thus, any treatment approach must focus on all three aspects of human existence (emotions, cognitions, and behaviors) to help people change.

In summary, I believe that people are influenced by both their biology and their environment, particularly early experiences that contribute to the development of attachment to others and self-esteem. Furthermore, although people are influenced by past experiences, they have some choice and free will. It is also important to recognize that people develop defenses as strategies for coping with the demands of the world.

I believe that people can change within limits. They cannot discard past learning or biological predispositions, but they can come to understand themselves more, live with themselves, and accept themselves. They can develop more adaptive behaviors, thoughts, and feelings. People can adjust to their inner potential, make the best of what they have, and make choices about how they want to live their life within the limits imposed by biology, early experiences, and external circumstances. These assumptions lead to an optimistic, but cautious, view about the possibility of change.

Three-Stage Model

As Figure 2.1 illustrates, the helping process involves three stages: an exploration stage (helping clients explore their thoughts, feelings, and actions); an insight stage (helping clients come to understand their thoughts, feelings, and actions); and an action stage (helping clients decide what action to take on the basis of their exploration and insight).

Before focusing on specific skills, I introduce helpers to the philosophy and theory underlying the model. Helpers need to be aware of the tasks and goals for each of the stages (see Figure 2.2) and to be clear on what they are trying to accomplish with clients. When helpers understand the general philosophy and the underlying theories, they can more easily learn the skills required for each stage of the process.

EXPLORATION STAGE

In the exploration stage, helpers seek to establish rapport, develop a therapeutic relationship with clients, encourage clients to tell their stories, help clients explore their thoughts and feelings, facilitate the arousal of client emotion, and learn about their clients. They accomplish these goals through attending nonverbally to clients; listening carefully to everything clients say verbally and nonverbally; and encouraging clients to explore thoughts and feelings through restating the content of what clients say, reflecting feelings, and asking open-ended questions.

Exploration is crucial to give clients an opportunity to express their emotions and to think through the complexity of their problems. Having another person act as a sounding board or mirror is often extremely helpful because it is difficult to examine one's concerns objectively without external feedback. When they think about issues by themselves, clients often become blocked by their own defenses and anxieties. Being blocked can make clients feel that they are going around in circles rather than gaining insight and making changes.

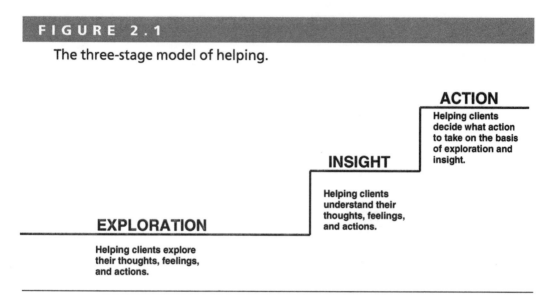

FIGURE 2.1

The three-stage model of helping.

The exploration stage also provides helpers with an opportunity to learn more about their clients. Helpers cannot assume that they know clients' feelings or problems. Helpers might be imposing their own standards and values on clients if they assume that they know how clients feel about problems or what solutions clients should choose. Even when clients are the same age, race, gender, religion, and sexual orientation as helpers, helpers cannot assume that clients have similar problems and feelings. For example, Jennifer, who was similar in age, race, and gender to her helper, disclosed that she had just become engaged. The helper had just recently gotten married and was very happy, so she assumed that the client felt similarly and started congratulating her. Jennifer broke down in tears and ran out of the room. Fortunately, the helper realized her mistake, called Jennifer, and asked her to return for a session. It turned out that Jennifer felt pressured to get engaged and, in fact, felt quite ambivalent about the relationship. When the helper could listen without assumptions, she was able to learn how Jennifer truly felt.

The exploration stage is informed primarily by Rogers's client-centered theory (Rogers, 1942, 1951, 1957, 1967, 1980), as well as by others closely affiliated with Rogers (Gendlin, 1978; Greenberg, Rice, & Elliott, 1993). Rogers believed that people are inherently good and that if nurtured properly and loved for who they are without others trying to change them, could achieve their full potential. He thought that when people try too hard to please others instead of following their own internal experiencing, they become disturbed and lose touch with their inner experiencing. He believed that if helpers accept clients completely and communicate empathy, respect, and genuineness to the clients, clients come to accept themselves and learn to trust their inner experiencing

FIGURE 2.2

Tasks of the helping skills model.

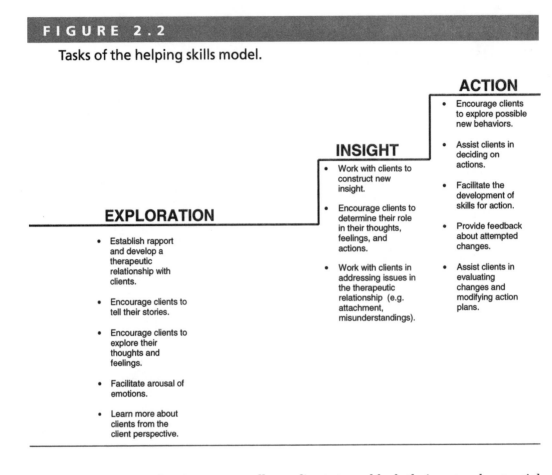

ACTION

- Encourage clients to explore possible new behaviors.
- Assist clients in deciding on actions.
- Facilitate the development of skills for action.
- Provide feedback about attempted changes.
- Assist clients in evaluating changes and modifying action plans.

INSIGHT

- Work with clients to construct new insight.
- Encourage clients to determine their role in their thoughts, feelings, and actions.
- Work with clients in addressing issues in the therapeutic relationship (e.g. attachment, misunderstandings).

EXPLORATION

- Establish rapport and develop a therapeutic relationship with clients.
- Encourage clients to tell their stories.
- Encourage clients to explore their thoughts and feelings.
- Facilitate arousal of emotions.
- Learn more about clients from the client perspective.

once again. Acceptance allows clients to unblock their natural potential and, hence, to live more fully and productively.

INSIGHT STAGE

In the insight stage, helpers collaborate with clients to achieve new understandings about clients' inner dynamics and attain new awareness of their role in perpetuating their own problems. Insight is important because it helps clients see things in a new light and enables them to take appropriate responsibility and control. Insight helps clients understand why they think, feel, and behave as they do. When clients have some understanding about their behavior, it is easier for them to change. For example, it was easier for Jacques to take a chance on getting involved in another relationship once he understood that he became scared of getting close to others because of his punitive relationship with his mother.

Understanding, however imperfect, guides future behavior. Insight may also lead to long-lasting change because it provides clients with a template for making sense out of events and helps them make better choices. Although people can and certainly do attain insight on their own, hearing new ideas and receiving feedback from a caring helper who has a different perspective can enable clients to develop a deeper level of awareness and understanding.

In contrast to the purely client-centered stance in the exploration stage, helpers more actively work with clients in the insight stage to construct meanings and reframe experiences. They not only maintain the empathic and collaborative stance but also occasionally challenge client perspectives, tentatively offer their own ideas, and use their own experiences in helping clients see things in a new way. Clients sometimes need the helper's external perspective to give them new ideas and feedback, especially when they are stuck or blocked. Of course, helpers do not necessarily have the "right" perspective, but they may have alternative perspectives that clients can consider.

In addition, helpers provide clients with feedback about their behaviors in sessions and assist them in understanding how these behaviors have developed and what function they now serve. By understanding how they are perceived by their helpers, clients are often better able to understand how other people react to them. Thus, the relationship itself is a focus of learning and change in the insight stage.

The insight stage is informed by psychoanalytic and interpersonal theories, particularly by theorists such as Freud, Erikson, Mahler, Bowlby, Kohut, Greenson, Cashdan, Teyber, and Kiesler. An important feature of psychoanalytic theory for this model is the emphasis on early development (particularly attachment and individuation) as the foundation of personality. The need to survive often requires that children form defenses to cope with the world. These defenses, while adaptive at the time of formation, can prevent people from functioning well as adults. For example, a person who has formed a defense of avoiding all adults because they might punish him could have a hard time relating to other adults as equals when he grows up. In therapy, clients need to dig deep into themselves and come to understand how these defenses developed and what maintains the defenses so they can reduce the defenses and change maladaptive behavior patterns. They also need to understand what currently helps them maintain defenses and maladaptive behavior patterns.

The contribution of interpersonal theory to the insight stage is the force on interpersonal relationships. By understanding how one comes across to others, one can then develop new and more adaptive ways of relating. Examining the immediate therapeutic relationship is particularly valuable because it is a microcosm of relationships that the client develops with others. By examining how the client interacts with the therapist, the client can learn about relationships in a safe place; then, of course, the goal is to help the client transfer this knowledge to other relationships.

ACTION STAGE

In the action stage, helpers guide clients toward making decisions and changes that reflect their new understanding of themselves. Helpers and clients together explore the idea of changing. They try to determine whether clients want to change and explore the meaning of change in clients' lives. They might brainstorm possible changes and help clients make decisions about which changes to pursue. In some cases, helpers teach the skills clients need to make changes in their lives. They also might help clients develop strategies for trying new behaviors and asking for feedback from others outside the helping relationship. In addition, helpers and clients continually evaluate the outcome of action plans and make modifications to assist clients in obtaining the desired outcomes. As in the first two stages, the process is collaborative. Helpers continue to ask about clients' feelings about changing and the change process. Again, helpers are not experts but guides who assist clients in exploring thoughts and feelings about action and about making positive changes in their lives.

By putting their new ways of thinking into practice, clients are able to consolidate the changes in their thinking. Without action, changes in thinking from the insight stage are typically short-lived. Psychoanalytic theorists assume that insight naturally leads to action and thus that helpers do not have to be concerned with encouraging clients to think about making specific changes. For some clients, this may be true. However, several things can block clients from moving to action after they attain insight. First, clients might not have the skills to make the desired changes. For example, Jamilla now realizes that she is unassertive because she was raised by controlling parents. Although Jamilla accepts responsibility for changing, she might have a hard time becoming more assertive unless she has assertiveness skills in her repertoire. She may need to learn to make eye contact and state her needs directly. Second, even though a person might attain insight during the helping process, change is difficult because old habits are hard to break. People are often willing to settle for what they know rather than risking change and the unknown. For example, although Harold realizes that he would like to be more affectionate and loving with his wife, he is unwilling to change because he is afraid of being rejected as a result of negative experiences in his previous marriage. The role of a helping relationship here might be to prepare Harold for thinking about possible changes. Third, significant others often have strong reactions to changes made by clients, and clients need assistance in figuring out how to deal with interpersonal obstacles to change. Continuing our previous example, Harold's wife may have difficulty adjusting to his greater spontaneity and affection because she is also anxious about closeness. Hence, clients often need help in learning more appropriate skills and in overcoming obstacles to change.

Exploration and insight provide the foundation for clients to understand their motivations and take responsibility for changing. Both helpers and clients need an adequate understanding of the scope and dynamics of the client's problem before developing an action plan. Unlike radio and television talk show psychologists who listen for three sentences and then advise clients, helpers rely on careful, thoughtful listening and probing to help clients fully explore their problems and gain new insights for themselves.

The theoretical foundation for the action stage is behavioral and cognitive–behavioral theories, particularly as articulated by B. F. Skinner, Wolpe, Lazurus, Bandura, Ellis, and Beck. These theorists believed that behaviors (including thoughts) are learned according to learning principles (e.g., reinforcement, punishment, shaping, generalization, extinction, modeling, thoughts mediating actions) and thus can be changed using these same learning principles. Hence, these therapists view helping as an application of behavioral and cognitive principles to specific problems, and so help clients assess current behaviors, teach new behaviors, reinforce changes, and help to modify action plans that are not working effectively.

Empathic Collaboration

Empathic collaboration is a major feature of all three stages of the model and merits attention as I describe the stages. Helpers need to try to understand their clients as much as possible while realizing that it is never possible to understand another person fully. Empathy implies understanding clients at both a cognitive level (what they are thinking and saying) and an affective level (what they are feeling; Duan & Hill, 1996). Although helpers sometimes feel the same emotions as their clients, empathy requires that they recognize that the pain, anger, frustration, joy, or other emotions belong to the client and not the helper. Empathy is sometimes confused with a certain type of response to clients (e.g., reflection of feelings), but empathy is not a specific response type or skill; rather, it is an attitude or manner of responding with genuine caring and a lack of judgment. Empathy involves a deep respect for clients and for the clients' willingness and courage to explore their problems, gain insights, and make changes. This attitude is typically implemented through a variety of helping skills, depending on what helpers perceive clients need at specific times.

Furthermore, the whole helping process is collaborative, in that helpers guide or coach clients in working through problems. Helpers are not experts in how clients ought to live their lives, but they are experts at facilitating the process of exploring feelings and values, achieving understanding, and making choices and changes. Rather than giving answers to clients, helpers try to teach clients how to think through problems, make decisions, and implement changes. This whole model is essentially client-centered in that clients are helped to determine their own solutions to the problems they face. A good metaphor is the parable about teaching a hungry person to fish: Giving someone a fish feeds the person for one meal, whereas teaching her or him to fish enables the person to eat for a lifetime.

Although both empathy and collaboration are crucial components of the helping process, they are not specific skills that can be taught directly. Rather, they are outcomes of the successful implementation of helping skills and a reflection of an attitude that the helper feels toward the client. As helpers, we can be knowledgeable about our implementation of verbal and nonverbal behaviors, aware of how we come across when using these interventions, aware of our intentions for using different interventions, and aware of client reactions to these interventions. However, we cannot always control the outcome of the helping session. We can strive toward empathy and collaboration but cannot always attain these goals because much depends on the client and how well we "match" or "click" with clients. Even so, however, through knowledge, self-awareness, and a genuine desire to understand, respect, and work with another person, empathic collaboration is more likely to emerge and to be experienced by helpers and clients.

Culture

Culture is a major issue that pervades any theoretical approach to thinking about and working with people. Our ideas about helping are based on our cultural values, and these cultural values may differ from those of the clients we serve. We must be aware of our values and the impact of them on our work with clients because it would be a disservice to impose our cultural values on clients (American Psychological Association, 2003).

Culture has been defined as the customs, values, attitudes, beliefs, characteristics, and behaviors shared by a group of people at a particular time in history (Skovholt & Rivers, 2003). In addition, culture can be considered the "shared constraints that limit the behavior repertoire available to members of a certain sociocultural group in a way different from individuals belonging to some other group" (Poortinga, 1990, p. 6). It can also be thought of as "a convenient label for knowledge, skills, and attitudes that are learned and passed on from one generation to the next. Accordingly, this transmission of culture occurs in a physical environment in which certain places, times, and stimuli have acquired special meanings" (Segall, 1979, p. 91). An even broader definition of a cultural group is "any group of people who identify or associate with one another on the basis of some common purpose, need, or similarity of background" (Axelson, 1999, p. 3).

Culture includes such things as race–ethnicity, gender, age, ideology, religion, socioeconomic status, sexual orientation, disability status, occupation, and dietary preferences (Pedersen, 1991, 1997). Each of us belongs to many cultures, any one of which may become salient depending on the time, place, or situation (Pedersen & Ivey, 1993, p. 1). Some cultural groups require admission (e.g., one has to attend school and pass tests to become a psychologist). Others are biologically determined (e.g., age, gender), and still others are a person's choices, although they are influenced by environmental factors (e.g., religion, vegetarianism).

Although it is important to learn about general characteristics of a culture (e.g., what it is like to be an Irish Catholic woman), it is important not to assume that everyone within that group is the same. In fact, there are generally more differences within groups than there are between groups (Atkinson, Morten, & Sue, 1998; Pedersen, 1997). For example, not all African Americans are the same, not all men are the same.

Individuals within groups vary in terms of racial identity, or how much they identify with their racial or ethnic culture (Fouad & Brown, 2000; Helms, 1990; Helms & Cook, 1999). Furthermore, people can develop over time in their sense of racial identity. For example, in the United States, racial and ethnic minority group members (e.g., African Americans) move from a depreciative perspective of their own race or culture to a more appreciative perspective, whereas European Americans come to understand the privilege inherent in their status.

Enculturation and *acculturation* are also key constructs to consider for people who have moved from one culture to another (e.g., when a person emigrates from Vietnam to the United States). Enculturation refers to retaining the norms of one's indigenous culture, whereas acculturation refers to adapting to the norms of the dominant culture (Kim & Abreu, 2001). For example, adults who come to the United States from another country often remain closely aligned with their culture of origin, whereas their children quickly acculturate to American ways. This difference in cultural values often causes rifts and strains in the family, with parents being upset that their children are not retaining the traditional cultural values and dress but are behaving according to different cultural norms.

Clearly, the helping process differs for both clients and helpers at different levels of racial identity and enculturation–acculturation. Helpers need to be aware of and sensitive to cultural differences in the helping process. Skovholt and Rivers (2003) suggested that helpers need to consider (a) the general experiences, characteristics, and needs of the client's cultural groups; (b) the client's individual experiences, characteristics, and needs; and (c) basic human needs—those common to all people (e.g., food, shelter, dignity, and respect). Hence, knowledge of general cultural characteristics can provide some background, but helpers still need to learn about the individual from the individual.

In terms of the relationship of these cultural constructs to the three-stage helping process, helpers need to be aware of cultural issues as they help clients explore their concerns. Helpers need to ask clients about their culture so the helpers can get a context for clients' current functioning, and they also need to educate themselves about cultural backgrounds and values by reading relevant texts (e.g., Pedersen et al., 2002; Sue & Sue, 1999). In terms of the insight and action stages, helpers need to be aware that not all clients value insight and action and should not impose their values on them. More details about the relationship between cultural issues and the specific skills are discussed within the ensuing chapters.

Concluding Comments

Each of the stages is important in the helping process. Thorough exploration sets the stage for the client to gain insight, and deep insight prepares the path for the client to make good decisions about action. Furthermore, making changes encourages the client to come back for exploration of other problems. Hence, helpers need to give due attention to all three stages. Furthermore, helpers need to remember to be empathic and sensitive to individual differences among clients throughout the helping process.

Although it sounds straightforward to move from exploration to insight to action, things do not flow quite so smoothly with some clients, and stages are not always as differentiated and sequential as they appear when reading about them. Within sessions, helpers and clients sometimes move back and forth among the stages. For example, helpers often have to return to exploring new facets of a client's problem during the insight and action stages. In addition, attaining insight often forces a client to explore newly recognized feelings and thoughts. Realizing that a client is reluctant to change in the action stage might necessitate more exploration and insight about obstacles. Sometimes action needs to be taken before much exploration has taken place, such as when a client is in crisis and needs help immediately. For example, a client who has medical problems caused by anorexia might first need to learn to eat in a healthy manner and only later might be ready and able to explore motives underlying her eating disorder. In other cases, clients cannot really explore until they have been taught to relax. Other clients cannot handle insight and are resistant to having anyone "poke around in their heads"; they only want guidance about very specific problems. With such clients, helpers may need to move more quickly to the action stage. However, I caution helpers to explore enough to make sure they know what is going on, what actions have been tried, and what help is needed before they rush to generate possible actions.

In summary, the three-stage model provides an overall philosophy and plan for the helping process, but helpers must attend to individual needs of clients and environmental pressures before determining how to respond at any given moment. This book is not meant to be a simplistic "cookbook" or manual of what to do at every specific moment in helping. That would not be possible, given the infinite number of situations that could arise with different helpers and clients. Instead, I hope you learn to think about what you are trying to accomplish at each point in the helping process, become skilled at delivering the various possible skills, and then observe the client's reactions to help you devise better interventions for that client.

WHAT DO YOU THINK?

▮ What are your assumptions about human nature in terms of genetics, temperament, environment, early experiences, attachment, individuation, self-esteem, defenses, determinism, free will, and the balance of emotions, cognitions, and behaviors?

▮ What view of development (client-centered, psychoanalytic, or cognitive–behavioral) appeals to you most? Provide several reasons for your choice.

▮ Discuss the roles of empathic collaboration and cultural differences in helping.

▮ Describe the types of clients who would be most suited for client-centered, psychoanalytic, or cognitive–behavioral approaches to helping.

▮ If you were to choose a therapist for yourself, would you choose someone who was client-centered, psychoanalytic, cognitive–behavioral, or integrative (combining all three approaches as I do in this book)? Provide your rationale for this choice.

▮ Debate whether all three stages are needed for a complete helping process or whether another model is better.

▮ What is your definition of culture?

LAB 1

Multicultural Awareness

Goal: To help beginning helpers become aware of their own cultural values and begin to appreciate other cultures.

Instructions

1. Get in a dyad with someone who is culturally different from you in terms of race/ethnicity, socioeconomic status, sexual orientation, gender, or religion. Each person should talk for at least five minutes about some aspect of his or her culture experienced while growing up (e.g., holiday customs, a time when one was sharply aware of one's culture). The other person should listen without talking.
2. Get back together in the large group. Each person can introduce the other person and talk about something they learned about that person's culture.

Personal Reflections

■ What did you learn that is new about yourself?
■ What did you learn that is new about a different culture?

A Model for the Process and Outcome of Helping | 3

We ought to respect the effect we have on others. We know by
our own experience how very much others affect our lives,
and we must remember that we in turn must have the same
effect on others.

—*George Eliot*

James, a 21-year-old European American beginning helper, who
tentatively felt an affinity for a Rogerian theoretical orientation, was in
the middle of his first session with an 18-year-old Japanese American
male college student. The client was having problems with shyness and
was contemplating whether he wanted to become less shy. At a
particular moment in the session, James noticed that the client was
feeling down. He formulated an intention to help the client identify
and express his feelings and chose to use a reflection of feelings to
implement that intention. The client felt understood by the helper,
perceived the helper as trying to help him, and so revealed more about
his feelings of isolation. James then wanted to help the client explore
more about his feelings and so asked an open question about how he
felt about making friends. The process continued with James carefully
watching the client and reassessing what skills to use at each moment
in the changing process.

Much of what happens in helping situations is so complex that it is
often difficult for helpers, especially beginning helpers, to have a full awareness of the process. Furthermore, the helping process occurs at lightning
speed, which does not give helpers time to give conscious thought to every component and decision that accompanies interactions. Helpers must
learn to react quickly because clients constantly present new needs and
challenges.

Web Forms referred to in text can be found on the book's companion online guide described in the Preface.

In this chapter, I break down the helping process into what happens moment by moment. By slowing down the process, helpers can begin to understand their reactions and responses in different situations and learn about clients' reactions to their interventions. Greater self-awareness allows helpers to be more psychologically available for clients and more intentional in their behaviors.

Analyzing each part of the helping process initially feels uncomfortable and cumbersome because beginning helpers are not used to breaking down their interactions and examining them so carefully. Furthermore, most beginning helpers are not used to thinking about their reasons for doing things and are not used to examining the reactions of others. As most beginning helpers continue with it, they become more comfortable taking apart and analyzing the process and then are able to put it all together to function more effectively in sessions.

I begin by examining background variables that influence the helping process. Then I focus on context variables that set the stage for the moment-by-moment interaction. Next, I discuss the moment-by-moment interactional sequence and how interactions with the external world influence the helping process. Finally, I discuss how all of these variables lead to the outcome of the helping process. Figure 3.1 summarizes the variables that are involved in the helper–client interaction.

Background Variables

Background variables are what helpers and clients bring with them to the helping process. These variables influence the process and so need to be considered in any discussion of helping.

HELPER BACKGROUND

Helpers bring unique ways of viewing the world to the helping process. They contribute their personalities, beliefs, assumptions about the world, values, experiences, and cultural and demographic characteristics. In addition, helpers bring their theoretical orientation (beliefs about how to help) and their previous experiences in helping (both informal and formal). For example, one could imagine that an introverted, young, European American female helper with a psychodynamic theoretical orientation would have a very different impact on the helping process than an extroverted, middle-aged, Iranian American male helper with a cognitive–behavioral theoretical orientation. It is very important for helpers to be aware of their values and biases when they engage in the helping process.

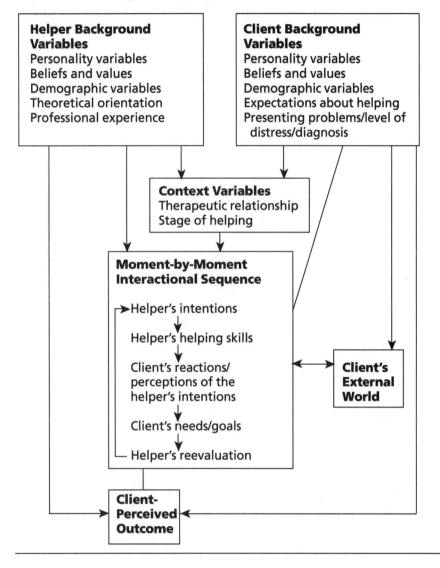

FIGURE 3.1

Factors influencing the helping process.

CLIENT BACKGROUND

A young, bright, attractive college student who is away from home for the first time and is feeling lonely and homesick would be very different to work with than a substance-abusing, older man who has been ordered by the court to attend counseling sessions because he batters his wife. Clients bring unique ways of viewing the world to the helping process in terms of their individual personalities, beliefs, assumptions about the world, values, experiences, and cultural and demographic characteristics. Furthermore, clients bring their expectations about what the helping process should entail, readiness to change, presenting problems, level of distress, and diagnoses. In this section, I focus on readiness to change and presenting problems because of the centrality of these variables to the helping process.

Client Readiness for Change

Clients are at various stages of readiness for change: some are reluctant to participate in any form of helping; others are eager to learn more about themselves; and yet others are ready to make changes in their behaviors. Prochaska, Norcross, and DiClemente (1994) identified six stages of change: precontemplation, contemplation, preparation, action, maintenance, and termination.

In the precontemplation stage, clients are unaware of the need to change or have no desire to change. Precontemplators lack information about their problems, engage in denial about their problems, and often blame other people or society for their problems. Other people are typically more bothered by the precontemplator's behavior than is the precontemplator.

In the contemplation stage, clients are aware of and accept responsibility for problems. They are beginning to think about changing but have not yet actively decided to change. Fear of failure often keeps clients stuck at this stage. Clients in this stage often spend time thinking about the causes of their problems and what it would be like to change.

In the preparation stage, clients have made a commitment to change and are preparing themselves to begin the change process. Some clients make public announcements that they plan to change (e.g., "I plan to lose 30 lbs"). Some clients prepare themselves mentally for how their lives will be different (e.g., "When I lose weight, I will feel healthier and be more attractive and it will be easier to exercise").

In the action stage, clients actively begin to modify their behaviors and their surroundings. They might stop smoking cigarettes, begin studying at regularly specified times, start taking more time for themselves, or decide to get married. The commitment and preparation done in the contemplation and preparation stages seem to be crucial for success in this stage, in that prepared clients are more aware of what they are striving for and why.

In the maintenance stage, clients have changed and are trying to consolidate their changes and deal with lapses. The process of change does not end, then, with the action stage. It takes several weeks for change to become incorporated into one's lifestyle, suggesting that it is not easy to make changes that stick. This stage is very challenging and can last a long time, because permanent change is difficult and often requires major lifestyle alterations.

In the termination stage, clients no longer are threatened by the original temptations, the problem behaviors do not return, and clients have confidence that they can cope without relapse. The effort to change and maintain the changes is no longer salient for people in this stage. In other words, clients do not have to think as much about changing or maintaining changes, and other things become more central.

Our goal as helpers is to assist clients in moving through the stages so that they become aware of problems, take responsibility for their behaviors, make decisions about how to change, make the actual changes, and then work on consolidating their changes. Movement through the stages can often take considerable time; thus, a client might be in one of the stages for a given problem for several months or even years. Furthermore, clients can be at different stages of change for different problems (e.g., a client could be in the maintenance stage for stopping smoking but at a precontemplation stage for resolving spiritual issues in his life).

Working with precontemplative clients can be difficult (but not impossible) because they often come to helping under duress (e.g., court referral) rather than because they genuinely want to change. One can compare working with precontemplative clients to trying to push carts with square wheels: It is more difficult to push a cart with square wheels than to push a cart with round wheels—the cart with square wheels does not budge no matter what the helper does. In contrast, working with clients in the contemplation, preparation, action, and maintenance stages tends to be easier because these clients are more eager to work on themselves. The process works better when clients are interested in, rather than resistant to, change.

Helping skills also vary with clients who are at different stages of readiness for change. Helpers typically spend more time in the exploration and insight stages of the helping process with clients in the precontemplation, contemplation, and preparation stages of readiness for change. In contrast, they spend more time in the action stage of helping with clients in the action, maintenance, and termination stages of readiness for change.

Presenting Problems

Clients seek help for a variety of problems. Issues that can be dealt with by beginning helpers using this model involve problems with identity; relationships; educational and career concerns; existential issues; spiritual issues; and maladaptive thoughts, feelings, and behaviors. Clients who present these types of relatively straightforward problems in adjustment and living typically need someone to listen empathically, help them sort out and understand their thoughts and feelings, and decide what actions to pursue. Some people, however, have long-standing psychological or organic problems (e.g., schizophrenia) and require treatment from more experienced therapists. Other people have problems with poverty or medical or legal problems and need help from trained professionals who specialize in dealing with these concerns.

Context Variables

Context variables are global factors that influence the process of helping. In this section, I discuss the therapeutic relationship and stages of helping.

THERAPEUTIC RELATIONSHIP

Researchers have consistently found that the therapeutic relationship is a robust predictor of the outcome of therapy (Gelso & Carter, 1985, 1994; Horvath & Bedi, 2002; Orlinsky, Grawe, & Parks, 1994). Clients typically report that the most helpful aspect of therapy is feeling understood and supported. For some people, the relationship itself is curative, and they need nothing else from the helper. Others need more in the way of helper skills. Because the therapeutic relationship is so important, it is necessary to explore and define what it is.

Gelso and Carter (1985, 1994) theorized that the therapeutic relationship is made up of the real relationship, the working alliance, transference, and countertransference. The real relationship is the genuine, nondistorted connection between the helper and client. The working (or therapeutic) alliance is the part of the relationship focused on the therapeutic work. Bordin (1979) further divided the working alliance into three components: a bond (i.e., the connection between the helper and client); an agreement on goals (a consensus about changes the client needs to make); and an agreement on tasks (a consensus about what is to take place during the helping process to meet the goals). A strong working alliance might involve a helper and client genuinely liking and respecting each other, deciding together to work on exploration and insight in the sessions, and agreeing about their goals to help the client develop better interpersonal relationships. Note that different types of working alliances may fit better for different types of clients. For example, Bachelor (1995) found that some clients prefer helpers who are warm and supportive, whereas others are put off by too much warmth and prefer helpers who are objective and businesslike.

In contrast to the straightforward concepts of the real relationship and the working alliance, transference and countertransference involve distortions in the relationship. Transference involves client distortions of the helper, and countertransference involves helper distortions of the client, both on the basis of experiences in previous significant relationships. In effect, transference and countertransference are like lenses or filters through which one views the world. For example, a female client may expect that the helper will be bored with her because her parents ignored her. Likewise, the helper might react poorly to client anger because anger was not an acceptable emotion in her or his family.

Although most researchers agree that a good therapeutic relationship facilitates the helping process, they are much less clear about how to establish good relationships with clients. I postulate that helpers establish good therapeutic relationships by attending and listening carefully to clients, using the appropriate helping skills at the right times, treating clients according to their individual needs, being aware of their own feelings and limitations, being aware of clients' reactions to their interventions, and being open to feedback from clients.

I propose that the therapeutic relationship works as follows. Clients often come to helpers feeling that no one listens to them or cares about them. Helpers try to pay full attention to their clients and communicate an understanding of clients' feelings and experiences. Helpers are empathic and nonjudgmental and accept clients as they are, which allows the clients to feel safe enough to express their hurt and pain. Finally, helpers are skilled in their interventions, which helps clients explore, gain insight, and make decisions about action and builds clients' confidence that they can be helped. In this type of setting, clients begin to feel that if their helper accepts them for who they are, they must be okay. It also allows them to see that not all people are like the significant others with whom they experience difficulty. Furthermore, it helps to reduce their anxiety and thus increases their capacity for facing interpersonal pain and anxiety. Clients slowly begin to build self-esteem, which is the foundation for change. They also feel it is safe to explore thoughts and feelings, come to new understandings, and make changes. It is clear, then, that the relationship and skills are interrelated in influencing the therapeutic process.

Helpers cannot establish relationships with all clients, especially those who are not motivated or ready to be helped. For example, an adolescent girl might be forced by her parents to go for helping but not want to be there. Moreover, some clients have been so hurt and their capacity to trust so seriously impaired that they cannot benefit from a facilitative relationship. One therapist suggested that some clients are like leaky gas tanks—you can never fill them up. Clients who have been seriously damaged in relationships often have difficulty attaching to therapists.

The fault sometimes lies with the helpers, however. All helpers have limitations related to their backgrounds and personal problems. I like to think of helpers as wounded healers who have personal issues that they have not resolved completely. All of us have issues, but most us can set them aside most of the time when we are helpers. If the personal issues are too salient, helpers are less likely to go beyond their own needs to focus on clients' needs. For example, a helper who just had a major fight with his or her spouse may not be able to concentrate on listening to a client's problems with studying. This does not mean that helpers must have all their problems resolved (which would be impossible); but problems must be resolved enough so that they do not interfere with the work.

Some matches between helpers and clients are not ideal and do not result in positive therapeutic relationships. For example, a female client who has been raped recently might not be able to talk to a male helper because she is terrified of all men. An alcoholic client might not want to see a helper who has never had problems with alcoholism because he fears that such a helper could not understand his struggle to stay sober. Helpers who have not resolved their experiences of traumatic sexual or physical abuse might not be able to hear a client's story of abuse without having strong emotional reactions or being distracted by their own pain.

No one can fully understand another person. We can try to empathize and imagine how the other person feels, but we can never fully remove ourselves from our own experiences to understand another person completely. Similarly, although we might try to have unconditional positive regard (i.e., caring about, understanding, and appreciating clients for who they are, regardless of how they behave), our regard for clients often has conditions (e.g., that they allow us to help them, that they talk openly about their problems, or that they not get angry at us). Unfortunately, we are not always fully aware of all of our personal issues and the conditions that we place on clients. Helpers need to do their best to form positive therapeutic relationships with clients; but when they are not able to establish good relationships, they need to examine their own issues as well as think about possible client dynamics influencing the interaction.

STAGES OF HELPING

As discussed in chapter 2, helpers have specific tasks during each of the stages of helping for what they want to accomplish (see Figure 2.2). During the exploration stage, the tasks are to establish rapport and develop a therapeutic relationship; to enable clients to tell their stories; to facilitate clients in exploring their feelings and thoughts; to arouse emotions; and to learn about the clients. The typical skills used to facilitate these exploration tasks are open question, restatement, and reflection of feelings. In the insight stage, the tasks are to assist clients in developing understanding of their concerns and insight into the ways in which they contribute to problems and to deal with the therapeutic relationship. In addition to continuing to use the exploration skills, helpers also use challenge, interpretation, self-disclosure, and immediacy to facilitate insight. In the action stage, the tasks are to assist clients in deciding how they want to change and to help them figure out how to implement these changes in their lives. In addition to continuing to use the exploration and insight skills, helpers use information and direct guidance to facilitate action.

The stages provide a blueprint or structure for how helpers proceed through sessions. Remembering the philosophy behind the model and the stage-specific tasks is crucial so that helpers remain focused on what they are trying to accomplish with their clients. Learning and practicing the skills can aid helpers in accomplishing the tasks that accompany each stage. These tasks and skills are discussed in detail throughout this book.

Moment-by-Moment Interactional Sequence

Given the background variables and the specific context, the helper needs to act at a given moment in the session. How does the helper select an intervention? I hypothesize the following sequence of events: Helpers formulate intentions on the basis of their assessment of the current situation. These intentions lead to the choice of specific helping skills. In turn, clients react to the helpers' interventions, which lead them to reevaluate their needs and goals and decide how to behave with the helpers. Helpers then assess clients' reactions and reevaluate what they need to do for their next intervention. The process thus continually unfolds with each person reacting both overtly and covertly, trying to determine the intentions of the other and deciding how to interact. The process thus changes depending on the perceptions, needs, and intentions of the moment. In the subsequent sections, I describe each of the components of the process.

HELPER'S INTENTIONS

A helper thinks about what can be accomplished with the next intervention on the basis of everything he or she knows at the time. The helper develops an intention (e.g., give information, identify feelings) for how to influence the client to respond (see the helper intentions list in Web Form D). The intentions guide the helper's choice of verbal and nonverbal interventions. Thus, the helper's intention is the reason behind the intervention. The helper might have several intentions for a single intervention (e.g., the helper might intend both to support and to identify and intensify feelings).

Intentions are covert and are not necessarily apparent to clients or helpers (Fuller & Hill, 1985). In fact, helpers are not always aware of their intentions at the time of delivery. For example, beginning helpers sometimes inadvertently self-disclose to make themselves feel better rather than to be helpful to clients. As helpers become more experienced, however, they typically become more aware of their intentions and develop better rationales for their interventions. Reviewing audio- or videotapes after sessions (alone or with a supervisor) and thinking about or writing down intentions for each intervention is an excellent way to increase awareness of what one is trying to accomplish. Helpers are typically able to identify intentions pretty easily when they review tapes within 24 hours of the session and recall how they were feeling and reacting at a given moment in the session (rather than how they currently feel about their interventions). By slowing down the process and examining it piece by piece, helpers can discover the different layers of feelings, thoughts, and actions. After gaining experience with examining intentions during videotape replays, helpers are often able to obtain an awareness of intentions while they are in sessions with clients. I encourage beginning helpers to become intentional in their interventions and to think about what they are trying to accomplish during each intervention.

HELPING SKILLS

Moment by moment, helpers make decisions about which helping skills to use to implement their intentions. They might ask an open question to encourage the client to talk more about the problem or challenge the client to become more aware of discrepancies. The helping skills system (HSS), shown in Web Form B, lists a variety of helping skills that can be used in helping. (Web Form C presents guidelines for using the HSS in research.)

Matching the helping skill to the helper's intention at a given moment is important. An open question may be the optimal choice if the helper's intention is to encourage the client to talk about problems, but it would not be as good a choice as reflection of feelings if the intention is to support the client, build the relationship, or communicate an understanding of the client's feelings. Hill and O'Grady (1985) and Hill, Helms, Tichenor, et al. (1988) found that therapists' intentions were connected consistently to their helping skills. For example, when therapists wanted to encourage their clients to express and experience feelings, they used open question, reflection, or interpretation. In contrast, when therapists wanted to give information to clients, they used information, direct guidance, or self-disclosure. These results suggested that therapists' intentions influenced which skills they used but that therapists did not always pair the same helping skill with a given intention (e.g., helpers could implement the intention of identifying and intensifying feelings with either an open question about feelings or a reflection of feelings).

Applying the helping skills in sessions with clients is both an art and a science. In addition to matching the skill to the intention, helpers should bear in mind that there are verbal and nonverbal components to the skills and that the same intervention can have a different impact depending on the manner of delivery. If the helper says, "You seem to be feeling anxious," in a supportive, gentle tone and makes appropriate eye contact, the client has a different reaction than if the helper uses a critical, judgmental tone and does not look at the client. Appropriate nonverbal behaviors vary across clients and situations, so helpers need to use nonverbal behaviors carefully and intentionally (see chap. 6).

The choice of intervention is limited to those skills in the helper's repertoire. Most helpers use the skills that are familiar to them and that fit their style. For example, some helpers do not feel comfortable challenging clients, so they use only supportive interventions. Research on intentions has indicated that helpers use skills that fit their theoretical orientation (Elliott et al., 1987; Hill, Thames, & Rardin, 1979; Mahrer, Sterner, Lawson, & Dessaulles, 1986; Stiles, 1979; Stiles, Shapiro, & Firth-Cozens, 1988; Strupp, 1955, 1957). In these studies, psychoanalytic therapists used more interpretation, behavioral therapists used more information and direct guidance, and Rogerian therapists used more reflection of feelings. In addition, helpers in different roles used different helping skills in ways that were consistent with what they were required to do in their roles. For example, psychotherapists in brief psychotherapy used mostly information and paraphrase (Hill, 1989). Radio psychology talk show hosts and career counselors used mostly information and direct guidance (A. Levy, 1989; Nagel, Hoffman, & Hill, 1995). Family practice lawyers used mostly information, whereas mental health professionals (e.g., counselors and social workers) used mostly information and closed questions (Toro, 1986). Nonprofessional group leaders used mostly information and self-disclosure (Toro, 1986). School counselors working with children used mostly closed questions and information, whereas the same school counselors working in a consultation with teachers used mostly information, paraphrase, and closed questions (Lin, Kelly, & Nelson, 1996).

Hill, Helms, Tichenor, et al. (1988) examined the effects of helping skills on immediate outcome (defined by client and therapist ratings of helpfulness, client reactions, and client experiencing levels). They found that helping skills had a small but significant effect on immediate outcome. It is actually surprising that they found any such overall effect, given the large number of uncontrolled background and situational variables. Specifically, interpretation, self-disclosure, paraphrase (restatement and reflection), and approval were very helpful interventions. Open question, confrontation, and information were moderately helpful interventions. In contrast, direct guidance and closed questions were not perceived as being very helpful. In a number of studies that investigated the effects of helping skills, interpretation is the only one that has consistently been found to be helpful (Elliott, 1985; Elliott, Barker, Caskey, & Pistrang, 1982; Hill, Carter, & O'Farrell, 1983; O'Farrell, Hill, & Patton, 1986).

In addition, Hill, Helms, Tichenor, et al. (1988) found evidence for a more complex process, such as that posited in this chapter. Specifically, preceding client behavior (client's experiencing levels in the turn preceding the helper's intervention), therapist intentions, and therapist helping skills were all important in predicting immediate outcome. When clients were at low levels of experiencing (i.e., telling stories rather than expressing their feelings), the most helpful interventions involved intentions of exploring feelings and behaviors, with the associated helping skills of paraphrase (restatement and reflection of feelings), interpretation, and confrontation. The least helpful interventions involved the intentions of setting limits, giving information, and attending to helper needs, with the associated helping skills of closed questions, open questions, and direct guidance. In contrast, when clients were at moderate to high levels of experiencing (experiencing their feelings and having some insight), almost anything helpers did was perceived as helpful. These results suggest that helper skills are most crucial when clients are not very involved in the helping process.

CLIENT'S REACTIONS

An intervention is met by one or more client reactions. When helpers are successful, the client's reactions match the helper's intentions and helping skills. For example, if the helper's intention is to provide emotional support and the helping skill used is an encourager such as "I understand what you're going through," the client's reaction might be feeling understood and supported. However, if the intervention is not successful, the client might feel that the helper did not really hear what was being expressed or that the helper made incorrect assumptions.

Hill, Helms, Spiegel, and Tichenor (1988) developed a measure of client reactions by asking clients how they felt about therapist interventions. About 60% of the reactions were positive (e.g., "felt understood"), although clients also reported many negative reactions (e.g., "felt worse"). The client reactions system is presented in Web Form G. Clients are sometimes consciously aware of their reactions, although at other times they might be unaware of their reactions. In addition, clients sometimes have difficulty admitting to reactions that are not socially acceptable (e.g., feeling angry at a helper's intervention). Admitting negative feelings about helpers can be difficult if clients respect and need the helpers or if clients cannot allow themselves to have negative emotions. For example, a client might react negatively to something a helper says because it is similar to something her parents said, but the client might not allow herself to express these negative feelings for fear of hurting the helper. Instead, this client might smile politely but feel somewhat distant and unengaged, not understanding consciously why she withdrew from the interaction.

Client reactions are sometimes covert (i.e., not displayed). The research suggests that clients often hide negative reactions from their therapists out of fear of retaliation or out of deference to the helper's authority (e.g., Hill, Thompson, Cogar, & Denman, 1993; Hill, Thompson, & Corbett, 1992; Rennie, 1994). For example, clients who feel angry at or misunderstood by their helpers are not likely to reveal those feelings if they feel unsafe in the therapeutic relationship.

In addition to hiding negative reactions during sessions, clients often do not disclose important material in sessions (Hill et al., 1993; Kelly, 1998; Regan & Hill, 1992). Clients in these studies indicated that they left things unsaid because the emotions felt overwhelming, they were ashamed or embarrassed, they wanted to avoid dealing with the disclosure, they feared that the helpers would not understand, or they thought that either they or the helpers could not handle the disclosure. These results are important because they remind us that helpers cannot "read" clients' minds and hence cannot assume that they know how clients are reacting.

Given that clients have negative reactions (and often hide them), it seems crucial to see whether one can detect these hidden negative reactions. Hill and Stephany (1990) looked at whether specific client nonverbal behaviors were associated with client reports of positive and negative reactions. The only result they found was that clients had fewer head nods when they were experiencing negative reactions. Clients seemed to become more still and less animated when they did not like what helpers were doing. These results suggest that helpers need to look closely at client lack of nonverbal movements as a possible sign of dissatisfaction or distress.

What Influences Client Reactions?

A number of factors influence the reactions clients have to helper interventions. First, clients' reactions are influenced by their needs at the time. For example, clients in severe crisis might tolerate almost any intervention because they are desperately in need of help. In contrast, a high-functioning client might have a specific need to make a decision about a career and therefore be more demanding that the helper be knowledgeable about how to help him with this decision.

I also speculate that clients' reactions are moderated by the therapeutic relationship. In generally positive relationships, clients might tolerate some mistakes from helpers without an adverse reaction because they feel that helpers are genuinely trying to be helpful. If the relationship is problematic or rocky, however, anything helpers do might elicit negative reactions from disgruntled clients.

In addition, clients' reactions seem to be influenced by their impressions of the helper's intentions. For example, if clients think that their helpers were acting out of their own personal needs and not in the best interest of the clients (regardless of what the helpers' actual intentions were), clients might have negative reactions. If clients think that therapists want to extend therapy to make more money rather than because their clients need help, clients might become quite angry and become uncooperative. In contrast, if clients think that their helpers are beginners who are struggling to be helpful (perhaps with limited success), they might feel sympathetic and have positive reactions. Clients' perceptions, even though they might not match the "reality" of helpers' intentions, seem to influence clients' reactions.

Helper Awareness of Client Reactions

In two studies (Hill, Thompson, & Corbett, 1992; Thompson & Hill, 1991), helpers were found to be better at detecting positive client reactions (e.g., felt supported, therapeutic work) than negative reactions (e.g., no reaction, challenged). One could postulate that helpers could not detect the negative reactions because clients did not express these reactions. Indeed, Hill, Thompson, and Corbett (1992) and Hill, Thompson, Cogar, and Denman (1993) found evidence that clients hid negative reactions more often than positive reactions. One could also postulate that some helpers are better than others at decoding reactions, as was found in the above studies and has been shown in the emotion literature (J. A. Hall, Rosenthal, Archer, DiMatteo, & Rogers, 1978; Rosenthal, Hall, DiMatteo, Rogers, & Archer, 1979). Hence, not detecting client reactions can be due either to clients hiding their reactions (particularly the negative ones) or to helpers having difficulty in perceiving reactions (particularly the negative ones.)

The findings from the research about reactions are sobering for helpers, who need to be aware that they might not know when clients have negative feelings or are hiding things in sessions. I would speculate that the more helpers can become aware of what clients are feeling, the better they perform as helpers. Furthermore, helpers need to be trained to understand and work with negative affect, especially when that negative affect is directed toward them (Hill, Kellems, et al., 2003). Such training is useful to enable helpers to deal more effectively with clients during sessions, to enable clients to experience a relationship in which negative feelings can be expressed and responded to in a healthy manner, and to provide a model for clients of how to deal effectively with conflict in their lives.

CLIENT'S NEEDS OR GOALS

Clients decide what they need and want from the interaction and what is possible to obtain from helpers at a particular time. Clients are not passive recipients of helpers' interventions but are actively involved in getting what they need from interactions. For example, one client might feel a need to retreat to avoid further confrontation. Another client might decide that he wants to reveal more because his helper is accurate in understanding him and can be trusted with secrets.

Clients also want to have an impact on their helpers. They might want to impress or please their helpers by doing whatever the helpers suggest. For example, Sam wanted to please his helper and so kept telling her what a good job she was doing. Other clients might decide not to reveal shameful secrets because they do not want to tarnish the helper's opinion of them.

I do not mean to imply that clients consciously plot the reactions they want to elicit from their helpers. Rather, I believe that clients act on the basis of their past experiences in ways that maximize the probability of getting their needs met. Most of this decision process about what they need from the interaction and what impact they want to have on helpers is intuitive rather than consciously planned. Some of these client goals are influenced by transference, which occurs when clients project how significant people in their lives (e.g., parents) behaved onto how they expect their helpers to behave (see Gelso & Hayes, 1998; Gelso, Hill, Mohr, Rochlen, & Zack, 1999). For example, if a client feels that no one listened to her as a child, she might not be able to believe that anyone could possibly want to listen to her now. Hence, even though the helper is attentive, the client might want the helper to "prove" that he really wants to listen to her or she will not talk in the session. Rather than recognizing that the helper is silent because he does not know what to say, this client might perceive the silence as occurring because the helper is bored by her. Another example is the client who believes that all older men are critical, like his father was; it may be hard for him to believe that an older male helper could be any different.

CLIENT'S BEHAVIORS

Clients engage in specific behaviors on the basis of their reactions, feelings about the therapeutic relationship, needs in the interaction, and goals for a desired impact. The client behavior system, shown in Web Form H, indicates that clients can resist, agree, make an appropriate request, recount, engage in cognitive–behavioral or affective exploration, come to insight, or discuss therapeutic changes. Clients' behaviors are determined not only by the interaction but also by their communication ability, awareness of needs, level of pathology, and personality structure. Hence, one client might be very articulate and insightful about describing the causes of his pain, whereas another client might be unskilled at communicating feelings and be unaware of what she is feeling in the moment.

HELPER'S ASSESSMENT OF CLIENT'S REACTIONS

Helpers, in turn, try to assess clients' reactions to their interventions. For example, they observe whether clients felt supported and understood or confused and misunderstood. Unfortunately, helpers are not always accurate in determining clients' reactions. A popular perception is that helpers can read clients' minds. In fact, our research suggests that helpers are not particularly adept at perceiving negative client reactions to their interventions, although they are somewhat more accurate at perceiving positive client reactions (Hill, Thompson, & Corbett, 1992). The lesser ability to perceive negative client reactions might occur because, as noted earlier, clients hide negative reactions from helpers. People often learn as young children not to show negative reactions for fear of evoking displeasure or being punished (e.g., imagine what would happen if an elementary school student told her teacher that she or he did not like what the teacher said). Hence, helpers have to be vigilant not to assume that clients have positive reactions just because the clients are not displaying negative reactions.

In addition, helpers might be reluctant to recognize when clients have negative reactions. Just as client perceptions may be distorted by transference, helper perceptions are sometimes distorted by their own past experiences, a phenomenon that has been called *countertransference* (see Gelso & Hayes, 1998; Hayes et al., 1998). For example, many helpers have a hard time with clients' anger directed at them. They want everyone to like them, and having clients get angry at them feels scary and upsetting. When clients are angry, these helpers might misinterpret the anger as a rejection of them personally, rather than appreciating that clients are able to express their anger (as they might other feelings). Other helpers might have difficulty allowing clients to become upset and cry, because they feel obligated to make everything better and have all clients be happy. Again, this is why it is critical for people considering a career as a helper to explore their own issues, needs, and limitations.

Unfortunately, not all helpers have received skills training or have learned to examine the effects of their interventions on clients, so they use interventions that feel comfortable rather than ones that match the client's needs in the specific situation. In addition, there is a danger that over time helpers can become insensitive to the influence of their behavior on clients and assume that they know how the clients are reacting internally. Helpers, even when they are experienced, must strive to be aware of their reactions and the impact of their interventions on clients.

HELPER'S REEVALUATION: AN ONGOING PROCESS

On the basis of their perceptions of the client's reactions (whether accurate or not) and observation of the overt behaviors, helpers reevaluate and devise new intentions and accompanying skills for the next intervention. If a helper perceives that the last intervention was successful and thinks that a similar intervention would be appropriate, she might continue with the same intention–skill combination. For example, if a reflection resulted in the client talking about sadness, the helper might use another reflection to help the client delve even deeper into these feelings. If a helper perceives that the last intervention was helpful but that something new is needed, he might choose a different intention–skill combination. For example, if a helper had reflected feelings and the client responded by talking about deep feelings but seemed to have a sense of completion, the helper might decide to use an open question to find out more about other aspects of problems.

If a helper perceives that the last intervention was not received well by the client, the helper tries to determine why the intervention was not successful. If the timing was poor, the helper might decide not to continue that intervention but to go back to a more exploratory intervention to learn more about the problem. In contrast, if the helper decides that the intentions for an intervention were on target but the wrong skill was used, the helper might use a different skill to implement the same intention. For example, a beginning helper might implement the intention of encouraging the client to talk about feelings by asking a closed question such as, "Did you have any feelings about that?" If the client responds, "No," and adds nothing further, the helper might realize that the closed question stopped rather than facilitated exploration. The helper might then use a reflection of feeling (e.g., "Perhaps you feel scared right now") in the next intervention and observe how the client responds. Thus, by paying attention to client reactions, helpers can devise new interventions to fit the immediate need.

Given that the most important criterion for the effectiveness of the helper's intervention is the client's response, helpers need to monitor client reactions to determine whether their interventions are helpful and make adjustments when clients respond negatively. I like to think of helpers as personal scientists, investigating the effects of each intervention on clients, testing what works and what does not work, and then deciding what needs to be done next. Helpers thus have to be very attentive to what works with individual clients. Even if a helper finds that certain helping skills work well with one client, those same skills might not work with the next client.

Of course, such constant awareness demands that helpers be open to feedback, have the skills in their repertoires to try something different, and have a good enough relationship with their clients to allow for misunderstandings. Unfortunately, many helper issues can interrupt this process: a bad day, a lack of openness and awareness, a lack of skills, or a lack of a good enough relationship with the client.

No helper can ever be perfect because there is no such concept as perfection in helping. One could argue that being a perfect helper would not be helpful for clients because it would not present a realistic relationship—everyone makes mistakes, and learning how to deal with mistakes can be very therapeutic. Helpers who recognize their mistakes, apologize, and process the event can provide a powerful example for clients about how to deal with problems in relationships. Helpers should relax, do the best they can, and try to learn from their experiences. Furthermore, helpers should seek a lot of training and supervision to help them deal with obstacles to their effectiveness.

External World

Typically, helping sessions last only one hour or so a week for a few weeks, whereas clients live the rest of their lives outside of the helping sessions. As helpers, we hope that clients take what they have learned from helping sessions and try to apply it to "real life." In one case of brief psychotherapy presented in Hill (1989), the therapist confronted the client with the fact that she did not seem to need him or listen to anything he said. The client was very surprised because she had never viewed herself this way. She thought that she was working intensely on the relationship. She discussed this with her friends, who agreed with the therapist's assessment that she seemed self-possessed and did not appear to need anything from them. Hearing this feedback from both the therapist and her friends forced the client to look at her behavior. In this case, the client successfully used the feedback from the friends to validate what she was learning in therapy. Ideally, clients think about what helpers have said and keep working on issues between sessions.

In intensive psychotherapy, clients sometimes form images, or what have been called *internal representations*, of their therapists to remind them of their helpers in between sessions (Farber & Geller, 1994; Geller, Cooley, & Hartley, 1981; Geller & Farber, 1993; Knox, Goldberg, Woodhouse, & Hill, 1999; Orlinsky & Geller, 1993). For example, some clients might hold imaginary discussions with their helpers to figure out what the helpers would suggest they do in difficult situations. Others might imagine their helper comforting them in difficult situations. These internal representations often help clients cope between sessions.

However, relationships in the external world can sometimes present obstacles to progress in therapy. Perhaps the clearest example is when a client's changes threaten the status quo of family life, causing family members to undermine the client's progress. For example, a severely overweight man's weight loss may threaten his marital relationship. The wife may fear that the husband is now attractive to other women and might lose interest in her. She may begin to cook tasty, fattening desserts to tempt the man to regain the weight and thus stabilize the relationship. These behaviors are not necessarily performed consciously but often are desperate attempts to maintain stability in relationships (see Watzlawick, Weakland, & Fisch, 1974). Thus, events in the external world can both help and hinder the therapeutic work. Helpers cannot just attend to what goes on in session; rather, they need to be aware of how external events influence the helping process. They also need to encourage clients to work on issues outside of helping to enhance the helping process and encourage clients to take responsibility for making changes in their lives.

Outcome

All of the variables discussed to this point (helper and client background variables, context variables, moment-by-moment interactional sequences, and the external world) interact to determine the outcome of the helping process. Thus, the outcome is influenced by many factors, and individuals react idiosyncratically to different aspects of the process.

Generally, the outcome of helping can be examined in terms of three areas: (a) *remoralization*, or the enhancement of well-being; (b) *remediation*, or the achievement of symptomatic relief; and (c) *rehabilitation*, or the reduction of troublesome, maladaptive behaviors that interfere with functioning in areas such as family relationships and work. Outcome research indicates that remoralization happens first and is the easiest thing to change in therapy; remediation follows at a slower pace; and rehabilitation takes the longest time to accomplish (Grissom et al., 2002; Howard et al., 1993). Hence, a client might feel more hopeful after a few sessions of therapy, but it may take longer for the client to feel less depressed and anxious, and even longer for the client to make changes in terms of new ways of behaving in relationships and work.

Another way to talk about outcome is in terms of *intrapersonal, interpersonal*, and *social role performance* (Lambert & Hill, 1994). Intrapersonal changes refer to outcomes that occur within the client (e.g., decreased symptoms, increased self-esteem, improved problem-solving abilities, new behavioral skills such as assertiveness, or increased subjective feelings of well-being). Interpersonal changes take place in the client's intimate re-lationships (e.g., improved communication, increased marital satisfaction, or healthier relationships). Social role performance refers to the client's ability to carry out responsibilities in the community (e.g., improved job performance, increased participation in community activities, greater in-volvement in school, or reduced antisocial behaviors). For example, a client with good outcome in all three areas might feel better about her-self, have a clearer sense of who she is and the meaning of her life, have an improved relationship with her husband, and have fewer days of ab-sence at work related to illness.

Helpers, clients, and clients' significant others often have different perceptions of the outcome of the helping process (see Strupp & Hadley, 1977). For example, a helper might feel pleased with her performance as a helper with Jack and believe that Jack benefited a great deal from the helping because he said he was going to change his major. In contrast, Jack might feel that he only participated in counseling to please his par-ents, that he listened politely and responded compliantly in the session to appease the helper, but dismissed all the helper's advice as soon as he left. Jack's parents might feel sad because their son is not choosing the career they want for him and resigned that even helping did not improve their relationship with their son. Thus, the outcomes of helping can be quite different depending on the individual's perspective.

Empirical Research on the Three-Stage Model of Helping

Because it is helpful to understand the empirical basis of the model, I summarize the results of some studies on the process model (see also Hill, 1992; Hill & Williams, 2000):

1. Helpers used intentions and response modes that fit their theo-retical orientations (e.g., psychoanalytic vs. behavioral) and pro-fessional roles (e.g., career counseling vs. psychotherapy).
2. Helpers had different intentions for using the same helping skill (e.g., open questions can be used to get information, focus, clarify, promote catharsis, explore cognitions, explore feelings, and deal with the therapeutic relationship). Thus, a complete description of the helper's verbal intervention must include both the inten-tion and the helping skill.
3. Helping skills had a small but significant impact on immediate outcome in sessions.

4. Interpretation and self-disclosure have generally been found to be helpful response modes, although both were used infrequently by helpers.

5. Client involvement (i.e., level of experiencing) in the helping process was related to the immediate outcome of helper interventions, so that specific helper interventions made the most difference when clients were at lower levels of experiencing (i.e., were recounting or telling stories) but made less difference when clients were at moderate levels of experiencing (i.e., talking about their feelings or thoughts).

6. Helpers were better at detecting positive than negative client reactions.

7. Clients used fewer head nods when they were experiencing negative reactions.

8. Clients hid negative reactions and left important material unsaid during sessions.

Research in helping skills is very difficult because the helping process is complex and research methods for studying this helping process are crude. I hope that others become excited about helping skills and find new methods for investigating the helping process. In particular, new measures need to be developed to assess other components of the process model (e.g., how helpers go about devising new intentions–skills on the basis of their evaluation of the client reactions). Research is also needed to determine how the components of the process model interact with one another and with the external world to lead to outcome.

Concluding Comments

The whole helping process undoubtedly seems incredibly complex, especially to the beginning trainee. Similarly, all the components of driving at first seem overwhelming to a person learning to drive, but later driving becomes so familiar that the driver often does not even think about the separate steps (e.g., turning the wheel to make a turn). At this point, I am trying to present you with a broad overview of the model so that you can have a framework for understanding the individual skills. Then I focus on learning and practicing each skill individually; only then do I discuss how to integrate them in the helping process.

WHAT DO YOU THINK?

■ I have described the helping process as being very complicated. Do you agree? What components have I left out of the helping process, and where have I included irrelevant components?

- What parts of the helping process are unconscious (i.e., not open to awareness)?
- How might helpers and clients increase awareness of their intentions and reactions?
- Why do you think that helpers and clients experience the same interaction differently?
- How important do you think helping skills are to the therapeutic relationship in terms of leading to client change?
- Is helping an innate trait, or can people be trained to be more effective helpers?

Ethical Issues in Helping | 4

Intellectual integrity, courage, and kindness are still the virtues
I admire most.

—*Gerti Cori*

magine that you are ending your first session with a client. You were
initially quite anxious but focused on the client during the session. You
enjoyed the session and felt that you became a better helper as a result
of working with this client. The client says that the session was very
helpful and then asks if the two of you might get together for coffee.
What do you do?

Beginning helpers may encounter ethical dilemmas similar to the one
described above as they learn and practice helping skills. When they face
an ethical quandary, beginning helpers are often uncertain about how to
respond in a professional and ethical manner. This chapter is designed to
help you work through ethical dilemmas and make responsible decisions
about how to resolve ethical questions.

An Overview of Ethics

WHAT DOES BEING ETHICAL MEAN?

Ethics are principles and standards that ensure professionals provide quality
services and are respectful of the rights of the people with whom they
work. Acting in an ethical manner also involves following the laws and
rules governing one's profession. Hence, the principles and standards are
aspirational guidelines that have been agreed on by a consensus of people

within the profession, whereas the laws and rules are legally binding prescriptions to do certain things and prohibitions against doing other things. It is important to contrast these principles and laws (which are agreed on by the profession or law) with one's personal morality (e.g., being for or against abortion rights).

Although beginning helpers are not yet professionals, they should follow the ethical standards of the profession. In the example of the client who asked the helper to go out for coffee, the helper might consider the ethical issues that arise in this situation before formulating a response. She or he would contemplate whether meeting for coffee would be therapeutic for the client, or whether this extension of the relationship could encourage dependency (and thus be harmful). In addition, although the helper might be tempted to accept the offer to go out for coffee and become friends with the client, she or he should ponder the impact of doing so on the therapeutic relationship.

ETHICAL CODES OF CONDUCT

Most helping professions (e.g., counseling, medicine, nursing, psychology, social work) have developed ethical codes that are intended to protect both the practitioners and the clients. These codes describe the underlying ethical principles to which professionals aspire in making their decisions. These principles encourage professionals to act in a responsible manner, ensure quality client care, and contribute to society through their work. Rather than providing "the right answer," the principles provide guidelines to helpers for behaving in a responsible manner and resolving ethical dilemmas. The codes also involve specific standards of conduct. These standards are the rules and indicate things that professionals must do (e.g., talk about confidentiality) and are prohibited from doing (e.g., having sexual relations with clients). Exhibit 4.1 provides a list of several professional organizations and their Web sites to review their ethical codes.

GENERAL ETHICAL PRINCIPLES

Many ethical codes stress the importance of six basic ethical principles: autonomy, beneficence, nonmaleficence, justice, fidelity, and veracity (Beauchamp & Childress, 1994; Kitchener, 1984; Meara, Schmidt, & Day, 1996).

Autonomy refers to the right (of both the consumer and the provider) to make choices and take actions, provided the results do not adversely affect others. This principle grants individuals the opportunity to determine their actions on the basis of their belief systems, which is a value of extreme importance in American society. For example, a helper may be working with a client to assist her in determining her future career direc-

EXHIBIT 4.1

Ethical Codes

American Association for Marriage and Family Therapy (2002)
   www.AAMFT.org
American Counseling Association (1995)
   www.counseling.org
American Psychological Association (2002)
   www.apa.org/ethics
American School Counselor Association (1998)
   http://www.schoolcounselor.org
National Association for Social Workers (1996)
   www.naswdc.org

tion, independent of her parents' hopes for her to pursue law school. Suddenly, the client announces that she is ending counseling and giving up her scholarship to pursue a career as a country music singer. The helper might suggest that the client reevaluate this decision and consider the pros and cons of life as a country music singer. However, the principle of autonomy allows the client the right to make her own decisions, provided these decisions are not harmful to others. In this example, the helper supported the client's decision to attend college in Nashville and simultaneously pursue her dream of becoming a musician.

Beneficence refers to the intent "to do good" by helping and promoting growth in others. This principle clearly states that helpers should be committed to the growth and development of their clients. Helpers who strive to provide the most comprehensive, up-to-date services to their clients are embodying the principle of beneficence, whereas helpers who see clients solely to make money violate this important principle.

Nonmaleficence can be described with the phrase "above all, do no harm." Professionals are asked to ensure that their interventions and actions do not inadvertently harm their clients. Thus, neglect on the part of the helper (even if unintentional) would be problematic. For example, a student in a helping class might be out drinking margaritas with friends and telling them about the practice helping session he had in class that day. Later, he might notice that his practice client was in the booth next to him and had probably overheard him telling his friends about her issues. Although the helper may not have used the client's name or intended to harm her, he would be responsible for the unintentional harm that results from having disclosed confidential information about his practice client.

Justice can be defined as fairness or ensuring equality of opportunities and resources for all people. One could interpret this to mean that helpers have an ethical responsibility to rectify the unequal distribution of helping services by making their services more accessible to those who are unable to pay. For example, helpers can contribute to building a just society by volunteering at not-for-profit agencies (e.g., shelters for battered women, clinics for people with AIDS). An additional method of promoting justice involves attempts to influence public policy or legislation to ensure that mental health services are available to those in need, regardless of their ability to pay, location, language preference, or disability status.

Fidelity refers to keeping promises and being trustworthy in relationships with others. Fidelity is a critical component of the relationship between helpers and clients. Without confidence in the helper's ability to be faithful to the agreements articulated in the helping session, minimal progress can be made. For example, the agreement between helpers and clients typically involves both parties meeting at a certain time, for a specified number of sessions. If helpers are consistently 20 minutes late for each session, they are breaking the promise to be available to clients at an arranged time. Violations like these can have a detrimental impact on the development of the helping relationship.

Veracity, which refers to telling the truth, is a powerful and necessary principle in dilemmas encountered in both helping and research settings. Clients often rely on their helpers to provide honest feedback about their interactions in the helping sessions. One example involves a 21-year-old client who worked with a helper for many months. Takiesha had not made much progress in the last few sessions and asked the counselor for some direct feedback about her work in the helping sessions. The helper provided several positive remarks and also indicated that at times, Takiesha appeared to place responsibility for her problems on others instead of empowering herself. Although Takiesha was upset about hearing this feedback, she was grateful to the helper for being honest and was able to understand how her reluctance to take responsibility prevented her from making necessary changes in her life.

Ethical Standards Relevant for Beginning Helpers

Although there are a number of important ethical issues for professional therapists and counselors, I focus here only on a few that beginning helpers may encounter.

CONFIDENTIALITY

Students learning helping skills may encounter confidentiality issues when they practice with classmates or volunteer clients who present real problems (and of course later on if they continue training to be mental health professionals). It is important that helpers respect a client's confidentiality by not divulging information shared in the helping session, except in limited circumstances (e.g., with their supervisor or as required by law). Sometimes, maintaining confidentiality can be challenging if students interact with clients outside of the sessions or if they have friends in common. However, the success of the helping relationship is due in part to a client's ability to trust that information shared with a helper in sessions will be held in confidence.

There are a few limits to confidentiality. First, you need to be able to talk about your client with supervisors so you can learn from your errors and grow as a helper. Second, if the client reveals to you an intent to harm self or others, you are legally obligated to report this threat. Third, if the client reveals childhood abuse to you, you are obligated to report this abuse to the authorities. It is important for you to inform the client at the very beginning of the first session about the general principle of confidentiality, as well as the specific limits to confidentiality. In addition, it is crucial for both of you to sign an informed-consent form, similar to the one shown in Exhibit 4.2, before the session.

RECOGNIZING LIMITS

It is critical that helpers recognize and practice only within the areas for which they have been trained and are competent. For example, after going through this course, you will have expertise in delivering basic helping skills (e.g., listening and reflecting feelings), but you will not have expertise in such things as crisis intervention or working with patients who are severely mentally ill. As an example, a friend may discover that you are learning helping skills. This friend then asks you to speak to her cousin, who has been acting in a strange manner and hearing voices that tell him to destroy the psychology building at the university. Appropriate ethical behavior in this case would involve telling your friend that meeting with her cousin is outside of your area of competence. You might offer to speak to your supervisor or professor to obtain a referral to a competent practitioner who has training and expertise in working with people who hear voices.

In a related vein, I encourage helpers to be honest about their qualifications. Helpers who describe themselves as counselors or advertise that they provide psychological interventions they have not been trained to use would be violating ethical behaviors. For example, a practice client may refer to you as his "psychologist." Ethical behavior would involve telling the client that you are in training to learn helping skills and do not yet have a degree or license to practice psychology.

Furthermore, beginning helpers must consult with supervisors to enable them to best serve their clients. In one helping class, a student met with a client who mentioned that she had considered suicide because of

---

EXHIBIT 4.2

Informed Consent

I understand that my helper is a student-in-training.

I understand that my helping session(s) may be audio- or videotaped for training and supervisory purposes; that only my helper and those involved in the course will review any tapes; and that confidentiality will be strictly maintained in accordance with the law. Recordings will be destroyed in a timely manner.

I understand that all information shared in this session will be kept confidential, with a few key exceptions:
(a) supervisors may listen to the session or read transcripts of sessions (transcripts will have no identifying information); (b) intention to harm self or others, as required by law; (c) reasonable suspicion of current or previous child abuse or neglect, as required by law; (d) court orders.

With the understanding that I may withdraw my consent to the above conditions at any time, I grant my permission to participate in the session(s) and to be audio/videotaped by the helper whose signature appears below.

Signature of Client: _____ Date: _____

Signature of Helper: _____ Date: _____

---

all of the stressors in her life. The student immediately contacted her lab leader and they consulted with the instructor, who then intervened with the client to provide the necessary assistance. Furthermore, when one's own issues threaten to interfere with the helping process, helpers need to consult supervisors. For example, at the same time John was struggling with his decision to marry his long-term girlfriend, his client was also considering whether to make a lifelong commitment to his partner. John realized the potential for harm in this situation and discussed with his supervisor how to ensure that his personal issues related to commitment would not have a negative impact on the helping sessions with his client.

EDUCATING CLIENTS ABOUT THE HELPING PROCESS

Clients have a right to understand the nature of the helping relationship. Many clients have never experienced a formal helping relationship and are uncertain about what to expect. Helpers have an ethical responsibility to educate clients about the process of helping, so that clients can make an informed decision to participate in the process (see Exhibit 4.2). For example, helpers should provide information about fees, length of the helping relationship, techniques used, and whether anyone will be observing or supervising. As noted above, beginning helpers must also inform clients about the limits of confidentiality and their status as helpers (e.g., that they are not professionals).

Furthermore, clients have the right to understand what procedures will be used and what outcome can be expected. If helpers plan on audiotaping or videotaping helping sessions, they must obtain permission from their clients before taping the interactions. Furthermore, when providing services to families or couples, helpers must clarify their roles and the relationships that occur during the time of service. For example, a helper was seeing an adolescent client whose parents were divorcing. The mother was struggling during this time and asked if she could talk privately with the helper to discuss some of her issues related to the divorce. The helper gently reminded her of the importance of having a special relationship with the client (the daughter) and indicated that this relationship might be jeopardized by even one helping session with the mother. The mother was given referrals to other qualified helpers.

FOCUSING ON THE NEEDS OF THE CLIENT

At times, the best interests of clients may conflict with the needs of helpers. For example, a helper may enter a helping session preoccupied because he needs to study for an exam. The helper may have a difficult time focusing on the client, and he may even hope to end the session early to go home and study. However, it is critical that the helper focus on listening carefully to the concerns of the client and be as present as possible in the helping session.

An interesting situation results when the client's unresolved issues result in behaviors that benefit the helper. For example, Himee noticed that her helper often had a soft drink on his desk. Himee then began to give the helper a soft drink at the beginning of each helping session. Although it might be in the best interest of the helper to accept his favorite drink, ethical behavior requires that the helper try to understand the meaning of Himee's behavior and act in a manner that places her needs first. In this case, the helper might assist Himee in uncovering her desire to please the helper and her fear that the helper might abandon her if she did not bring gifts to the sessions. Perhaps it would be in the best interest of the client to assist her in viewing herself as valuable in relationships, independent of the gifts she presents to others.

As the helping relationship progresses, helpers are responsible for ensuring coverage of psychological services if they are out of town or unavailable. Helpers are also responsible for ending helping when the client has met the treatment goals or is no longer benefiting from the helping sessions. When ending a helping relationship, counselors need to assist clients in terminating the relationship and in mobilizing internal and external resources to enable healthy functioning. Strategies for ending the helping relationship are outlined in chapter 22.

AVOID HARMFUL DUAL RELATIONSHIPS

A potentially harmful dual relationship occurs when someone in power (e.g., a helper, professor, or supervisor) adds another role to his or her interaction with a less powerful individual (e.g., a client, student, or supervisee), and that interaction may lead to the harm or exploitation of the less powerful person. For example, it would not be unusual or problematic for a supervisor also to be a student's professor and evaluator; however, if the supervisor–professor also took on the role of therapist, the dual relationship would be considered harmful because confidential information disclosed in therapy could potentially be used to the student's detriment. Helpers need to be aware of the power differential when working with others and ensure that clients are not harmed by their interactions. For example, if a beginning helper is assigned a client for whom she or he is also a teaching assistant, harm might occur if the client–student felt that disclosures could be used against him or her when the helper was grading exams. Hence, helpers should not take on clients with whom they have other relationships if that would interfere with the helping process.

Helpers also should not provide helping sessions to friends or family members. Although helping skills can be used to communicate more effectively in personal relationships, taking on the role of helper with friends can be detrimental for several reasons. First, it is difficult to be objective when listening to the problems of friends or family members. A lack of objectivity could have a negative impact on a helping session because the helper's own agenda could interfere with assisting the client to act in her or his best interests. Second, the role of helper is powerful and could disturb the power dynamics in the relationship. For example, Alfonso began to rely on his friend to be his helper while he was going through a divorce. In time, Alfonso became dependent on this friend for assistance when problems emerged at work or with his children. His relationship with his friend-turned-helper was harmed because their interactions were always focused on Alfonso's problems. Perhaps the most harmful example of dual relationships involves having a sexual relationship with a client. Research has shown that sexual involvement with clients (and former clients) results in negative outcomes (Pope, 1994). Thus, many professions have developed explicit rules prohibiting sexual intimacies between helpers and clients. In addition, providing counseling to someone with whom one has been sexually involved in the past can be very destructive to the client. Helpers typically cannot be objective and provide quality services to clients with whom they have been intimately involved. (For information on feelings of sexual attraction, see chap. 22.)

BE AWARE OF YOUR VALUES

Empirical literature has shown that helpers' values influence clients (e.g., Beutler & Bergan, 1991), so helpers need to be aware of this influence of values and beliefs in their interactions with clients. For example, a helper who believes that all women should work outside the home in high-status, nontraditional occupations may inadvertently discourage a client from selecting a traditional career that seems to be a good fit for her interests and that would enable her to focus on her family. Beginning helpers, like advanced clinicians, should work to understand their biases. Thus, I encourage helpers to increase their awareness of their values and to ascertain the influence of these values on the helping process.

The influence of values in helping can be subtle. Helpers can influence the direction of sessions and clients' selection of actions through nonverbal behavior they are unaware of, such as smiling or nodding their heads at particular moments. Beginning helpers sometimes struggle with inadvertently encouraging clients to talk about situations that are comfortable for or interesting to the helper. For example, a helper might use nonverbal behaviors to indicate great interest when the client is talking about her romantic relationship but seem somewhat disinterested when the discussion moves to roommate concerns.

BE AWARE OF CULTURE

Ethical Behavior Related to Culture

Ethical behavior mandates that helpers be mindful of differences among individuals and use basic helping skills that reflect an understanding of the people with whom they are working (see also American Psychological Association, 2003). It is important that beginning helpers do not assume that the helping skills transfer across cultures and individuals. One example is the assumption that maintaining eye contact is a sign of openness, interest, and willingness to participate in the session. In some cultures (e.g., Asian cultures), a lack of eye contact signifies respect for an authority figure and thus should not be interpreted according to American societal norms in helping sessions.

At times, helpers who are working with clients from a different culture either neglect or attach too much significance to the culture of their clients when providing interventions. It is important for helpers to realize that helping in the traditional manner may (or may not) be sufficient for these clients. For example, heterosexual helpers who are working with lesbian or gay clients should investigate the literature about working with these clients and be aware of the special challenges that may be present for these clients (while also understanding that lesbian and gay clients may share many similarities with heterosexual clients). For example, Shawn was depressed and felt hopeless when he sought help at the university counseling center. His helper assumed that because Shawn was a gay man, his depression ensued from the discrimination that gay men experience on campus. The helper told Shawn that he understood how painful it must be to be a gay man on a predominantly heterosexual college campus. Shawn was stunned and angry at the helper: He had sought assistance because his sister had recently been killed in a car accident and he was having trouble grieving the loss, not because of problems related to his sexual orientation. Thus, it seems critical to be aware of the client's culture as influencing the client deeply but never to assume that the client's cultural background and related experiences are the primary motivators for seeking assistance.

Furthermore, a helper who is working with a client from a different culture should not assume that the client's goals are to assimilate (or not assimilate) into the majority culture. For example, Bridget immigrated to the United States from another country and asked for assistance in selecting a career. She explained to her helper that her parents wanted her to go to medical school, but she was doing poorly in her science courses. The helper incorrectly assumed that Bridget did not want to pursue a medical career and directed her to select a different occupation on the basis of her interests, values, and abilities (because making career decisions in terms of individual needs and abilities is a cultural value for many people living in the United States). However, if the helper had listened carefully to Bridget, he would have discovered that she was feeling devastated about her inability to meet her parents' expectations and dreams (in part because of her cultural background, which valued familial harmony and parental approval).

Demonstrating interest in clients' cultures is important, but reliance on clients to educate helpers about diverse cultures is inappropriate. Helpers should educate themselves about their clients' cultures through obtaining supervision, reading relevant materials, and seeking exposure to the culture through the people and food. An African American client who worked in a battered women's shelter expressed frustration not only with being a member of a group of people who have less power in American society but also with being asked to train and educate European American people about her culture.

In addition, ethical behavior goes beyond having an awareness of individual and cultural differences to embracing a commitment to eliminate bias and discrimination in one's work. This commitment may involve actively examining our biases, confronting colleagues who act in a discriminatory manner, advocating for those with less power, and working for social change. For example, some helpers facilitate growth or empowerment groups for clients who have been marginalized in society. Another helper used her experience as a counselor, teacher, and researcher to write a book about empowering clients through the process of counseling (McWhirter, 1994).

Cultural Self-Awareness

All of us need to engage in serious self-examination to discover our cultural values and beliefs as well as our prejudices and biases. Being aware of our cultural beliefs (e.g., valuing independence, autonomy, and family) is important so that we can recognize what we value; but it is also important so that we do not automatically assume these values are right for everyone else. Understanding our prejudices and biases is important so that we do not harm clients who are culturally different from us. All of us are raised with prejudices and biases which can surface when we are least aware of them. In fact, sometimes we are so used to these feelings that we do not even question their validity.

As an initial step, think about what your "hot buttons" are. How would you feel if you were assigned different types of clients: male versus female, homosexual versus heterosexual, old versus young, African American versus European American versus Latino–Latina versus Asian American, Jewish versus Christian versus Muslim versus Buddhist versus Hindu, poor versus rich, educated versus not educated, disabled versus not disabled? If you had different reactions to one side of the contrast (e.g., different reactions to seeing a male vs. female client), you need to step back and think about your reactions. Talk over your reactions with a supervisor or therapist and try to understand them.

As a next and crucial step, beginning helpers can become familiar with other cultures by reading about them. There are several excellent texts that provide further information about multicultural counseling and counseling with specific groups (Atkinson & Hackett, 1998; Atkinson et al., 1998; Helms, 1990; Helms & Cook, 1999; McGoldrick, 1998; McGoldrick, Girodano, & Pearce, 1996; Pedersen, 1997; Pedersen et al., 2002; Ponterotto et al., 2001; Sue & Sue, 1999).

Being a Culturally Competent Helper

Sue and Sue (1999) asserted that becoming a culturally skilled helper is an active, ongoing process that never reaches an end point. It is something we aspire to, and work toward, rather than accepting complacency. The following are characteristics of culturally sensitive helpers (Arredondo et al., 1996; Skovholt & Rivers, 2003; Sue & Sue, 1999):

■ They strive to understand their culture and how it influences their work with clients.
■ They strive to understand how their beliefs about helping (e.g., style, theoretical orientation, definition of helping) are influenced by their culture.
■ They honestly confront their biases, prejudices, and discriminatory behaviors and work to keep them out of the helping process.
■ They have a wide range of helping skills and use them flexibly to fit the needs of clients from different cultures.
■ They are knowledgeable about the cultures of their clients.
■ They understand the extent to which discrimination and oppression influence clients' lives and contribute to their problems.
■ They acknowledge and address cultural differences between themselves and their clients while still communicating willingness to help.
■ They seek supervision or refer when necessary.

ACT IN A VIRTUOUS MANNER

Professionals concerned with ethical behaviors have begun to move from a focus on behaving in an ethical manner (i.e., following the guidelines delineated in an ethical code) to behaving in a virtuous manner. Virtue differs from ethics in that one is not as concerned with laws and rules as much as with striving to be a person of positive moral character (Meara et al., 1996). Part of this change results from the reality that ethical codes, in and of themselves, cannot provide exact specifications for behaviors. Helpers need to be trained to internalize the six basic ethical principles, practice a comprehensive ethical decision-making model, and monitor themselves and their behaviors to ensure respectful interactions with clients. For example, a helper had a very successful helping session with a client at the university counseling center. She used her basic helping skills to provide a safe and open environment. The client shared much personal information in the session and struggled with concerns of importance in his life. The following weekend, the helper ran into the client at a party. She was confused about how to deal with this situation because her training had not addressed guidelines for meeting clients in social situations. This was a case in which knowledge of the "right" behavior or rule for intervention was missing. However, the helper was a sensitive and respectful woman, so she waited for the client to speak to her first and returned his brief greeting as they passed. Her response was consistent

with virtuous behavior and provides yet another reason to promote virtuous interactions with others. It is not possible to provide helpers with
answers to every ethical situation they might encounter; instead, I suggest that helpers behave with clients in a caring and respectful manner
that is consistent with acting in a virtuous manner (which is most likely
also ethical).

TAKE CARE OF YOURSELF TO ENSURE
THAT YOU CAN CARE FOR OTHERS

One final dimension of ethical behavior that is often ignored involves
helpers taking care of themselves. Helping can be an exhausting enterprise that requires helpers to give much of themselves to others. The fast-
est road to burnout involves taking care of others without paying attention to relaxation and caring for one's own needs. Helpers who assist clients
in their jobs and then, during their free time, also take care of the needs of
friends and relatives should examine this potentially unhealthy pattern
carefully.

It also behooves helpers to monitor their health and energy to ensure
the provision of quality services. Helpers might evaluate regularly the
presence of added stressors, poor health, and exhaustion. I would encourage helpers to achieve balance by integrating rewarding work, supportive relationships, regular exercise, and healthy eating habits into their
lives. I also strongly encourage helpers to seek counseling when they need
support or assistance with pressing concerns.

Working Through
an Ethical Dilemma

Although beginning helpers may not encounter many ethical dilemmas,
learning how to work through these situations can be helpful so that helpers can be prepared when ethical dilemmas arise. Ethical dilemmas occur
when there are competing ethical reasons to act in ways that are mutu-
ally exclusive (Kitchener, 1984). At times, the actions that helpers would
take to uphold one ethical principle could violate another ethical principle. Kitchener described inherent contradictions that exist in ethical codes
(e.g., individual autonomy vs. making decisions for clients; confidentiality vs. protecting others). For example, ethical codes often ensure a client's
right to privacy and confidentiality. They also endorse the importance of
working to minimize harm to others. These important standards can, at
times, conflict with one another. For instance, one helper worked with an

adolescent client who was threatening to kill herself but did not want the helper to discuss this with her parents. The adolescent felt her parents would not take her seriously and might punish her for disclosing these thoughts to her helper. The helper was faced with an ethical dilemma that was not easily resolved by examining the profession's ethical code. In this case, the helper talked with the adolescent about the importance of disclosing this information to her parents to ensure that she would be safe from harm. Then, in the presence of the client and with the client's permission, the helper discussed the client's concerns with her parents.

The A–B–C–D–E strategy for ethical decision making (Sileo & Kopala, 1993) is a framework that can be followed when helpers are confronted with ethical dilemmas. To illustrate its application, let us consider an example of an ethical dilemma in which a client discloses to a helper that she was raped the previous night by an acquaintance. The helper in this case is a beginning helper who feels outraged by the crime and wants to call the police immediately. The client, however, is concerned about her relationship with her boyfriend and definitely does not want the rape to be reported. The helper realizes that this is not a situation in which he is legally required to break confidentiality and report the rape, but instead is an ethical dilemma between reporting a crime against the client's wishes and maintaining confidentiality. The helper uses the A–B–C–D–E strategy for ethical decision making to work toward resolving how to proceed in this challenging situation.

A: ASSESSMENT

The helper identifies the situation; the client's status and resources; and the helper's values, feelings, and reactions to the situation. In this case, the helper notes that the client is a well-adjusted, bright, and competent young woman who is finishing her fourth year in college, majoring in business administration. She reports having a good relationship with her boyfriend. Two close friends have promised to support her through her recovery from the rape, and she has indicated an interest in attending a rape survivors' group. The helper, however, feels strongly that the rapist should be punished for what he did to the client. When he reflects more on the issue, the helper acknowledges that the strength of his emotions may result from his feeling helpless when he discovered that his younger sister had been raped during her first year in college.

B: BENEFIT

The helper evaluates what is most likely to benefit the client, the helping relationship, and the client's significant others. In this case, the helper believes that disclosure of the rape to the police and subsequent prosecution of the rapist could benefit the client, her boyfriend, and possible future victims. However, he also acknowledges that the client believes that she would be helped most by discussing the rape with her helper, her best friends, and a rape survivors' support group. As with many ethical dilemmas, different benefits are present for several possible solutions.

C: CONSEQUENCES AND CONSULTATION

Moving on to the ethical, legal, emotional, and therapeutic consequences that could result from possible actions, the helper consults with a supervisor who provides assistance in identifying and working through salient issues. In this case, the supervisor helps him identify that his disclosure of the rape to the police would undermine the trust he had worked to develop with the client. Moreover, the helper would be violating the client's confidentiality and right to privacy. His reporting of the rape might reinforce feelings of powerlessness that the client felt after being raped.

D: DUTY

The helper next considers to whom a duty exists. In this case, the helper's primary duty or responsibility is to the client, rather than to her boyfriend or other women that the rapist might harm. His job as a helper is to do no harm to his client and to provide services that enhance her growth and potential. The helper is beginning to realize how important it is to abide by the client's wish for nondisclosure, despite his own desire to prosecute the rapist.

Sometimes, the helper may have a duty to protect someone other than the client (i.e., an identifiable person whom the client is threatening to harm). In situations where a child is being abused, helpers are mandated by law to report the abuse or to assist the client in reporting the abuse. Furthermore, in cases where the client threatens to harm self or others, the helper must ensure the safety of the individuals identified to be at risk for harm. For example, if this client told her helper that she planned to murder the rapist and had enlisted the assistance of an assassin to carry out the plan, the helper would have a responsibility to prevent harm to the rapist.

E: EDUCATION

The helper reviews his education to determine what he has learned about appropriate actions to take in dealing with similar ethical dilemmas. The helper refers to his notes from his courses, consults current Web sites (see Exhibit 4.1), and determines that in this situation, the best strategy is to maintain the client's confidence and assist in her recovery from the rape. The helper also decides to go for therapy to address his residual feelings about his sister's rape.

Concluding Comments

Ethical dilemmas can be aptly described by the two Chinese symbols representing *crisis*: danger and opportunity. Ethical dilemmas can be dangerous in that the welfare of the client may be compromised, but they also present an opportunity for helpers to reflect on what they have learned and what they value and then to act in a manner consistent with professional and (one hopes) personal values. Ethical dilemmas provide a unique challenge for helpers to confront and resolve important questions and to ensure, to the best of their abilities, that their clients' needs are being served.

WHAT DO YOU THINK?

- How do you feel about professional groups imposing ethical restrictions on helpers?
- What do you think the consequences should be if someone violates the ethical standards?
- What is your opinion about cultural considerations in ethics? Discuss how your response may be influenced by your cultural background.
- Is there a value in identifying "hot buttons?"
- Discuss the possible positive and negative consequences of discussing confidentiality and informed consent and how they influence the therapeutic relationship.
- What are some ways, other than those covered in the chapter, that could inadvertently cause harm by the helper?
- Do you believe that taking care of oneself as a helper helps to prevent problems in the helping role?

LAB 2

Ethical Awareness

Goal: For helpers to become knowledgeable about how to resolve ethical issues that might emerge during their helping sessions.

Instructions: Gather into four small groups. Identify the ethical issues in each situation and then apply each step of the A–B–C–D–E strategy for resolving ethical dilemmas to the case. Afterward, get together as a large group and present your conclusions.

Case 1: A beginning helper (Jack) wants to practice his helping skills and notices someone in his residence hall (Sam) who seems to have a lot of problems and few friends. What issues should Jack consider if he wants to act in accordance with the ethical guidelines described in this chapter?

Case 2: A beginning helper is interested in working with clients who have eating disorders because she went through counseling for this issue. Recently, she has been under a lot of stress and her eating has become erratic and uncontrollable. She is assigned a client who has an eating disorder. What should be the helper's response if she were acting in accordance with the ethical guidelines described in this chapter?

Case 3: A beginning helper has been working with a client for three sessions. The client is a single, attractive male who has many qualities that the helper (also a single male) admires in a romantic partner. During the third and final session, the client indicates an interest in talking more over drinks. The helper is attracted to the client yet uncertain about what to do, given that the helping relationship is ending and that it may or may not have risen to the level of "real" counseling. What should be the helper's response if he were acting in accordance with the ethical guidelines described in this chapter?

Case 4: Using the knowledge you have gained from the material and exercises in this chapter, indicate the action you would take with regard to the ethical dilemma presented at the beginning of this chapter. Describe the strategy you used to make your decision.

Personal Reflections

■ What issues arose for you personally in trying to apply the A–B–C–D–E strategy to these cases?

■ What would you do to prevent yourself from making ethical "mistakes" if you were a practicing therapist?

■ How do the ethical principles and standards mesh with your personal morality?

II

Exploration Stage

Overview of the Exploration Stage 5

When one pours out one's heart, one feels lighter.

—Yiddish proverb

Yusef was feeling miserable, lonely, and worthless after his recent move to the United States. He desperately wanted to have a close friend with whom he could talk about his deepest feelings. His parents were concerned about him and suggested that he talk with a helper. During his first session with the helper, Yusef indicated that he felt like he was going to "burst from loneliness." Since moving to this country, he had not talked to anyone other than his parents. He was hesitant to tell them how badly he felt because he worried that they would get too concerned and he felt they could not really do anything to help him. The helper listened carefully and reflected Yusef's feelings of isolation, sadness, and rejection. Yusef began to cry and was able to talk about how he felt different from the other kids because he was from another culture. The helper let him talk and express all his feelings. She accepted him and listened nonjudgmentally, interested in understanding his experiences. At the end of the session, Yusef told the helper that he felt much better. He felt like he was different but okay; he had renewed energy to make friends. Just talking to a caring, understanding person helped lift the burden that had been bothering him and made him feel better about himself.

In this overview chapter, I present the theoretical background for the exploration stage and then describe the major goals of this stage: establishing rapport and developing the therapeutic relationship, encouraging clients to tell their stories and explore feelings and thoughts, facilitating

---

Web Forms referred to in text can be found on the book's companion online guide described in the Preface.

arousal of emotions, and allowing helpers to learn about their clients. Chapters 6 through 9 describe the major skills (attending and listening, open question, restatement, reflection of feelings) used to reach the goals of the exploration stage. Chapter 10 presents several additional skills (information about the process of helping, approval and reassurance, closed question, self-disclosure for exploration, and silence) that are used infrequently but can sometimes be valuable. In Chapter 11, I present an integration of the skills used in the exploration stage, discuss some common obstacles that trainees face in meeting these goals, and suggest several strategies that helpers can use to overcome these obstacles and manage anxiety.

Theoretical Background: Rogers's Client-Centered Theory

Much of what takes place in the exploration stage is influenced by Carl Rogers's theory of personality development and psychological change (see Rogers, 1942, 1951, 1957, 1959, 1967; Rogers & Dymond, 1954). Rogers had a profound influence on the field of psychology with his optimistic and hopeful assertion that all people have the potential for healthy and creative growth. His orientation was client-centered and was rooted in phenomenology, which means that he placed a strong emphasis on the experiences, feelings, values, and inner life of the client. Rogers believed that perceptions of reality vary from person to person, that subjective experience guides behavior, and that people are guided by their internal experience rather than by external reality. Similarly, he believed that the only way to understand individuals is to enter their private world and understand their internal frame of reference. In other words, to understand another person, one needs to suspend judgment and try to see things as they see them.

According to Rogers (1942, 1951, 1967), the only basic motivational force is the tendency toward self-actualization, which propels people to become what they are meant to become. He believed that each person has an innate "blueprint," or set of potentialities, that can be developed. Rogers likened the forces toward self-actualization in people to the natural order. He noted that plants and animals grow without any conscious effort, provided that the conditions for growth are optimal. Similarly, he believed that people have an inherent ability to fulfill their potential. Furthermore, Rogers believed that people are resilient and can bounce back from adversity given this innate growth potential.

THEORY OF PERSONALITY DEVELOPMENT

According to Rogers (1942, 1951, 1967), infants evaluate each experience in terms of how it makes them feel, which he called the *organismic valuing process* (OVP). Rogers believed that because behavior is governed by OVP, infants can perceive experiences as they actually occur without distorting them. In OVP, no experiences are more or less worthy; they just are. In other words, every event is interesting and open for investigation without prior prejudice. Infants evaluate experiences as to whether they enhance or maintain the organism. For example, if an experience (e.g., being hugged) enhances the organism, the infant feels good and is satisfied and might smile or laugh. However, if experiences do not enhance the organism (e.g., being cold or having a dirty diaper), the infant does not feel good, is not satisfied, and so might cry. Infants evaluate events by how they actually feel, not by how someone else tells them they should feel. The OVP, then, is an internal guide that everyone has at birth; and OVP leads the person toward self-actualization (see Figure 5.1). People freely seek those experiences that enhance them when they trust this internal guide. Rogers believed that infants could trust these inner feelings because they have positive strivings toward self-actualization and a natural curiosity about life.

In addition to having the OVP, children also have a need for unconditional positive regard. In other words, they need acceptance, respect, warmth, and love without conditions of worth (i.e., they need to be loved just because they are themselves and not because they do anything). When children feel prized, accepted, and understood by others, they begin to experience self-love and self-acceptance and develop a healthy sense of self with little or no conflict. These prized children are able to attend to their OVP and make good choices on the basis of their inner experiencing.

Unfortunately, because parents themselves are not perfect, they place conditions of worth (COW) on their children, demanding that they fulfill certain requirements to be loved. For example, parents may give messages such as, "I will not love you unless you are a 'good girl,'" "I will not love you unless you keep your room clean," or "You must be beautiful to receive my love." Because parents communicate (through words or actions) that children are lovable and acceptable only when they behave in accordance with imposed standards, children come to believe that they must be and act in certain ways to earn their parents' love.

Consequently, the COW, rather than the OVP, guide a person's organization of their experiences (see Figure 5.2). In other words, children sacrifice their OVP to receive love from their parents (e.g., children give up being spontaneous and playful to sit "properly" and be "good" to please their parents). When a child introjects (i.e., internalizes) his or her par-

The hypothesized path between the organismic valuing process (OVP) and self-actualization if there are no conditions of worth.

```
┌─────┐                                    ┌──────────────────────┐
│ OVP │ ────────────────────────────────► │  SELF-ACTUALIZATION  │
└─────┘                                    └──────────────────────┘
```

ents' COW, these conditions become a part of the child's self-concept and prevent the child from functioning freely. The more COW there are, the more distorted the person becomes from his or her own experiencing.

Conditions of worth lead children to feel conflict between their self-concept and their inner experience. For example, a mother may communicate to a young girl that it is not acceptable for her to hate her brother. The girl may feel that to be loved, she must be a good girl, and so she may disown the hate as not being part of herself. Hence, rather than learning that she may feel hate but cannot hurt her brother, she learns that her feelings are not acceptable. Another example is parents who punish or ridicule a boy for crying when he is hurt or needs help with a difficult task. The boy might repress his feelings of pain and dependency and become extremely independent to maintain his parents' approval. These two examples illustrate how externally imposed values can substitute for the OVP. When feelings of hate or dependency get aroused, these children misidentify or repress these feelings and, thus, are not in touch with their inner experiencing. Children experience positive self-regard only when their self-experiences are consistent with feedback that they get from others (e.g., if a girl feels talented in playing the violin and others tell her that she is talented). Feelings of self-worth become dependent on the conditions of worth that are learned in interaction with significant others. A child with too many conditions of worth would not be open to experience, accepting of feelings, capable of living in the present, free to make choices, trusting, capable of feeling both aggression and affection, and creativity. He or she would have a conflicted sense of self.

Obviously, children must become socialized so they are able to live in their families and society. Children cannot act on all their innate desires or get all of their needs met immediately because the world is not a perfect place and other people also have needs. Parents, for example, cannot always immediately meet the infant's needs because they have other demands on their time. In addition, parents cannot allow a child to hurt a sibling or another child. The manner, however, in which parents socialize their children is crucial. For example, a parent can empathize with a young girl but still place limits on her (e.g., "I know you are angry at your brother, but you cannot hurt him"). The girl may feel frustrated but does not learn

FIGURE 5.2

The hypothesized path between the organismic valuing process (OVP) and self-actualization when the path is derailed by conditions of worth (COW). When more conditions of worth are placed on a person, there is more of a discrepancy between the real self and the ideal self.

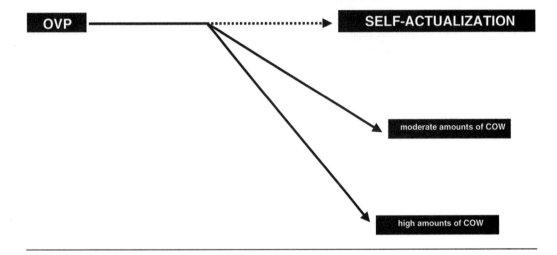

to deny her feelings. Instead, she learns to experience her feelings but channel them in a more socially acceptable direction. In contrast, when parents humiliate a child (e.g., "Real men don't cry") or deny that the child has feelings (e.g., "You don't hate your teacher," "You don't feel hurt"), children become confused about their feelings. The child may feel sad or feel hatred, but the parents say he or she does not have these feelings. What do children trust—their inner experience or what their parents tell them they feel? If they do not pay attention to their parents, they risk losing parental approval and love. If they do not pay attention to their inner feelings and instead try to please others who place COW on them, they lose their sense of self. One can easily see how children come not to trust their inner experiences. Children must survive, so they often choose parents' attention and "love" over inner experiencing.

When COW are pervasive and the OVP is disabled, the sense of self is weakened to the point where a person is unable to label feelings as belonging to the self. For example, a woman might not even be aware of feeling angry and hurt when being verbally and physically abused by her husband because she thinks she deserves the abuse. When people cannot allow themselves to have their feelings, they often feel a sense of emptiness, phoniness, or lack of genuineness. This lack of genuineness about one's feelings leads to a split or incongruence between the real and ideal self and is the source of anxiety, depression, and defensiveness in relationships.

DEFENSES

Rogers suggested that when there is an incongruence between experience and sense of self, the person feels threatened. For example, a person who acts pleasant and happy but is actually feeling grumpy and depressed is in danger of losing touch with his inner self. If he were to perceive his depression accurately, his self would be threatened because he has built an image of himself as always happy. When people feel such a threat, they respond with anxiety, a signal that the self is in danger. Feeling this anxiety, the person invokes defenses to reduce the incongruity between experience and sense of self, thereby reducing anxiety.

One major defense is perceptual distortion, which involves altering or misinterpreting one's experience to make it compatible with one's self-concept. By distorting experiences, clients avoid having to deal with unpleasant feelings and issues and can maintain their perceptions of themselves. For example, a man may perceive himself as being of average weight even though he is quite overweight and no longer fits into chairs. He might tell himself he does not eat any more than other people. In another example, a person with a sense of worthlessness who is promoted at work might misinterpret the reason for the promotion to be congruent with his negative sense of self. He might say that the only reason he got the promotion was that "the boss had to do it" or "no one else wanted the job."

A second defense is denial, which involves ignoring or denouncing reality. In this situation, people refuse to acknowledge their experiences because they are inconsistent with the images they have of themselves. By denying their experiences, clients avoid anxiety. For example, a woman who is treated unfairly at work might ignore her anger at her boss because she has internalized her parents' belief that anger is bad and that she will not be loved if she expresses anger. Rather than allow herself to experience her anger, she may say she is not trying hard enough or she is not smart enough for the job.

Defenses block incongruent experiences from full awareness and minimize threats to one's sense of self and allow the self to function and cope. A certain level of defenses is necessary for coping, but excessive use of defenses can take a toll on the self in at least three ways. First, the subjective reality (what one allows oneself to experience) can become incongruent with the external reality (the world as it is). At some point, the person may no longer be able to distort or deny the experience, which could lead to overwhelming feelings of threat and anxiety and disintegration of the self. For example, a child might struggle to maintain the illusion that things are fine between his parents despite their nightly battles.

However, when his mother leaves without warning, the boy may not be able to handle the loss and may stop attending school and talking to others. In another example, a person might partition off parts of self that are unacceptable and exclude them from awareness (e.g., deny to oneself that sexual abuse occurred). Second, a person might develop a rigidity of perception in areas where she or he has had to defend against perceiving reality. For example, a woman might have such a strong need to believe in the curative effects of a quack medicine for cancer that she does not listen to any disconfirming evidence, resulting in her not seeking proven strategies for treating her cancer. Third, the real self can become incongruent with the ideal self, suggesting a discrepancy between who one is and who one wishes to be. A woman might be average in intelligence but feel a need to be smart (particularly if she has internalized parental COW that she should be extremely intelligent). If the real–ideal discrepancy is large, the person may feel dissatisfied and may be maladjusted (e.g., depressed or anxious).

REINTEGRATION

To overcome disintegration, rigidity, or discrepancies between real and ideal selves, Rogers thought a person must become aware of the distorted or denied experience. In other words, a person must allow the experience to occur and accurately perceive the event. The woman described above must acknowledge to herself that she has average intelligence and accept and value herself rather than distort or deny her feelings. Rogers theorized that for reintegration to occur, the person must (a) reduce the COW and (b) increase positive self-regard through obtaining unconditional positive regard from another person. Conditions of worth lose their significance and ability to direct behavior when another person accepts the person as he or she is. In effect, individuals return to the OVP and begin to trust their inner self, thus becoming more open to experience and feelings (see Figure 5.3).

A person can reintegrate without unconditional positive regard from another person if there is minimal threat to the self and the incongruity between self and experience is minor, but this is a relatively rare occurrence. Typically, individuals respond to years of having COW imposed on them by becoming increasingly defensive. Once developed, defenses are difficult to let go because the person anticipates being vulnerable and hurt again. In effect, defenses are adaptive to help children cope, but fear and habit make them difficult to shed when they are no longer needed.

A helping relationship, then, is often crucial for assisting individuals in overcoming their defenses and returning to trusting their OVP. A helping relationship allows the individual's self-actualizing tendency to overcome the restrictions that were internalized in the COW. In a helping

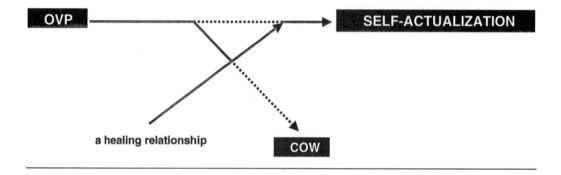

FIGURE 5.3

The reparative function of a healing relationship in terms of getting a person back on path so that the organismic valuing process (OVP) is once again directly related to self-actualization. COW = conditions of worth.

relationship, the helper attempts to enter the client's subjective world and understand the client's internal frame of reference. The helper also tries to provide an experience in which the client is accepted and cared for without COW. This helping relationship does not necessarily need to be from a professional helper, and in fact, people often seek healing relationships from supportive people in their environment (e.g., friends, relatives, rabbi, minister, or priest). A person who has received training in helping skills, however, is more likely than an untrained person to provide the important conditions to facilitate change.

Rogers believed that the helping relationship, in and of itself, produces growth in the client. He said, "I launch myself into the therapeutic relationship having a hypothesis, or a faith, that my liking, my confidence, and my understanding of the other person's inner world, will lead to a significant process of becoming" (Rogers, 1951, p. 267). Rogerian helpers believe that most clients benefit greatly from being listened to, understood, and accepted. The power of this kind of relationship can be highly therapeutic and constructive. In the Rogerian approach to helping, the helper enters the therapeutic relationship with the facilitative attitudes of congruence (genuineness), unconditional positive regard, and empathy. Rogers (1957) postulated six conditions that he considered to be necessary and sufficient for change to occur.

1. The client and helper must be in psychological contact. A therapeutic relationship or emotional connection between the helper and client is essential.
2. The client must be in a state of incongruence, so that there is a discrepancy between self and experience that leads the client to

feel vulnerable or anxious. If a client feels no anxiety, she or he is unlikely to be motivated enough to engage in the helping process.

3. The helper must be congruent (genuine) or integrated in the relationship. The helper must be open to her or his own experiences and be genuinely available to the client. The helper cannot be phony in the helping relationship.

4. The helper must feel unconditional positive regard for the client. The helper values all feelings (although not necessarily all behaviors) and places no judgment on the feelings. Essentially, a helper is trying to understand a client's feelings and experience but is not trying to judge whether the person "should" or "should not" have the feelings or whether the feelings are "right" or "wrong."

5. The helper must experience empathy for the client. The helper tries to immerse her- or himself in the client's feeling world and understand the client's inner experiences. The understanding comes out of the helper's experiencing of the client's feelings, using the helper's inner processes as a referent. The helper not only experiences the client's feelings but also has his or her own reactions to the client's feelings; the helper is thus able to go beyond words to understanding the client's implicit feelings (Meador & Rogers, 1973). The helper tries to feel "as if" she or he were the client and temporarily living in the client's life, without ever losing the awareness that they are separate individuals. The helper tries to sense and uncover feelings of which the client is unaware because they are too threatening. Rogers emphasized that empathy is not passive but requires thinking, sensitivity, and understanding. He described *empathy* as follows:

> It means entering the private perceptual world of the other and becoming thoroughly at home in it. It involves being sensitive, moment by moment, to the changing felt meanings which flow in this other person, to the fear or rage or tenderness or confusion or whatever that he or she is experiencing. It means temporarily living in the other's life, moving about in it delicately without asking judgments (Rogers, 1980, p. 142).

Emphathy can be distinguished from sympathy, in which the helper feels pity for the client and often acts from a position of power rather than as an equal. I can also distinguish empathy from emotional contagion, in which a helper feels the same feelings as the client (e.g., becomes just as depressed as the client) and cannot maintain objectivity. Empathy involves a deep understanding of the client's feelings. Bohart et al. (2002) indicated that empathy is effective because it creates a positive relationship, provides a corrective emotional experience, promotes exploration, and supports the client's active self-healing efforts.

6. The client must experience the helper's congruence, unconditional positive regard, and empathy. If the client does not experience the facilitative conditions, for all practical purposes they do not exist for the client, and the sessions are not likely to be helpful.

In summary, Rogers speculated that if helpers can accept clients, clients can come to accept themselves. When clients accept themselves, they can allow themselves to experience their real feelings and accept that the feelings come from themselves. Hence, the OVP is unblocked, and the person becomes open to his or her experiences. The client can begin to experience love, lust, hatred, jealousy, competitiveness, anger, pride, and other feelings. For Rogers, the most important thing is accepting the feelings and coming to accept oneself.

CURRENT STATUS OF CLIENT-CENTERED THEORY

Recent reviews of the empirical literature have confirmed the importance of the facilitative conditions, particularly of empathy, in leading to positive outcome of therapy (Bohart, Elliott, Greenberg, & Watson, 2002; Farber & Lane, 2002; Klein, Kolden, Michels, & Chisholm-Stockard, 2002). It appears that empathy is important to allow clients to feel safe and supported, to help clients have a positive relationship experience, to promote exploration, and to support clients' active self-healing efforts. Recent research, however, has focused more on the working alliance, or the relationship between the therapist and the client, rather than just the therapist-offered facilitative conditions (e.g., Horvath & Bedi, 2002).

In a reformulation of Rogers's theory, Bohart and Tallman (1999) stressed that clients are self-healing but can get off track. They suggested that when helpers provide appropriate conditions, clients are once again able to be self-healing. Similar to Rogers's argument that an empathic attitude is more important than the use of specific skills, Bohart and Tallman argued that specific techniques are not as important as using whatever techniques work to help the client get back to self-healing.

HOW ROGERS'S THEORY RELATES TO THE THREE-STAGE HELPING MODEL

Rogers's theory forms the foundation for the exploration stage and informs the insight and action stages. I agree with Rogers that helpers should maintain an empathic client-centered stance of trying to understand the client's experience as completely as possible with as little judgment and as few prior assumptions as possible. Empathy and a therapeutic relationship can be very effective in helping clients begin to accept themselves and trust their experiences.

For some people, being understood and encouraged to express their feelings is enough to get them back to a self-healing mode so they can function again and make needed changes. Others need more assistance in learning how to deal with feelings and experiences, many of which may be new to them. It is important to note that acceptance of feelings is distinct from decisions about what to do about the feelings. Furthermore, some people need to be assisted in moving toward insight and action. In addition to maintaining the facilitative conditions, helpers also need to be able to facilitate insight and action. Additional theories (psychoanalytic, cognitive, behavioral) provide the foundation needed to assist some clients in moving beyond exploration of thoughts and feelings; these are described in later chapters.

Furthermore, I do not completely agree with Rogers that people are inherently good and striving for self-actualization. There seems to be minimal evidence for these postulates. As discussed in chapter 2, my assumption is that people are neither good nor bad at birth but rather develop depending on temperament, the environment, and early experiences. Despite this difference in beliefs about human nature, I agree with Rogers about the importance of the facilitative conditions for establishing the therapeutic relationship and helping clients explore concerns and achieve self-acceptance.

Goals for the Exploration Stage

The goals for the exploration stage are establishing a relationship of trust, helping clients tell their stories, facilitating the expression of emotion and emotional arousal, and learning about clients. The sections that follow define these goals in more detail.

ESTABLISHING RAPPORT AND DEVELOPING A THERAPEUTIC RELATIONSHIP

Helpers establish rapport (i.e., an atmosphere of understanding and respect) with their clients, so that clients feel safe to explore. Rapport sets the stage for development of the therapeutic relationship, which is very important in helping. Clients are most likely to reveal themselves when they believe they have a caring, therapeutic relationship with their helpers. Clients generally need to feel safe, supported, respected, cared for, valued, prized, accepted as individuals, listened to, and heard. In everyday relationships, people often do not fully listen to others, so it is a gift to clients for helpers to listen attentively to them without rushing to say something next (e.g., telling a competing story, as friends often do). If friends and relatives would listen as carefully as I hope helpers learn to do in the exploration stage, communication would be greatly improved and people would live in greater harmony.

During this stage, helpers are trying to understand their clients from clients' frame of reference. Helpers attempt to "walk a mile in the clients' shoes" and view the world through their clients' eyes. They try to understand clients' thoughts and feelings without imposing their thoughts or values on clients. They attempt not to judge clients and figure out whether they are "right" or "blameworthy," but instead try to understand how clients came to be the way they are and how it feels to be who they are. Helpers try to align or attune themselves (i.e., try to feel what it is like to be the client) so they can understand each client's feelings.

If helpers can assist clients move to an awareness of their inner experiencing, they can begin to trust and then to heal themselves. I agree with Rogers (1957) that clients typically need to feel accepted and prized by others before they can begin to accept and value themselves. To do this, helpers need to accept clients as they are as much as possible and provide them with the facilitative conditions of empathy, unconditional positive regard, and genuineness. As mentioned earlier, *empathy* refers to understanding another person and feeling "as if" you are the other person (i.e., trying to put yourself in her or his place even though you are not that person and can never understand them completely). *Unconditional positive regard* refers to accepting and appreciating another person without judgment. *Genuineness* (or what has also been termed *congruence*) refers to helpers' being open to their own experiences and genuinely available to clients, rather than being phony or inauthentic. A large part of establishing a relationship is having an attitude of acceptance, empathy, and respect. Helpers need to want to listen and understand clients without judging them. In addition, having knowledge of helping skills, feeling competent in being able to use the skills, and the appropriate use of skills places helpers in the framework whereby they are more likely to have a therapeutic attitude.

Helpers should not think they can simply establish a relationship at one point in time and ignore it thereafter. They need to be aware of maintaining the relationship throughout the helping process. At any time throughout the process, the relationship can, and often does, rupture and need repair (see Hill, Nutt-Williams, Heaton, Thompson, & Rhodes, 1996; Rhodes, Hill, Thompson, & Elliott, 1994; Safran, Muran, Samstag, & Stevens, 2002).

Beginning helpers often worry about the consequences of not liking their clients or of not being able to establish a rapport with their clients. For example, many beginning helpers think they could never work with rapists or child abusers because they would be repulsed and horrified. However, the goal of being a helper is not to make friends. Helpers do not need to "like" clients in the same way they like or choose to spend time with close friends. Rather, helpers have a responsibility to understand and assist clients and to feel compassion for the human beings underneath the exterior presentations. The greatest challenge for one helper was working with women in prison. The crimes committed by the women made it difficult for her to empathize and respect them. However, after getting to know the women and their life circumstances, she became aware that these women had feelings similar to hers. Although actions are not universal, feelings are. Even though helpers may not have experienced the same life events as their clients, they have surely experienced many of the same emotions; thus, helpers can empathize with clients' feelings, even if they disagree with their behaviors.

TAPPING INTO THOUGHTS AND HELPING CLIENTS TELL THEIR STORIES

Clients need a chance to talk about their problems. It often helps to talk out loud about what is going on inside. All too often, people just continue with their ordinary routines without exploring their problems in any depth. As Frank and Frank (1991) noted, "How can I know what I think until I have heard what I have to say?" (p. 200). Having a forum to express one's thoughts allows one to hear and think about the content of what one is saying. Clients need to realize what they are thinking and have a chance to express these thoughts out loud.

Furthermore, by realizing what one is thinking, one has a better chance to hear the inconsistencies and logical fallacies. Talking about one's thoughts provides the person the opportunity to think about whether she or he really believes what is being said, especially when she or he knows someone else is hearing it. In addition, the process of talking to a helper about a problem is useful because it allows one to think about it, take it out and examine it, put thoughts into words, and get another person's reactions.

TAPPING INTO EMOTIONS

Earlier, I discussed the importance of emotions in Rogers's theory and suggested that emotions reflect a core part of human experience. Emotions are a key element in the helping process because they represent fundamental experiencing and are connected integrally to cognitions and behavior. In fact, mental health could be defined as allowing oneself to have a whole range of feelings and expressing these feelings in an appropriate manner.

One major goal of the exploration stage is for helpers to assist clients in experiencing feelings about their presenting problems. Many clients learned as children to suppress their feelings. They had to distort or deny their actual feelings to survive and gain approval from parents or other significant persons, so many clients are not aware of their feelings. For example, if clients cannot allow themselves to feel hurt, they limit their range of emotions and might feel hollow or empty inside. Some clients feel that their "inner cores" are rotten. Clients might not know who they are and might rely on other people to tell them how they feel. In significant relationships, they might ignore their feelings of hurt and feel distant without knowing why.

Sometimes the content of what the client says is not as important as the feelings about the topic, particularly if there is a discrepancy between content and feelings. Helpers need to listen to the "music" (i.e., the underlying message) in addition to the words. They need to try to hear both the content and what the client feels about the content.

In addition, I want clients to focus on what they are feeling immediately in the present moment. Experiencing immediate feelings often is not comfortable, so clients may want to run away and avoid their feelings. Through support and encouragement by helpers, clients often are able to tolerate the anxiety and discomfort of exploring their immediate feelings. For example, Joel spent much of the session relaying to the helper events that occurred during the week. When the helper gently encouraged him to explore his feelings in the present regarding these past events (e.g., "How do you feel right now about the event?"), Joel talked about his feelings and sessions became more intense and productive than they previously had been.

Helpers sometimes need to be assertive and ask about feelings that clients are not discussing. For example, clients might need to be invited to talk about difficult feelings such as shame or being depressed or suicidal. In friendships, people often do not probe beyond what their friends choose to reveal because they feel that would be overstepping implicit boundaries. In helping relationships, helpers need to encourage clients to explore painful feelings that are hard to express. Some clients do not reveal certain feelings unless helpers inquire, so helpers need to ask about personal, sometimes uncomfortable, issues. However, helpers need to respect the rights of clients not to answer any questions or to go deeper than they choose. Helpers walk a fine line between inviting clients to disclose feelings and not forcing them into unwanted disclosure.

Another reason for encouraging clients to talk about feelings is that emotional arousal seems to be necessary for change to occur (Frank & Frank, 1991). Without emotional arousal, clients typically are not involved in the helping process and are not motivated to change. Many times, people deny or defend against their feelings because they do not want to deal with the overwhelming or painful nature of their feelings. In contrast, when people have strong emotional arousal (e.g., fury, despair), they are most aware of feelings and more likely to be open to changing. Because emotional arousal is important in terms of setting the stage for change to occur, helpers need to assist clients in becoming aware of and experiencing their emotions.

LEARNING ABOUT CLIENTS

The exploration stage provides an important opportunity for helpers to learn about their clients. When a client first comes to a session, the helper has no way of knowing how to help that particular person. Helpers cannot assume they know anything about particular clients or their problems, even (or perhaps especially) if helpers have similar problems. Encouraging an individual client to explore often requires a substantial amount of time because most people and problems are quite complex. In addition, because our goal is to help clients come to their own conclusions and decisions, helpers need to listen carefully to what clients say and how they feel before constructing an action plan to help them solve their problems.

In learning about clients, helpers must follow the lead of the individual client. Helpers can be prepared in general by knowing theories of therapy and helping skills, but they must learn more specifically about how to help each client from that client. A parallel example is having a baby. Expectant parents can read lots of books about babies and generally be prepared for having a child, but they really learn parenting skills from attending to the needs of their own infant. Similarly, each client is different because of culture, family, and experiences; helpers cannot make assumptions about who the client is or what she or he needs.

Furthermore, helpers need to start conceptualizing clients' problems during the exploration stage so they can best help them through the insight and action stages. The helper needs to determine whether the client can profit from talking therapy or whether he or she needs an alternate form of intervention. Knowing something about the origin of and factors maintaining the problem can aid helpers in making these determinations.

Concluding Comments

The exploration stage is important because it facilitates the development of the relationship, gives clients a chance to explore concerns and immerse themselves in their immediate experiencing, and provides helpers with an opportunity to learn about clients' presenting issues and to assess clients' appropriateness for what helpers can offer. For Rogerians, the exploration stage is all that is needed for helping. Rogerians believe that the facilitative attitudes of empathy, unconditional positive regard, and genuineness allow clients to begin to accept themselves, which releases the inner experiencing and unblocks the potential for self-actualization. Indeed, some clients need only a listening ear to get them back to their own self-healing processes. Hence, I believe helpers should spend a lot of time in the exploration stage because it can be helpful by itself. However, because many clients cannot make progress with exploration alone, insight and action are often necessary to help them change. In this case, exploration sets the stage for everything else that follows.

An important caveat throughout the exploration stage (and the rest of the helping process) is that there are no absolute "right" interventions to use. Although I can provide general guidelines, I cannot provide a cookbook to tell helpers exactly what to do in different circumstances. Individual clients require different things from helpers. It is up to helpers to determine which interventions are productive and which are not useful by paying attention to the individual client's reactions and responses.

WHAT DO YOU THINK?

▪ How well do the tasks of the exploration stage fit your personal style?
▪ Discuss whether establishing a relationship is more a matter of attitudes or implementing helping skills.
▪ Describe the challenges you would face in developing a relationship with someone you believe has done awful and despicable things (e.g., rape, murder).

Initial Session

In this lab, you will meet with a classmate and try to be as helpful as possible.

Goal: To get a baseline of what skills are used in a 20-minute session prior to training.

Helper's and Client's Tasks During the Helping Interchange

1. Students take turns being helper, client, and observer for 20-minute sessions.
2. Helpers bring copies of the Session Review Form (Web Form A), Helper Intentions List (Web Form D), Client Reactions System (Web Form G), and Session Process and Outcome Measures (Web Form I) to the session. Obervers bring copies of the Supervisor Rating Form (Web Form B).
3. Helpers bring an audio- or videotape recorder (tested ahead of time to ensure it works) and a tape, and turn the recorder on at the beginning of the session.
4. Helpers introduce themselves and assure clients of confidentiality.
5. Each helper conducts a 20-minute session with his or her client, being as helpful as possible. Clients talk about an easy topic (See Exhibit 1.1 in chap. 1). Observers record what they thought was the most and least helpful thing the helper did.
6. While watching the session, the observer completes the Supervisor Rating Form.
7. Helper and client complete the Session Process and Outcome Measures.
8. The observer and client give feedback to the helper.

Helper's and Client's Tasks During the Postsession Review of the Tape

1. After the session, the helper and client review the tape (takes about 40–60 minutes). Helpers stop the tape after each helper intervention (except minimal utterances such as "um-hmm" and "yeah") and write the key words on the Session Review Form (so the exact spot on the tape can be located later for transcribing the session).
2. Helpers rate the helpfulness of the intervention and record the numbers of up to three intentions (using the Helper Intentions List) for the intervention, responding according to how they felt *during* the session rather than while listening to the tape. Helpers should try to use the whole range of the helpfulness scale and as many intentions as possible. Do not complete these ratings in collaboration with clients.
3. Clients rate the helpfulness of each intervention and record the numbers of up to three reactions, responding according to how they

continues

LAB 3 (Continued)

Initial Session

felt *during* the session. Clients should try to use the whole range of the helpfulness scale and as many reactions as possible (helpers learn more from honest feedback than from "nice" statements that are not genuine). Clients should not collaborate with helpers in doing the ratings.

Lab Report

1. Helpers should type a transcript of their 20-minute session (see the sample transcript in Web Form C). Skip minimal utterances (e.g., "okay," "you know," "er," "uh").
2. Divide the helper speech into response units (see Web Form F).
3. Using the Helping Skills System (Web Form E), determine which skill was used for each response unit (i.e., grammatical sentence) in your transcript.
4. Erase the tape. Make sure no identifying information is on the transcript.
5. Compare the helper and client scores on the Helping Skills Measure, Relationship Scale, and Session Evaluation Scale with those of other students (see Web Form I; all these measures are included in the Session Process and Outcome Measures).

Personal Reflections

▌ What did you learn about yourself from this experience?
▌ What was it like for you to be a helper and a client?

Attending and Listening 6

The one who listens is the one who understands.

—African [Jabo] proverb

The students in one class prearranged to manipulate their professor's behavior through nonverbal responding. Whenever the professor moved to the right, they looked up, paid rapt attention, and smiled encouragingly. Whenever the professor moved to the left, they looked down, rustled their papers, coughed, and whispered. The professor soon had moved so far to the right, he fell off the stage! This example illustrates the power of attending skills.

Attending and listening are basic skills helpers use throughout the entire helping process to enable clients to feel safe and to explore their thoughts and feelings. *Attending* refers to helpers orienting themselves physically toward clients. The goal of attending is for helpers to communicate to clients that they are paying attention to them and to facilitate clients in talking openly about their thoughts and feelings. In effect, attending lays the foundation for the implementation of all the other helping interventions. Clients feel they are valued and worth being listened to when helpers attend to them. Attending can encourage clients to verbalize ideas and feelings because they feel helpers want to hear what they have to say. Furthermore, attending behaviors can reinforce in clients an active involvement in the session.

Attending is communicated mostly through nonverbal behaviors. Through nonverbal behaviors, people convey both what they are trying

---

Web Forms referred to in text can be found on the book's companion online guide described in the Preface.

to express and what they do not intend to express (or might be trying to hide). For example, although a helper might try hard to be empathic and look concerned, he or she might feel bored and irritated with the client, which might be expressed through foot tapping or stifled yawns. Helpers need to be aware of both the intended and unintended consequences of their nonverbal behaviors in helping interactions.

Attending orients helpers toward clients, but listening goes beyond just physically attending to clients. *Listening* refers to capturing and understanding the messages that clients communicate, either verbally or nonverbally, clearly or vaguely (Egan, 1994). Listening involves trying to hear and understand what clients are saying. Reik (1948) talked about listening with a third ear, which involves listening carefully to what the client really means, not just what she or he says overtly. In effect, the helper puts the verbal and nonverbal messages together and hears what the client is thinking and feeling at a deep level.

Attending behaviors set the stage for allowing helpers to listen, but attending does not necessarily ensure listening. Helpers could attend physically but not be listening (e.g., they could be thinking about dinner that night and not hear what clients are saying). Listening provides the raw material from which helpers develop their verbal and nonverbal interventions, but listening should not be confused with the ability to deliver these interventions. Helpers could listen without being helpful, but it would be very difficult to be helpful without listening. Thus, from watching sessions, one could not actually tell if helpers were listening; however, one could infer they were listening if they were able to produce statements that reflected they heard the client.

Several nonverbal behaviors have been shown to be important in the helping setting (see Highlen & Hill, 1984) including smiling, body orientation directly facing the client, forward trunk lean, vertical and horizontal arm movements, and a distance of about 55 inches between the helper and client.

Some researchers (e.g., Archer & Akert, 1977; Haase & Tepper, 1972) have suggested that nonverbal behaviors play a more important role in the communication of emotions than verbal behaviors. These researchers suggested that people communicate more about true emotions through nonverbal than verbal expressions. The results also suggest that if there is a discrepancy between verbal and nonverbal behaviors, nonverbal behaviors are more reliable indicators of true emotion. In my opinion, there is not enough empirical evidence to indicate the relative importance of verbal and nonverbal behaviors; however, the existing evidence suggests that helpers should pay attention to what they communicate nonverbally and that helpers need to pay attention to clients' nonverbal behaviors.

How to Attend and Listen

Numerous attending skills can be delineated, all of which are important for the helping process. To make it easier to remember them, I use the acronym ENCOURAGES (Exhibit 6.1).

EYE CONTACT AND FACIAL EXPRESSION

Eye Contact

Eye contact is a key nonverbal behavior. Looking and gaze aversion are typically used to initiate, maintain, or avoid communication. With a gaze, one can communicate intimacy, interest, submission, or dominance (Kleinke, 1986). Eyes are used to monitor speech, provide feedback, signal understanding, and regulate turn taking (Harper, Wiens, & Matarazzo, 1978). One could say we meet people with our eyes or that "the eyes are the windows into the soul." In contrast, gaze avoidance or breaking eye contact often signals anxiety, discomfort, or a desire not to communicate with the other person.

In typical noncounseling interactions, people make eye contact with each other (i.e., mutual gaze) in 28% to 70% of their interactions (Kendon, 1967), although usually for no more than one second at a time. Dyads typically negotiate when and how much to look at each other, although this is not a conscious negotiation and it takes places at a nonverbal level. Too little eye contact can make one feel the listener is uninterested in the conversation; too much eye contact can make one feel uncomfortable, intruded on, dominated, controlled, and even devoured.

Norms for eye contact differ among cultures. In White middle-class North America, people tend to maintain eye contact while listening but look away when speaking; in African American culture, people typically look at others while speaking but look away when listening (LaFrance & Mayo, 1976; Sommers-Flanagan & Sommers-Flanagan, 1999). In some Native American groups, sustained eye contact is considered offensive and a sign of disrespect, especially if by a younger to an older person (Brammer & MacDonald, 1996). Several cultural groups (some Native American, Inuit, or Aboriginal Australian groups) avoid eye contact, especially when talking about serious topics (Ivey, 1994).

I suggest helpers use moderate amounts of nonintrusive eye contact. They should use enough that clients feel attended to, but not should stare or look intently without a break.

Facial Expression

Darwin (1872) speculated that before prehistoric people had language, they communicated threats, greetings, and submission through facial ex-

---

EXHIBIT 6.1

Overview of Attending and Listening

Definition	*Remember*	*Attending* is orienting oneself physically toward the client. *Listening* is capturing and understanding the client message.
Types		**E** = maintain moderate levels of *Eye contact (avoid looking away frequently or staring)* and interested *facial expression.* **N** = use moderate amounts of head *Nods.* **C** = respect *Cultural differences* in nonverbal behaviors. **O** = generally maintain an *Open stance* toward clients (arms open, lean forward, face client squarely). **U** = use acknowledgments such as *"um-hmm."* **R** = *Relax* and be natural but professional. **A** = *Avoid distracting nonverbal behaviors, interruptions, note-taking, and touching.* **G** = match the client's *Grammatical style and pace of speech.* **E** = listen with a third *Ear.* **S** = use *Space* appropriately.
Typical helper intentions		To support, to encourage catharsis (see Web Form D).
Possible client reactions		Supported, understood (see Web Form G).
Desired client behavior		Affective and cognitive–behavioral exploration (see Web Form H).
Potential difficulties		Being distracted by internal thoughts and feelings. Not being sensitive to cultural differences. Not being attentive to client reactions to them. Not being able to relax and be natural.

---

pressions. He believed that this shared heritage explains why all humans express basic emotions through similar facial expressions. He wrote,

> the movements of expression in the face and body, whatever their origin may have been, are in themselves of much importance for our welfare. They serve as the first means of communication between the mother and her infant; she smiles approval, and thus encourages her child on the right path, or frowns disapproval . . . The movements of expression give vividness and energy to our spoken words. They reveal the thoughts and intentions of others more truly than do words, which may be falsified . . . These results follow partly from the intimate relation which exists between almost all the emotions and their outward manifestations. (p. 366)

The face is perhaps the body part most involved in nonverbal communication because people communicate so much emotion and information through facial expressions (Ekman, 1993). People pay a lot of attention to facial expressions because they give clues about the meaning of the verbal message. In Shakespeare's (1623/1980) *Macbeth*, Lady Macbeth says to her husband, "your face, my thane, is a book whereon men may read strange matters" (Act 1, Scene 5, p. 17).

Many facial expressions have similar meanings to people all over the world (Ekman, 1993; Izard, 1994). Ekman and Friesen (1984) showed photographs of facial expressions to people in different parts of the world and found that several facial expressions had the same meaning across cultures. People around the world cry when distressed, shake their heads when defiant, and smile when happy. Even blind children who have never seen a face use the same facial expressions to express emotions as sighted people (Eibl-Eibesfeldt, 1971). In addition, fear and anger are expressed mostly with the eyes and happiness mostly with the mouth (Kestenbaum, 1992).

Although people in different cultures share a universal facial language, they differ in the manner and depth of emotion they express. For example, while emotional displays are often intense and prolonged in Western cultures, Asians display emotions of sympathy, respect, and shame but rarely display self-aggrandizing or negative emotions that might disrupt communal feelings (Markus & Kitayama, 1991; Matsumoto, Kudoh, Sherer, & Wallbott, 1988).

An important facial feature used in helping is smiling. Although smiling makes a person look friendly and can encourage exploration, I caution helpers against smiling too much during helping sessions because smiling can be perceived as ingratiating or inappropriate when clients are talking about serious concerns. Helpers who smile excessively could be seen as not genuine or as mocking the depth of clients' problems.

Helpers need to be aware what they are communicating through their facial expressions. Expressing active interest and concern is important, and matching facial expression to what the client is saying is crucial. In other words, helpers might smile or laugh when clients say something funny, and they might cry when clients say something very sad.

HEAD NODS

The appropriate use of head nods, especially at the end of sentences, can make clients feel helpers are listening and following what they are saying. Indeed, verbal messages are sometimes unnecessary because helpers communicate through head nods that they are "with" clients and clients should continue talking. As with other nonverbal behaviors, however, there is an optimal level of head nods. Too few head nods can make clients feel anxious because they might think that helpers are not paying attention; too many can be distracting. For example, one student nodded her head constantly to show support, but her nodding distracted the client because she looked like a puppet attached to a string.

CULTURAL ISSUES IN ATTENDING

Each culture develops rules for nonverbal communication (Harper et al., 1978). An example of such a cultural rule is the pattern of greeting that might take no more than one third of a second. This pattern involves looking at the other person, smiling, lifting the eyebrows, and nodding the head. These behaviors seem to act as a releasor in that they elicit the same response from another person. Rules for nonverbal behaviors are typically outside of conscious awareness. Most people probably could not articulate the nonverbal rules in their own culture because they learn these rules as young children through social interactions and example rather than by explicit verbal instruction.

Nonverbal behaviors that are appropriate in one culture might not be in another. A whole industry has developed to teach diplomats and travelers about nonverbal rules of other cultures. For example, in Asia, it is important for people not to praise themselves and instead to appear humble (Maki & Kitano, 2002). Therefore, an American visiting Asia who started to boast might not be well received.

If you are involved in interpersonal interactions in which your rules for nonverbal behaviors are not followed, you might feel intense discomfort. You might not be able to understand or articulate why you feel uncomfortable, but you know something is not right. For example, if you are caught staring at someone, you might feel embarrassed because it is inappropriate in your culture to stare for a long time. If someone stands too close and grabs your arm when you are talking, you might feel an urge to move away because the person has violated your personal space.

Helpers need to adapt their style to fit clients' nonverbal styles, rather than expect clients to adapt to them. Helpers can take their cues from clients as to what makes them feel comfortable. For example, if a client acts nervous and initiates too much eye contact, the helper might look away and observe whether the client responds differently. In addition, helpers might ask clients for feedback about what feels comfortable or uncomfortable for them.

OPEN STANCE TOWARD CLIENTS

A body posture often recommended is for helpers to lean toward clients and maintain an open body posture with the arms and legs uncrossed (e.g., Egan, 1994). This leaning, open body posture effectively conveys that the helper is paying attention, although helpers can appear rigid if they stay in this position too long. Also, if the open, leaning position is uncomfortable, it can be hard for helpers to attend to clients.

One body posture some students (especially men) use is slouching back in their chairs with legs spread wide apart. This posture, although comfortable, can seem like a sexual advance, so helpers need to be aware what they convey with their body posture.

USE ACKNOWLEDGMENTS SUCH AS "UM-HMM"

Helpers encourage clients to keep talking through nonlanguage sounds, nonwords, and simple words such as "um-hmm," "yeah," and "wow." Helpers use minimal encouragers to acknowledge what the client has said, communicate attentiveness, provide noninvasive support, monitor the flow of conversation, and encourage clients to keep talking. Minimal encouragers are often used in conjunction with and serve the same purpose as head nods.

Helpers sometimes use too few or too many minimal encouragers. Too few can feel distancing, whereas too many can be distracting and annoying to the client. I suggest helpers use minimal encouragers and acknowledgments, mostly at the end of client sentences or speaking turns (i.e., everything a client says between two helper interventions), to encourage clients to keep talking (assuming they are actively involved in exploration). Interrupting a client to provide minimal encouragers can be distracting, so helpers should pay attention to the appropriate timing of this intervention.

RELAX AND BE NATURAL BUT PROFESSIONAL

Each helper needs to determine which attending behaviors feel comfortable to use. A suggestion is to first try the ENCOURAGES stance and then modify these behaviors according to what makes the helper and client most comfortable.

I also strongly encourage helpers to observe the reactions of clients to their attending behaviors. A helper slouching back in his or her seat might feel relaxing for one client, whereas another client might feel that the helper is not paying full attention to him or her. Helpers can ask for feedback about their attending behaviors during training to become aware of how they affect others. As noted earlier, many attending behaviors have different meanings in different cultures, so helpers need to be sensitive to possible misunderstandings with clients from different cultures.

It is important not to just appear, but actually to be, relaxed. Many beginning trainees try so hard to maintain an attending stance that they appear artificial or posed. They perform all the "right" behaviors but end up being too attentive, which makes clients feel they are being examined too closely. One of the most difficult tasks facing helpers is to relax and be themselves. However, when helpers integrate attending and listening behaviors into their way of being, clients often respond by exploring their concerns.

When you are not able to relax, you can try to learn more about what is going on inside you. For example, if you feel your muscles tensing or note you are withdrawing physically from clients, you might ask what is going on for you at that moment. Awareness is the key to handling situations. Once you know how you feel, you can make informed decisions about how to act rather than having the reactions "leak out." Paying attention to bodily reactions provides an incredible amount of information about clients. If you feel bored, anxious, attracted, or repulsed by a client, chances are other people feel this way toward the client. See the chapter on immediacy for ideas about how to use these reactions therapeutically in the insight stage.

Helpers of course want to maintain a professional stance while still behaving naturally. One way to accomplish this is through the manner of dress. I often suggest that beginning helpers dress one notch better than their clients. Rather than jeans and halter tops, helpers can wear nice slacks and a shirt. It is particularly important to avoid seductive clothing.

AVOID DISTRACTING NONVERBAL BEHAVIORS, INTERRUPTIONS, NOTE-TAKING, AND TOUCHING

Distracting Nonverbal Behaviors

Before I discuss distracting behaviors, it is important to describe different kinds of nonverbal behaviors. *Kinesics* refers to the relationship of bodily movements (arm and leg movements, head nods) to communication. Bodily movements can be categorized into several types, each of which has a different function (Ekman & Friesen, 1969). *Emblems* are substitutes for words (e.g., a wave is a universal greeting). *Illustrators* accompany speech (e.g., measuring the size of a fish with the hands). *Regulators* (e.g., head nods, postural shifts) monitor the conversation flow. *Adaptors* are habitual acts that are often outside awareness and have no communicative purpose (e.g., head scratching, licking one's lips, playing with a pen).

Helpers generally want to use emblems, illustrators, and regulators to accompany verbal messages but want to avoid using adaptors. Adaptors detract from the helper's effectiveness by turning the focus away from the client to the helper's inappropriate nonverbal behaviors. Too many adaptors or an inappropriate use of emblems, illustrators, or regulators is often a sign of "nonverbal leakage" (i.e., the person does not want to communicate or is trying to hide, but the feeling leaks out through nonverbal channels).

Bodily movements provide information one often cannot obtain from either verbal content or facial expression. As Freud (1905/1953a) eloquently stated, "he that has eyes to see and ears to hear may convince himself that no mortal can keep a secret. If his lips are silent, he chatters with his fingertips, betrayal oozes out of him at every pore" (p. 94). Ekman and Friesen (1969) noted that leg and foot movements are the most likely sources of nonverbal leakage because they are less subject to conscious awareness and voluntary inhibition. The hands and face are the next best sources of clues for nonverbal leakage. Hence, if a helper finds him- or herself repeatedly tapping his or her foot, the helper might think about what he or she is feeling.

One particularly distracting behavior is interruptions. When the client is exploring productively (i.e., talking about innermost thoughts and feelings), the helper does not need to interrupt. Often the helper simply has to attend and listen and stay out of the client's way, so she or he has the opportunity to keep talking. If the client is stuck and cannot think of what to say or if the client is talking nonstop but not exploring productively (i.e., telling stories, rambling), the helper may need to help the client get back on track. Matarazzo, Phillips, Wiens, and Saslow (1965) stressed that helpers should not interrupt and should delay talking for several seconds after the end of client statements. This pause (noninterruption) allows clients to continue thinking and talking without undue pressure from helpers. Matarazzo et al. found a significant difference between inexperienced and experienced helpers in this interruption variable.

Another potentially distracting behavior is note-taking, which tends to reduce the ability of helpers to attend to clients. While the helper is taking notes, the client is often unengaged, passively waiting for the helper to finish writing; this reduces the intensity of the immediate experience. Clients may be suspicious about what helpers are writing and curious about why they record some things and not others. Helpers often take notes to remember what occurred during sessions; a less intrusive method is to tape sessions and later listen to the tapes to recall specific details of the session.

Finally, a controversial behavior is touching. Touching is a natural inclination when helpers want to indicate support to their clients, and in fact can make clients feel understood and involved in a human relationship (Hunter & Struve, 1998). Montagu (1971) noted that touch is a natural physical need and that some people hunger for touch because they do not receive enough physical contact. Unfortunately, touch can have negative effects if clients feel invaded, if the touch is unwanted, and if clients have a history of unwanted touch. Highlen and Hill (1984) reported that the few studies conducted on touching in therapy were inconclusive. Some studies have shown positive effects of touching, whereas others have found no effects. It requires clinical judgment to know when to use touch; therefore, it is better that beginning helpers refrain from any touching because of possible misunderstandings about the meanings of the touch and because of the ethical issues associated with touching clients.

MATCH THE CLIENT'S GRAMMATICAL STYLE AND PACE OF SPEECH

Another way helpers communicate attending is through matching the client's language and grammatical style. Language must be appropriate to the cultural experience and educational level of the client, so the helper can form a bond with the client. If a client says, "I ain't never gonna make it with chicks," it would be better for the helper to say something like, "You're concerned about finding a girlfriend," rather than "Your inferiority complex prevents you from establishing relationships with appropriate love objects." The latter statement sounds too divergent from the client's statement. The helper must sound natural and helpful rather than stilted or condescending.

In addition, helpers need to match the client's pace of speech, within some limits. Helpers need to use a slower pace of speech with clients who speak slowly. In contrast, helpers might speak somewhat faster with clients who talk rapidly. If a client is manic and is speaking rapidly, the helper might use a slower pace to calm him or her down.

Helpers should not compromise their integrity by using a language style or pace of speech that feels uncomfortable to them, but they can modify their style to be more similar to that of their client. Each of us has a comfortable range of behaviors, and helpers need to find the place within that range to meet each client. After all, the goal of helpers is to facilitate client change rather than to add additional barriers to change.

LISTEN WITH A THIRD EAR

Listening involves paying attention to both the verbal and nonverbal messages of the client and trying to determine what the person is thinking and feeling.

Verbal Messages

Clients communicate with helpers in a variety of ways, the most obvious being the words they use to express thoughts, feelings, and experiences. Helpers can listen carefully to the words. Helpers get into a listening stance by using attending skills, minimal encouragers (e.g., "um-hmm"), and freeing their minds from distractions. Helpers can imagine themselves in the client's position. Thus, helpers listen by seeking to understand what a client is experiencing from the client's perspective rather than from the helper's viewpoint. For example, an adolescent client, Kathleen, complained she felt devastated and worthless because she had not been asked to the prom. From the perspective of the helper, a 35-year-old married woman, not being asked to the prom was not a catastrophic event. However, while listening to Kathleen, the helper tried to imagine how this experience might feel for the young woman.

A key to listening is for helpers to pay attention to clients without formulating their next response. All too often, people are half listening to what someone is saying because they are thinking about what to say next. It is better to listen during this stage and say nothing (especially if the client is exploring productively) than to rush in and say something that interrupts the client's flow of exploration.

Clients who have different verbal styles than their helpers can cause confusion for their helpers. Helpers who are introverted might assume that talkative clients are comfortable, when they could be talking too much out of anxiety. It is important for helpers not to project their feelings and personal style onto their clients.

Nonverbal Messages

Not only is it important that helpers listen to clients' words, but they also can learn a lot by "listening" to their nonverbal behaviors. Clients who are nervous often use a lot of adaptors, are very quiet, stutter, or cannot speak coherently. Clients who are defensive or closed often cross their arms and legs, almost as a barricade to the helper. Clients who are ashamed might look down as they speak. Clients who are scared might speak softly, look away, or have a closed posture. In contrast, clients who are comfortable and in tune with the helper often lean forward and talk with animation and feeling in their voices.

Helpers need to be aware of possible misinterpretations when someone from another culture uses nonverbal behaviors differently than they do. For example, if a European American helper greets an African American client who does not make eye contact, the helper should not assume the client suffers from guilt or low self-esteem, but should pay close attention to whether this nonverbal behavior has a different meaning in the client's culture.

I want to emphasize that helpers should not interpret nonverbal behaviors as having fixed standard "meanings." Fidgeting can reveal anxiety, but it can also reveal boredom; folded arms can convey either irritation or relaxation. For example, if a client sits with arms and legs crossed, he or she is not necessarily withholding or defending. It could mean he or she is cold or is in the habit of sitting with arms and legs crossed. Helpers cannot "read" another's body language as having universal meaning but can use observations as hints or clues about what a client might be feeling. If a client is sitting with arms and legs crossed and has scooted the chair back, the helper might hypothesize that the client needs distance from the helper. However, the helper needs to investigate this hypothesis further by talking about it with the client (using skills covered in this volume). Thus, helpers can use nonverbal data to form hypotheses and then gather more data to determine the accuracy of these hypotheses.

Clients who have different nonverbal styles than their helpers can cause confusion for helpers. For example, a helper who does not like to make a lot of eye contact might assume that a client who makes eye contact feels comfortable and in control of the situation. However, too much eye contact can be as much a defense or indication of anxiety as too little eye contact; both styles make it difficult for people to get close to others.

A key to listening is to pay attention to context. Rather than becoming fixated on the meaning of specific nonverbal behaviors, helpers need to pay attention to everything about the client: the verbal and nonverbal behaviors, the setting, the culture, and the presenting problem. For example, Archie appeared angry and hostile, but his behavior made sense when he revealed he had just been stopped and frisked by a police officer for no apparent reason other than that he was an African American man in a White neighborhood. Hence, context is important to take into account when thinking about behaviors.

Some people are better listeners and more sensitive to nonverbal cues than others. When Rosenthal, Hall, DiMatteo, Rogers, and Archer (1979) showed clips of emotionally expressive faces and bodies, they found some people were better at detecting emotion than others. In addition, they found women were generally better at detecting emotion than men. Miller (1976) provided a social learning explanation why women might be better at detecting emotion than men:

> Subordinates (women), then, know much more about the dominants than vice versa. They have to. They become highly attuned to the dominants, able to predict their reactions of pleasure and displeasure. Here, I think, is where the long story of "feminine intuition" and "feminine wiles" begins. It seems clear that these "mysterious" gifts are in fact skills, developed through long practice, in reading many small signals, both verbal and nonverbal. (p. 10)

Helpers who are aware that they are not as natively sensitive to nonverbal cues can try harder to pay attention to these behaviors. A few studies have suggested that trainees can be taught to increase their sensitivity to nonverbal communication (e.g., Delaney & Heimann, 1966; Grace, Kivlighan, & Kunce, 1995). It seems that self-awareness and practice can help people become more sensitive to nonverbal cues.

USE SPACE APPROPRIATELY

The term *proxemics* refers to how people use space in interactions. E. T. Hall (1968) described four distance zones for middle-class Americans: intimate (0–18 inches), personal (1.5–4 feet), social (4–12 feet), and public (12 feet or more). If rules for prescribed distances are not followed, people can feel uncomfortable, although they are not usually aware of what is making them uneasy. Hall noted that once these patterns for space are learned, they are maintained largely outside of conscious awareness. Typically, the personal to social distance is considered appropriate for seating arrangements in helping relationships, although individuals vary in the amount of distance that feels comfortable for them. Some helpers place chairs close together, whereas others, when they have control over the arrangements, place the chairs far apart. I know of therapists who place a number of chairs in their offices and allow clients to choose where they sit.

Space is used in very different ways in different cultures (E. T. Hall, 1963). American and British people generally prefer to be relatively distant from other people and rarely touch. In contrast, Hispanic and Middle Eastern people generally prefer less distance. For example, Arabs and Israeli Jews often stand close, touch, talk loudly, and stare intently. Helpers need to take cultural considerations into account rather than just reacting unconsciously to someone from another culture who uses different proxemic patterns. In addition, helpers need to be aware of differences within cultures. For example, a helper should not assume all Latino–Latina clients want to be hugged at the beginning and end of each session just because some Lattino people hug when greeting and leaving. Differences exist within cultures, and acculturation to the dominant culture may influence clients' comfort with physical closeness.

Examples of Attending and Listening Skills

EXAMPLE OF INAPPROPRIATE ATTENDING AND LISTENING

Helper: (leaning back, arms folded, and looking at the ceiling) So, how come you came today anyway?

Client: (very softly) Well, I'm not sure. I just haven't been feeling very good about myself lately. But I don't know if you can help me.

Helper: (shifts forward in seat and looks intently at client) Well, so what is happening?

Client: (long pause) I just don't know how to . . .

Helper: (interrupts) Just tell me what the problem really is.

Client: (long pause) I guess I really don't have anything to talk about. Sorry I wasted your time.

EXAMPLE OF APPROPRIATE ATTENDING AND LISTENING

Helper: (using all the ENCOURAGES behaviors) Hi. My name is Debbie. We have a few minutes to talk today so that I can practice my helping skills. What would you like to talk about?

Client: (very softly) Well, I'm not sure. I just haven't been feeling very good lately about myself. But I don't know if you can help me.

Helper: (matches the client's soft voice) Yeah, you sound kind of scared. Tell me a little bit more about what's been going on lately.

Client: I've been kind of down. I haven't been able to sleep or eat much. I'm behind on everything, and I don't have the energy to do any schoolwork.

Helper: (pauses, softly) It sounds like you feel overwhelmed.

Client: (sighs) Yes, that's exactly how I feel. It just seems like there's a lot of pressure in my first year of college.

Helper: Um-hmm (head nod)

Client: (continues talking)

Effects of Attending and Listening

Helpers need to evaluate the effectiveness of their attending and listening behaviors. Helpers can watch videotapes of their sessions and use a three-point scale to assess the effectiveness of their attending and listening behaviors. This scale stresses the effects of attending and listening on clients' reactions:

1 = When attending and listening are unhelpful, a client might move away from the helper, get fidgety, appear uncomfortable, or become distracted. For example, if a helper sits back with his legs spread apart, some clients might interpret this as a sexual advance, look away, and become very uncomfortable. If a helper fiddles with her hair or plays with pens, some clients might become dis-

tracted and feel irritated that they are not important enough to receive the helper's full attention.

2 = If the attending and listening behaviors are at least moderately adequate, clients are able to continue talking but may not feel completely comfortable.

3 = If the attending and listening behaviors are very good, clients feel comfortable in the setting and feel helpers are listening and concerned. Clients probably feel safe to continue talking about personal concerns.

Of course, helpers must be aware that clients are not always responding to the helper's attending and listening behaviors. Sometimes clients are upset because of the content of their presenting concerns and are not responding at all to the helper's attending behaviors. Helpers need to try to determine to what clients are reacting.

Difficulties Helpers Experience in Attending and Listening

One of the problems helpers have in attending and listening is being distracted by internal thoughts and feelings. For example, helpers often engage in negative self-talk (e.g., "I'm not doing this right," "I'm not sure the client likes me," "I wonder if I'm giving too much eye contact?"). If they are distracted by what they are thinking, helpers will have a hard time focusing on clients and listening attentively.

Another difficulty is that some helpers are not sensitive to cultural differences in nonverbal behaviors. When someone from another culture does something nonverbally that is different from their custom (e.g., using eye contact differently), some helpers judge these clients according to their own cultural standards.

In addition, some helpers do not pay attention to client reactions to their nonverbal behaviors. Clients rarely tell helpers directly that a nonverbal behavior is annoying or intrusive, but they often provide subtle cues when they feel uncomfortable (e.g., becoming more quiet, looking away). Helpers need to attend to clients' nonverbals to detect reactions.

Finally, beginning helpers frequently assume the "correct" nonverbal position rather than find a nonverbal position that feels natural and relaxed. Helpers need to try out different positions and ask for feedback about their nonverbals. An effective way for helpers to obtain feedback is to videotape themselves in a helping situation (with the client's permission) and later carefully observe their nonverbal behaviors and the client's reactions. Helpers can also experiment with nonverbal behaviors with friends or classmates. When friends are talking about something important, helpers might use attending behaviors appropriately and observe the friend's reaction. Helpers then might use attending behaviors inappropriately (or not at all) and see if friends react differently. Helpers can later tell their friends what they were doing and solicit feedback about reactions to the different nonverbal manipulations.

HELPFUL HINTS

- Try out the attending behaviors suggested in the acronym ENCOURAGES and see how they fit for you.
- Discover how you feel comfortable in attending. Develop your own style.
- Ask for feedback from friends and clients about the impact of your nonverbal behaviors. Watch yourself on videotape.
- Do not interrupt clients unless absolutely necessary (e.g., a client is talking nonstop about irrelevant things).

Concluding Comments

In conclusion, attending behaviors set the stage for helpers to listen and to let clients know they are being heard. Helpers also need to listen carefully to clients' verbal and nonverbal behaviors to hear what clients are saying and to pick up clues about underlying thoughts and feelings. In addition, attending and listening set the foundation for all the other skills taught in this book, so helpers should be particularly attentive to learning these skills.

WHAT DO YOU THINK?

- What are the differences between attending and listening?
- What are some rules for nonverbal behavior in your culture?
- How are rules established for nonverbal behaviors? Can these rules be changed?
- What do you think about the role of culture in attending and listening?
- What are your thoughts about manipulating your nonverbal behaviors to achieve desired goals with clients?

LAB 4

Attending and Listening

Please note that the first few labs might feel somewhat artificial because each helping skill is first practiced separately. In real helping sessions, you will not use just one skill at a time, but the best way to master the helping skills is to focus on each one intensely and separately before trying to integrate them.

In addition, some students feel overwhelmed with these lab exercises because they worry that they will not remember everything they are "supposed" to do. You probably will *not* remember everything. It takes a lot of practice before you can begin to use everything you have learned. Try to relax and do your best—you do not have to be perfect. Just get in there and try the exercises and see what happens. These exercises are designed to give you the opportunity to practice the skills in a relatively safe place.

Exercise 1: Attending

Goals
1. To allow helpers a chance to communicate empathy just through attending behaviors.
2. To enable helpers to become accustomed to being in the helper role.

Helper's and Client's Tasks During the Helping Exchange
1. Students pair up and take turns being helper and client.
2. The helper uses appropriate attending behaviors with the client, who talks about an easy topic (See Exhibit 1.1 in chap. 1). The helper should communicate empathy *but not say anything verbally*.
3. Continue for three minutes. Switch roles.

Exercise 2: Listening

Goals
1. To enable helpers to become accustomed to the helper role.
2. To allow helpers an opportunity to try different attending behaviors to see which feel most comfortable and congruent.
3. To provide feedback to helpers about their attending behaviors.
4. To allow helpers an opportunity to observe and learn about the meanings of clients' nonverbal behaviors.
5. To give helpers an opportunity to practice listening skills without interpreting, making judgments about what clients say, or thinking of what they want to say.

Helper's and Client's Tasks During the Helping Interchange
1. Students should be arranged in groups of three, alternating roles so each person participates at least once in each role (helper, client, and observer).
2. The helper can relax, use appropriate attending skills, introduce him- or herself, and ask what the client would like to talk about.

continues

Attending and Listening

3. The client should talk *briefly* for one or two sentences about an easy topic.
4. The helper should first pause to think and then repeat verbatim what the client said. Repeating verbatim probably will feel awkward to many helpers, but it enables helpers to listen carefully and make sure they hear what clients are saying. Be sure to focus on this task and not talk about life in general.
5. Continue for eight to ten client speaking turns. Although it is difficult (especially the first time), stay in the helper and client roles.

Observer's Task During the Helping Interchange

1. Take notes on your observations of the helper's ability to repeat exactly what the client said. Note one positive and one negative attending behavior.
2. Encourage the helper and client to stay on task.

After the Helping Interchange

1. The helper first discusses which attending behaviors felt comfortable and how it felt to repeat what the client said.
2. The client can give feedback about the helper's attending and listening skills.
3. The observer can give positive and then negative feedback to the helper.

Exercise 3: Attending and Listening

Goals

1. To give helpers an opportunity to attend and listen to clients.
2. To encourage helpers to focus on the most important part of the client's statements.

Using the same format as in Exercise 2, the helper repeats the single most important word or phrase the client has said. For example, if the client says, "I am having a terrible dilemma. I just found out my best friend's boyfriend cheated on her. I don't know whether I should tell her because she would be so hurt," the helper might say, "dilemma" or "unsure." Continue for eight to ten client-speaking turns and then follow the same feedback procedures as in Exercise 2.

Personal Reflections

- What was it like for you to be silent in the first exercise?
- What was your experience in the roles of helper, client, and observer?
- Which attending behaviors did you find most helpful as a helper and as a client?
- How did you feel about repeating everything verbatim?
- What multicultural issues (e.g., gender, race, ethnicity, age) arose in your dyads?

Open Questions and Probes 7

Questioning is the door of knowledge.

—*Irish proverb*

Miya said she was very nervous about taking a trip to France for business by herself. She had never been out of the country before, and she was concerned about traveling on her own and being able to communicate when she did not know the language. The helper asked, "What is it like for you to be alone?" Later, the helper asked, "What are your fears about not being able to communicate with others in a foreign country?" and "What experiences have you had before when you didn't know the language?" These open questions helped Miya explore her reluctance to travel independently.

Open questions and probes help clients clarify and explore their thoughts and feelings. When using these leads, helpers do not want a specific answer from clients but instead want clients to explore whatever comes to mind. In other words, helpers purposely do not limit the nature of clients' responses to a "yes," "no," or one- or two-word answer, even though clients may respond that way. Open questions and probes can be phrased as queries ("How do you feel about that?") or as directives ("Tell me how you feel about that") as long as the intent is to help the client clarify or explore.

The focus in this chapter is on four different types of open questions and probes: those that ask for clarification or focus, those that encourage exploration of thoughts, those that encourage exploration of feelings, and those that request examples (see Exhibit 7.1). Open questions can be dis-

---

Web Forms referred to in text can be found on the book's companion online guide described in the Preface.

tinguished from closed questions (e.g., "How old are you?" "When did you first start chewing your fingernails?"), which are presented in chapter 10. Open questions for insight and action are discussed in later chapters.

Why Use Open Questions and Probes?

Many researchers have found that open questions are used frequently in therapy and are generally perceived as being moderately helpful for the therapy process (Barkham & Shapiro, 1986; Elliott, 1985; Elliott et al., 1982; Fitzpatrick, Stalikas, and Iwakabe, 2001; Hill, Helms, Tichenor, et al., 1988; Martin, Martin, & Slemon, 1989). These studies suggest that open questions can be a useful intervention by encouraging clients to talk longer and more deeply about their concerns.

Open questions enable clients to explore the many aspects of their problems. They can be particularly useful when clients are rambling, repeating the same thoughts but not really exploring deeply. They can also be used to help clients clarify their thoughts when they are confused, lead clients to think about new things, help clients unravel conflicting thoughts or feelings, or provide structure for clients who are not very verbal or articulate. Clients often get stuck describing their problems and need questions to help them think about different aspects of the problem.

Open questions demonstrate that the helper is listening and interested in the client. They show the helper is tracking what the client says and is interested enough to encourage the client to keep talking.

The four types of open questions and probes are used for different reasons, all of which are fundamental to the exploration stage. First, open questions used to clarify or focus are particularly helpful when clients are starting the session, rambling, being vague or unclear, or are stuck. Second, open questions for thoughts are used to enable clients to say what they are thinking and to reveal irrational thinking. Third, open questions for feelings help clients express and experience specific feelings and emphasize the importance of feelings. Fourth, probes for examples are needed when clients are talking generally and vaguely about problems. Providing specific examples gives helpers a clearer picture of what the client is talking about. All four types of open questions and probes can be useful to help clients explore, but each takes clients in a different direction. Given that most problems are complicated, different ways of questioning are useful for eliciting full exploration.

For all the reasons stated above, open questions and probes are useful for the helping process. Open questions and probes are introduced as the

EXHIBIT 7.1

Overview of Open Questions–Probes

Definition	*Open questions and probes* are interventions that ask clients to clarify or explore thoughts or feelings. Helpers do not request specific information and do not purposely limit the nature of the client response to a "yes," "no," or one- or two-word answer, even though clients may respond that way. Open questions and probes can be phrased as queries ("How do you feel about that?") or as directives ("Tell me how you feel about that"), as long as the intent is to help the client clarify or explore.
Types and examples	*Clarification/Focus*: "What did you mean by that?" *Thoughts*: "Tell me more about your thoughts about that." *Feelings*: "What feelings do you have about your mother?" *Examples*: "Give me an example of what you do when you're angry. Walk me through your behaviors step by step."
Typical helper intentions	To focus, to clarify, to encourage catharsis, to identify maladaptive cognitions, to identify and intensify feelings (see Web Form D)
Possible client reactions	Clear feelings (see Web Form G)
Desired client behaviors	Recounting, cognitive–behavioral exploration, affective exploration (see Web Form H)
Potential difficulties	Using the same format of open question repeatedly Using only open questions instead of a variety of interventions in sessions Asking open questions to satisfy their curiosity instead of to help clients explore Asking multiple questions at one time Using closed instead of open questions Asking too many "why" questions Focusing on someone other than the client in the open question Focusing on past instead of present feelings Focusing on too many parts of the issue at once

first verbal helping skill in this book because they are most commonly used in interpersonal relationships outside of helping and thus are generally easier for students to use when they are initially learning helping skills. Helpers learn when and how to use open questions and probes rather than how to formulate a whole new behavior.

How to Ask Open Questions and Probes

Helpers should maintain the appropriate attending behaviors because the manner of presenting open questions is very important. The tone of voice should be kept low to convey concern and intimacy, the rate of speech should be slow, and the questions should be phrased tentatively to avoid sounding as though helpers are interrogating clients. Helpers should be supportive, nonjudgmental, and encouraging no matter what clients say because there are no "right" or "wrong" topics to explore and no "right" or "wrong" answers to questions.

Open questions should be short and simple. Clients may have difficulty following lengthy questions. Helpers should also avoid asking several questions at once because this can be confusing for clients. Multiple questions ("What did you do next, and how did you feel, and what did you think she was feeling?") can have a dampening effect on the interaction if clients do not know which question to respond to first or feel bombarded. Clients might ignore important questions because they cannot respond to all of them.

Another guideline is that open questions are most effective when helpers focus on one part of the problem at a time. Clients cannot talk about everything at once and may have difficulty choosing a single topic, so helpers need to pick the most important or salient issue to focus on and return to others later. Typically, the issue helpers should focus on is the one for which clients have the most energy or affect, or for what is at the "cutting edge" of a client's awareness. For example, if Juan is talking about several different topics, the helper might ask Juan a question about the topic that seems most provocative.

Similarly, if a client just cannot think of what to talk about, open questions are a good way for helpers to provide direction. For example, if Justin has been talking about receiving a bad grade and has explored his feelings and then the dialogue stops, the helper might ask Justin what a bad grade means for the future and compare how this situation relates to past experiences with grades or how this grade affects his relationship with his parents. These questions could help Justin talk more completely about other important aspects of the problem. I like comparing problems to a ball of yarn; with each intervention helpers encourage clients to take out a bit of the yarn and talk about it. When one piece is explored thoroughly, helpers gently guide them to another piece.

Helpers should keep the focus of the open question on the client ("How did you feel about your mother's behavior?") rather than turning the attention to other people ("What did your mother do in that situation?").

Keeping the focus on the client helps him or her explore what is going on inside rather than deflecting to other people. For example, if Jean often argues with her mother, the helper can ask about Jean's feelings and thoughts ("What makes you angry?") rather than asking Jean about her mother's feelings and thoughts ("Why do you think your mother gets so angry with you?"). Although it could be helpful to understand more about the mother, she is not in the room, and the helper is likely to get a one-sided view of her. The person the helper is most likely to help is the client, so it is typically better to focus on the client.

It is also important for helpers to avoid interrupting to ask questions or probes if clients are already exploring productively. It is better to allow clients to keep talking and only ask questions when clients are stuck or need guidance about what to explore further. In addition, the focus should be on the present instead of the past (e.g., "How do you feel now about how your mother treated you?" rather than "How did your mother treat you?"). The former question encourages the client to search deeply for current experiencing, whereas the latter encourages the client to tell stories that may not be deeply involving. The details are often not as important as the feelings about the situation.

Helpers should avoid closed questions (questions that have a specific desired answer, e.g., "yes," "no," or specific information) because these tend to limit exploration. One way to differentiate between closed and open questions is to see whether the question can be more open; if it can be, it is probably a closed question. For example, the closed question "Did you get an A?" can be changed to "How do you feel about how you did on the test?" In contrast, the latter question is much more open. A particularly egregious type of closed question occurs when the helper is condescending or tries to coerce the client into responding a particular way (e.g., "You really don't want to keep drinking, do you?"). Such questions take the focus away from the client and make the helper seem like an expert who knows how the client should behave. (See chap. 10 for more about closed questions.)

Helpers should also avoid "why" questions (e.g., "Why did you blow up at your boyfriend the other night?" "Why are you not able to study?"), especially in the exploration stage (note that "why" questions can be helpful in the insight stage when used appropriately). As Nisbett and Wilson (1977) indicated, people rarely know why they do things. If they knew why they act as they do, they probably would not be talking to helpers. Furthermore, "why" questions often make clients feel challenged and defensive. When someone asks why you did something, you might feel she or he is judging you and deriding you for not being able to handle the situation more effectively. Instead of "why" questions, helpers use "what" or "how" questions (e.g., instead of "Why didn't you study for your exam?" the helper could ask, "How did you feel about your performance on the exam?" "What was going through your mind when you were trying to study?" or "What is going on that makes it difficult for you to study?").

Finally, helpers should be aware of cultural differences in clients' responses to questions. Sue and Sue (1999) noted that people from some cultures may be uncomfortable when they are questioned or asked to initiate the dialogue (e.g., "What would you like to talk about today?") because it may be disrespectful. In such cases, helpers may have to be more direct, either in educating the client about the helping process or in suggesting topics to discuss. Helpers cannot assume clients from other cultures will not like open questions, but they can notice if clients seem uncomfortable with questions and can instead try other skills.

EXAMPLE OF OPEN QUESTIONS

Client: My younger sisters are fighting a lot with each other. They really get nasty and have been hurting each other. My youngest sister was caught stealing from a store recently. My parents aren't doing anything about it, and my sisters are just going wild.

Helper: *How do you feel about your sisters going wild?*

Client: I'm really upset. I wish there was more I could do to help them. If I were still at home, they would listen to me. I think they don't have anyone to turn to. My parents are divorcing, so they're just not available to my sisters.

Helper: *Tell me more about what it's like for you not to be there.*

Client: On one hand, I'm delighted to be away from the mess. On the other hand, I feel guilty, like I survived the Titanic crash and came out alive but they're sinking.

Helper: *What is it like when you are with your family?*

Client: My parents are still living together, but they fight all the time. Things are pretty scary around the house because my parents get pretty violent with each other. I have to look out for my sisters. I am really more their parent than either of my parents are. I got to be pretty strong by having to fend for myself so much.

Helper: *How are you feeling right now as you think about your family?*

Client: I feel helpless, like there's nothing I can do. I guess I could go home, but actually I know that wouldn't do any good. Maybe I'm selfish too because I want to be here at college. This is what I need to be doing at this stage of my life. But I still feel badly that they are there in that situation.

Helper: *What do you mean when you say that you feel badly?*

Client: I feel bad for them, I really do. But as I think about it more, I also feel bad for myself having grown up in that home. I'm really glad to be away from there. It was just awful being around my parents when they fight. I would get all knotted up inside and just felt like running away.

Helper: *Give me a specific example of a time when you felt all knotted up inside?*

Client: Oh, yeah, just last night when I called home. My mom started yelling at me for spending too much money. And then my dad started saying yelling at my mom to leave me alone. I felt caught in between.

Helper: *What were your thoughts when they were yelling at you?*

Client: I just felt so horrible because I thought that I could never please them. (Client continues exploring.)

Effects of Open Questions and Probes

Helpers can watch tapes of their sessions and rate the effects of their open questions on clients using the following three-point scale:

1 = If open questions are not very helpful, the client will not respond or will respond in a minimal way or with hostility. For example, clients often get annoyed and frustrated when helpers repeatedly ask the same question (e.g., "How do you feel about that?").

2 = If open questions are at least moderately helpful, the client continues talking but might repeat or rephrase without exploring new things.

3 = If open questions are very helpful, the client explores deeper thoughts and feelings and clarifies important aspects of the problem.

Difficulties Helpers Experience in Delivering Open Questions and Probes

A common problem is that helpers tend to ask the same type of open questions repeatedly, most often "How do you feel about that?" Many clients become annoyed when they continually hear the same type of question and have a hard time responding. I recommend that helpers vary the phrasing of open questions and ask about different types of things (e.g., thoughts, feelings, examples, past experiences, future expectations, and a client's role in maintaining the problem).

Similarly, some beginning helpers use only open questions rather than interspersing open questions with other types of interventions, such as restatement and reflection of feelings (which are covered in chaps. 8 and 9). Helpers tend to use open questions excessively when anxious, because this skill is relatively easy and already exists in most helpers' repertoires. Unfortunately, the interaction can become one-sided if helpers ask too many open questions. In this situation, helpers are not demonstrating that they are listening to what the clients are saying or struggling to understand the clients. The tone of the session can become stilted rather than being a mutual struggle to explore and understand the client's concerns.

Helpers sometimes use open questions inappropriately to satisfy their curiosity. They might ask for information out of voyeurism rather than to help the clients explore. For example, Martha has been working on her feelings of jealousy and competitiveness with her older sister. Martha comes into the session and announces that her sister had a date with a "hot" movie star. The helper might exclaim, "Wow, how did she meet him?" or "What was he like?" Although extreme, this example illustrates how helpers can get carried away with asking for specific information to satisfy their own curiosity rather than to help clients explore. It also illustrates how the focus can easily shift away from the client to others.

HELPFUL HINTS

- Make sure your questions are open (i.e., do not ask questions that purposely limit the client's response to a "yes" or "no" answer).
- Rephrase closed questions into open questions (e.g., ask "What could you do tonight?" rather than "Have you thought about calling a friend tonight?").
- Remember that the goal of asking open questions is to facilitate exploration. If the client is already exploring, there is no need to interrupt to ask a question.
- Vary questions so you are not always asking the same thing. If you feel stuck because the client is going in circles or repeating everything, think about asking a different type of open question (clarification, thoughts, feelings, example).
- Focus on one part of the issue rather than trying to cover everything at once.

▪ Keep the focus on the client rather than on other people (e.g., "What was your reaction to her statement?" rather than "What did your friend say?").

▪ Be aware of attending behaviors, specifically tone of voice: Keep your tone low to convey concern and intimacy, keep the rate of speech slow, and make the questions tentative to avoid sounding as though you are interrogating the client.

▪ Have an intention for every question. The ultimate test of the appropriateness of an open question is "Will the question that I am about to ask be helpful to the client?"

▪ Avoid asking multiple questions without giving the client a chance to respond between questions (e.g., "What did you do then, and how did you feel, and what happened after that?").

▪ Avoid asking too many questions in a session. Too many questions can make clients uncomfortable. Clients also often wait passively for the next question when a helper is in a questioning mode.

▪ Avoid "why" questions. They put people on the defensive and are difficult to answer candidly. "Why" questions ask for speculation about motives, but clients may be unaware of their motives. "Why" questions also can imply criticism. Rephrase the "why" questions to make them less blaming. Rather than "Why did you fight with your husband?" ask "How did you and your husband start fighting?"

▪ Avoid questions that already have an answer or convey condescension (e.g., "You don't really feel that it's right to act that way, do you?").

▪ Avoid asking a closed question immediately after an open question because that often stops exploration (e.g., "What does that feel like? Is it scary?")

▪ Be aware of cultural differences: Clients from some cultures may have difficulty responding to open questions.

PRACTICE EXERCISES

Pretend that a client makes the following statements to you. Read each of these statements, and then write an open question. Compare your responses with the possible helper responses provided at the end of the section. The helper responses that are given are not the "right" or "best" open questions, but they are provided to give you some idea of the different possibilities of ways to respond.

Statements

1. Client: "I got my exam grade yesterday."
   Helper response: _____

2. Client: "I heard on the news that a college student died because she drank too much in too short a time."
   Helper response: _____

3. Client: "We talked in class about the concept of a "chilly climate" and how female students don't get called on in the classroom as often as male students."
   Helper response: _____

4. Client: "I don't want to be here. I wouldn't be here if I didn't have to be, but my parole officer told me I had to come."
   Helper response: _____

Possible Helper Responses

1. "How do you feel about your grade?"
   "How does your grade make you feel about yourself?"
   "Talk to me about your thoughts about your grade."

2. "What was your reaction to hearing this news?"
   "Tell me more about your reaction to that."
   "How do you feel about your drinking behavior?"

3. "How do you feel about the climate here?"
   "How do you feel about the ways your teachers treat you?"
   "How does the climate here compare with what you've had in the past?"

4. "How does it feel to have someone make you come here?"
   "What do you generally do when someone makes you do something?"
   "What would you like to do with our session today?"

WHAT DO YOU THINK?

▪ How do you respond when people use open questions in conversation with you?

▪ What cultural considerations can you think of in using open questions?

▪ Do you agree that helpers should not ask "why" questions?

LAB 5

Open Questions and Probes

Goal: For helpers to practice using open questions to help clients explore their thoughts and feelings.

Exercise 1

In a group, the group leader should present an example of a client statement (keep it simple). Each student can write an open question for each of the types (clarification, thoughts, feelings, example). The leader can go around the group, asking for different types of open questions. Continue with examples until the leader is certain that students understand and can deliver the different types of open questions.

Exercise 2

For this exercise, students should be arranged in groups of three. Initially, one person should be the helper, one the client, and one the observer. Then, students can switch roles, so each person has the opportunity to participate in each role.

Helper's and Client's Tasks During the Helping Interchange

1. Helpers should introduce themselves.
2. Clients should talk about a topic for a few sentences (See chap. 1 for suggestions for topics).
3. After each client statement, the helper should ask an open question. For this exercise, helpers should use only open questions and no other interventions. Keep the open questions short and simple.
4. Continue for five to ten turns. The helper should try to use all four types of open questions (clarification, thoughts, feelings, behaviors). Remember to focus on the client rather than on others.

Observer's Tasks During the Helping Interchange

Take notes about the helper's questions. Note the number of closed versus open questions. Write down the specific questions so they can be discussed in the feedback. Note which were effective (e.g., enabled client to explore deeper) compared with which were less effective (e.g., were confusing, distracted the client from the main topic). Note the manner of delivery of the questions—was the helper gentle and supportive or intrusive like an interrogator?

After the Helping Interchange

1. Helpers should talk about how it felt to ask open questions.
2. Clients should talk about how it felt to be the recipient of questions.
3. Observers should give positive and negative feedback to helpers about the appropriateness of the open questions and the manner in

continues

LAB 5 (Continued)

Open Questions and Probes

which they were delivered. Discuss specific questions that were helpful and less helpful.

SWITCH ROLES

Personal Reflections

- What did you learn about yourself in trying to use open questions?
- What difficulties did you have asking open questions?
- How did the client respond when you asked open questions?

Restatement | 8

The world is made of stories, not atoms.

—*Muriel Rukeyser*

fter Jason's parents were killed in a random drive-by shooting, he was filled with rage and needed a chance to talk. His helper listened supportively, showed appropriate and encouraging attending behaviors, and rephrased the content of what Jason was saying (e.g., "You're still trying to understand what happened," "You can't make sense of their deaths," and "You want to hurt their murderer"). These restatements helped Jason express his thoughts about the shooting.

When Jackie talked in great detail about difficulties with her job because of changes in technology, the helper restated Jackie's message, "So the new technology is changing the way you do things." This restatement helped Jackie focus on what she was saying and further explore her situation. Jackie replied that it was not the new technology as much as her resistance to learning new things that made it difficult.

Restatements are a repeating or paraphrasing of the content or meaning of what a client has said (see Exhibit 8.1). Restatements typically contain fewer but similar words, are more concrete and clear than the client's statement, can be phrased either tentatively (e.g., "I wonder if maybe she said something like that you were kind of late?") or more directly (e.g., "So she said you were late"), and refer to things the client just said or to things the client said earlier in the session or treatment. The emphasis of restatements is on the substance or content rather than on the feelings or inner experience (reflection of feelings is covered in chap. 9).

Web Forms referred to in text can be found on the book's companion online guide described in the Preface.

EXHIBIT 8.1

Overview of Restatement

Definition	*Restatement* is a repeating or rephrasing of the content or meaning of the client's statement(s) that typically contains fewer but similar words and is more concrete and clear than the client's statement. The restatement can be phrased either tentatively or as a direct statement. Restatements can paraphrase either immediately preceding material or material from earlier in session or treatment.
Examples	"You want to be an effective helper." "Your parents are breaking up." "To summarize, you seem more clear on what you would like to do about attending the wedding."
Typical helper intentions	To clarify, to focus, to support, to encourage catharsis (see Web Form D)
Possible client reactions	Supported, understood, clear, negative thoughts or behaviors, stuck, lacking direction (see Web Form G)
Desired client behavior	Cognitive–behavioral exploration (see Web Form H)
Potential difficulties	Parroting Restating only surface thoughts Feeling frustrated because of not "doing" enough for client Focusing on someone other than the client

Summaries, a kind of restatement, tie together several ideas or pick out the highlights and general themes of the content expressed by the client. They do not go beyond what the client has said or delve into the reasons for feelings or behaviors but consolidate what has been said.

Why Use Restatements?

The use of restatement goes back to Rogers (1942), who believed that helpers need to be mirrors or sounding boards, enabling clients to hear what they are saying without judgment. Thinking about one's problems alone is often difficult because one can get blocked or stuck, may not have enough time or energy to examine problems thoroughly, may rationalize behaviors, or may give up and quit trying. Another person who listens and serves as a mirror of the content offers clients a golden opportunity to hear their thoughts.

Given that clients often feel confused, conflicted, or overwhelmed by their problems, receiving accurate restatements allows them to hear how their concerns sound to others. It is important that clients hear back what they have said, so they can evaluate what they are thinking, add things they had forgotten, think about whether they actually believe what they have said, and think about things at a deeper level. Because statements often sound different when repeated by someone else, restatements allow clients to ponder what they really think. Restatements also can enable clients to clarify matters, explore certain aspects of the problem more thoroughly, and think about aspects they had not considered before. Just taking the time to think through a problem carefully with the benefit of an interested listener can lead to new insights. In fact, with healthy clients who are trying to understand major problems or make decisions, helpers might never need to go beyond this type of intervention because these clients only need an opportunity to hear what they are thinking.

An additional reason for helpers to use restatements is that helpers are required to put their listening into words and play an active role in the helping process. Rather than assuming they have understood what clients have said, restatements enable helpers to check out the accuracy of what they have heard. Having to listen to clients and summarize their words in fewer and more concise terms requires that helpers attend carefully and determine the key components of what clients have revealed. Saying "I understand how you feel" or asking questions can be easy but is often empty; restating clients' statements is much harder and requires that helpers not only listen but also struggle to understand enough of what clients have said so they can restate the essence of their messages. Although at first it may seem that restatements are a passive mode of responding, helpers actually are engaged actively in trying to capture the essence of clients' experiences and paraphrase it back for clients to hear.

Helpers also use summaries to reassure clients that they have been listening and to check the accuracy of what they have been hearing. Summaries can be particularly useful when clients have finished talking about a particular issue or at the end of sessions, as a way of helping clients reach a sense of closure regarding what has been explored. Summaries also can be helpful at the beginning of subsequent sessions to recap past sessions and provide a focus for the upcoming session.

Although there is no empirical evidence, restatements seem most appropriate for clients who are cognitively oriented rather than affectively oriented. Such cognitively oriented clients like to analyze their thoughts about problems and might be threatened if asked to focus too much on feelings, especially early in a helping relationship. Restatements also seem to be appropriate when affectively oriented clients are talking about issues that are too affect laden because the feelings might be overwhelming and need to be contained.

How to Restate

Restatements are generally shorter and more concise than clients' statements, focusing on the most important material rather than repeating everything verbatim. For example, if the client has been talking at some length about the many things that have been getting in the way of studying, the helper might give a restatement such as, "so you have not been able to study lately" or "studying has been difficult for you lately," because these statements focus the client on what is important to explore at a deeper level.

The goal of restatements is to enable clients to focus and to talk in more depth about an issue, as well as to assist clients in figuring out issues rather than just restating what the client already knows. Focusing on one piece of an issue at a time is important to allow clients the opportunity to delve deeply into a concern. Helpers can return later to other important aspects of the problem after one part is explored thoroughly.

Rather than paraphrasing everything clients say, helpers try to capture the essence of what they have said. Specifically, helpers try to capture the "cutting edge" of what clients have revealed—what clients are most uncertain about, what is still unexplored, or what is not completely understood. A student used a metaphor of Wayne Gretzy, a star hockey player, saying that it is important in hockey to go to where the puck is going, not where it has been. Helpers, then, should pick out the salient message or the issue clients are still working on to facilitate further exploration.

Helpers often worry that selecting the most important part of the client's statement requires a judgment call and removes them from a client-centered approach to helping. I would argue that restatement allows helpers to stay within a client-centered approach because they are trying to use their empathic skills to figure out the most important aspect for the client. Helpers have to listen to clients at a deep level to understand what they are most concerned about. The attitude of being client-centered is very important for helpers when formulating restatements. The emphasis is on helping clients explore more deeply rather than on helpers having agendas for what content should emerge. Helpers should not be judgmental and should not assume they know or understand what clients are experiencing. Helpers should not be invested in solving problems or disclosing their own problems; rather, they should be focused on hearing the client's story and facilitating exploration.

Clues for determining what is most important to restate can be gathered by attending to what the client focuses on most, what the client seems to have the most involvement in talking about, what the client seems to have questions or conflicts about, and what is left unresolved. Attention to nonverbal messages (e.g., vocal quality might indicate that the client is deeply engaged in what he or she is talking about) can also assist helpers in determining the salient content of the client's message.

Although it is helpful when restatements are relatively close to what the client has said, it is not necessary (or often even possible) for the restatements to be perfectly accurate. For example, if a client presents a confused and jumbled statement of her concerns and a helper provides restatements that do not encapsulate the content accurately, the client can clarify what she means so both of them understand the situation better. Restatements thus allow clients a chance to clarify helpers' mistaken impressions.

The emphasis of restatements should be on the client's thoughts rather than on other people's thoughts. This client focus enables a client to focus inward rather than blaming others or worrying about what others think. For example, a client was discussing her decision to change jobs and move to the West Coast. During the session, she continuously focused on her colleagues' and friends' reactions to her decision. The helper worked to focus the restatements on the client ("You keep thinking about how your friends will react if you move") rather than on her friends and colleagues ("Your friend doesn't want you to move").

To reduce the tendency to become repetitive, helpers can vary the format of restatements. There are several ways to introduce restatements, such as,

- "I hear you saying . . . "
- "It sounds as though . . . "
- "I wonder whether . . . "
- "You're saying that . . . "
- "So . . . "

Alternatively, helpers can just repeat and slightly draw out a key word clients have said, such as *divorce, music,* or *headache.* If the key word is presented in a questioning or inviting tone, it encourages the client to tell the helper more about the topic. For example, if a client has been talking about her daughter having just been tested and found to have an incredibly high IQ score, and the helper wants the client to explore more about IQs, she might simply say, "IQ . . . ?," thereby inviting the client to tell her more about what IQ means to her.

Formulating a restatement can be difficult when the client has talked for a long time. Beginning trainees often think they need to capture everything the client has said. Capturing everything not only would be impossible but would probably be counterproductive. The focus would shift from the client to the helper because the repeating would take too much time and would take the emphasis off the client. The momentum would be lost in the session. The client would be put in a position of trying to remember everything he or she said to determine whether the helper repeated everything accurately. In contrast, an effective restatement keeps the focus on the client and is almost unnoticeable in subtly guiding and encouraging the client to keep talking.

EXAMPLES OF RESTATEMENTS

Client: I have to go on a pilgrimage to Mecca. I don't really want to go because it's the middle of my last semester in college and I'm worried that my grades will suffer if I leave for two weeks, but I don't have much choice. According to my religion, I have to go.

Helper: *You have to go.*

Client: Yeah, for my religion, we all have to do a pilgrimage before we get married. It's just expected. My father has to go with me because a man has to be on the pilgrimage, but I don't have a very good relationship with him, and he's not well, so I don't know if he can withstand the rigors of the trip. The last time he went with my brother, it was pretty disastrous.

Helper: *You said you don't have a very good relationship with your father.*

Client: Right. He wasn't around much when I was growing up. He was always too busy. And now to spend two weeks with him is a lot. I don't even know what we could talk about. I feel like I don't know him. I get anxious just thinking about spending a lot of time with him. But on the other hand, I wish I knew him better, so maybe this is an opportunity to get to know him.

Helper: *Really know him.*

Client: Yeah, really know him. I've always wanted to have a good relationship with him. People say that we're a lot alike. And he could teach me a lot about my religion and culture, things I don't know much about, given that I came to the United States when I was very young.

Helper: *So you could learn something from your father.*

Client: Oh yeah, I think I could learn a lot from him. He is a wise person. I just hope I can be myself with him. I've always felt like such a little kid, and I would rather feel like an adult with him the way I can with my mother.

Helper: *Feel like an adult.*

Client: Yeah, I want to feel like myself when I am around him. I want to be able to behave like I do with other people. I want to get to know him as a person instead of feeling afraid of him. (Client continues to explore.)

Effects of Restatement

Helpers need to be aware of the impact of their restatements on clients. To become more aware, helpers can watch tapes of their sessions and rate the impact of each restatement, using the following three-point scale:

1 = Very ineffective restatements stop exploration because clients do not know what else to say and do not feel encouraged to talk further. Clients may also respond with frustration and anger if they perceive helpers are parroting what they have said (e.g., they might feel or say, "I just said that").

2 = With moderately ineffective or neutral restatements, clients keep talking but repeat themselves, doing what is called *circling*. They do not have a sense of what is important to talk about next and do not feel guided by the restatement.

3 = Effective restatements capture the "cutting edge" of what clients are talking about and helps clients elaborate on their thoughts. When restatements capture the essence of the communication, clients feel understood.

Difficulties Helpers Experience in Restating

Many helpers initially feel awkward and stilted using restatements because people do not typically paraphrase what the other person has said in regular social communication. Many beginning helpers worry that clients will feel annoyed and say something like "I just said that." In fact, the reaction of clients is usually quite different when they are given a good restatement—they feel heard. Once students learn how to use restatements, they can be very useful not only in helping relationships, but also with friends and family to demonstrate that one is really listening.

Another difficulty beginning helpers face is sounding like parrots if they continually use the same format to introduce restatements (e.g., "I hear you saying . . . ") or if they repeat clients' messages verbatim. Clients often get annoyed with parroting and become distracted from focusing on their concerns. In a related vein, some helpers are so afraid of making a mistake when choosing key aspects of clients' messages that they repeat everything, taking the focus off the client and halting the flow of the interchange. Not surprisingly, clients quickly become bored and annoyed with such restatements, saying things like, "That's what I just said." Moreover, clients might feel stuck and aimless when restatements are mere repetitions of what they have said. By choosing the key components, focusing on the "cutting edge" of clients' concerns, varying the format, and keeping the restatements short, helpers can deal with these problems.

It is also important to focus on being empathic rather than restating robotically. Some helpers get so caught up in capturing the content accurately that they forget the most important thing is to show the client that they are struggling to understand.

Some helpers feel frustrated when they use restatements because they feel they are not "doing" anything or giving the client specific answers. Restatements are used to help clients explore and tell their stories rather than come to insight or action, so helpers rarely feel brilliant when using them. In fact, clients often are not able to remember restatements because the focus is on them rather than on the helper.

HELPFUL HINTS

- The cardinal rule: Do not assume you understand anything about the client. Even if you are the same age, gender, race, ethnicity, and so on, you have not had the same experiences as the client and cannot assume your experiences and feelings are similar. It is best to assume you know nothing and then learn as much as you can from the client.
- Pick the most important part of the client's statements to restate. Do not try to paraphrase everything. Even though several points of information in a statement may be important, only one issue can be dealt with effectively at a time. Clues for determining what is most important can be gathered by attending to nonverbal messages and to what the client focuses on most, what she or he seems to have the most involvement in talking about, what she or he seems to have questions or conflicts about, and what is left unresolved.
- Keep restatements short and concise. The goal is to turn the attention back to the client right away, so she or he continues exploring. Remember that in helping, helpers typically talk only 20% to 40% of the time.
- Give the restatement slowly and supportively (take a deep breath before responding) rather than just rushing to say something.

- Use a tentative tone so the client can disagree with restatements.
- Focus on the client rather than on another person, even when the client's focus is on another person. Remember that you cannot often influence the other person, so your best bet is to focus on the client. For example, when a client talks about her husband's nagging, focus on what the client thinks about the nagging rather than on how terrible the husband is for nagging.
- Remember that by definition, restatements do not include feelings even if a client has expressed feelings. The focus is on the content of the client's statements, to help the client hear what he or she said. I am not suggesting that feelings are not important (in fact, I believe that reflection of feelings, covered in chap. 9, is a very helpful skill); but in restatements, the focus is on thoughts.
- Use restatements (as opposed to reflection of feelings) when you want to assist a client in clarifying or focusing or when you want to summarize what a client has said.
- Use the client's language style as much as possible, but avoid too much repetition.
- Do not rush to give a restatement when the client is productively exploring thoughts and feelings. When the client stops talking completely, a restatement can be given.
- Pause before restating because it gives the client a chance to keep talking if she or he has something more to say. In addition, deep breathing before delivering restatements can help you relax when you feel anxious.
- Vary the manner in which you deliver restatements. Use a sentence (e.g., "You are having trouble with your mother"), a key word or two (e.g., "mother," "trouble with mother"), or begin with lead-ins such as, "I hear you saying . . . ," "It sounds as though . . . ," "I wonder whether . . . ," or "You're saying that. . . . "
- If you truly do not understand what the client has said, asking the client to repeat her- or himself is better than pretending you understand. If you ask for clarification too many times, a client might feel you are not listening or they are bad communicators, but an occasional query is appropriate.

PRACTICE EXERCISES

Pretend that a client makes the following statements to you. Read each of the following and then write a restatement. Compare your responses with the possible helper responses provided at the end of the section. The helper responses provided are not the "right" or "best" restatements but give you an idea of different ways to respond.

Statements

1. Client: "I have a lot of work to do for my classes. But I don't know when I'm going to do it because I have to work 20 hours a week at my job. When I come home from classes and working, I just don't have any energy for doing schoolwork. I feel like I need a chance to just 'veg' out and watch TV."
    Helper response: _____
2. Client: "After I graduate, I am going to take a cross-country trip. At first I was just going to go by myself, but then my roommates heard about it, and both of them said they wanted to go. I rearranged my schedule to accommodate them, and now one of them says he isn't going."
    Helper response: _____
3. Client: "My mother is going through a divorce. She calls me every night to talk. She says she has no one else to talk to. The guy she married after my father left her is a real jerk. He beat her up and is an alcoholic."
    Helper response: _____

Possible Helper Responses

1. "You don't have much energy right now for your schoolwork."
    "When you get home from work, you don't really want to do schoolwork."
    "I hear you saying that you're not getting your homework done."
2. "You've made a lot of adjustments in your plans for your friends."
    "You just learned that your friend will not accompany you on your trip."
    "You are planning a trip with another person."
3. "You're thinking a lot about your mother lately."
    "You talk to your mother every night and are very involved in her problems."
    "You think your mother needs you a lot right now."
    "Lots of responsibility."

WHAT DO YOU THINK?

▮ Debate the efficacy of restatements compared with responses that are more typically used in friendships, such as advice and self-disclosure.

▮ Have you experienced feelings similar to those of the client in the first example of the practice exercises? If so, was it difficult for you to focus on the client because of thinking about your own issues?

∎ Compare and contrast restatements and open questions about thoughts.

∎ In his early theorizing, Rogers (1942) promoted restatement as the most important skill, whereas later he focused more on other skills. What do you think about restatements?

LAB 6

Restatement

Goal: For helpers to learn to restate the *content* of client's speech.

Exercise 1

In a large group, the group leader verbally gives an example of a client statement (keep it simple, brief, and unemotional). Each student writes a restatement and then reads his or her restatements out loud. Continue with examples until the leader is certain that students understand and can deliver restatements.

Exercise 2

Students should be arranged in groups of three, with lab leaders monitoring the groups. Within groups, roles should be switched so that each person gets a chance to participate at least one time as the helper, client, and observer.

Helper's and Client's Tasks During the Helping Interchange

1. The helper introduces him- or herself (see Lab 1 for possible format).
2. The client talks briefly on a topic about which he or she has few emotions. (See Exhibit 1.1 in chap. 1 for suggestions for topics.)
3. The helper listens attentively during the client statement without thinking of what she or he is going to say next. After the client statement, the helper pauses, takes a deep breath, thinks of what to say, and then restates what the client said using fewer words and focusing on the most essential part of the statement. For this exercise, the helper focuses on content rather than feelings. Remember to use appropriate attending behaviors throughout the exercise.
4. Continue for five to ten turns.

Observer's Task During the Helping Interchange

Take notes about the helpers' restatements and attending behaviors.

After the Helping Interchange

1. The helper talks about how it felt to do restatements.
2. The client says how it felt to receive restatements and gives feedback to the helper.
3. The observer gives feedback to the helper about the restatements and attending skills.

SWITCH ROLES

Personal Reflections

■ How did you handle any anxiety you experienced giving restatements?
■ What were your strengths and weaknesses in giving restatements?

▪ In the past, students have had difficulty formulating short concise restatements, focusing on content instead of feelings, figuring out what to focus on in the client's statements, talking too much, and taking the focus off the client. Which of these experiences did you have? How can you handle these challenges in the future?

Reflection of Feelings 9

It seems to me that clients who have moved significantly in
therapy live more intimately with their feelings of pain, but
also more vividly with their feelings of ecstasy; that anger is
more clearly felt, but so also is love; that fear is an experience
they know more deeply, but so is courage.

—Carl Rogers

Tyler, an aspiring actor, had been in an automobile accident that left
him with a disability and made it unlikely he would ever be able to act
again. Throughout the session, his helper used a number of reflections
(e.g., "You feel angry because you can no longer do what you love to
do," "I wonder if you feel afraid that people will laugh at you," "It
sounds like you feel anxious about going out in public") to help Tyler
talk about his many feelings so he could identify and accept what was
going on inside him.

A reflection of feelings is a repeating or rephrasing of the client's statements with an emphasis on the client's feelings (see Exhibit 9.1). The
feelings may have been stated by the client (in either the same or similar
words), or the helper may be able to infer what the feelings are from the
client's nonverbal behavior or from the content of the client's message.
The reflection may be phrased either tentatively (e.g., "I wonder if you're
feeling angry?) or more directly (e.g., "It sounds to me like you're feeling
angry"). The emphasis can be just on the feeling (e.g., "You feel upset") or
on both the feeling and the reason for the feeling (e.g., "You feel upset
because your teacher did not notice all the work you have done").

Why Reflect Feelings?

Reflection of feelings is probably the most important skill in the helper's
repertoire. If beginning helpers could learn and use only one skill, reflec-

Web Forms referred to in text can be found on the book's companion online guide described in the Preface.

EXHIBIT 9.1

Overview of Reflection of Feelings

Definition	A *reflection of feelings* is a repeating or rephrasing of the client's statements, including an explicit identification of feelings. The feelings may have been stated by the client (in exactly the same or similar words), or the helper may infer feelings from the client's nonverbal behavior, the context, or the content of the client's message. The reflection may be phrased either tentatively or as a statement.
Examples	"You feel angry at your husband for not being home." "You seem pleased that you told your boss you didn't want to work late."
Typical intentions	To identify and intensify feelings, to encourage catharsis, to clarify, to instill hope, to encourage self-control (see Web Form D)
Possible client reactions	Feelings, negative thoughts or behaviors, clear, responsibility, unstuck, scared, worse, misunderstood (see Web Form G)
Desired client behavior	Affective exploration (see Web Form H)
Potential difficulties	Dealing with intense feelings such as anger and sadness Capturing the most intense feeling to reflect to the client Separating one's own feelings from the client's experiences Stating feeling words too adamantly, so that clients have difficulty correcting you or expressing other feelings

---

tion of feelings would be the one. It is often more difficult to learn to use reflections than open questions, though, because most people are often not used to reflecting feelings in everyday conversations.

Helpers use reflections to help clients identify, clarify, and experience feelings on a deeper level. Reflection is one of the most important skills for facilitating client exploration because it encourages clients to become immersed in their inner experiences. In addition to articulating an intellectual label of a feeling, however, it is important to stress that helpers aid clients in experiencing feelings in the immediate moment. For example, a couple might recount an incident in which they became angry with one another. The helper would encourage them to express their current feelings and talk to each other about how they are feeling about the incident now. Another intention is to encourage emotional catharsis with reflections. Cathartic relief occurs when feelings begin to flow rather than being stuck or bottled up and when clients begin to accept their feelings.

IMPORTANCE OF EMOTIONS

As Rogers noted, emotions are a key part of our experience. They tell us how we are reacting to the world. Often we ignore, deny, distort, or repress feelings because we have been told they are unacceptable. Hence, we grow apart from our inner experiencing and cannot accept ourselves. We need to return to and allow ourselves to feel our emotions, because only then can we decide what to do about them.

Many beginning helpers are concerned about learning the details of events, as they might in a friendship or when asked to solve a problem, but they ignore the feelings behind the events. Gathering details implies that helpers are going to do something to solve the problem, and it allows the client to move away from painful or confusing affect.

Feelings are at least as important as content in client communication. Clients are best able to solve their problems when they get in touch with their feelings. Experiencing feelings allows clients to evaluate events in terms of their inner experiencing.

Clients' expression of emotions enables helpers to know and understand them. People respond differently to events, so helpers need to know how experiences are interpreted by individual clients. For example, when Varda came to a helper's office because her father died, the helper initially assumed that Varda felt sad, depressed, and lonely because that is how she felt when her father died. In fact, Varda felt angry because she had been having intrusive memories of childhood sexual abuse since her father died. It was safe for Varda to remember the abuse only when her father was no longer able to hurt her. In addition, Varda felt relief that her father died because she no longer had to deal with him. This example illustrates that helpers must listen carefully and not impose their assumptions on clients.

If clients accept their emotions, they can become open to new feelings and experiences. Feelings are not static but change once they are experienced. When a person experiences a feeling fully and completely, new feelings emerge. For example, once Varda experienced her anger, she became aware of other feelings such as sadness, which then led to feelings of acceptance and peace.

In contrast, unaccepted feelings are likely to "leak" out, sometimes in very destructive ways. For example, Robert might become subtly rude or hostile to a friend who was accepted into a prestigious law school after Robert learned his own application was rejected. All of us know people who do not directly say they are angry but indirectly communicate subtle, nasty messages that make it difficult to respond to them. Other people get stuck because they cannot accept their feelings. Similar to the obstruction that occurs when a river gets dammed up, these people get blocked if they do not allow themselves to have and express their feelings.

Feelings are rarely simple or straightforward; therefore, it is important to note that clients might have several conflicting feelings about a topic. For example, Diana might feel excited about taking a new job and pleased that she was selected over other candidates. However, she might also feel anxious about what is required of her, afraid of working too closely with the boss (who reminds her of her father), insecure about how others may view her, and worried about whether she can make enough money to pay the rent. As helpers, it is important to encourage clients to express as many feelings as possible without worrying about whether the feelings are rational, ambiguous, or contradictory.

Anger, sadness, fear, shame, pain, and hurt seem to be the most important emotions involved in therapeutic change (Greenberg, 2002). These negative emotions are often bottled up and not expressed or experienced because of shame and fear of disapproval. Many people cannot allow themselves to even think about such feelings. Hence, it requires a supportive environment for clients to feel safe enough to express these feelings openly.

In addition, it is important to note that sometimes emotions exist in layers (Greenberg, 2002; Teyber, 2000). For example, after anger is expressed and experienced, sadness and shame often emerge. Inversely, after sadness is expressed and experienced, anger and guilt often emerge. Similarly, Gestalt therapists believe every feeling has two sides. If clients talk only about fear, helpers might wonder about wishes; if clients talk only about love, helpers might wonder about hate. By fostering deeper thought about the feelings, helpers enable clients to admit the multitude of feelings they might not otherwise have been able to acknowledge.

SEPARATION BETWEEN FEELINGS AND BEHAVIORS

Clients who can experience, accept, and own their feelings can then decide how to behave. Clients do not have to act on the feelings but can make more informed decisions about what to do when feelings are out in the open. In other words, when one feels murderous, one does not have to kill someone but can figure out other avenues of expression. Being aware of one's feelings makes one less likely to act on them unintentionally.

BENEFITS OF REFLECTION OF FEELINGS

Reflections of feelings are ideal interventions for enabling clients to enter into their internal experiences, especially if delivered with concern and empathy for clients' reluctance to experience the painful feelings. Clients often need such assistance to recognize and accept their feelings and themselves.

Reflections also validate feelings. Laing and Esterson (1970) suggested that people stop feeling "crazy" when their subjective experience is validated. It is easy to feel that one is the only person who has ever felt a certain way, so hearing the helper calmly say the feeling can help clients see that such feelings are acceptable.

Clients often have difficulty identifying and accepting feelings on their own, perhaps because they do not know how they feel or are ambivalent or negative about the feelings. Furthermore, it can be difficult to articulate feelings because they are often sensations rather than fully understood awarenesses. People often do not have words to symbolize feelings, so struggling to label feelings helps one discover what they are.

Hearing reflections also enables clients to rethink and reexamine what they really feel. If a helper uses the term *disgusted*, this forces the client to think about whether *disgusted* fits his or her experience. This searching can lead to deeper exploration of the feelings in an attempt to clarify the feeling. It is often difficult for clients to verbalize their deepest, most private thoughts and feelings. In a safe and supportive relationship they can begin to explore the feelings, which are often complex and contradictory. They can feel a combination of love, hatred, and guilt toward the same person in the same situation. Being allowed to admit these ambivalent feelings to another person without rejection can enable clients to accept feelings as their own.

If clients have difficulty identifying their feelings, they might feel very anxious and unsure when helpers ask, "How are you feeling about that?" Such questions can confuse or concern clients because they are not sure what helpers want to hear or how they "should" feel. Sometimes asking how they feel stimulates defenses and makes clients shut down. Clients can also feel annoyed that helpers are not really listening to what they are saying or trying to empathize with their feelings. In contrast, reflecting feelings ("You seem upset about that") often feels more facilitative and less threatening to clients.

Reflecting feelings can also model the expression of feelings, which could be useful for clients who are out of touch with their emotions. Many people experience an emotion but do not have a label for the feeling. For example, saying "I wonder if you feel frustrated with your sister" suggests that frustration is a feeling a person might have in this situation. By labeling feelings, helpers also imply that they are not afraid of feelings, that feelings are familiar, and that clients are acceptable regardless of their feelings. By suggesting a feeling, reflections might circumvent defenses or possible embarrassment about having the feelings. Helpers indicate through reflections that the feelings are normal and that they accept the person who has the feelings, which can be a relief to clients.

Coming up with reflections requires that helpers work at least as hard as clients are working. Reflections demonstrate that the helper is actively engaged in trying to understand the client. It also forces the helper to communicate his or her understanding of the client's feelings so the helper can investigate the accuracy of his or her perceptions. One could say, "I understand exactly how you feel," but this statement does not demonstrate to the client the content of the understanding. Reflections provide an opportunity for helpers to show their understanding. Beginning helpers quickly discover that accurately perceiving how another person feels is difficult. We can never truly understand another person, but we can struggle to get past our own perceptions and try to immerse ourselves in the client's experiences.

Reflections of feelings are ideal interventions for encouraging client expression of feelings because helpers give examples of what clients might be experiencing. Clients can then begin to recognize and accept feelings, and helpers accept clients' feelings as natural and normal. In addition, clients can give helpers feedback about what they did or did not understand if helpers clearly articulate what they think clients are feeling. Finally, reflections can help to build the relationship because helpers communicate their understanding to clients.

HOW REFLECTION OF FEELINGS RELATES TO EMPATHY

Some authors have equated reflection of feeling with empathy (e.g., Carkhuff, 1969; Egan, 1994). I disagree with this stance because it is too narrow to define *empathy* as just reflection of feeling (see also Duan & Hill, 1996). I agree with Rogers (1957) that empathy is an attitude or way of being in tune with the experience of another person. If delivered appropriately, a reflection of feelings could be a manifestation of empathy, but a technically correct reflection of feelings could be unempathic if it is delivered at the wrong time or in an inappropriate manner. For example, if a helper says, "you feel humiliated" in an all-knowing, firm voice, the client might feel put down or misunderstood. The client may feel that the helper understands her better than she understands herself, which could make her mistrust her own feelings and submit to the helper as the authority.

There are times when it is more empathic to use a helping skill other than a reflection (e.g., a challenge). A helper responding to a client who feels stuck in an abusive relationship might challenge her to seek help in a program for battered women. This response might be very empathic given the dangerous situation in the home and the helper's valuing of the client as a person deserving of a healthy relationship.

CAUTIONS ABOUT USING REFLECTION OF FEELINGS

Reflecting feelings can have positive benefits by helping clients experience relief from tension, come to accept their feelings, and feel proud that they had the courage to express and face their feelings. Reflection of feelings, however, can be problematic if clients reveal more feelings than they can tolerate at the time. If their defenses are overwhelmed, clients can deteriorate under prolonged emotional catharsis. They may not be ready for the feelings and may not feel supported enough to risk deep exploration.

Some suggestions about when *to focus* on emotions are taken from Greenberg (2002):

- When there is a therapeutic bond between a helper and a client
- When a helper and the client agree on the task of working on emotions
- When a client is avoiding feelings (e.g., the client obviously has a feeling but is interrupting it or is avoiding emotion by intellectualizing, deflecting, or distracting)
- When a client behaves maladaptively because of a lack of awareness of feelings (e.g., becomes passive when abused, depressed when angry, overly inhibited from feeling happy or sad and so lacking vigor)
- When a client needs to reprocess traumatic experiences (although not usually immediately after the event)

Some suggestions about when *not to focus* on emotions are taken from Brammer and MacDonald (1996) and Greenberg (2002):

- When the therapeutic relationship is not strong (e.g., the client does not feel safe or does not trust the help, or the helper does not have enough information about the client)
- When the client feels overwhelmed by emotions due to severe emotional disorder, delusional thinking, or extreme anger
- The client is going through severe emotional crises, and discussing feelings would add more pressure than he or she could handle
- The client has a history of aggression, falling apart, substance abuse, self-harm, not being able to regulate emotions, or lack of coping skills
- The client shows strong resistance to expressing feelings
- There is not enough time to work through the feelings

▮ The helper is not experienced in dealing with emotionally distraught
clients

During crises or when the client is feeling emotionally overwhelmed
or distraught, it is more appropriate to teach clients emotion regulation so
they can manage the overwhelming emotions (Greenberg, 2002). Emotion regulation techniques such as relaxation training are discussed in
chapter 20.

An additional concern is that clients might accept the helper's reflection as accurate, not because it necessarily is, but because the helper is in
a position of authority. Clients might feel their helpers know more about
them than they actually do. Helpers thus need to observe whether clients
comply too readily with what helpers say rather than experiencing their
own feelings. As tempting as it might be, acting as an omniscient authority with regard to clients' feelings often leads to dependency, misunderstandings, or a difficult realization of the helper's limitations.

Helpers should also be aware of cultural considerations in using reflections, given that cultures differ in beliefs about how emotion should
be expressed. In the United States, people are generally encouraged to be
open about their feelings and experiences. One only needs to turn on
radio and television talk shows to see how people share their innermost
experiences freely. People from non-American cultures, however, are often more reserved about admitting and expressing feelings, especially with
non-family members (Pedersen et al., 2002). There are also gender differences in the expression of emotion, in that men may have a harder time
expressing feelings than women. Men are not typically socialized to be
sensitive to feelings and often feel threatened if asked to say what they
are feeling (Cournoyer & Mahalik, 1995; Good et al., 1995; O'Neil, 1981).

My intent in presenting these cautions is not to discourage helpers or
make them fearful about dealing with their client feelings but to increase
helpers' awareness about potential hazards of reflecting feelings. In general, reflection of feelings is appropriate and beneficial but can occasionally lead to clients feeling overwhelmed by uncontrollable feelings, so
helpers need to be aware and responsive to client reactions.

How to Reflect Feelings

Clients need to feel safe enough in the therapeutic relationship to risk
delving into their feelings. They must feel that they will not be dispar-
aged, embarrassed, or shamed, but rather accepted, valued, and respected
when they reveal themselves. Hence, reflections must be done gently and
with empathy.

FORMAT OF REFLECTION OF FEELINGS

When learning to do reflections, helpers can use one of two formats:

■ You feel ___ OR
■ You feel ___ because ___.

In other words, helpers can say just the feeling word to highlight the feeling (e.g., "You feel angry"), or they say both the feeling and the reason for the feeling (e.g., "You feel frustrated because you didn't get your way"). The "because" clause paraphrases the content of what the client has been discussing and provides supporting data for why the client has the feeling.

Once helpers grasp how to do reflections, they can vary the format so clients do not become annoyed with repetitiveness. If the helper says, "It sounds like you're feeling ___" 20 times in a row, it is not surprising that the client would notice, which would take away from the client's exploration. Alternate formats are as follows:

■ "I wonder if you're feeling ___"
■ "Perhaps you're feeling ___"
■ "You sound (or seem) ___"
■ "If I were you, I might feel ___"
■ "Could you be ___?"
■ "From your nonverbals, I would guess you're feeling ___"
■ "It sounds like you feel ___"
■ "Perhaps you feel ___"
■ "If I were you, I would feel ___"
■ "So you're feeling ___"
■ "And that made you feel ___"
■ "I hear you saying ___"
■ "My hunch is that you feel ___"
■ "You're ___"
■ "Upset" (or whatever feeling word is most appropriate)

Helpers should only pick what they perceive to be the most salient feeling rather than reflect all of the feelings in a single reflection. Selecting the most salient feeling requires a judgment call, so helpers need to be attentive to clients' verbal and nonverbal behavior. To detect the most powerful immediate feelings, helpers can pay attention to where the most energy is in what the client is saying or how they are reacting nonverbally.

Not only is the specific feeling important, but helpers also need to try to match the intensity of the feeling (Skovholt & Rivers, 2003). For example, the intensity of anger could range from a mild "irritated," to a stronger "mad," to an even stronger "enraged." Similarly, the intensity of happiness could range from "okay" to "happy" to "ecstatic." Helpers can also vary the intensity of a feeling word by using modifiers such as "somewhat" or "very" (e.g., "somewhat upset" vs. "very upset").

It is also useful for helpers to state the feelings tentatively (e.g., "Perhaps you're feeling upset?") to encourage clarification. Stating feelings too definitely (e.g., "You obviously are angry at your mother") can preclude exploration because clients might feel that there is no reason to struggle to identify the inner feeling. Hence, it is best to adopt a quizzical tone, such as "I wonder if you might be feeling ___?"

In addition, given that our goal is to allow clients to immerse themselves in their feelings so they can come to accept them, helpers should focus on present, rather than past, feelings. By focusing on feeling present in the moment, clients can experience their immediate feelings rather than telling stories about past feelings (e.g., "You sound irritated right now as you talk about your mother" rather than "It sounds like you were upset with your mother"). Remember that a person can have feelings in the present about something that happened in the past (e.g., "You still feel angry as you think about what he said").

I also suggest that helpers allow clients time to absorb and think about the reflections that are presented rather than rushing quickly to the next feeling. If the client starts crying or getting upset, the helper can encourage him or her to experience and express these feelings rather than trying to "take away" the feelings or make the client feel better. Pause, go slowly, and do not interrupt when the client is experiencing feelings.

Because the goal is to reflect feelings and keep the focus on the client, helpers need to be aware of staying in the background and facilitating exploration. Helpers can reach this goal by maintaining a supportive and listening stance. Good reflections should almost not be noticed by clients because these interventions help clients continue exploring and paying more attention to themselves than to the helper.

IDENTIFYING FEELING WORDS

Many beginning helpers have difficulty coming up with a range of words to describe the emotions expressed in a given situation. Exhibit 9.2 contains a checklist of emotion words developed from several sources (Greenberg, 2002; Hill, Siegelman, Gronsky, Sturniolo, & Fretz, 1981; student feedback, lists collected from various unknown sources). Each of you can highlight favorite words and add words to the list to personalize it.

Note that this list includes both positive and negative emotions. Negative emotions outnumber positive emotions by about two to one (Izard, 1977), especially in a helping situation; however, helpers need to remember to focus on positive as well as negative emotions so clients feel encouraged about changes they are making.

EXHIBIT 9.2

Emotion Words Checklist

Calm–relaxed

at ease	at peace	calm	comforted	comfortable
complacent	composed	contented	easygoing	mellow
peaceful	quiet	relaxed	relieved	safe
satisfied	serene	soothed	tranquil	warm

Joyful–excited

amused	animated	blissful	captivated	cheerful
delighted	eager	elated	ecstatic	enchanted
energized	enthusiastic	euphoric	exhilarated	excited
fantastic	glad	gleeful	happy	high
hopeful	joyful	jubilant	lighthearted	loved
lucky	marvelous	optimistic	overjoyed	pleased
positive	superb	thrilled		

Vigorous–active

active	adventurous	alert	alive	ambitious
animated	bubbly	busy	daring	energetic
free	invigorated	lively	motivated	reckless
refreshed	renewed	revitalized	spirited	vibrant
vigorous	vivacious	wild		

Proud–competent

accomplished	admired	attractive	beautiful	bold
brave	capable	competent	confident	courageous
deserving	effective	efficient	empowered	fearless
forceful	gifted	handsome	heroic	important
independent	influential	intelligent	invincible	looked up to
lovely	mighty	pleased	powerful	prosperous
proud	purposeful	respected	responsible	satisfied
self-reliant	steady	strong	successful	sure
talented	triumphant	victorious	wise	worthy

Loved–loving

accepted	affectionate	attached to	cared for	desire for
devoted to	encouraged	fond of	included	love–loved
needed	protected	safe	secure	supported
trust–trusted	understood	wanted		

Concerned–caring

accepting	caring	charitable	comforting	compassionate
concerned	considerate	cooperative	empathic	forgiving
generous	gentle	giving	helpful	interested
kind	loving	nice	pity	protective of
receptive	responsive	responsible for	sensitive	sorry for
sympathetic	tender	understanding	unselfish	warm
worried about				

continues

EXHIBIT 9.2 (Continued)

Emotion Words Checklist

Luck–deserving

appreciative	deserving	entitled	fortunate	grateful
justified	lucky	thankful	warranted	

Inspired

enlightened	enriched	impressed	inspired	transported
uplifted				

Completed–finished

completed	done	finished	fulfilled

Surprised–shocked

amazed	astonished	astounded	awestruck	flabbergasted
immobilized	numb	paralyzed	shocked	shaken
speechless	startled	stunned	surprised	taken aback

Anxious–afraid

afraid	agitated	alarmed	anxious	apprehensive
at a loss	defenseless	desperate	dread	edgy
fearful	fidgety	frantic	frightened	horrified
hysterical	ill at ease	impatient	insecure	jumpy
jittery	out of control	overwhelmed	panicky	petrified
nervous	on edge	restless	scared	stressed
tense	tentative	terrified	threatened	uncomfortable
uneasy	vulnerable	worried		

Bothered–upset

annoyed	bothered	burdened	distressed	disturbed
perturbed	troubled	rattled	restless	shaken
shook	upset	uptight	unbalanced	worried

Angry–hostile

aggravated	agitated	angry	bitter	defiant
displeased	dissatisfied	enraged	exasperated	frustrated
furious	hateful	heartless	hostile	incensed
indignant	infuriated	irate	irked	irritated
mad	miffed	nasty	outraged	pissed off
provoked	rebellious	resentful	resistant	ruthless
spiteful	unforgiving	vehement	vengeful	vindictive
violent	vicious			

Contempt–disgust

better than	contemptuous	disgusted	indignant	look down
nauseated	repelled	repulsed by	revulsion	righteous
scornful	sickened	superior	turned off	

Sad–depressed

blue	distraught	down	defeated	dejected
demoralized	depressed	despondent	discouraged	down
gloomy	glum	grief	heartsick	low
melancholy	miserable	morose	mournful	numb
pessimistic	resigned	sad	somber	sorrowful
tearful	unhappy			

Shame–guilt

apologetic	ashamed at	fault	bad	belittled
blameworthy	culpable	degraded	disgraced	embarrassed
exposed	foolish	guilty	humbled	humiliated
mortified	naughty	put down	mocked	regretful
remorseful	ridiculous	rotten	scorned	shamed
sorry	stupid			

Inadequate–weak–helpless

cowardly	deficient	feeble	fragile	helpless
hopeless	impaired	inadequate	incapable	incompetent
ineffective	inefficient	inept	inferior	insecure
insignificant	overwhelmed	pathetic	powerless	rejected
small	stupid	unable	unacceptable	unfit
unimportant	unqualified	unworthy	useless	vulnerable
weak	worthless			

Intimidated–controlled

bossed	bullied	controlled	dominated	intimidated
intruded on	obligated	overpowered	picked on	pressured
pushed around	put upon			

Lonely–unloved–excluded

abandoned	alienated	alone	apart	cut off
discounted	distant	empty	homesick	ignored
isolated	left out	lonely	lonesome	neglected
overlooked	rejected	uncared for	unimportant	unloved
unpopular	unwanted	unwelcome		

Hurt–cheated–criticized–blamed

abused	accused	belittled	betrayed	blamed
cheated	criticized	crushed	degraded	deprived
devastated	disappointed	disliked	forsaken	hurt
judged	injured	let down	mistreated	misunderstood
overlooked	pained	put down	rejected	victimized
wounded				

Burdensome–tolerated–obligated

burdensome	endured	indebted	in the way	obligated
put up with	tolerated			

continues

EXHIBIT 9.2 (Continued)

Emotion Words Checklist

Manipulated–exploited

abused	exploited	imposed upon	manipulated	managed
maneuvered	overworked	placated	pressured	used

Tired–apathetic

apathetic	bored	disinterest	drained	exhausted
fatigued	indifferent	lukewarm	resigned	run down
sleepy	sluggish	tired	unconcerned	unimpressed
uninterested	unmoved	weary		

Confused–bewildered

baffled	bewildered	conflicted	confused	disorganized
doubtful	flustered	hesitant	lost	mixed up
mystified	perplexed	puzzled	stuck	torn
uncertain	undecided	unsure		

Reluctant

cautious	guarded	hesitant	inhibited	reluctant
shy	timid	wary		

Compelled–determined

compelled	determined	driven	haunted	obsessed
obstinate	stubborn	tormented		

Jealous–mistrustful

envious	jealous	mistrustful	paranoid	suspicious

SOURCES OF REFLECTIONS

Clues about what a client is feeling can be found in four sources: the client's portrayal of his or her feelings, the client's verbal content, the client's nonverbal behavior, and the helper's projection of his or her own feelings onto the client. Helpers need to be aware that the last three sources only provide clues and may not necessarily be accurate reflections of a client's feelings.

Client's Expression of Feeling

Sometimes clients are aware of their feelings and express them openly. For example, a client might say, "I was really upset with my teacher. I was so mad that she wouldn't even listen when I told her my feelings." The helper might use another word (e.g., "furious") to describe the feelings so the client can experience feelings at a deeper level and explore other aspects of the feelings. The client has signaled her or his readiness to talk about feelings, so the helper can help the client move into deeper exploration. I recommend using synonyms rather than repeating the exact feeling word the client has used. In this way, the client can find the best label for the feelings and also experience the different parts of the feelings.

Helpers need to remember that feelings are multifaceted and change over time. New feelings emerge as old feelings are experienced and expressed. Understanding and reflecting feelings at one point in time are just the beginning of entering into an experiential process; helpers need to constantly look for new feelings that emerge during the exploration process.

Client's Verbal Content

Another source for clues about feelings is verbal content. Although the client may not be mentioning feelings directly, it may be possible to infer the feelings from the client's words. For example, clients often respond to a major loss with feelings of sadness; people often respond to success with feelings of pleasure; clients often respond to anger directed at them with fear. Hence, helpers can make preliminary hypotheses about what clients might feel. For example, an adolescent client might mention that she received her report card and had improved her grades in almost every subject. The helper might say, "You must feel proud of yourself for raising your grades." However, helpers need to be cautious, tentative, and ready to revise their reflections on the basis of feedback from the client. Helpers cannot know everything about clients and may need to amend their reflections as they gather more information and as the feelings emerge and change in sessions.

Nonverbal Behaviors

How the client appears nonverbally is a third source of clues for feelings. For example, if the client is smiling and looks pleased, the helper might say, "I wonder if you feel happy about that." Helpers need to look at all the nonverbal behaviors for clues. As discussed in chapter 6, there is often nonverbal leakage in arm and leg movements because people do not monitor themselves as closely in these areas as in their facial expressions. For example, when a client is kicking his or her foot, a helper might wonder out loud if the client is nervous or angry. The meaning of nonverbal behaviors is not always the same (discussed in chap. 6), so helpers must use nonverbals as clues to possible feelings rather than assuming that nonverbal behaviors have fixed meanings.

Projection of Helper's Feelings

A final source for detecting client feelings is ourselves: How would I feel if I were in that situation? For example, if a client is talking about an argument with a roommate over cleaning their apartment, helpers can recall how they have felt in arguments with roommates, siblings, or friends. Helpers are not judging how the client "should" feel but are attempting to understand the client's feelings by placing themselves in a similar situation. Helpers can use these projections as long as they remember that the projections are possibilities rather than accurate representations of the client's reality. The helper's feelings might not apply to someone else. However, the helper can hypothesize about the client's feelings using her or his own projections and then search for supporting evidence in the client's verbal content and nonverbal behaviors.

ACCURACY OF REFLECTION

The feeling word provided by the helper does not have to be perfectly accurate to be helpful, although it does need to be "in the ballpark." If the feeling word is relatively close to what the client is feeling, it can enable the client to clarify the feeling. For example, if a client has been talking about feeling scared and the helper uses the word *tense*, the client can clarify and say the feeling is more like *terror*. Clarifying the feelings gives the helper a clearer understanding of the client and allows the client to clarify what he or she is experiencing internally. One could argue that reflections that are too accurate could halt client exploration because there would be no reason for the client to try to clarify or explore the feelings. On the other hand, feeling words that are "out of the ballpark" can be damaging. If a helper uses the word *happy* after the client has said *tense*, the client might feel that the helper was not listening or does not understand and might quit exploring.

Helpers are rarely accurate with every reflection. More often, helpers struggle in each reflection to understand the client more completely. Clients often appreciate the helper's struggle to understand as much as the specific reflection. Understanding another person's feelings is something helpers strive for but remain humbly aware of how difficult it is to achieve. Hence, helpers should not be as concerned with assessing the accuracy of a particular reflection as with trying to understand clients and communicating to clients that they are struggling to understand.

REFLECTION EXAMPLE

The following shows a helper using reflection of feelings (in italics) in a session:

> *Client:* I had to miss classes last week because I got a call right before class that my father had been in a serious car accident. He was on the Beltway and a truck driver fell asleep at the wheel and swerved right into him, causing a six-car pile-up. It was really awful.

Helper: *You sound very upset.*

Client: I am. All the way to the hospital, I kept worrying about whether he was okay. The worst thing is that he already had several bad things happen to him recently—his third wife left him, he lost money in the stock market, and his dog died. He just doesn't seem to have anything left.

Helper: *You're concerned because of all the bad things that have happened lately.*

Client: Yeah, he doesn't have much will to live, and I don't know what to do for him. I try to be there, but he doesn't really seem to care.

Helper: *It hurts that he doesn't notice you.*

Client: Yeah, I have always tried to please my father. I always felt like I couldn't do enough to make him happy. I think he preferred my brother. My brother was a better athlete and liked to work in the shop with him. My father just never valued what I did. I don't know if he liked me very much.

Helper: *Wow, that's really painful. I wonder if you're angry too?*

Client: Yeah, I am. What's wrong with me that my father wouldn't like me? I think I'm a pretty nice guy. (Client continues to explore the situation.)

Effects of Reflection

Helpers can determine whether their reflections are effective by attending to the client's response (see also Egan, 1994). A three-point scale can be used to assess the impact of the reflection:

1 = When a reflection is not accurate or is very unhelpful, the client might not respond at all, might reject the helper's statement (e.g., "No, I don't feel that at all"), or might say something like, "That's what I just said" and not explore further.

2 = When a reflection is at least moderately effective, the client might continue talking but not go deeper into feelings. He or she might say something like, "you're right" or "yeah" but not go on to explore.

3 = When a reflection is very helpful, the client might pause and say something like, "Wow, you're right, I never thought of it that way before, but that is what I have been feeling, and I also feel . . . " and go on to talk in greater depth about feelings. Often new feel-

ings emerge as clients immerse themselves in their immediate experiences.

Difficulties Helpers Experience in Delivering Reflection of Feelings

Beginning helpers are often nervous about dealing with clients' expressions of intense negative feelings, such as sadness or anger. They get anxious when clients cry because they feel uncomfortable with crying, uncertain about how to handle emotions, and unsure about ever really understanding another person. Feelings of guilt might also emerge when clients cry because helpers might think their interventions upset the clients or caused the pain. Furthermore, helpers might be afraid that if they encourage clients to express their feelings, the clients will get stuck in the feelings and not be able to emerge from them. In addition, helpers might have difficulty accepting intense feelings both in themselves and in their clients. It is important to stress, however, that feelings are natural and clients need to express their feelings so they can begin to accept them. When helpers accept clients' feelings, it conveys to the clients that their feelings are okay. Helpers are encouraged to learn to accept and cope with their anxieties so they can enable clients to express and accept their feelings. Many helpers find that taking a deep breath and focusing on the client and the client's feelings rather than focusing on themselves helps them allow clients to express and accept their feelings (Williams, Judge, Hill, & Hoffman, 1997).

At times, beginning helpers have difficulty capturing the most salient feeling to reflect back to the client. They might hear several feelings and be confused about which is most important to reflect first. Helpers should pay attention to the feeling that seems to elicit the most intensity or depth of feelings. They can always come back later and reflect other feelings when they become more salient. There is plenty of time in the exploration stage to cover the feelings in depth, so it is better to focus on each feeling individually and thoroughly. Practice helps tremendously. Helpers can practice by guessing the most salient emotions displayed in movies, reflecting strong feelings of friends when they are talking about problems, and role playing in practice exercises.

Some helpers also have difficulty separating their own feelings from the client's feelings. They assume clients must have the same feelings they do. Other helpers overidentify with a client and feel the client's emotion so strongly (i.e., feel sympathy or emotional contagion) that they cannot be objective and helpful. Helpers need to become aware of their own feelings so that they can differentiate what is coming from clients and what is coming from themselves. As mentioned before, personal therapy and supervision can be invaluable in this task.

Finally, helpers sometimes state the client's feelings too definitely (e.g., "You obviously feel angry") rather than tentatively (e.g., "I wonder if you feel angry"). If clients are passive and have difficulty disagreeing with their helpers, direct statements of feelings by helpers can be problematic because clients are not thinking for themselves or examining their experiences. A tentative statement about feelings can be more respectful and encourages clients to verify, dismiss, or modify the feeling words.

HELPFUL HINTS

- Listen for the basic underlying feeling. Look for what the client says with the most intensity. Further clues for feelings include listening for feeling words, hearing the verbal content, watching the nonverbal expressions, and projecting one's own feelings from similar situations. Remember, however, that these latter things provide clues and may not necessarily accurately reflect the client's feelings.

- When learning to do reflections, use the format, "You feel ___" to focus directly on the feelings ("You feel upset."), or "You feel ___ because___" to make sure you capture the feeling word and the possible reasons for the feeling (e.g., "You feel upset because your mother won't talk to you.")

- Use an empathic tone, convey concern, and show you are trying to understand. Clients can tell whether you are parroting and using a pat phrase or whether you are genuinely interested. Don't judge clients (e.g., "You feel angry about *that?*"). Speaking softly and slowly can make your voice sound warmer.

- Use a tentative tone to encourage clients to determine what feelings are going on internally rather than paying attention to feelings imposed from the outside.

- Reflect present rather than past feelings to keep clients involved in the immediate moment. Remember that clients are often upset in the present about events that occurred long ago. For example, "You sound angry right now when you describe the situation," rather than "You felt angry when he said that."

- You do not have to say the perfect feeling word. If the feeling word is close, the client can correct it and let you know more about how she or he feels. If the feeling word is too different than the client's experience, however, the client might feel misunderstood and communication might stop.

▪ Reflect what you think is the most important or intense feeling at the moment rather than trying to capture everything the client has stated. You will have more opportunities throughout the session to reflect emerging important feelings. Your goal is to enable the client to focus and experience feelings at a deep level; reflecting too many feelings at once can be distracting and diffusing.

▪ Keep the reflection short and concise.

▪ Focus on the client instead of other people, even if the client focuses on another person (e.g., "You feel angry at your mother" rather than "Your mother sounds angry").

▪ Vary the format to avoid sounding like a machine. Clients often feel irritated when helpers sound like parrots repeating the same phrases.

▪ Vary the feeling words that you use. Add words to the list in Exhibit 9.2 to make it as personalized as possible.

▪ Use feeling words the client can understand. For example, a 9-year-old might respond better to "You are mad that you were treated badly" than to "You feel aggrieved that your rights were abridged."

▪ Take a deep breath before you give your reflection to relax and give you a chance to think about what you want to say. There is no need to rush.

▪ When the client is stuck or cannot think of what to say, the helper can reflect immediate feelings (e.g., "You feel stuck right now," "You're not sure what to say next," or "You feel irritated that I didn't understand what you said").

▪ If a client responds with something like "that's it" but does not explore further, pause for a minute and give the client an opportunity to reflect on her or his experience and see if anything new emerges. After that, offer a new reflection that seems appropriate for the immediate moment (e.g., "Even though you are aware that you feel upset, you feel unsure what to do about that feeling" or "You feel stuck with where to go with your feeling"). By focusing on the immediate feelings, the client can explore more about the experience in the moment and might even give you feedback about how to be more helpful to her or him.

▪ Some students have expressed concerns about what to do if a client starts crying. If you reflect feelings and clients begin to experience their feelings, undoubtedly some of their feelings are sadness and pain. I encourage you to stay with the client and not try to "take away" their sadness, but to accept the client and the feelings. You might want to be silent for a minute, allow the client to cry, and then give a reflection in a soft tone of voice to help the client verbalize the feelings.

▪ If you make an inaccurate reflection or if a client does not respond well to your reflection, ask the client to explain more about how he or she feels and try again to understand the feelings. Try to avoid negative self-talk (e.g., "I'm a lousy helper because I didn't give a perfect reflection"). Try instead to view the "mistake" as an opportunity to learn more about how the client really feels.

PRACTICE EXERCISES

Write a reflection of feelings in response to the following client statements. Compare your responses to the possible helper responses provided at the end of the section.

Statements

1. Client: "I'm really having difficulty with my schoolwork right now. I have a hard time concentrating because there are so many other things going on. My mother is in the hospital and I wish I could be there to be with her because she may die soon. When I'm thinking about her, it's hard to get into my work. But I know that what would upset her most is if I got bad grades and didn't finish school."
   Helper response: _____

2. Client: "They're constructing a new building next to my apartment complex. The noise is really loud. I have a hard time sleeping early in the morning. I complained to the landlord, but he said there's nothing he can do. What do you think I should do? Do you think I should talk to the landlord again or move out? What would you do?"
   Helper response: _____

3. Client: "My roommate is really nice. I really like her. She is so much like the sister I wish I had when I was younger. It's really nice to have somebody to do things with. I was so lonely on campus last year, but having her as a roommate makes me feel like I belong. She's from a really poor family and she hardly has any money. Fortunately, my parents send me a lot of money, so I'm glad I can share some with her."
   Helper response: _____

4. Client: "I just got in a fight with my mother. She was saying awful things to me, like I would never succeed in school because I'm lazy. I got so angry at her, I was shaking. I just don't know what to say to her when she does that. Why can't she be supportive like my friends' mothers? The worst thing is that I still have to live at home because I don't have enough money to move out."
   Helper response: _____

Possible Helper Responses

1. "So you're feeling torn between your schoolwork and worrying about your mother" (intent: to identify and intensify feelings, to encourage catharsis).

   "You're so worried about your mother that you can't concentrate on anything else."

   "You feel trusted because your mom counts on you to do well in school."

2. "You're unsure about how you should handle the noise situation at your apartment."

   "I hear you saying that you feel upset about not being able to sleep."

   "You feel exhausted."

   "It sounds like you feel irritated because your landlord was so unresponsive."

3. "I hear you saying that you feel very close to your roommate."

   "You're really pleased that you can help your roommate financially."

   "You feel relieved that you finally feel like you belong."

4. "You are full of rage at your mother."

   "I can see how mad you are at your mother."

   "You feel trapped because you have to live at home."

   "You feel hurt that your mother doesn't believe in you."

WHAT DO YOU THINK?

▪ How does your culture influence how you feel about experiencing and expressing your feelings and talking about other people's feelings?

▪ How do you choose which feeling to reflect if a client has a lot of different feelings?

▪ How can you tell if clients agree with your reflections because they are accurate, because you are in the "power position," or because they want to please you?

▪ How much should you mirror feelings that the client is aware of versus encourage clients to experience feelings of which they might not be aware?

▪ Compare and contrast restatements, reflections of feelings, and open questions in terms of their ability to facilitate exploration.

LAB 7

Reflection of Feelings

Goal: For helpers to learn to reflect feelings. The focus is on paraphrasing the person's feelings, although content can be added to indicate why the client has the feelings.

Exercise 1

1. In a large group, each student says three feeling words that reflect how she or he is currently feeling. Students should practice using feeling words that they would not typically use so they can broaden their feeling word vocabulary. See Exhibit 9.2 for ideas but remember to add words to personalize the list.
2. In a large group, the leader role plays a brief emotionally laden example of a client problem. Each student writes down a reflection of feeling. The leader asks the group members to take turns delivering their reflections. The leader continues with examples until students grasp the concept of reflections.

Exercise 2

Students should be arranged in groups of four, with students taking turns being the client. One person will be the client while the other three are helpers. Note that focusing on feelings can be threatening for some people and lead to issues that students may not want to reveal (especially in class), so students in the role of client should stop any time they feel uncomfortable. Also remember that the focus in these exercises is on the helper learning the skills rather than the helper trying to fix the client.

Helper's and Client's Tasks During the Helping Interchange

1. The client talks for a few sentences on a topic about which he or she has strong feelings (e.g., an instance in which the client felt put down or angry or a time when the client felt particularly proud).
2. Helpers listen without trying to think of what to say. After the client finishes talking, helpers should pause for a moment and think of reflections of feelings. Helpers take turns giving a reflection using the format, "You feel __" or "You feel __ because __." For purposes of this exercise, helpers should give only reflections of feelings, even if other skills seem more appropriate.
3. Clients respond briefly to each reflection so helpers see the effects of their reflections.
4. After all helpers have delivered reflections, clients discuss which reflections were most helpful and why.
5. Helpers who were the most helpful describe how they came up with their reflections.

Exercise 3

Divide into groups of three students. Everyone takes turns with each role (helper, client, and observer).

continues

Reflection of Feelings

Helper's and Client's Tasks During the Helping Interchange

1. The helper introduces herself or himself.
2. The client talks briefly about a topic for which he or she has strong feelings.
3. After the client finishes speaking, the helper gives a reflection of feelings, using the format, "You feel __" or "You feel __ because __." For purposes of this exercise, the helper should do only a reflection and not other interventions. Helpers should take their time, pause, and then consider how the client is feeling, what nonverbal behaviors reveal about feelings, and how they would feel if they were the client. Keep the reflection short and simple and vary the feeling words used.
4. Continue for five to ten turns.

Observer's Task During the Helping Interchange

Take notes about the helper's reflections and attending behaviors, writing down the exact feeling words used to have a record for later discussion. Note the accuracy of the feeling words and the manner of delivery (e.g., were a variety of feeling words used; were the reflections short and concise?). Also note the client's reactions to the reflections (e.g., did the reflections facilitate or hinder exploration of feelings?).

After the Helping Interchange

1. The helper should talk about how it felt to give reflections.
2. The client should talk about how it felt to be the recipient of the reflections. Discuss specific reflections that were more and less helpful.
3. The observer should give positive and negative feedback to the helper about her or his reflection skills and attending behaviors.

SWITCH ROLES

Personal Reflections

- What did you learn about yourself when delivering reflections?
- What would you do if a client started to cry?
- In the past, some students have had a hard time selecting the most important feeling; some have become overwhelmed by lengthy client descriptions and could not differentiate the forest (the feelings) from the trees (all the words); some were worried about hurting the client if they gave a "bad" reflection; some had difficulty figuring out the feelings if the client did not explicitly state feelings; and some had trouble when clients were very articulate about their feelings because they did not want to repeat the client's feeling words. What was your experience?

- Are there particular feelings (e.g., anger, guilt) that you have difficulty using with clients because of your own discomfort or problems?
- In the past, many students have reported that their confidence dropped dramatically after beginning to learn helping skills but then increased with practice. What pattern do you see emerging with regard to your confidence as a helper?

Additional Skills for the Exploration Stage

10

To truly hear, you must quiet the mind

—Anonymous

arina was a Ukrainian woman who traveled to the United States to obtain her PhD. She sought help because she was unable to complete her dissertation even though she soon had to go back to her country. She was not sure what the helper expected from her, and she knew very little about helping. The helper explained the process of helping to Karina and reassured her that he would help her identify and express her feelings. He also let her know that he thought she was very courageous to come to another country to gain an education and to pursue counseling so she could resolve her anguish and achieve her goals. He revealed that he had experienced difficulty in finishing his dissertation. The helper asked Karina a few closed questions to identify exactly what her problems were in completing the dissertation and then asked her to explore her feelings about finishing her degree and returning to her country. Finally, he was silent for a moment while Karina gathered her thoughts about her feelings.

Although open question, restatement, and reflection of feelings can be used in most situations to help clients explore, there are some situations in which other skills are more likely to facilitate exploration:

- when clients need specific information about what to expect in helping
- when clients want to know about the helper's credentials
- when clients need reassurance, support, or reinforcement

Web Forms referred to in text can be found on the book's companion online guide described in the Preface.

- when helpers need specific information about the client to make treatment decisions
- when clients need help recognizing or expressing their feelings
- when helpers want to allow clients time to think or get into their feelings
- when helpers want to encourage clients to take the lead

In this chapter, I present several skills (information about the process of helping, approval and reassurance, closed questions, self-disclosures for exploration, and silence) that helpers can use in the exploration stage to intervene in situations such as these. These skills can be useful additions to a helper's repertoire; however, each has significant drawbacks so helpers should use them appropriately and with caution.

Information About the Helping Process

Providing information about the process of helping can educate clients about what to expect (see Exhibit 10.1). Clients need to know about the helping process and the expected appropriate behavior so they can determine whether they want to participate in the process and how to do so. They need to know the length of sessions, fees associated with sessions, rules of conduct in sessions, limits of confidentiality in helping, and whether it is appropriate to contact the helper outside of sessions. Helpers often tell clients their rules at the beginning of the initial session. They inform clients about other rules as the need arises (e.g., when clients ask for information that is too personal, the helper might explain why he or she chooses not to divulge such information; when a client repeatedly asks for hugs, the helper might explain why that is not a good idea). Helpers might also deliver information about helping throughout the process to let clients know what they might encounter. For example, helpers might inform clients about what to expect as they move into the action stage. By informing clients about what to expect, helpers hope clients will become more involved and collaborative in the helping process. Additional uses of information for the action stage are discussed in chapter 19.

Although it is crucial to provide relevant information to clients, some helpers give too much detail. They might feel a need to explain limits of confidentiality or their theoretical orientation, for example, in great depth. For the most part, clients do not need great detail about the process because they are more interested in talking about what brought them to helping. Hence, helpers must find a way to provide relevant information

---

EXHIBIT 10.1

Overview of Information About the Helping Process

Definition	*Information about the helping process* educates clients about what to expect during helping
Examples	"Our first task today is to complete some measures about how you are feeling." "We will be using a three-stage model of helping where you first explore, then try to come to some insight and figure out what you want to do differently in your life."
Typical intentions	To give information, to set limits (see Web Form D)
Possible client reactions	Educated, hopeful, no reaction (see Web Form G)
Desired client behavior	Agreement (see Web Form H)
Potential difficulties	Becoming too didactic Wanting to be the expert Having the focus shift to the helper

---

to clients in such a way that clients do not get bored, become passive, or tune out. Once again, helpers need to gauge client reactions and be responsive to client needs.

EXAMPLE OF USING INFORMATION ABOUT THE HELPING PROCESS

> *Helper:* *I wanted to let you know a few things first about the way we operate here. This is a training clinic, and I'm a beginning helper learning the skills. I have a supervisor who will be watching us through a one-way mirror, and as you know, I'm taping the session so I can listen to the tape and improve my skills. I also want to tell you that everything we talk about is confidential except if you talk about an intent to harm yourself or someone else or childhood sexual abuse.* Do you have any questions?
>
> *Client:* Yes. Why is the supervisor there?
>
> *Helper:* *The supervisor is there to observe me and give me feedback about my skills.*
>
> *Client:* What kind of program are you in?
>
> *Helper:* *I'm taking a class on helping skills.* What would you like to talk about today?

Note that the helper provides a brief introduction and answers questions briefly but turns the focus back to the client so she can explore her concerns.

Approval–Reassurance

Approval–reassurance is a helpful skill that can be used occasionally to provide emotional support and reassurance, indicate helpers empathize with or understand clients, or suggest that clients' feelings are normal and to be expected (see Exhibit 10.2). The key is to use approval–reassurance to foster exploration and to make clients feel safe enough to keep talking at a deep level about their concerns. For many clients, approval–reassurance that their problems are normal and that they are not alone in their feelings can be empowering and help clients go further in exploring their concerns. Examples of approval–reassurance include

- "That's really hard to handle."
- "That's a devastating situation."
- "How awful!"
- "Wow! That's an awesome opportunity!"

Approval–reassurance can also be used to provide reinforcement, indicating that the helper values something the client has said or done and wants to encourage the client to continue the effort to change. Some clients need support or acknowledgment that they have done something well. In addition, approval, reassurance, and reinforcement can help some clients persist in exploring because they know someone is listening and sympathetic; this is especially important if clients are exploring difficult or painful topics. Examples of support and acknowledgment include

- "Good try!"
- "It was really terrific that you were able to express your feelings to him!"

Although helpful in some situations, approval–reassurance can sound false if done excessively, prematurely, or insincerely. If such interventions are used to promote helper biases (e.g., "I think you're right to feel guilty about getting an abortion"), they can be problematic because they stop client exploration or make clients feel compelled to agree or comply with helpers.

In addition, approval–reassurance is inappropriate if used to alleviate anxiety or distress, to minimize feelings, or to deny feelings (e.g., "Don't worry about it," "Everyone feels that way"). When used in this manner, approval–reassurance is typically counterproductive to our work as helpers because it stops rather than facilitates clients' exploring and accepting feelings. Such statements can make clients feel they have no right to their feelings. Helpers sometimes use these interventions as misguided attempts to reassure others that everything is okay. Unfortunately, problems typically do not go away because they are minimized or denied. Most of us

EXHIBIT 10.2

Overview of Approval and Reassurance

Definition	Approval and reassurance provides emotional support, reassurance, encouragement, and reinforcement
Examples	"It's very hard to have a parent who is dying." "It's so good that you were able to get your homework done."
Typical intentions	To support, to instill hope, to encourage catharsis, to reinforce change, to relieve helper's needs (see Web Form D)
Possible client reactions	Supported, hopeful, relieved (see Web Form G)
Desired client behavior	Recounting, cognitive–behavioral exploration, affective exploration (see Web Form H)
Potential difficulties	Being too giving Being too sympathetic and not being able to separate from client Minimizing or denying client feelings, especially negative feelings

have heard the old sayings, "Give it time" or "Time cures all." It is not "time" that makes feelings go away; in fact, feelings often fester when they are bottled up or denied. Rather, it is awareness, acceptance, and expression of feelings that aid in resolution of painful affect. To reiterate, our goal is to help clients identify, intensify, and express feelings rather than minimize or deny them.

In general, then, approval–reassurance needs to be used judiciously and sparingly to encourage clients and facilitate exploration of thoughts, feelings, and experiences. Approval–reassurance should not be used to diminish feelings, deny experiences, stop exploration, or provide a moral judgment. When helpers find themselves using approval–reassurance in a counterproductive way, they might want to think about what is going on in their own lives.

EXAMPLE OF POSITIVE USE OF APPROVAL REASSURANCE

Client: I just learned that my sister needs to have a kidney transplant. She's been sick a lot lately and hasn't been getting better.

Helper: *That's too bad.*

Client: Yeah, I feel terrible for her. She's only 21 and has always been active, so this is a real shock for her. I feel guilty that she got this horrible disease while I'm healthy and able to function.

> *Helper:*   *It's pretty natural to feel some guilt.*
> *Client:*   Really? I'm glad to hear that. I have been trying to do more for her. I'm thinking of organizing a campaign to find a donor and raise money for her treatment. Because she has an unusual blood type, it will be difficult to find the right person, and it's going to cost a lot of money.
> *Helper:*   *That's terrific that you would do that for her.*
> *Client:*   I feel like it's the least I can do. It does interestingly bring up a lot of issues for me about obligation versus doing things because I want to. (Client continues exploring her thoughts.)

Closed Questions

Closed questions request a one- or two-word answer ("yes," "no," or a confirmation) and are used to gather information or data (see Exhibit 10.3). Closed questions can ask for specific information:

- "What was your test grade?"
- "How old were you when your parents were divorced?"
- "Did you call the counseling center?"

Helpers sometimes ask closed questions because they did not hear what the client said or because they want to determine if clients understood or agreed with what they said.

- "What did you say?"
- "Am I right?"
- "Is that what happened?"
- "Does that sound right to you?"
- "Did I understand you correctly?"

Closed questions have a limited but important role in the helping process. The primary reason for using closed questions is to obtain specific information from clients, perhaps because the client has been vague and the helper needs more information to understand the situation. The most direct way to get this specific information is through closed questions. For example, when a client is vague about his or her family situation and the helper is struggling to understand the family dynamics, the helper might ask, "Are you the oldest child?" or "Where are you in the birth order?" In such situations, asking for needed information is better than making assumptions or being confused. The key is that the information is important for the therapeutic process.

EXHIBIT 10.3

Overview of Closed Questions

Definition	*Closed questions* request a one- or two-word answer (a "yes," "no," or a confirmation) and is used to gather information
Examples	"How old are you?" "What is your major?"
Typical intentions	To get information (see Web Form D)
Possible client reactions	No reaction (see Web Form G)
Desired client behavior	Recounting (see Web Form H)
Potential difficulties	Not listening enough to the client The focus might turn onto the helper Getting into an interrogator mode with the client becoming passive and dependent on getting more closed questions Being viewed as the expert who will then provide a diagnosis or solution to a problem

When helpers use closed questions, they follow the same guidelines for implementation as were proposed for open questions. In other words, helpers should use an empathic and inviting manner to encourage the client to explore rather than just answer the simple question. Furthermore, helpers should refrain from asking using multiple closed questions. As with too many open questions asked at once, clients can feel bombarded and have a hard time knowing which questions to answer first. More important, helpers need to notice what happens when they use closed questions. Helpers should determine for themselves whether control of the interaction shifts back to them when they use too many closed questions. Do closed questions make you feel like a grand inquisitor? Helpers can also ask clients for their reactions to closed questions to determine the effects of these interventions.

One situation in which closed questions are important is during a crisis situation. If there is a crisis (e.g., the potential for suicide, homicide, violence, or abuse of any kind or decompensation into serious mental illness), the process changes from helping to crisis management. In these situations, helpers need to ask directly about what is happening so they can make appropriate referrals. If such a situation occurs while you are in training, immediately seek out supervisors who can help you figure out how to handle the situation.

EXAMPLE OF APPROPRIATE USE OF CLOSED QUESTIONS

The following is an example of the appropriate use of closed questions (in italics) to assess suicide risk (see also the section in chap. 22 about suicide):

> *Client:* I get so depressed, I just feel like life isn't worth living sometimes. I want to crawl into my bed and sleep all the time. I just don't want to face anyone.
>
> *Helper:* *Have you had thoughts of killing yourself?*
>
> *Client:* Yes, quite often I wish I were dead. I would be better off.
>
> *Helper:* Sounds like you're pretty depressed. *Do you have a plan for how you would kill yourself?*
>
> *Client:* I am not sure I would actually do it. I more fantasize that I would like to do it.
>
> *Helper:* *Do you have any way to do it?*
>
> *Client:* No, I hate guns, I don't have any pills, I wouldn't like jumping. I think it's more of a fantasy of doing it and imagining how people would respond.

After assessing for suicidal risk, the helper would move on to other skills to help the client explore thoughts and feelings and underlying issues that make him feel helpless and hopeless.

Closed questions are also appropriate for certain types of interview situations, such as a medical doctor gathering information to make a diagnosis, interrogations by lawyers during courtroom trials, or job interviews. In these situations, the roles between the interviewer and interviewee are often distinct. The interviewer asks the question to get the desired information; the respondent answers the questions. The control of the interview usually stays with the interviewer, who directs the interaction by asking questions.

An example of another situation in which closed questions are useful is in academic advising. When a student comes to me in my role as an academic advisor asking about her or his chances of being accepted into graduate school, my goal is to gather enough information about the student's credentials (e.g., grade point average, Graduate Records Exam (GRE) scores, research and clinical experience, and career goals) to make an assessment. The best and most efficient way of gathering such information quickly is typically through closed questions (e.g., "What are your grade point average and GRE score?" "What research experiences have you had?" "Where do you hope to be employed after graduate school?"). I try to ask the closed questions in a supportive, empathic, nonjudgmental fashion, without attempting to determine what students should do with their lives or pass judgment on their effectiveness as human beings. Once I have the information, I can assess how likely it is that the student will be admitted to graduate school. If I think the student needs help in exploring values, feelings, options, and talents, I typically refer the student to the campus counseling center because these tasks are not part of my role as an academic adviser.

Although closed questions can be helpful in interview situations, they have limited applicability in helping settings because they typically do not help clients explore. Helpers slip into an interviewer role and become responsible for directing the interaction. They become interviewers rather than helpers. Once trapped in the interviewer role and having to think about the next question, helpers may have difficulty changing the course of the session and focusing on clients. In these situations, clients can become dependent on helpers for the next question. Rather than exploring problems deeply, clients respond passively to questions.

Helpers are trying to facilitate clients in their self-healing efforts, not acting as experts who diagnose and "treat" clients, so they do not typically need much specific information. Specific information does not help facilitate exploration of values, feelings, options, and talents. Before asking questions, helpers should think about what they are going to do with the information once it is provided. Helpers can ask themselves, "Whose need am I fulfilling with the information I gain from closed questions?" If the information will be used to facilitate the process of exploring for the client, helpers should ask the question. If the information is desired for voyeurism, curiosity, to fill the silence, or to make a diagnosis and fix the problem, helpers should not ask the closed question.

Most beginners use too many closed questions because this skill is a familiar way of interacting outside of the helping situation. In social interactions, people often ask a lot of closed questions to get the details of exactly what happened. The goal in these social interactions is to get the facts of the story rather than to help another person express or explore feelings, as it is in helping.

I do not suggest that helpers never use closed questions, as they can occasionally be helpful; I do, however, encourage helpers to reduce the number of closed questions they use and instead use more open questions, restatements, and reflections of feelings. When helpers do use closed questions because specific information is needed, they can follow up with the other exploration skills to help clients get back to exploration.

Self-Disclosures for Exploration

There are three types of self-disclosures that are appropriate for the exploration stage: disclosures of similarity, disclosures of information, and disclosures of feelings (see Exhibit 10.4). Disclosures of insight and strategies will be covered in the insight and actions stages, respectively.

SELF-DISCLOSURE OF SIMILARITIES

Disclosing similarities allows helpers to communicate approval and reassurance. Basically, the helper is saying, "I understand because I went

EXHIBIT 10.4

Overview of Self-Disclosures for Exploration

Definition	*Self-disclosures for exploration* reveal personal, nonimmediate information about the helper.
Types and examples	*Self-disclosure of similarities*: "I have a hard time working out my relationship with my roommate too." *Self-disclosure of history–credentials*: "I am working on my PhD in psychology." *Self-disclosure of feelings*: "I felt sad when my father died."
Typical intentions	To support, to instill hope, to encourage catharsis, to identify and intensify feelings, to encourage self-control, to relieve helper's needs (see Web Form D)
Possible client reactions	Supported, hopeful, relief, feelings, clear, responsibility, unstuck, negative thoughts–feelings, scared, worse, misunderstood (see Web Form G)
Desired client behavior	Cognitive–behavioral exploration, affective exploration (see Web Form H)
Potential difficulties	Difficulty dealing with intense feelings, such as anger and sadness Being too sympathetic and not being able to separate from client Projecting own feelings onto client Turning focus from client to helper

through something similar." Hearing that someone else had a similar experience can help the client feel that her or his experience is normal and that she or he is not alone. Many people feel isolated, so it is often reassuring to hear that others have had similar experiences. For example, Suzanne felt mortified that she had gotten a C on a math test because she thought it ruined her chance to go to graduate school. Her counselor, a graduate student, revealed that she had not done well in math as an undergraduate. This disclosure initially surprised Suzanne, but then she felt relieved and more hopeful that she too could make it to graduate school. The helper then led Suzanne in exploring her overly harsh demands on herself and her belief that she had to succeed in order for her parents to love her.

Helpers, of course, must be cautious not to minimize clients' feelings or cut short exploration. Helpers must also be careful not to disclose similarities because of their own needs. Sometimes clients' problems are so similar to helpers' that they feel a need to spill out their problems, but the focus then shifts from the clients to the helpers. Helpers must ask themselves whether disclosure would facilitate client exploration. If not, they should use other skills to help the client (and seek help for their own unresolved issues).

SELF-DISCLOSURE OF INFORMATION

Disclosing personal facts is sometimes appropriate to inform clients briefly about the helper and his or her professional background and training. Many helpers believe it is beneficial to share information about their professional training or background:

- ▮ "I am a beginning helper just learning helping skills."
- ▮ "I am a counseling psychologist with a PhD and have been practicing for 20 years."

Clients from oppressed groups often want to know about the helper's beliefs and values to determine whether it is safe, or whether they will feel comfortable, working with the helper. For example, a religious client might want to know if the helper is religious or tolerant of other religions. A gay client may need reassurance that the helper is not homophobic and will not try to alter his sexual orientation. A stay-at-home mother might be concerned about the helper's feelings about her lifestyle. A recovering alcoholic may want to know whether the helper is a recovering alcoholic. An African American man might be interested in learning whether the helper has any experience working with African Americans.

Helpers' self-disclosure can be particularly appropriate with clients from other cultures, who often approach helping situations with considerable distrust (Ivey, 1994; Sue & Sue, 1999). Some clients doubt that helpers from other cultures can understand or help them and fear the information they disclose might be used against them. Helpers might start an initial session by asking, "Do you have any questions you'd like to ask me?" and then honestly answer questions so clients get to know them. Self-disclosure can be particularly important with people who have difficulty talking about problems because of cultural prohibitions against revealing personal and family matters to outsiders. By disclosing, helpers model that disclosure is acceptable and expected. Too much helper self-disclosure, however, can be problematic because it can be considered unprofessional.

An interesting dilemma arises when clients ask helpers for personal information. Although it is sometimes appropriate for clients to ask questions and for helpers to respond authentically with disclosures of facts, helpers might sometimes want to ask clients what is motivating their questions (especially if the questions are excessive or personally intrusive). They might also want to ask how clients feel about the disclosures that are given. Holding a dialogue about the issues behind the questions is crucial for establishing a therapeutic relationship and for understanding salient client issues. I suggest that helpers not reveal much personal information unless it is for an identifiable therapeutic reason.

SELF-DISCLOSURE OF FEELINGS

Disclosure of feelings can be used to model for clients what they might be feeling (e.g., "When I was applying for my first job, I felt terrified about what I would say in the interview"). Helpers can say how they would feel if they were the client (e.g., "If I were you, I would feel mad at your father"), or they might state how they feel hearing the client talk ("I feel angry at your father"). After hearing a disclosure of feelings, clients might recognize that they had similar (or very different) feelings. In other words, disclosures of feelings can stimulate clients to recognize and express their feelings. In effect, the disclosure of feelings is similar in intention and consequences to reflection of feelings. Disclosure of feelings can be helpful for clients who are afraid to experience their feelings, especially feelings of shame and embarrassment.

An additional goal of disclosure of feelings is to help clients feel more normal because they learn other people have similar feelings. Many of us think we are the only ones who ever feel lousy, inadequate, phony, or depressed. Hearing that others have felt the same way can be tremendously relieving. In fact, Yalom (1995) posited that universality (i.e., a sense that others feel the same way) is a curative agent in therapy.

Disclosures of feelings can be a good way for helpers not to impose feelings on clients. Rather than saying, "You feel ____," the helper says, "I felt ____ in the past, and I wonder if you might feel that way?" Helpers are being respectful by owning that they are the ones who have the feelings. They acknowledge their projections and then ask how clients feel.

As indicated before, it is important that beginners not use self-disclosures for their own needs. Beginning helpers often want to disclose feelings because they want to shift attention to their own problems or show clients how knowledgeable they are about certain issues. Helpers have to be thoughtful about their intentions for disclosing feelings and must be careful to turn the focus back on the client after disclosing feelings.

In summary, disclosures can sometimes be helpful to inform clients and help them recognize their feelings, but helpers need to be careful that the attention does not shift from the client to them.

EXAMPLE OF SELF-DISCLOSURE

> *Client:* How did you learn to be a therapist?
> *Helper:* *I am just in the process of learning to be a helper. It will be many years and lots of training before I am qualified to consider myself a therapist.* Perhaps you're curious about my credentials?

Client: I just wonder if you're going to be able to help me.

Helper: I can understand that fear. *I was very nervous about going to see a therapist the first time too.*

Client: I am a bit nervous. This is the first time I've talked to anyone about my problems. I feel like I'm weak if I talk to anyone. My father always used to say that only crazy people go to therapists.

Helper: *My father was pretty negative about therapy too, but I found it useful.*

Client: I can see that it could be helpful. I really want to have an opportunity to talk more about my feelings about my family—they are pretty messed up, and I guess I am too.

The helper would probably shift at this point to using other helping skills (e.g., reflections and restatements) to help the client explore more about her feelings about her family.

Silence

A silence is a pause during which neither helper nor client is speaking (see Exhibit 10.5). The silence can occur after a client's statement, within a client's statement, or after a simple acceptance of the helper's statement. For example, after the client says something like, "I just feel so confused and angry and don't know what to say," the helper might pause to allow the client time to reflect on the feelings. If the client pauses in the middle of saying something and is obviously still processing the feelings, the helper might be silent to let the client think without interruption. If the client responds minimally to something the helper said, the helper might be silent to see if the client can think of something to say. It is important to note that to say nothing is not necessarily to do nothing. Helpers can be attentive and supportive, and they can listen without saying anything. In fact, sometimes the most useful thing a helper can do is to say nothing.

Silence can be used to convey empathy, warmth, and respect and to give clients time and space to talk (Hill, Thompson, & Ladany, 2003). Silence can allow clients time to reflect or think through what they want to say without interruption. Some clients pause for a long time because they process things slowly and thoroughly or because they are in the middle of thinking through something and need time to get in touch with their thoughts and feelings. At such times, silence is respectful because it provides space for clients to think without feeling pressured to say anything. Warm, empathic silences give clients time to express their feelings. By

---

E X H I B I T   1 0 . 5

Overview of Silence

Definition	*Silence* is a pause during which neither helper nor client is speaking.
Examples	A pause after something the client says; a pause between two things the client says; a pause after a simple acceptance of a helper's statement.
Typical intentions	To support, to focus, to encourage catharsis, to encourage self-control (see Web Form D)
Possible client reactions	Supported, feelings, responsibility, scared, worse, stuck, lacking direction (see Web Form G)
Desired client behavior	Cognitive–behavioral exploration, affective exploration (see Web Form H)
Potential difficulties	Anxiety Desire to fill the void and take care of client

---

allowing clients the space, helpers can encourage clients to express feelings from which they might otherwise run away. Silence can indicate to clients that helpers are patient and unrushed and have plenty of time to listen to whatever comes out. During these empathic silences, helpers can sit attentively focused on being with the client while the client is deeply immersed in thoughts and feelings. Hence, I suggest that helpers avoid interruptions and give clients several seconds after speaking to see whether they have anything else to say (see also Matarazzo et al., 1965, who found that when therapists were able to delay speaking, clients talked more).

In contrast to the use of silence to provide empathy and warmth, silence can also be used to challenge (Hill, Thompson, & Mahalik, 2003). In this use of silence, helpers challenge clients to take responsibility for what they want to say. Rather than rushing in and taking care of the client, helpers wait and try to force the client to say something. Silence is used by psychoanalytic therapists during long-term therapy to encourage free association (i.e., saying whatever comes to mind; see Basch, 1980). During free association, silence can be used to raise the client's anxiety because the client does not receive feedback about what the helper wants or feels. Like a stimulus deprivation experiment, silence sometimes increases discomfort and forces clients to rely on their inner resources and to examine their thoughts, or as one therapist said, "to let clients stew in their juices." Although challenging silences might be helpful in long-term therapy when there is a good working alliance, it can be potentially damaging to use silence for these reasons if the client does not trust the helper or understand the purpose of the silence. Silence can be frightening for clients who feel isolated and out of touch with the helper or who do not know how to express themselves. Helpers have to assess what is going on for clients during the silence and determine whether it is better to continue the silence or break it.

Silence also can be used for negative or inappropriate reasons (Hill, Thompson, & Mahalik, 2003). Some helpers are silent because they do not know what to say, are anxious, angry, bored, or distracted. Many beginning helpers are uncomfortable with silence. They do not know what to do and are often concerned about how clients might perceive them. I suggest that helpers breathe deeply, relax, and think about the client and what might be going on inside the client. In other words, helpers should try to establish an empathic connection with clients during silence rather than focusing on themselves. If silences go on for a long time (i.e., more than a minute) or a client is obviously uncomfortable, helpers should break the silence and ask the client how she or he is feeling.

As with other skills, the acceptability of silence varies by culture. Sue and Sue (1999) have noted that in Japanese and Chinese cultures, silence can indicate a desire by the person to continue talking after making a point. In contrast, European Americans are less comfortable with silence and often rush to fill the space.

EXAMPLE OF THE THERAPEUTIC USE OF SILENCE

Client: My dog "Sam" just died. I'm really upset because I've had that dog since I was very little. I grew up with the dog.

Helper: *(Silence of about one minute.)* How are you feeling?

Client: I was just thinking about how I got the dog. I begged my parents forever to get me a dog. I said I would take care of it. Of course I didn't much at first, but I did later. Sam was kind of like Red Rover in the comics— he waited for me at the bus stop, and we had great adventures together. I could tell Sam everything.

Helper: *(Silence of 30 seconds.)*

Client: Sam helped me get through my parents' divorce. I felt like I could rely on him then like no one else. It's like losing my best friend—we went through so much stuff together. I felt so terrible when I left for college and couldn't take him with me. He looked so sad. And I didn't even get to say goodbye to him.

Concluding Comments

The helping skills described in this chapter can be useful at specific points in sessions but typically will not be used as extensively as other exploration skills. For example, sometimes clients need explicit reassurance to let them know that they are okay. Other times, helpers need to gather or to provide specific information to be able to help clients. Furthermore, by hearing helpers self-disclose, clients can sometimes acknowledge having similar thoughts and emotions and feel less judged. Finally, silence can sometimes be helpful for allowing clients time to think or for encouraging clients to take responsibility. With all these skills, however, helpers need to be particularly attuned to clients' reactions because of the potential negative consequences. Helpers should observe clients' reactions and consider shifting to other skills if clients respond negatively.

Integrating the Skills of the Exploration Stage | 11

It is a luxury to be understood.

—*Ralph Waldo Emerson*

D mitry, a new helper, was in his first session with a client. He asked several closed questions, which the client answered briefly and then sat waiting for more questions. Dmitry panicked because he did not know what to do next. He felt himself sweating and wanted to run out of the room. Instead, he paused, took a deep breath, and thought about what he had learned about helping. His teacher's words echoed in his head, "Try reflections of feelings, restatements, and open questions." So he asked, "How do you feel about school?" and was amazed when the client started talking about feeling scared and depressed because he was doing poorly in his courses. He then reflected the client's feelings, and the client talked about feeling angry and shamed because of his poor performance. Dmitry learned firsthand how to help clients explore.

Now that helpers are able to identify (discriminate) and use (communicate) each of the individual exploration skills, they need to learn to integrate them. Helpers need to determine which skills to use at different times to facilitate exploration. They need to pay attention to client reactions and use different skills when indicated.

Before talking about when to use the different skills, it is important to remind helpers that the goals of the exploration stage are to establish rapport and help clients explore. It is important foremost to be empathic and to accept clients unconditionally so they can begin to accept them-

---

Web Forms referred to in text can be found on the book's companion online guide described in the Preface.

selves. Rather than make assumptions, helpers must learn about clients from the clients themselves. In the process of productive exploration, clients might not even notice what helpers are doing because helpers are facilitating clients in the exploration process rather than coming up with new insights or suggesting actions. Jung (1984) phrased this well in talking about dream interpretation: "The greatest wisdom [a dream analyst] can have is to disappear and let the dreamer think he [the dream analyst] is doing nothing" (p. 458). Our job as helpers is to have clients so immersed in exploration that they do not notice our skills—the interventions should facilitate, rather than intrude on, the process. In addition, helpers are laying the foundation during the exploration stage to move to insight and action. By keeping an awareness of the goals in this stage, helpers can be more grounded in trying to facilitate the process. Otherwise, it is easy to get lost and let clients talk aimlessly or in circles.

In this chapter, I first discuss how to integrate skills to manage the flow of the exploration stage. I then talk about the need for helpers to develop self-awareness and begin to make hypotheses about clients. Finally, I cover difficulties helpers have in this stage and strategies they can use for coping with the difficulties. Reading through this material, helpers can imagine themselves conducting a brief session focused only on exploration, as recommended in the lab at the end of this chapter.

Integrating the Exploration Skills

Exhibit 11.1 presents ideas about which skills to use at different points in helping sessions. These suggestions are based on clinical experiences rather than empirical data because, unfortunately, minimal empirical data regarding the timing of interventions are available.

START THE SESSION

Helpers begin the session by providing information about the helping process. First, the helper explains the structure of the process and talks about expectations for what should happen (e.g., "We are going to be spending 30 minutes together, and our goal is to help you explore whatever topic you would like to address"). Helpers can also briefly self-disclose about facts or credentials to educate clients about their background as helpers (e.g., "I am a beginning helper"), especially if clients ask for such information. Second, helpers need to clarify issues of confidentiality (e.g., "Everything you say will be kept in strict confidence, with a couple of excep-

E X H I B I T   1 1 . 1

A Guide for When to Use Each Exploration Skill During the Exploration Stage

Marker in session	When helper intends to	Helper might try
At all points	Support	Appropriate attending behaviors Listening attentively Approval and reassurance
When helper wants client to know what to expect in helping	Give information	Information about the helping process
To get the dialogue started	Get information Focus	Open question Restatement Reflection of feelings
When client is exploring thoughts and feelings productively	Promote catharsis Identify maladaptive cognitions–behaviors	Silence Refrain from interrupting Restatement Reflection of feelings
When helper wants to elicit thoughts or explanation	Identify maladaptive cognitions–behaviors	Restatement Open question
When client has a lot of feelings; when helper wants to elicit client feelings, demonstrate understanding, or model expression of feelings	Identify and intensify feelings	Reflection of feelings Disclosure of feelings Open question about feelings
When client is rambling, confused, or stuck	Focus Clarify	Open question Restatement Reflection of feelings
After client response to helper question	Clarify Identify maladaptive cognition–behavior–feeling	Restatement Reflection of feelings
When helper has not heard, needs information, or wants to know if client has heard or understood or agrees	Get information	Closed question
When client is talking about someone else rather than about self	Focus	Switch focus to client using open question or reflection of feelings

tions. If you reveal anything about abuse or intent to harm yourself or others, I will need to report that to the authorities"). Third, helpers should inform clients at the beginning of the session if they will be recorded, observed live, or supervised (e.g., "I will be recording this session, and my supervisor is watching through that one-way mirror"). Helpers then ask clients if they have any questions about what to expect from the process (e.g., "Is there anything you want to know about me or about the process?"). Rather than talking more, helpers then turn the focus onto clients by asking an open question, such as "What would you like to talk about?" or "What's on your mind?" to encourage clients to share their concerns.

If clients do not respond right away or respond to the opening comments by saying "I don't have anything to talk about," helpers might pause to give clients a chance to think and talk. It is important not to rush clients, but to give them the message that it is their turn to talk. If the client still does not talk, the helper might reflect possible feelings (e.g., discomfort, uncertainty) to allow clients to focus on and accept their feelings. When helpers listen patiently and empathically, clients often begin talking within a few minutes. Some clients are anxious about whether what they have to say is important enough to be discussed in helping and need reassurance that the helper is listening and thinks what they are talking about is important. The most important thing helpers do at this point in the session is to listen empathically to encourage the client to begin talking and exploring.

ATTEND AND LISTEN

Throughout the session, helpers should use appropriate attending behaviors. Using the acronym ENCOURAGES as a guide, helpers should maintain moderate levels of *eye* contact (avoid looking away frequently or staring); use moderate amounts of head *nods*; maintain a respect and awareness of *cultural* differences in attending; maintain an *open* stance toward clients (i.e., arms should not be closed tightly; helper should lean toward and face client squarely); use acknowledgments such as *"um-hmm"*; *relax* and act natural but professional; *avoid* distracting behaviors (e.g., too many adaptors, too much smiling, giggling, playing with hair or objects, interruptions, note-taking, touching); match the client's *grammatical* style and pace of speech (i.e., use the same language style and speech pace as client within the limits of one's own style); listen with a third *ear* (i.e., listen attentively to verbal and nonverbal messages); and use *space* appropriately (e.g., do not sit either too close or too far). These attending behaviors enable helpers to listen carefully to what clients are saying and encourage clients to explore. Helpers should also note clients' responses and modify attending behaviors accordingly (e.g., if clients draw away from eye contact, helpers should not look at them intensely). In addition, helpers offer approval and reassurance (e.g., "That's tough," "You're doing a good job talking about the problem") if the client seems to need encouragement. Most important, when clients are talking productively about their concerns, helpers can sit quietly and listen attentively and empathically.

KEEP THE EXPLORATION GOING

The best exploration tool for most clients is reflection of feelings. When in doubt, helpers can rely on reflection of feelings because it demonstrates that helpers are listening and struggling to understand the client's experience. Reflections are particularly helpful when clients pause and need encouragement to keep talking, when clients need to experience their feelings (whether or not they are actively expressing the feelings), or when helpers want to show support or understanding. Reflection of feelings is also a useful way to identify possible feelings for clients who are out of touch with their feelings. Helpers can self-disclose about their own feelings as a softer, more tentative way of proposing feelings that clients might have. Most clients respond to reflections of feelings or disclosure of feelings by talking about their feelings. However, some clients do not, perhaps because reflections do not request that clients talk about their feelings. For these clients, helpers can alternate reflecting feelings with asking open questions about the feelings. This way, helpers not only suggest possible feelings but also encourage clients to identify and express their own feelings. This method helps clients become comfortable expressing their feelings.

If helpers want to focus the discussion or clarify what clients are talking about, they might use restatements (e.g., "so you flunked your exam" or a repetition of the key word *exam*). When clients are confusing, rambling, or just need to talk, restatements can serve as mirrors that reflect back to clients what they are saying. Restatements help clients clarify and think more deeply about what they are saying.

Throughout the session, a helper can use open questions and probes to maintain the session's flow (e.g., "How are you feeling about that?" or "Tell me more about that"). If clients seem stuck or are repeating the same material over and over, helpers can use open questions to ask about other aspects of problems the client has not addressed. Helpers can ask open questions for different purposes: to help clients clarify or focus (e.g., "What do you mean when you say anxious?" "What would you like to talk about?"); to help clients reflect on their thoughts (e.g., "What is going through your head right now?" "What did you think about what she said?"); to help clients experience and express their feelings (e.g., "How do you feel about going to medical school?" "What is going on right now in your body?"); or to solicit examples (e.g., "Go through the situation and tell me exactly what you said"; "Tell me about the last time that you felt immobilized by your anxiety"). Using a variety of open questions and probes helps clients explore the complexity of situations and think about things they might not have considered.

Helpers can follow clients' responses to open questions with a reflection or restatement to show they understand what clients have said and to encourage them to say more. Open questions are demanding interventions that require clients to respond. In contrast, reflections of feelings are a gentler way of suggesting feelings without seeming as demanding. Alternating among open questions, restatements, and reflections can keep helpers from getting stuck in an interviewer mode. Restatements and reflections shift the responsibility for initiating dialogue back to clients and show that helpers are listening to clients.

When the client is productively exploring, the helper should fade into the background as much as possible and not intrude on the client. The client is obviously able to work and needs the helper just to be there supporting the work. This might involve giving only minimal head nods, being silent, and working to be empathic. Of course, the helper needs to monitor the situation carefully and make sure the client is comfortable and eager to explore.

Occasionally, helpers ask closed questions to gather specific, important information from clients (e.g., "Is your mother alive?" or "When did you graduate from high school?"). Helpers always need to remember to use closed questions to benefit clients rather than to satisfy their own curiosity. Before using closed questions, then, helpers need to be clear about what they are going to do with the information and whose needs are being met (the helpers' or the clients'). Generally, I recommend that helpers rephrase closed questions into open questions or reflection of feelings.

Beginning helpers may have problems in the exploration stage if they are not able to facilitate deep exploration in their clients. Their clients seem to go around in circles, repeating themselves over and over, rather than going deeper into their problems. Generally, circling occurs when helpers use too many closed questions or use restatements or reflections that are focused on someone other than the client, are too general or vague, or do not ask about other aspects of the problem. Beginning helpers sometimes worry about being too intrusive, so they often skim the surface of issues rather than helping clients explore deeply with the skills suggested in this book. They might forget to attend and listen, or they might forget to be empathic and caring. It is not enough just to use the right skills; helpers must use them in an empathic manner to fit what clients need at the time.

In summary, to help clients explore, helpers can use a combination of reflection of feelings, restatements, and open questions, with an occasional sprinkling of approval and reassurance, silence, closed questions, self-disclosure of facts or credentials, self-disclosure of feelings, and information about the helping process, all within the context of appropriate attending behaviors and listening.

KEEP THE FOCUS ON THE CLIENT

At all times, helpers need to remember to keep the focus on the client, even when the client talks primarily about others. For example, if a client says, "My mother is really awful," the helper can say, "You are really irritated with your mother," thereby changing the focus from the mother to the client's reaction to her or his mother. The guiding principle is that it is easier and more efficient (and more ethical) to help a client change than to attempt to help the client change another person.

Helpers also need to maintain the focus on a specific concern (although each specific concern has many parts). Many beginning helpers let clients jump from topic to topic (e.g., academic concerns, interpersonal relationships, spirituality), so that by the end of a session, clients have covered a lot of things superficially but have not explored anything in depth. Focusing on a specific issue is important to make progress, especially in brief treatments. Helpers can use a combination of skills to assist clients in focusing on one issue in depth. Specifically, they can observe clients to determine which issue has the most salience for them (e.g., where is the most intense affect?). After identifying the most important issue, helpers can reflect the feelings clients are experiencing about that issue. Helpers can branch off to explore aspects of the central focus but should always remember to come back to the central focus. For example, if the helper determines that academic concerns are the central focus for Sam, the helper might ask Sam to explore parental expectations for academic performance; ask Sam to explore thoughts about his future occupational preferences; and encourage Sam to talk about study skills. In this way, the helper is sticking to the central topic of academic concerns but is helping Sam explore many aspects of it.

PAY ATTENTION TO CLIENTS' REACTIONS

Helpers should pay attention to clients' reactions to their interventions. If the client is exploring and going deeper into problems, that is great. The helper is obviously on the right track. However, if the client becomes very quiet, passive, or does not explore, the helper should assess what is not working. Perhaps the helper is not attending or listening, is asking too many closed questions, is focusing on someone other than the client, or is giving inaccurate restatements and reflections. The client might be bored, confused, or overwhelmed with negative feelings and retreating from further exploration. Using an assessment of the problem, a helper can change what she or he is doing and try different skills. It is crucial that the helper pay close attention to the client's reactions in order to select appropriate interventions.

MULTICULTURAL CONSIDERATIONS

There are a number of multicultural considerations to consider when implementing the exploration stage. First, the humanistic theory behind the exploration stage is in tune with a western philosophy, which encourages open examination of thoughts and feelings and emphasizes self-healing and self-actualization. Other cultures, particularly eastern cultures, value collectivism more than a strong emphasis on self (Pedersen et al., 2002; Sue & Sue, 1999). Helpers must be mindful of not imposing their own values about open communication on people from other cultures.

Clients from non-western cultures may be less amenable to exploration than to action, so the exploration stage may need to be shorter than with a western client (note that some western clients are also uncomfortable exploring feelings). I caution, however, that some exploration is necessary to get a firm foundation of understanding before rushing to action.

Helpers must be careful not to stereotype clients from other cultures or assume all people from a given culture have similar values. Remember that there is more variation within a given culture than between cultures (Atkinson et al., 1998; Pedersen, 1997). Being knowledgeable and having an appreciation and curiosity about other cultures are important in establishing a working alliance with clients from other cultures.

A general guideline is that it is important to explore cultural differences when these seem salient to the client. The helper can mention cultural differences early in the first session and ask about these (e.g., "I am aware that we are from different cultural backgrounds. I wonder how that is for you?"). The helper can be attentive to client discomfort throughout the helping process and question whether this discomfort is due to cultural differences (e.g., "I notice you seem uncomfortable when I probe for feelings. I wonder if opening up to a stranger is frowned on in your culture?"). It can also be helpful to ask about cultural values related to the helping process (e.g., "What is the reaction in your family and culture to people seeking help from counselors or therapists?"). I suggest that helpers read about the client's culture to educate themselves generally (see chap. 2). In addition, helpers should ask clients to talk about their culture, so helpers can learn more about what it is like for each client particularly (e.g., "Tell me about what it is like for you to be a Korean student who just arrived in the United States").

DECIDE WHEN CLIENTS HAVE EXPLORED ENOUGH

Clients have explored enough when helpers can answer the following questions:

■ What is the client's problem?

■ What is motivating the client to seek help now?

■ How does the client think and feel about the problem?

When helpers sense that clients have explored the situation thoroughly, they might use a restatement to summarize, to see whether the client has anything else to add, to provide closure, and to set the stage for insight. For example, a helper might say, "You've been talking a lot today about your feelings about your roommate. You seem concerned that the two of you are not as close as you have been in the past. You are not sure what you can do to fix the relationship. How does that fit for you?" Alternatively, helpers might ask clients to summarize (e.g., "How would you sum up what you learned so far?") to get a sense of how much clients have absorbed. Ideally, summaries are a joint effort, with helpers and clients trying together to explicate what has been learned. Helpers can either state a summary and check with the client whether it is accurate (e.g., "Does that fit for you?") or ask the client to summarize what he or she learned (e.g., "What do you think you have learned about yourself today?"). Sometimes, of course, summarizing is not necessary because clients naturally move directly to insight.

DEVELOP OWN STYLE

As one last caveat, there is no "right" way to implement this (or any other) stage in this helping model. Each helper has a different style, and each client needs different interventions and has unique reactions. It is not possible to provide an exact road map or cookbook for helpers. I stress again that once helpers have learned how to deliver the specific skills, they need to develop their own intervention styles and integrate helping skills into their way of being. Helpers also need to apply the scientific method to each helping interaction (e.g., observe what does and does not work in each situation and modify behaviors accordingly). Being open to feedback from clients, teachers, and supervisors is an excellent way to improve one's skills.

Helper Self-Awareness

Helpers can use their inner experiences as tools for understanding what is happening in the helping process. By being aware of their reactions, helpers can make better decisions about how to intervene and are less likely to act out their reactions in helping situations (Williams, Hurley, O'Brien, & DeGregorio, in press). Moreover, helpers' reactions can provide valuable clues about how other people react to clients. For example, if the helper feels bored when a client talks in a monotone voice, chances are that other people in the client's life also feel bored when the client talks that way. Hence, helpers have firsthand information about how the client comes across to other people, which is important data for the insight stage.

One clue that something is going wrong in a session is when the helper does not use the most appropriate skills with a client (assuming that the helper has the appropriate skills in her or his repertoire). Helpers can ask themselves, "What keeps me from doing what would be most helpful with this particular client at this moment?" It could be due to client resistance, but helpers first need to rule out that it is not related to their personal issues. Before assuming that clients are disturbed, helpers need to think about their contribution. In other words, if a helper feels bored by a particular client, it is possible that the client reminds him of his father, with whom he is angry. A helper who has no romantic involvements and is lonely might be attracted to a client; one who is insecure when dealing with male clients might be afraid of men. Helpers can ask themselves (see also measure of self-awareness in Web Form J): How do I feel when I am with the client? More specifically,

- Do I feel bored talking with the client?
- Do I feel attracted to the client?
- Do I feel irritated when the client does not agree with me?
- Do I want to solve the client's problems for him or her?
- Do I feel anxious or ill at ease with this client?
- Am I trying to impress this client?
- Am I acting differently with this client than I would like to act?
- What personal issues of mine might be stimulated by working with this client?
- How might I ensure that my personal issues do not have a negative impact on the helping sessions?

It is important that helpers learn about themselves so personal issues do not intrude on sessions with clients. An ideal place to examine these issues is in supervision. With the help of an experienced supervisor, helpers can begin to identify which feelings come from personal issues, which are stimulated by clients, and which are due to a combination of personal issues and client behavior.

I encourage helpers to become involved in psychotherapy for themselves. Therapy can enable helpers to recognize personal issues that could interfere with their ability to help if they are preoccupied with themselves and their problems. Furthermore, therapy can enable helpers to work on their own growth and self-understanding. An occupational hazard of being a helper is that the helping process stirs up personal issues that might otherwise lay dormant. For example, if a client talks about problems with alcoholism and the helper has not resolved similar problems, it might be difficult for the helper to attend to the client's pain instead of focusing on his or her own. Many people become helpers because they want to understand themselves. Although people learn a great deal about themselves through the process of being helpers, their personal therapy gives them the opportunity to work on themselves in an appropriate setting rather than taking time away from clients who have come for help and deserve full attention.

Being in therapy themselves as clients can also teach helpers about the process of helping. Being a client allows helpers to learn what it is like to be on the receiving end of helping skills, to see what is and is not helpful, and to experience how difficult it is to open up and reveal painful material about oneself. Being in therapy also provides a model for helpers about how they would (or would not) want to act in sessions with their clients. Hence, the firsthand experience of what it is like to be on the receiving end of helping is invaluable.

It is troublesome when helpers-in-need refuse to seek help themselves but are willing to be helpers for others. One worries about the motivations of such persons for wanting to be helpers. For example, some people want to be helpers to feel superior to others who are worse off and have problems (see Bugental, 1965). Helpers who have the attitude that helping is only for weak or defective people may inadvertently communicate that attitude and cause clients to feel ashamed for seeking help.

Developing Hypotheses About Clients

Thorough exploration allows helpers to develop hypotheses about clients that lay the foundation for choosing interventions in the next stages of the helping process. Hence, helpers might spend time during the exploration stage thinking about their clients. They should pay close attention to each client's personality and verbal and nonverbal behaviors. How does the client respond to interventions? How does the client's way of interacting influence the helping process?

Helpers can make observations about clients and develop hypotheses about what factors led clients to come to where they are, although I do not suggest helpers act on these hypotheses in this stage. Rather, these hypotheses can be stored away and revised as new information is obtained. These hypotheses and assessments of clients are useful during the insight stage of the helping model. After thinking about a client, helpers should be able to answer several questions.

■ How serious is the problem?

- How is the client behaving?
- How much does the client disclose or withhold about the problem?
- Are there discrepancies in what the client is saying?
- What is the client's role in the creation and maintenance of the problem?

An Example of an Extended Interaction

The following is a sample of an interchange in which the helper facilitates client exploration through an integration of the exploration skills. This example is not meant to be "perfect," but rather a realistic example of what might occur with a beginning helper. After each helper response, I label the skills used and give an explanation of what the helper was trying to accomplish. As you go through the example, cover the helper's responses and formulate your response first. You can then see how similar the helper's response is to yours and determine which is most effective and which you would be most comfortable trying.

Helper: Hi! My name is Sandra. We have 30 minutes today to explore whatever you would like to talk about. (The helper intends to set limits by providing information about what the client can expect from the session.)

Client: Okay.

Helper: So, where would you like to begin? (The helper asks an open question to focus the session.)

Client: I'm feeling anxious about a paper I have to write. I always end up waiting until the last minute to begin, and then I panic because I don't have enough time to write it. I know I do this, but I can't seem to stop myself.

Helper: You're really upset with yourself. (The helper gives a reflection to help the client experience feelings.)

Client: Yeah, I'm worried that I'm going to ruin my chances of getting into graduate school because I'm not doing as well in my courses as I should be.

Helper: You feel scared because your current behaviors might limit your future goals. (The helper gives another reflection because she wants to stay with the feelings and help the client explore futher.)

Client: Exactly, I really think I could succeed in graduate school, and I know I need a graduate degree to do what will make me happy. I'm so worried that I'll stay in this rut and ruin everything I've worked for.

Helper: Tell me about the last time you had a paper to write. Take me through what went on inside your head. (The helper wants more information about exactly what goes on and wants to get the client to talk more concretely about the problem, so asks open questions.)

Client: Well, actually, I have a paper due tomorrow, and I haven't started it yet. I've gathered all the material I need, and I've taken notes on the books, but I haven't written anything. And I've been up late several nights already this week, so I'm short on sleep.

Helper: I can hear the panic in your voice. (The helper reflects nonverbal behavior to help the client recognize feelings.)

Client: Yeah, I'm scared that I won't be able to pull it off this time. Usually I can just pull an all-nighter and get it done, but it seems too big this time. The paper's supposed to be 20 pages.

Helper: What are your plans for this evening? (The helper wants the client to get more specific about the situation to provide a clearer picture and again focuses by asking an open question.)

Client: Well, I just want to go home and sleep. I just don't want to do it.

Helper: Is anything else going on in your life that makes it difficult for you to work on the paper right now? (The helper notes that the client seems stuck and thinks that perhaps the situation is more complicated than the client has expressed. Hence, the helper asks an open question about other issues.)

Client: It's funny you should ask about that. I just had a big fight with my boyfriend, and I feel very upset. He wants to get married and have kids right away, but I really want to go to graduate school. But if I go to graduate school, I will have to move away, at least for a while.

Helper: So you feel conflicted between being with your boyfriend and going on to school. (The helper feels pleased that the client has opened up about other parts of the situation. Because the helper wants to get the client to talk about her feelings about this conflict, the helper uses a reflection that focuses on both parts of the problem.)

Client: That's really true. It just feels like everything has to go his way. Just because he's already finished his school and is working, he wants me to be done too.

Helper: I wonder if you're somewhat confused. (The helper's intent is to identify feelings through a reflection, but the helper has inappropriately projected her confusion onto the client because she is in a similar situation.)

Client: No, not really. As I think about it, I feel angry. I shouldn't have to give up my career for his. My mother did that, and she is very unhappy. She never even learned how to drive. She did everything for her kids, and now that we have all left home, she's depressed and lonesome. I think I want to have a career, but I don't know. I don't know if it's fair, and I don't want to risk losing my relationship with my boyfriend.

Helper: (in a softer voice) It sounds like you are really torn up inside. (The helper realizes that last intervention was inaccurate and shifts focus back to the client's feelings by using a reflection.)

Client: (cries softly) Maybe I can't write the paper because I'm so confused about this fight with my boyfriend and what's going on with my mother.

Helper: (The helper is silent for 30 seconds to give the client a chance to experience her feelings of sadness.)

Client: (cries and then blows her nose)

Helper: (softly) I'm sure this is very difficult for you to talk about. (The helper wants to support the client and gives a supportive statement.)

Client: Yeah, it sure is. What do you think I should do?

Helper: Well, I think you should go talk to your instructor and see if you can get out of writing the paper tomorrow. Then I think you need to talk to your boyfriend and try to work things out. Perhaps you should encourage your mom to get counseling. (The helper inappropriately gets caught up in the client's request for help and gives direct guidance about what client should do.)

Client: Oh. (silence) Well, I don't know. (The client stops exploring and becomes passive.)

Helper: Sorry, I got carried away with too much advice. How do you feel about a career? (The helper realizes that the client has stopped exploring and so apologizes briefly. She then tries to go back to the exploration by

returning to the last major issue they were discussing
before the client got stuck.)

Client: (Client continues to explore.)

Difficulties Helpers Experience in the Exploration Stage

Beginning helpers typically face several obstacles implementing the exploration stage. If helpers are aware of these obstacles ahead of time, they can cope when difficulties inevitably arise.

INADEQUATE ATTENDING AND LISTENING

Several factors might interfere with helpers being able to attend and listen adequately to their clients. Many helpers get distracted from listening because they get involved in their own thoughts or think about what to say next. Helpers sometimes judge the merits of what clients are saying rather than listening to understand them. One type of judgment that is hard to avoid is evaluating clients using one's own cultural standards. For example, a European American, middle-class, female helper might have difficulty listening to and understanding an upper-class African American man or a very poor Asian woman. Sympathy can be another impediment to listening because helpers sometimes become so involved with and feel so badly for clients that they cannot maintain objectivity; they try to "rescue" clients instead of attending to feelings.

ASKING TOO MANY CLOSED QUESTIONS

Beginning helpers often ask too many closed questions because they feel they need to gather all the details of a problem. Many helpers think the helping process is similar to a medical model in which they should collect a lot of information to diagnose the problem and provide a solution for the client. However, in this stage the helper's task is to aid clients in coming to their own solutions, so there is little need to know all the details. Instead, such skills as facilitating exploration of thoughts and feelings are important for helping clients explore before they can arrive at solutions.

Some helpers ask too many questions simply because they do not have anything better to say. These helpers do not necessarily want to hear the answers to their questions; they just want to fill the time or satisfy their curiosity. When asking questions, it is important to clarify for whom the question is being asked (i.e., to assist the client or to fulfill the helper's need).

TALKING TOO MUCH

Some helpers talk too much in helping sessions. They might talk because they are anxious, they want to impress clients, or they like to talk in general. However, if helpers are talking, clients cannot talk and, hence, cannot explore their concerns. Research has found that clients generally talk about 60% to 70% of the time (Hill, 1978; Hill et al., 1983). In contrast, in nonhelping situations, both people in an interaction ideally talk about 50% of the time; therefore, it can be difficult for beginning helpers to adjust to listening more than talking.

GIVING TOO MUCH (OR PREMATURE) ADVICE

Beginning helpers often rush into giving advice. They feel pressured to provide answers, fix problems, rescue clients, or have perfect solutions. Many clients and beginning helpers are under the misguided notion that helpers have a responsibility to provide solutions to problems. Giving clients answers or solutions is often detrimental, because clients have not come to the solutions on their own and, therefore, cannot own them. Furthermore, when given answers, clients do not learn how to solve future problems without depending on other people. Clients most often need a sounding board or someone to listen to them think through their problem or help them figure out how to solve their problems, rather than someone just telling them what to do. It is critical to realize that the need to provide answers often originates in the helper's insecurity and desire to help, which are normal feelings at the start of learning helping skills.

It is important to recognize that some clients *do* want answers from helpers and do not want to explore. It is sometimes appropriate to move more quickly to the action stage with such clients. Sometimes such clients will be more eager to explore after they have made some specific changes in their lives; other clients, however, just want changes without deep exploration and understanding. Helpers can educate clients about the benefits of coming to their own solutions after a thorough exploration of their problems, feelings, and situation. Helpers should be careful not to be judgmental about clients who do not want to explore.

BEING "BUDDIES"

Sometimes beginning helpers err by acting like "buddies" with clients instead of being helpers. The role of helper necessitates providing a connected yet clearly defined relationship to maintain objectivity and offer maximum assistance. Being a buddy can be limiting because helpers might choose interventions to make clients like them rather than to help clients change. For example, Sam, a beginning helper, began every session by talking with his client, Tom, about recent sporting events. Tom responded enthusiastically to talking about sports but was reluctant to discuss more personal issues. Sam avoided changing the topic because he wanted to maintain a friendly connection with Tom. Unfortunately, because of his desire to be buddies, Sam was not able to help Tom explore his personal issues.

NOT ALLOWING SILENCE

One of the most daunting tasks for beginning helpers is to cope with silence. Trainees often rush to fill voids in sessions out of fear that clients are bored, anxious, critical, or stuck. Rushing to fill voids can result in superficial and unhelpful comments.

Helpers should try to understand their fears about silence in sessions. Helpers can ask themselves what concerns they have (e.g., not appearing competent, not helping the client) and work on these fears outside of sessions, rather than rushing to fill silences in sessions.

INAPPROPRIATELY SELF-DISCLOSING

One of the biggest problems beginning helpers have is the urge to self-disclose. Because client issues are often similar to their own issues, beginning helpers want to share their experiences with their clients. It seems natural to disclose and tell one's stories, as one would with friends. Helpers also may want help for themselves and may be distracted by their own problems while listening to clients. It is can be difficult to listen to someone else's issues when one is going through the same thing. For example, beginning helpers in their early 20s often have difficulty listening to students their own age talk about identity issues, relationship difficulties, problems with parents, and plans for the future because these are issues for the helpers. Beginning helpers who are older might have difficulty listening to problems about parenting and aging. Adopting the professional identity of a helper who listens but does not disclose much is a major and challenging shift in perspective for beginning helpers. However, because inappropriate self-disclosure can be detrimental and can hinder the therapeutic relationship, helpers need to learn to restrain themselves.

DISCOURAGING INTENSE EXPRESSION OF AFFECT

Beginning helpers sometimes feel awkward when clients express intense affect, such as despair, intense sadness, or strong anger (especially if the anger is directed toward the helper). Sometimes helpers are uncomfortable with negative feelings because they do not allow themselves to feel their own negative feelings. They may deny or defend against their internal "demons." For these helpers, hearing clients' negative feelings can be very stressful. Sometimes helpers feel a need to make clients feel better immediately because they do not want their clients to suffer. They mistakenly think that if clients do not talk about their feelings, the feelings go away. They might be afraid to have clients get into the negative feelings because they feel inadequate to help them. Guilty feelings might emerge for helpers if their interventions result in clients crying. These helpers err on the side of keeping things "light" or minimizing feelings so they do not have to face "tough" situations where they feel helpless. Recently, an attractive adolescent client told her helper she felt totally fat and ugly. She expressed disgust with her body and astonishment that anyone would want to be around her. A helper who is uncomfortable with intense negative feelings might give the socially sanctioned response of reassuring this client that she is attractive and suggesting that her feelings are not accurate. Ironically, this response would negate the client's feelings and could make the client feel worse because she would feel misunderstood.

Now might be a good time to ask yourself how you feel about overt expressions of affect. What do you instinctively want to do when someone begins to sob uncontrollably? Most of us feel an urge to get the person to stop crying and to feel better. How do you react when someone is acting hostile and angry toward you? Many of us get defensive or react with hostility. Helpers need to be aware of their tendencies to respond in these types of situations so they can practice other, more appropriate ways, to respond. The exploration skills can be particularly valuable for giving helpers tools to allow clients to stay in moments of intense emotions.

DISSOCIATING AND PANICKING

Sometimes beginning helpers become so anxious about their performance that they feel they are outside their bodies observing themselves in the helping role, instead of being fully present and interactive in the helping session. At worst, these helpers become completely frozen and cannot say anything. These dissociative experiences can frighten helpers, who then panic and tell themselves they can never be good helpers. In fact, anxiety is often more of a problem than lack of skills, and I have seen students overcome their anxiety and become gifted therapists.

FEELING INADEQUATE

At about this point in the course, some students say they feel like they are getting worse at being a helper rather than getting better. They are so focused on each skill and on watching everything they do that it is hard to perform at all. An analogy can be drawn to learning to drive. When you first learn to drive, you are conscious of every little thing you do. Like beginning drivers, beginning helpers focus on each thing they do in the helping encounter. In learning helping skills, helpers practice the individual skills (and often unlearn habits that were not facilitative to helping) and then put all the skills together. Although difficult initially, it should begin to feel easier when you put them all together. If you are feeling badly about your skills as a helper right now, give yourself some time. Students often feel better after practicing for a few more weeks. (Of course, some students come to realize after additional practice that they do not want to be helpers.)

Strategies for Overcoming the Difficulties and Managing Anxiety

To overcome a lack of skills, helpers can learn and practice helping skills taught in this book. The skills can be compared to tools in a toolbox; helpers learn about the different tools available for different tasks. Some tools work better than others for some helpers and some clients. It is important that helpers have many tools (e.g., helping skills and methods for managing anxiety) in their toolboxes so they have a lot of options to help clients and to manage their own anxiety in sessions.

To manage anxiety, several ideas are offered in this section (see also Management Strategies Scale in Web Form J). The first few strategies helpers can use in sessions with clients; the last few helpers can use to prepare themselves for dealing with anxiety. I hope all helpers find some strategies they can use.

PREPARATORY SRATEGIES

Viewing Models

Watching skilled helpers in helping sessions is an excellent way to observe skills being used appropriately. The skills come alive when one sees them demonstrated by experts. Although reading about theories and skills is important, imagining how they come across is hard unless models are available. Bandura (1969) has shown the effectiveness of watching a model as one step in the learning process. I recommend watching many different helpers to illustrate that there are many ways and styles of helping.

Imagery

Through sports psychology, we know that when athletes have the requisite skills, practice through imagery can be a beneficial addition to actual practice (Suinn, 1988). Similarly, helpers can imagine themselves using appropriate attending behaviors and helping skills in different situations. For example, a beginning helper who feels uncomfortable with silence might close her eyes and visualize herself in a session with a quiet client. She might imagine herself sitting comfortably with the client and allowing the silence to occur. She might also visualize breaking the silence after a period of time by asking how the client is feeling.

Role-Play

Before sessions with clients, helpers can role-play using specific helping skills. Helpers can also role-play the mechanics of sessions, such as starting and stopping the session, responding to silence, and dealing with anger directed toward the helper. By using role-plays with supportive partners (e.g., classmates), helpers are more likely to learn the skills at a comfortable pace.

Practice

Perhaps the best method for managing anxiety is practice. The more helpers practice and pay attention to what they do well and how they can improve, the better and more comfortable they are likely to become in helping sessions. Throughout the book, I provide exercises for helpers to practice the helping skills. I encourage helpers to participate in many practice sessions with sympathetic and helpful volunteer clients.

IN-SESSION STRATEGIES

Deep Breathing

One way helpers can manage anxiety is to breathe deeply from the diaphragm instead of taking short breaths from high in the chest. To determine if you breathe from the diaphragm, put your hand over your stomach. When you breathe, you should feel your hand move in and out. Deep breathing serves several functions. First, it allows helpers to relax. When the diaphragm is relaxed, it is harder to be anxious physiologically. Second, taking a deep breath gives helpers a moment to think about what they want to say. Helpers can take time to focus their energy instead of being distracted by thinking about what to say in the next intervention. Third, it gives clients a chance to think and consider whether they have anything else to say. Sometimes helpers interrupt too quickly when clients are exploring. The goal is exploration, so helpers do not need to say anything if clients are working productively.

Focus on the Client

All too often, beginning helpers are so concerned with their own behavior that they cannot listen attentively to clients. By shifting focus to be more concerned with the client than with themselves, helpers can listen more attentively (Williams et al., 1997). The goal is to facilitate clients in exploring feelings, not for helpers to show off how much they understand clients. By focusing on the client and attempting to immerse oneself in the client's world, many beginning helpers are able to lessen their anxiety.

Positive Self-Talk

We all talk to ourselves as we do things. We say things like, "I can do this" or "I think I am going to panic." Some people have called this the "inner game" because it occurs beneath the surface. Positive self-talk has a positive influence on performance in helping sessions, whereas negative self-talk has a negative influence on performance (see Nutt-Williams & Hill, 1996), so helpers need to be attentive to what they are saying to themselves. Helpers can practice using positive self-talk before sessions so they have positive sentences ready to use to coach themselves. Alternatively, helpers can write down positive self-statements (e.g., "I know the skills," "I am competent") on index cards and glance at them before or during practice sessions.

WHAT DO YOU THINK?

- How would you have handled the situation as the helper in the extended example? Would you have used different interventions at any point?
- How do you explain the client's being able to gain insight (i.e., "Maybe I can't write the paper because of my fight with my boyfriend and what's going on with my mother") in the example when the helper did not provide interpretations?
- Discuss whether you think helpers need to go on to the insight stage or whether the exploration stage is necessary and sufficient for clients' change.
- How can you balance using the helping skills with empathic listening?

▪ How would you know when you have explored enough?
▪ Check the obstacles you are likely to face in your development as a helper:

_____ inadequate attending and listening

_____ asking too many closed questions

_____ talking too much

_____ giving too much or premature advice

_____ being "buddies"

_____ not allowing silence

_____ inappropriately self-disclosing

_____ discouraging intense expression of affect

_____ dissociating and panicking

_____ feeling inadequate

▪ Identify strategies you might use to cope with obstacles as a helper:

_____ viewing models

_____ imagery

_____ role-playing

_____ practice

_____ deep breathing

_____ focusing on the client

_____ positive self-talk

LAB 8

Integration of Exploration Skills

You are ready to integrate the skills you have learned so far. In this lab, you will meet with a client and use these skills to facilitate client exploration.

Goal: For helpers to participate in a 20-minute helping session using basic helping skills (restatement, reflection of feelings, and open questions) as well as minor skills (information about the helping process, approval and reassurance, closed questions, self-disclosures for exploration, and silence).

Helper's and Client's Tasks During the Helping Interchange

1. Each helper pairs up with a volunteer client selected from outside the class.
2. Helpers bring the necessary forms with them to the session: Session Review Form (Web Form A), Helper Intentions List (Web Form D), Client Reactions System (Web Form G), Session Process and Outcome Measures (Web Form I), and Self-Awareness and Management Strategies Scales (Web Form J). Supervisors bring the Supervisor Rating Form (Web Form B).
3. Helpers bring an audio- or videotape recorder (tested ahead of time to ensure it works) and a tape. They turn on the recorder at the beginning of the session.
4. Helpers introduce themselves, inform clients about confidentiality, and indicate whether sessions will be recorded and observed.
5. Each helper conducts a 20-minute session with a client who talks about any easy topic (see Exhibit 1.1). The helper should be as helpful as possible, using all the exploration skills. Watch for the client's reactions to each of your interventions and modify subsequent interventions when appropriate.
6. Watch the time carefully. About 2 minutes before the end of the session, let the client know that time is almost up. At the end, let your client know when time is up by saying something like, "We need to stop now. Thank you for helping me practice my helping skills."

Supervisor's Tasks During The Session

Supervisors use the Supervisor Rating Form to record observations and evaluations.

Postsession

1. Both helper and client complete the Session Process and Outcome Measures. Each helper also completes the Self-Awareness and Management Strategies Scales.
2. After the session, each helper reviews the tape with the client (review of a 20-minute session takes about 40 to 60 minutes). Helpers stop the tape after each intervention (except minimal acknowledgments such

continues

LAB 8 (C o n t i n u e d)

Integration of Exploration Skills

as "um-hmm" and "yeah"). Helpers write down the key words on the Session Review Form (so the exact spot on the tape can be located later for transcription).

3. Helpers rate the helpfulness of the intervention and record the numbers of up to three intentions (responding according to how they felt *during* the session). Use the whole range of the helpfulness scale and as many categories as possible on the intentions list. Do not complete these ratings collaboratively with clients.

4. Clients rate the helpfulness of each intervention and record the numbers of up to three reactions (responding according to how they felt *during* the session). Clients should use the whole range of the Helpfulness Scale and as many categories as possible on the reactions system (helpers learn more from honest feedback than from "nice" statements that are not genuine). Do not collaborate with helpers to complete the ratings.

5. Helpers and clients record the most helpful and least helpful event in the session.

6. Supervisors give feedback to helpers based on the Supervisor Rating Form.

Lab Report

1. Helpers should type a transcript of their 20-minute session (see the sample in Web Form C). Skip minimal utterances such as "okay," "you know," "er," and "uh."

2. Divide the helper speech into response units (essentially grammatical sentences), using the directions provided in Web Form F.

3. Using the Helping Skills System (see Web Form E), determine which skill was used for each response unit (grammatical sentence) in your transcript.

4. Indicate on the transcript which different words you would use for each intervention if you could do it again. Use the Helping Skills System (Web Form E) to indicate which skill fits for each response unit of what you would say differently.

5. Erase the tape. Make sure no identifying information is on the transcript.

6. Compare the skills used in this session with the skills in the first session (Lab 3).

7. Compare the helper and client scores on the Session Process and Outcome Measures and the Self-Awareness and Management Strategies Scales to those of other students (go to references cited in Web Forms I and J).

Personal Reflections

▮ What did you learn about yourself as a helper from this experience?

- Which skills did you and the client find to be most helpful? Why?
- How much did your intentions match your skills (compare your intentions with those listed in the exhibits on the skills, chaps. 7–10)?
- Some helpers have a hard time exploring because they want to rush to problem solving. If this was true for you, speculate about reasons.
- What skills do you still need to work on?

III

Insight Stage

Overview of the Insight Stage | 12

Daring as it is to investigate the unknown, even more so is it to question the known.

—*Kaspar*

uan had been to a behavioral helper who taught him relaxation, assertiveness skills, and time management skills. He was now more organized, relaxed, and better able to carry on a conversation, but he still felt empty inside. He could not understand why he felt life had no meaning. He went to a helper who believed in insight, and they began exploring his feelings about himself and his childhood. Through the helper's gentle questioning, challenges, interpretations, and self-disclosures of insight, he came to the understanding that perhaps his anxiety and loneliness had roots in the fact that his mother died when he was two months old and his father sent him to live with his grandparents. Although his grandparents were very loving, he had always felt that he was interfering with their retirement plans and that he was out of place. He realized that in social situations, he always placed himself on the outside so others would not have the chance to reject him. He lived his life as a defense against being abandoned again. He also came to realize that by removing himself from social situations, he had no opportunity to have close, satisfying relationships. In sessions, he found himself constantly worrying that the helper was bored and would rather be with other clients. Through the helper's talking about their immediate relationship, Juan came to understand that his feelings were a transference onto the helper of his feelings about his parents abandoning him. Once he understood more about himself and could see that the helper indeed cared about him, Juan began to rethink the idea that he was not lovable. He was able to reframe his perceptions of his grandparents to see that they did love him and had chosen to raise him. Juan felt better because he now had some explanations for his feelings and behaviors.

During the exploration stage, we established a therapeutic relationship and helped clients experience feelings at a deep level and explore thoughts about the many facets of their problems. The exploration stage was client-centered in that we suspended judgment to try to understand the client's perspective. For some clients, this supportive, nonjudgmental listening is all that is needed to motivate them to make important changes in their lives. The helper's acceptance enables these clients to experience their feelings and accept what is going on inside them. They become unblocked, able to think about how they want to be and what they want to do about their problems. Their actualization potential is released, and clients become creative and active self-healers and problem solvers. They no longer need outside intervention, although they might enjoy sharing their thoughts and feelings with a good helper.

Unfortunately, not all clients can progress on their own after exploring their thoughts and feelings. Some clients have a hard time understanding the origins and consequences of their feelings and behaviors. Other clients get stuck and need someone to help them get past obstacles and defenses they learned in childhood that protect them against internal pain and external harm. It is difficult to give up protective defenses because there is no assurance that the world is a safe place. When painful events occur, people often compartmentalize experiences in their minds so they do not have to think about them, making it difficult to integrate these experiences into their lives. Some people have done things a certain way for so long that they never question their actions or think about the reasons for what they do. Other clients are eager to learn more about themselves and their motivations but need an objective perspective to help them past blind spots. Helpers can challenge clients to help them gain awareness about their thoughts, feelings, and behaviors; encourage clients to gain insight; offer interpretations and self-disclosures of insight to help clients think in new ways; and work to help clients understand immediate problems in the therapeutic relationship in order to help them understand how they relate to others.

The insight stage is important to assist clients in coming to new understandings of themselves and their problems. I believe people strive to find meaning in their lives and often need to restructure maladaptive thinking patterns to actualize their potential. Frankl (1959) emphasized the importance of having a life philosophy to transcend suffering and find meaning in existence. He argued that our greatest human need is to find a core of meaning and a purpose in life. Frankl's experience in a German concentration camp bears out his theory: Although he could not change his life situation, he was able to change the meaning he attached to this experience. By drawing on the strengths of his Jewish tradition, he was able to survive and help others survive.

Finally, I reiterate that the insight stage builds on the foundation of the exploration stage. Going beyond exploration to insight and an understanding of inner dynamics requires a deep sense of empathy and belief in clients. Helpers have to see beyond defenses and inappropriate behaviors to the inner self and accept who clients are. Suspending judgment allows helpers to look deeper to understand and accept clients.

Theoretical Background: Psychoanalytic Theory

Psychoanalytic theory began with Sigmund Freud and has evolved through many subsequent theorists (e.g., Adler, Basch, Bion, Erikson, Fairbairn, Fenichel, Ferenczi, Fromm, Gill, Greenson, Horney, Jung, Klein, Kohut, Mahler, Rank, Sullivan, Winnicott). Over the century that psychoanalytic theory has existed, many changes have been made in the theory (Mitchell, 1993), with current emphasis given to the relationship between therapist and client (e.g., Teyber, 2000). In this section, the focus is on a few important aspects of psychoanalytic theory that are currently salient and applicable to the helping skills model.

THEORY OF PERSONALITY

Although Freud's (1940/1949) theory of psychosexual development (going through the oral, anal, phallic, latent, and genital stages) has been widely disputed, there are several components of Freud's theory that are relevant. The first is his description of the mind (it is important to emphasize that this theory is useful more as a metaphor than as a physiological reality). Freud postulated that at birth, infants are totally governed by the *id*, or primitive urges that seek immediate gratification. As the child develops, the *ego* forms to help the child delay gratification and negotiate with the world. As the child develops further and internalizes society's morals and values, she or he develops a *superego*. There are conflicts among these three aspects of personality as a person struggles between primitive impulses and societal restrictions.

A related Freudian concept is of consciousness, which again is more important as a metaphor than as a physiological entity. He divided awareness into the unconscious, preconscious, and conscious. He postulated that the largest percentage of mental activity is unconscious, or not available to immediate awareness. A small amount of energy is in the preconscious, suggesting that one can access these thoughts and experiences if a great deal of attention is paid to them. An even smaller amount of awareness is conscious, or currently in our awareness at any given time. Freud proposed that most people act out of unconscious motivations and are unaware why they act the way they do. To illustrate the power of the unconscious, think about a recent time you did something that seemed out of character for you (e.g., became suddenly angry, acted differently from your values)—these feelings and behaviors may have been motivated by unconscious feelings.

A third important Freudian construct relates to defenses. Not everything goes smoothly in the development of personality. Children do not always receive everything they need to develop psychologically. One way people cope with adversity is through developing defense mechanisms. Freud (1933) and more recent psychoanalysts have theorized that defense mechanisms are unconscious methods for dealing with anxiety through denial or distortion of reality. Everyone has defense mechanisms because everyone has to cope with anxiety. Defense mechanisms can be healthy if used appropriately and in moderation, but repeated and frequent use of defense mechanisms can be problematic. Examples of defense mechanisms include the following:

- Repression (not allowing painful material into one's conscious thought)
- Intellectualization (avoiding painful feelings by focusing on ideas)
- Denial (actively rejecting painful affect)
- Regression (engaging in behaviors from an earlier stage of development at times when one is anxious)
- Displacement (shifting uncomfortable feelings toward someone who is less powerful and less threatening than the individual from whom the feelings originated)
- Identification (emulating characteristics in others)
- Projection (perceiving that others have the characteristics that are unconsciously disliked in one's self)
- Undoing (behaving in a ritualistic manner to take away or make amends for unacceptable behaviors)
- Reaction formation (acting in a manner that is opposite to what one is feeling)
- Sublimation (changing unacceptable impulses into socially appropriate actions)
- Rationalization (making excuses for an anxiety-producing thought or behavior)

For example, Antonio has marital problems because he projects onto his wife that she is dominating like his mother. He is unable to see that her questions are motivated by concern rather than by a desire to control.

He is afraid of telling his wife about his anger at her for being dominating, and so he displaces his feelings by kicking the dog. If asked about his anger, he denies it and regresses to acting like a whiny 7-year-old who expects to be punished. These defense mechanisms protect Antonio from being aware of his anger at his mother and from learning how to deal with his feelings more appropriately.

A final important construct is attachment, which has been the focus of much recent theorizing and research (e.g., Bowlby, 1969, 1988; Cassidy, & Shaver, 1999; Meyer & Pilkonis, 2002). Bowlby developed attachment theory to explain the behavioral and emotional responses that keep young children in close proximity to caregivers. In optimal attachment, caregivers provide a comfortable presence for the infant that reduces anxiety and promotes a feeling of security. From this secure base, infants are able to explore their environment. Through an observational study of young children, Ainsworth, Blehar, Waters, and Wall (1978) found three patterns of attachment (secure, anxious–ambivalent, and anxious–avoidant). Infants who were securely attached explored freely in their mother's presence, showed some anxiety upon separation, and were easily comforted when reunited. Infants with an anxious–ambivalent pattern were excessively anxious and angry, and they tended to cling to their mothers to an extent that interfered with their exploration. They were also distressed during separation and were difficult to comfort on reunion with mothers. Anxious–avoidant infants showed minimal interest in their mothers and displayed minimal affect throughout the observation. These observations have been replicated with other children, and the results have been extended to adulthood, suggesting that attachment patterns in childhood carry over to relationships in adulthood (Ainsworth, 1989). Bowlby's theory has been used extensively in recent years to explain the difficulties clients have in forming relationships with other people, including therapists (e.g., Mallinckrodt, Gantt, & Coble, 1995).

PSYCHOANALYTIC TREATMENT

Freud (1923/1963) believed examination and insight into troubling issues could assist in the resolution of problems. As a foundation for treatment, the helper listens patiently, empathically, uncritically, and receptively (Arlow, 1995).

To facilitate insight, the helper encourages the patient to free associate—to say whatever thoughts come to mind without censure as a means to make the unconscious conscious, which is a primary focus of psychoanalytic treatment. When appropriate, the helper offers interpretations that are just beyond the client's current understanding to encourage the client to think more deeply about the issues (Speisman, 1959). The focus of interpretations is typically about the origins of behaviors and the influence of early childhood experiences on current behaviors. Psychoanalysts talk about the importance of doing an "archeological dig" to determine the early reasons for current behaviors.

The goal of psychoanalytic treatment is to make the unconscious conscious, or stated another way, to replace the id with the ego. Although the majority of our mind is unconscious, according to Freud, we can strive to make ourselves as aware as possible of these primitive influences. Because of the difficulty of dealing with unconscious material, Freud proposed that we analyze dreams, fantasies, or slips of the tongue, where the ego does not have as strong a control. Helpers also assist clients in developing an awareness of frequently used defense mechanisms and in gaining more control over the use of these unconscious strategies to reduce anxiety.

Freud believed that manifestations of unresolved problems from early in childhood are repeated throughout the client's life. Often, the repetition is uncovered through analysis of the way the client relates to the therapist. For example, a client whose mother was cold and unable to fulfill her attachment needs as an infant may demonstrate neediness in her relationship with the therapist. The client might call the therapist at home, ask for extra sessions, and try to get the therapist to extend the time limits of each session. The client might also project onto her therapist that the therapist is cold and unable to meet her needs. Placing on the therapist characteristics that belong to other people with whom one has unresolved issues is termed *transference* (Freud, 1920/1943). Freud indicated that the analysis and interpretation of transference can be a powerful therapeutic tool to facilitate understanding of the client's relationships with others and of significant unresolved issues for the client (see also Gelso & Carter, 1985, 1994). In addition, current interpersonal theorists stress the importance of understanding the therapeutic relationship. Recent research, however, suggests some caution in using transference interpretations, especially with clients who have a lot of difficulty with interpersonal relationships (Crits-Christoph & Gibbons, 2002). Helpers should be careful to make sure a solid relationship is established with such clients before dealing directly with transference issues in the therapeutic relationship.

The helper's unresolved issues can also influence the process and outcome of helping. This process has been called *countertransference* (see also Gelso & Hayes, 1998) and is defined as the helper's reactions to the client that originate in the unresolved issues of the helper. In the previous example, the therapist may have had unresolved needs to take care of others (perhaps related to having an alcoholic mother who relied on the helper to care for younger siblings) and so might respond to the client's neediness by allowing the client to call her at home, stop by the office at any time, and delay payment until the client earns more money. If unrecognized, countertransference behaviors can influence therapy in a negative way. However, awareness of countertransference feelings can ensure that the helping process is not harmed by the helper's unresolved issues and can actually facilitate the process by making helpers aware of what clients pull from them.

Therapists who follow strict Freudian principles are considered to be psychoanalytic. Therapists who modify the principles or who use them more liberally or in conjunction with other principles are considered to be psychodynamic.

Because psychoanalysis is complex, it is not possible to do justice to the richness of the theory here. I encourage interested readers to explore other sources to learn more about other psychoanalytic theories (e.g., Basch, 1980; Gelso & Hayes, 1998; Greenson, 1967; Kohut, 1971, 1977, 1984; Mahler, 1968; Mitchell, 1993; Patton & Meara, 1992).

How Psychoanalytic Theories Relate to the Three-Stage Model

The emphasis in psychoanalytic theories on the importance of early relationships, defenses, insight, and dealing with the therapeutic relationship is consistent with my thinking about the insight stage. More specifically, the emphasis on the importance of early childhood experiences is in concert with my thinking about the importance of early experiences, particularly with significant others. Similarly, the emphasis on defenses is very important in helping clients cope with establishing moderate levels of defenses that protect them yet allow them to interact with others. I also believe strongly that insight is helpful in enabling clients to make lasting changes and to solve new problems as they arise. Finally, dealing with problems as they occur in the therapeutic relationship is crucial because it provides clients with skills to handle relationships outside of therapy more effectively.

However, in contrast to traditional psychoanalytic theory, I emphasize the helper's role in the insight stage involves coaching the client to gain insight, rather than the helper being the one who provides the insight. Often, clients are capable of coming up with their own insights if helpers provide the appropriate atmosphere and ask thoughtful questions. In fact, clients often feel better about insights they have attained on their own rather than interpretations that were foisted on them. Some clients want more input from helpers, and such input can be helpful if offered in a collaborative, tentative manner.

Psychoanalytic approaches do not directly help clients move to the action stage. Therapists using psychoanalytic theories do not usually provide direct guidance or advice (Crits-Christoph, Barber, & Kurcias, 1991). I contend that the action stage can be very useful, especially when it follows the insight stage (although some clients want or need action before insight). Similarly, helpers using the three-stage model tend to be more active agents in helping, and the length of treatment tends to be shorter than in classic psychoanalytic therapy. Despite some differences in theoretical assertions, however, I would stress that psychoanalytic techniques are very helpful for guiding clients toward increased insight and self-understanding.

Goals for the Insight Stage

FOSTERING AWARENESS

It is important that clients become aware of their thoughts and behaviors. People have lived with themselves for so long and developed defenses to protect themselves from interpersonal injuries, so they are often unaware of thoughts and behaviors that are not adaptive. They need to hear how others honestly react to them so they can begin the self-examination process. For example, a client may be unaware that he comes across in a hostile manner, which makes others avoid him. Awareness involves becoming more conscious about one's thoughts, feelings, behaviors, and impact on others.

FOSTERING INSIGHT

Awareness often leads to a desire for insight, which is a major goal of the insight stage. In other words, once a person becomes aware of some feeling, thought, or behavior, he or she often wants to understand more about it.

Helpers work with clients to construct new understandings and learn more about their role in creating and maintaining their problems. One of the hallmarks of our existence as human beings is the desire for an explanation for our thoughts, feelings, and behaviors. An explanation, right or wrong, helps most people feel more in control of their world and is a potent ingredient in therapeutic change (Hanna & Ritchie, 1995). In the insight stage, helpers search for clues regarding what motivates people, what causes them pain and happiness, and what hinders them from achieving their potential.

Several theorists have recognized the importance of insight in the therapeutic process. Freud (1923/1963) believed psychological problems are developmental and resolution can only be reached by obtaining insight into the problems. Symptoms generally make sense in the context of past and present life experiences. For example, Jenna's fear of public speaking makes sense in the light of her reluctance to achieve and possibly outdo her passive and depressed mother.

Frank and Frank (1991) viewed insight as a reworking of the past that leads to the discovery of new facts, as well as a recognition of new relationships between previously known facts and a reevaluation of their significance. Hence, Jenna's insight that she has been limiting herself to placate her mother could lead her to understanding why she made the choices she did throughout her life. This understanding can also give her a sense that she can make different choices in the future.

What Is Insight?

When clients come to insights, they see things from a new perspective, are able to make connections between things, or have an understanding of why things happen as they do (Elliott et al., 1994). For some, gaining insight is like a light bulb going off, a sudden feeling of "aha." For example, Yinyin might suddenly realize her strong reactions to her boyfriend when he said he would not go to a party stems from her rarely having gotten her way as a child. Her anger may be due to perceived past injustices and a belief that her boyfriend is doing the same thing to her that her parents did. For others, however, insight comes more gradually. Rogers (1942) noted that "insight comes gradually, bit by bit, as the individual develops sufficient psychological strength to endure new perspectives" (p. 177). For example, Robert might slowly, and only after several challenges and interpretations, come to realize that his indecision over his career choice might be due to unhappiness with his wife.

Intellectual Versus Emotional Insight

Insight must be emotional as well as intellectual to lead to action (Reid & Finesinger, 1952; Singer, 1970). Intellectual insight provides an objective explanation for a problem (e.g., "I am anxious because of my Oedipal conflict"); it has a barren, sterile quality that keeps clients stuck in understandings that lead nowhere (Gelso & Fretz, 2001). Many of us know people who can give a comprehensive history of their psychological problems and the sources of their difficulty but who cannot express their feelings fully. Emotional insight, on the other hand, connects affect to intellect and creates a sense of personal involvement and responsibility (Gelso

& Fretz, 2001). For example, when Jason suddenly realizes his conflict with his wife for having her own interests is really due to the hurt he felt because his father did not spend much time with him, he can feel that hurt deep inside himself. He may feel the relief of a burden lifted from him. This emotional and intellectual insight might help Jason decide that it is okay for his wife to have separate activities. Jason might start thinking that he needs to develop his own interests and might begin to question why he allows his identity to be based on his wife. The deep insight Jason achieved would not have been possible if he had been given an interpretation that sounded right "on paper" but was not something he could acknowledge as his own or feel at a deep level.

The attainment of emotional insight is thought to result in behavioral change (Ferenczi & Rank, 1925/1956). For example, a client who understands intellectually that she screams at her boyfriend because she is angry with her father does not achieve the same kind of growth and change that both intellectual and emotional insight engenders. If this client were to experience the feelings associated with this intellectual understanding (e.g., how badly she feels about transferring negative feelings toward her mostly innocent boyfriend, and how deeply frustrated she is that her father continues to have a negative influence on her life), she might develop the motivation to change her behavior toward her boyfriend.

Emotional insight is typically easier for clients to attain when they are fully and actively involved in the helping process. They need to be personally involved and eager about trying to understand themselves. It is usually better for helpers to work with clients to help them achieve insight rather than telling them what to think.

Why Is Insight Necessary?

Frank and Frank (1991) asserted that the need to make sense of events is as fundamental to humans as the need for food or water. They suggested that people evaluate internal and external stimuli in view of their assumptions about what is dangerous, safe, important, good, bad, and so on. These assumptions become organized into sets of highly structured, complex, and interacting values, expectations, and images of self that are closely related to emotional states and feelings. These psychological structures shape, and in turn are shaped by, a person's perceptions and behaviors.

Clients' interpretations of events determine subsequent behaviors and feelings, as well as their willingness to work on certain topics in a helping setting. For example, John, an 18-year-old male client, is reluctant to learn to drive. If he believes his reluctance to drive is due to fears about having a major accident, John might say fear is the main problem. If John believes the fear is due to a reluctance to grow up and become independent, he might feel more of a need to work on separation issues. Helpers need to learn how clients currently construe events (both consciously and unconsciously) so they can help them develop more adaptive constructs.

It is usually best to attain insight before moving on to action. If clients did whatever helpers told them to do, with no understanding of or explanation for why these actions were important, they would not have a framework to guide their behavior when new problems develop. Clients would be dependent on others to tell them what to do as each new problem arose. In contrast, if clients are taught how to work with their problems, they are more likely in the future to explore their problems, achieve understanding, and decide what they would like to do differently on their own. In effect, helpers are teaching clients a problem-solving approach. In the example of the reluctant driver, if John comes to understand his reluctance is due to anxiety and guilt about leaving his sick mother, he can make an informed decision that fits his values about what he wants to do about his mother. Hence, insight is especially important in the helping process.

FOSTERING BETTER INTERPERSONAL INTERACTIONS

Another specific goal of the insight stage is for clients to gain awareness and insight into their interpersonal interactions. Clients are often unaware how they come across to others; therefore, one goal of helping is to provide them with feedback about how they come across in the helping relationship. The assumption is that they act toward others in similar ways as toward the helper, so looking closely at the therapy relationships provides a microcosm of their interpersonal relationships. Of course, clients do not behave exactly the same with everybody as they do with helpers, and helpers' countertransference influences the relationship, but observations of the therapy relationship provide an opportunity to work on one immediate relationship. Helpers can then work with clients in the action stage to generalize learning to other relationships.

Use of the Helper's Perspective

In comparison with the exploration stage, helpers in the insight stage rely somewhat more on their own perspectives and reactions to help clients understand where they are getting stuck and what might be motivating them. Thus, helpers move somewhat away from being immersed in client experiences to a more impartial stance of trying to help clients understand the issues that prevent them from full functioning.

I emphasize that helpers do not have "the" insight or right perspective and should not force clients to accept their perspectives. Rather, helpers primarily try to encourage clients to discover new things about themselves and occasionally offer their own perspectives to help clients come to new awarenesses and insights. There remains a sense of working together, with helpers aiding clients in discovering things about themselves. The goal is for clients to have a sense of discovery of the new understandings. Even when helpers suggest insights, clients need to try them on and discover if they fit rather than accepting them blindly. Understanding what is going on inside oneself is an "aha" experience that is invaluable, but it must be discovered and experienced by the client to be truly beneficial.

Helpers have to be careful when using their own perspective to make sure they are motivated by the best interests of the clients rather than by their own needs. When helpers are motivated by their own needs (i.e., countertransference), their interventions tend to be less helpful. Helpers need to be aware of their countertransference reactions so they do not inappropriately act on them in sessions.

Helpers also have to be prepared for clients' rejections of their challenges or interpretations. Sometimes these skills are used prematurely or are inaccurate or inappropriate, some are done insensitively, and sometimes clients become defensive and anxious. Helpers need to pay attention to these reactions to see how they can intervene differently with the client.

Skills Used in the Insight Stage

Probably the most important and frequently used helper skill in the insight stage is open questions. Open questions can be used two primary ways. First, this skill is used to stimulate the client's thinking about awarenesses and insights. Rather than providing a challenge or interpretation, the helper asks the client to challenge or interpret for him- or herself (e.g., "I wonder what might be going on right now?" "I wonder what you make of your behavior?" "What do you suppose is the meaning of that behavior?"). Guiding the client in a gentle and nonjudgmental manner to observe him- or herself and think about behaviors can be very empowering. A second use of open questions is to discern the client's reactions to the helper's provision of challenge, interpretation, self-disclosure, immediacy, or paradoxical interpretation (e.g., "How does that fit for you?" "What reaction do you have to that?"). Because the helper does not want to push anything on the client, it is important to check out the client's reaction and modify subsequent interventions to fit the client's needs.

The skills primarily associated with the insight stage are challenge, interpretation, self-disclosure for insight, and immediacy. Helpers use challenge to stimulate the client to think about the meaning of their behaviors, interpretation to offer suggestions about meanings, self-disclosures of insight to challenge clients or to help clients gain insights through example and modeling, and immediacy to help clients gain insight into relationship problems.

Although fundamental to the insight stage, these insight skills are used infrequently and after careful preparation. These skills all present more of the helper's perspective and must be presented cautiously, with great attention to remaining empathic and collaborative.

The skills unique to the insight stage are harder to learn and use than the skills in the exploration stage. I do not expect students to master the insight skills quickly in their initial exposure to the model. In fact, it takes most students many years and much practice to learn the insight skills and apply them in the appropriate situations in a helping setting.

The other exploration skills (attending and listening, restatement, reflection of feelings, and silence) are frequently used in the insight stage. Once the helper has presented a challenge, interpretation, self-disclosure, or immediacy, the client is at a new level, and the helper has to facilitate the client in exploring thoughts and feelings.

WHAT DO YOU THINK?

- What is the role of insight in your life? Describe several situations in which you naturally sought out (or avoided) insight.
- Describe your thoughts about whether insight is necessary before action.
- Describe your thoughts about how much interpretive input the helper should provide and how it should be done.
- Compare and contrast psychoanalytic theory with Rogers's client-centered theory. Which theory makes most sense to you personally in terms of the personality development and therapy?
- Which defense mechanisms do you use most often in your life?

Challenge 13

And the trouble is, if you don't risk anything, you risk even more.

—*Erica Jong*

Ethan says he wants to go to graduate school, but then he doesn't study and so ends up with bad grades. The helper challenges Ethan by saying, "You say you want to go to graduate school, but then you don't study. I wonder what's going on for you?" This challenge was presented in a gentle, nonthreatening manner and followed by an open question that checked out his reactions. It raised Ethan's awareness about his behaviors and encouraged him to think more about his commitment to attending graduate school. Ethan realized he was not ready for graduate school and began pondering why he might be sabotaging himself.

Challenges point out discrepancies or contradictions of which the client is unaware or unwilling to change (see Exhibit 13.1). Discrepancies and contradictions are important because they are often signs of unresolved issues, ambivalence, suppressed feelings, or repressed feelings. Often these discrepancies come up because clients have not been able to deal effectively with feelings as they arise. With challenges, helpers juxtapose two things to make the client aware of the contradiction between them, thus paving the way to understanding the cause of the discrepancy. Challenges are invitations to clients to become aware of their maladaptive issues, thoughts, feelings, and behaviors.

The helper can focus on several types of discrepancies:

Web Forms referred to in text can be found on the book's companion online guide described in the Preface.

EXHIBIT 13.1

Overview of Challenge

Definition	A *challenge* points out discrepancies or irrational beliefs of which the client is unaware, unwilling, or unable to change.
Example	"You're feeling sad that your husband died, but I wonder if you're also angry at him for leaving you."
Typical helper intentions	To challenge, to identify maladaptive behaviors, to identify maladaptive cognitions, to identify and intensify feelings, to deal with resistance, to promote insight (see Web Form D)
Possible client reactions	Challenged, unstuck, negative thoughts and feelings, clear, feelings, responsibility, new perspective, scared, worse, stuck, confused, misunderstood (see Web Form G)
Desired client behaviors	Cognitive–behavioral exploration, affective exploration, insight (see Web Form H)
Potential difficulties	Fear of offending clients Fear of being intrusive Being too invested in challenging Unconsciously using challenges to be mean or hurtful Minimizing painful feelings Using challenges in a culturally inappropriate manner

---

- Between two verbal statements (e.g., "You say there's no problem, but then you say you're annoyed with him.")
- Between words and actions (e.g., "You say you want to get good grades, but you spend most of your time partying and sleeping.")
- Between two behaviors (e.g., "You're smiling, but your teeth are clenched.")
- Between two feelings (e.g., "You feel angry at your sister, but you also feel pleased that now everyone will see what kind of person she really is.")
- Between values and behaviors (e.g., "You say you believe in respecting others' choices, but then you try to convince them that they are wrong about abortion.")
- Between one's self and experience (e.g., "You say no one likes you, but earlier you described an instance where someone invited you to have lunch.")
- Between one's ideal and real self (e.g., "You say you want to achieve, but you also say you can't.")
- Between the helper's and the client's opinions (e.g., "You say you are not working hard, but I think you are doing a great job.")

A number of studies show that challenges or confrontations are used infrequently, accounting for about 1% to 5% of all therapist statements (Barkham & Shapiro, 1986; Hill, Helms, Tichenor, et al., 1988). Furthermore, Hill, Helms, Tichenor, et al. found that clients and therapists rated confrontations as moderately helpful but that clients had negative reactions to confrontations (i.e., felt scared, worse, stuck, confused, or misunderstood; lacked direction). They also found that clients did not explore their feelings after hearing confrontations and that therapists viewed sessions in which they did a lot of confrontations as not very smooth or satisfactory. Other studies indicate that confrontations are powerful, arousing interventions that can lead to defensiveness and resistance (W. R. Miller, Benefield, & Tonigan, 1993; Olson & Claiborn, 1990; Salerno, Farber, McCullough, Winston, & Trujillo, 1992). These studies suggest that challenges can be helpful in pointing out contradictions but need to done carefully and empathically so clients can hear and use them.

The term *challenge* is used in this book instead of the more typical term *confrontation* because challenge conveys less of a confrontational or aggressive manner. However, I use the two terms somewhat interchangeably in the discussion.

Why Use Challenges?

Challenges can be useful to help clients recognize feelings, motives, and desires of which they are not aware. If clients are angry at others but unable to admit it, they might make a lot of sarcastic comments and inadvertently wound others. In other words, their anger "leaks" out. Furthermore, clients might be invested in not being aware of their inappropriate behaviors. They may blame other people rather than take responsibility for their actions. For example, a middle-aged person might continue to blame his parents for all of his problems rather than take responsibility for them, because taking responsibility would mean he would have to give up his rage at his parents and change his unhealthy behaviors. Challenges are often needed to nudge clients out of denial, help them see their problems in a different light, and encourage them to take appropriate responsibility for their problems.

Challenges can also help clients become aware of ambivalent feelings. Most of us have ambivalent feelings but cannot allow ourselves to feel both sides of issues because of beliefs about how we "ought" to be (e.g., "Nice girls don't get angry"). Challenges can be used to unearth thoughts and feelings so clients begin to experience and take responsibility for their thoughts and feelings.

Challenges also enable clients to admit to having different or deeper feelings than they were previously able to acknowledge. For example,

Angela said over and over that everything was going well until the helper challenged her about her poor grades. This challenge encouraged Angela to think about what might be going on at a deeper level and made her realize that she was trying too hard to ignore problems. Another example involves Gianni, who indicated that his relationship with his wife was great. The helper pointed out that Gianni's wife was never home and they had not had sex for three years. This challenge invited Gianni to examine closely what was happening in his relationship with his wife.

Challenges can also be used to help clients become aware of their defenses (go back to chaps. 5 and 12 for more discussion of defenses). Most of us have defenses that are not very adaptive. Sometimes we develop defenses to protect ourselves from unreliable, punitive, or abusive parents or others, and we rigidly use these defenses later in life even when they are no longer needed. Although everyone needs defenses sometimes, our goal is to help clients become aware of their defenses and make choices about when to use them. For example, a helper might challenge a client by saying, "You say that you keep up a wall to protect yourself against everyone, but I wonder if you really need to keep it so high with people you can trust." By providing a safe place to examine defenses, helpers can work with clients to distinguish situations in which defenses are needed to protect the client and when it is safe to let go of unnecessary defenses.

Our goal as helpers is not to break down or remove all of the defenses, but to give clients the option of choosing when and how often to use defenses. Defenses exist for a reason—they help clients cope. All of us need some defenses to survive in the world. However, we need to look carefully at our reasons for maintaining defenses and determine whether they are still valid. For example, in the face of a hostile attacker, a defense of withdrawal might be appropriate, whereas withdrawal might be counterproductive in an intimate relationship. Hence, helpers work with clients to figure out how to use their defenses in a more judicious manner.

Another reason for using challenges is to help clients gain insight. Although helpers are not interpreting or providing reasons when they challenge, sometimes simply hearing a challenge leads clients to insight. For example, a helper may challenge a client by telling him that he says he wants help, but he does not disclose anything about his situation. This challenge might lead the client to realize that he is reluctant to reveal anything because he is afraid of being rejected. Without the challenge, the client might have been unaware of his reluctance.

Carkhuff and Berenson (1967), humanistic theorists, stated that the purpose of pointing out discrepancies is to help reduce ambiguities and incongruities in the client's experiencing and communication. They suggested that confrontations encourage clients to accept themselves and become fully functioning. Confronting clients with the discrepant facets of their behaviors challenges them to understand themselves more fully. "At the point of confrontation the client is pressed to consider the possibility of changing and, in order to do so, utilizing resources that he *[sic]* has not yet employed" (Carkhuff, 1969, p. 93). "The challenge in a sense creates a crisis in the client's life. The crisis poses the client with the choice between continuing in his present mode of functioning or making a commitment to attempt to achieve a higher-level, more fulfilling way of life" (Carkhuff, p. 92).

Another perspective about confrontation comes from Greenson (1967), a psychoanalyst. Greenson defined confrontation as a demonstration to the client of his or her resistance (e.g., "all the forces within the patient that oppose the procedures and processes of psychoanalytic work," p. 35). He suggested that confrontations should be delivered before interpretations because defenses first need to be confronted and brought into awareness before they can be understood. For example, he noted that before he could interpret why a client was avoiding a certain subject, he would first have to get the client to face that she or he was avoiding something. Thus, the confrontation points out that the client is resisting; the questions of how and what the client is resisting are then addressed through clarification and interpretation.

How to Challenge

A major task for helpers is presenting challenges in such a way that clients can hear them and feel supported rather than attacked. Quite unlike the exploration skills that convey acceptance, challenges can imply criticism if done improperly. With challenges, helpers indicate that some aspect of a client's life is incongruent or problematic and imply that a client should change to feel, think, or act differently. I suggest helpers use challenges carefully because they have the potential for upsetting clients. Although it is sometimes important to confront clients' current ways of thinking, challenges should be done carefully, gently, respectfully, tentatively, thoughtfully, and with empathy.

Challenging someone's inconsistencies can be threatening and should be undertaken with caution. One might think of the client as building a wall around him- or herself. Rather than attacking the wall directly with major weapons or armaments, the helper might do better to point out the wall. When the client is aware of the wall, the helper and client together can try to understand the purpose for the wall and decide whether the wall is needed. Rather than battering down the wall, the helper might encourage the client to build a door in the wall and learn when to open and close that door.

Helpers can use the following steps to provide challenges to clients:

STEP 1: SET THE STAGE FOR CHALLENGE

Spending sufficient time in the exploration stage is important for two reasons. First, it allows the helper to establish a relationship with the client. Once they have a good relationship, it is easier for the client to hear a challenge. The client is more likely to feel that the helper is using challenges to facilitate the client than for other, less therapeutic reasons. Helpers need to assess whether the therapeutic relationship is strong enough to withstand challenges. Does the client feel safe? Does the client trust the helper? Has there been enough exploration? Has rapport been established adequately? Challenges are most effective in the context of a caring and respectful therapeutic relationship.

A second reason for taking adequate time is so the helper can observe the client. Helpers formulate challenges of discrepancies or contradictions from their observations of inconsistencies in clients, so they must be alert for inconsistencies and trust their observations. Before challenging, helpers need to collect an adequate amount of evidence to clarify what is going on rather than jumping hastily to conclusions.

STEP 2: LOOK FOR MARKERS THAT INDICATE CHALLENGES WOULD BE APPROPRIATE

Helpers can look for specific markers that indicate readiness for receiving challenges. These markers include expressions of ambivalence, contradictions, discrepancies, or confusion or feeling stuck or unable to make a decision. Helpers can observe and listen to clients carefully for "sour notes"—things that do not sound right, make sense, fit or go together, or things that are done out of "shoulds," cause ambivalences, or result in struggles. These sour notes can point the way to issues about which clients feel contradictions and uncertainties. These markers suggest that clients are ready to allow the problem to "come into awareness."

I also recommend that helpers think about why the client might feel confused or stuck. Rather than blaming or condemning the client, the helper tries to understand the client's dynamics. The empathy generated through this process can help the helper become curious about checking out the hypotheses rather than becoming invested in pointing out a discrepancy or trying to make the client change.

STEP 3: DETERMINE INTENTIONS

Helpers need to think carefully about why they would challenge. What do they want to accomplish? Are the goals to raise awareness; identify maladaptive feelings, thoughts, and behaviors; deal with resistance; or promote insight? These are appropriate goals.

However, helpers need to make sure they are not challenging to meet their own needs (e.g., to appear brilliant, to feel superior to the client). They need to evaluate whether any of their personal issues might be influencing their desire to challenge the client. For example, a helper who is irritated by passivity in a partner might be especially challenging of clients who become passive. A helper who has just gotten divorced might view all relationships as destructive, so he or she may challenge all clients about why they are staying married. In these examples, the problem really belongs to the helper, not the client.

Helpers also need to think about whether challenges are appropriate for the particular client. Direct, blunt challenges are not likely to be appropriate with Asian, Latino–Latina, and indigenous American clients (Ivey, 1994) because they are not culturally appropriate. Ivey presented the example of a Chinese counselor's first efforts to counsel in China after training in the United States. He confronted an older Chinese man using the standard format for challenges: "On the one hand you do X, but on the other hand you do Y; how do you put these two together?" The older man politely said his farewell and never came back. The counselor had forgotten that when Chinese people see the need to express disagreement, they generally take great care not to hurt the other person's feelings or cause the other person to "lose face." His direct confrontive technique was considered ill-mannered and insensitive, especially because it came from a younger person. Ivey suggested that it is not impossible to confront a Chinese person, but that one needs to be sensitive and gentle.

On the other hand, direct (but still empathic and respectful) confrontation may be more appropriate with some male European American or African American clients who find the soft and gentle approach meaningless and who may even denigrate the helper for using it. Ivey (1994) stressed the need for flexibility and responsiveness to each person.

Furthermore, the need for challenges varies on the basis of where the client is in the change process. Clients who are at precontemplation and contemplation stages of change (see the discussion in chap. 3) are more likely to need challenges to jolt them out of their complacency and encourage them to change (Prochaska, DiClemente, & Norcross, 1992). Clients in the later stages of the helping process (e.g., action, termination, and maintenance) are less likely to require challenges to get them past defenses and barriers to changing.

STEP 4: PRESENT THE CHALLENGE

When learning to challenge discrepancies, I recommend that helpers use the following formats to make sure they include both parts of the intervention:

- On the one hand _____, but on the other hand _____.
- You say _____, but you also say _____.
- You say _____, but nonverbally you seem _____.
- I'm hearing _____, but I'm also hearing _____.

Sometimes the first part of the discrepancy is implied, and the helper states only the "but" clause. For example, the client might say that there are no problems, and the helper might respond, "But you said he was angry at you" (implying "You just said there were no problems, but . . . "). Or the helper might challenge by simply saying, "really?" "oh yeah?" or "hmmm?" which questions the client in a challenging manner and indicates the helper does not completely believe the client.

Challenges should be used as soon as possible after an example of the client's inconsistent behaviors. If a helper waits too long, the client might not remember what the helper is talking about. For instance, if the helper says, "Last session when you spoke about your mother, you smiled in a strange way," the client is not likely to remember the incident. Thus, helpers should act fairly quickly (if they have enough data), while the behaviors and feelings are still recent.

Challenges should be delivered gently and respectfully. The helper's manner should be one of puzzlement rather than hostility, of trying to help the client figure out a puzzle and make sense of discrepant pieces. One can simply point out the discrepancy in a nonthreatening manner and ask the client to clarify. Similarly, Lauver and Harvey (1997) suggested using "collegial confrontations," which point out the helper's confusion about what he or she perceives as discrepant; they recommend against trying to persuade the client to come around to the helper's viewpoint. In essence, helpers empathically point out discrepancies and then follow these challenges with reflections of feelings and open questions about how it felt to be challenged.

Furthermore, it is important that helpers not make judgments when they challenge. A challenge should not be a criticism, but an encouragement to examine oneself more deeply. The goal is to work collaboratively with clients in raising awareness. If helpers are judgmental, clients may feel shamed and embarrassed and hence be more resistant to recognizing problems. Helpers need to remember that all of us have discrepancies and irrationalities and that we are not "better than" our clients. We need to be humble and empathize with how difficult it is to understand ourselves and make necessary changes. It is usually easier to see someone else's inconsistencies than it is to see our own.

Sometimes challenges can be softened by using humor, as long as the client feels that the helper is "laughing with" rather than "laughing at" him or her. Helping clients laugh at themselves can help them think about their problems in a different way. An example from Falk and Hill's (1992) study of the effects of therapist humor involved a case in which the client had just described how her daughter, an honor student at a prestigious college, had belittled her A average at a community college. The therapist said, "It's not quite so often that I've run into a daughter's being so overtly competitive with her mother. Not that competition between mothers and daughters isn't a hallmark of our society for heaven's sake, but it's usually masked or disguised or, you know, somewhat less overt." The client responded to this statement with laughter and it helped relieve some of the tension that she was feeling.

In another example from the Falk and Hill study, a helper and client were dealing with issues related to control and perfectionism in the client's life, particularly in regard to eating and schoolwork. The client excitedly described her weekend in which she contacted several friends, coordinated their activities, and eagerly took on the role of the designated driver. She exclaimed, "I had so much fun." The helper commented, "and so much control." They both laughed, and the client began to talk about how her need for control pervaded many aspects of her life.

If clients can start laughing, they can begin to see things in a different light. Of course, as with other types of challenges, helpers need to have established a relationship with clients and use the humor to raise awareness rather than to make fun of the client.

A final issue regards the timing of challenges. If you think your challenge was accurate but your client denies or dismisses it, you may need to back off until the client can handle the challenge or until you have more evidence for your observations. For example, you may experience a client as being extremely hostile and pushy with you although he perceives himself as being friendly and accommodating. Your first challenge, "You say you're easygoing, but you sound like you act somewhat aggressively with your friends," might be negated by the client ("Nah, they all love me"). You might want to obtain more examples from the client about how he behaves with friends, or you may want to ask the client to observe his own behavior or ask his friends for feedback. Despite his reaction, you can trust your impression that this client was aggressive with you (although of course you need to search yourself for countertransference issues). In time, you might present another challenge with more specific behavioral evidence. ("You say you are never hostile, but you sounded like you were hostile in your interaction with your friend yesterday. From what you said, you completely disagreed with everything your friend said and refused to talk about it. I wonder what your experience was?")

STEP 5: OBSERVE THE CLIENT'S REACTIONS

Because challenges can have such a strong impact on clients, helpers need to observe clients' reactions carefully. They need to listen attentively and observe the client's nonverbal behavior. Helpers need to remember the research cited in chapter 3 that suggested clients often hide negative reactions. Thus, helpers should not expect that they necessarily know when clients feel badly after a challenge. Clients could withdraw, and helpers would not know that they were upset. Hence, helpers often have to ask clients how they reacted to challenges and probe beneath the surface to understand the complete reaction. In addition, helpers need to remember to reflect feelings to encourage clients to talk about their reactions to challenges.

From observing the client's reactions, a helper can make more informed decisions about how to proceed:

- If clients respond to challenges with denial, helpers need to rethink how they are presenting the challenges, whether clients are ready to hear them, or whether a challenge was the right intervention.
- If clients say they have no reaction to the challenge, helpers might wonder whether they presented the challenges effectively, whether they were accurate, or whether the clients were defensive.
- If clients respond with partial examination or acceptance and recognition but no change, helpers can continue to confront gently to help clients move further. Helpers also can reflect how scary it is to change and help clients in exploring their fears.
- If clients respond with new awareness and acceptance, helpers can move on to interpretation.

Helpers should not be surprised when clients react strongly to challenges. Instead, they should help clients express and work through their emotions.

STEP 6: FOLLOW THROUGH

Helpers may need to repeat challenges several times, in different ways, and apply them to different situations, so clients can hear the challenge and think about the issue in different ways. It is often difficult for clients to hear a challenge the first time because it is threatening, no matter how gently it is done. Helpers might have to persist and gently present the challenge several times until the client is ready and able to hear the challenge.

AN EXAMPLE OF CHALLENGES

Client: My husband wants his parents to come and live with us. His father has Alzheimer's, and his mother takes care of his father, but she can't drive and is not feeling too well herself. They are both pretty old and need more help.

Helper: How do you feel about them moving in with you?

Client: Well, I think they need to do something. The situation is not improving, and they are getting old. My husband really wants to take care of them. He feels some obligation since he's the oldest child.

Helper: (gently) *I hear that your husband wants to take care of them, but I am not hearing how you feel about it.*

Client: I have been brought up to believe that family takes care of family when they need help. I didn't take care of my parents, so I feel like we should do what we can to help them if they want it. They may not even want to move in. They might rather do something else.

Helper: *I'm struck by how hard it is for you to talk about your feelings.*

Client: That's interesting. You're really right. I feel like I don't have a right to my feelings. I feel like it's something I "should" do. I don't have any choice, so I'm trying not to have any feelings. If I'm really honest with myself, I'm terrified of what it will be like if they move in. His mother can be very critical.

Helper: You sound upset.

Client: Yeah, but it makes me feel guilty. I just don't know what to do. I guess I've always had a hard time standing up to his parents. Actually, I have a hard time standing up to most people, so this is just another example. I think it stems from my childhood. (Client continues to talk.)

Effects of Challenge

Helpers can observe their sessions and use the following three-point scale to evaluate the effects of their challenges on clients:

1 = If challenges are very ineffective, clients might deny them (e.g., "I'm not angry about the divorce"), get upset with the helper (e.g., yell at the helper), or quit.

2 = If challenges are at least neutral, clients might accept and recognize the issue but not make any changes (e.g., "I guess I have mixed feelings about getting a divorce"). Alternatively, clients

might partially examine what the helper has said but not consider the challenge fully or experience it emotionally (e.g., "Yes, I'm hurt and perhaps I should be angry, but I'm not").

3 = If challenges are very effective, clients accept them and develop new, larger, and more inclusive constructs, patterns, or behaviors (e.g., "You've helped me see that mixed feelings and thoughts are part of every relationship. I need to express my feelings. Maybe if I had expressed them before, I wouldn't be facing divorce now. I'm going to call my wife and see if we can develop a new way of thinking about the relationship").

Difficulties Helpers Experience Using Challenge

Challenge is a difficult intervention for many beginning helpers. One set of difficulties relates to helpers not doing enough challenges. Many beginning helpers use too few challenges because they are afraid of being intrusive, forcing clients to examine their "dirty laundry," offending clients, sounding accusatory or blaming, destroying the therapeutic relationship, or causing clients to feel unsupported. Furthermore, confronting people is not considered polite in some cultures, and helpers from such cultures may feel reluctant to use challenges. However, if clients are being contradictory or confusing or are stuck, they often cannot clarify their thinking without outside feedback. In fact, if done appropriately, challenges can be a gift that lets the client know the helper is willing to say unpleasant things that others may not say (e.g., "You say you want to have friends, but you criticize everything anyone does").

Another set of difficulties involves using challenges inappropriately. Some helpers who feel afraid of negative feelings might use challenges to deny or minimize negative feelings. For example, if a client talks about suicidal feelings, a helper might use a challenge that indicates that the client has a lot to live for and should not be thinking about suicide. A statement that a client has a lot to live for might sound like the helper is pointing out strengths, but in this situation the helper is minimizing the negative feelings and falsely reassuring the client so he or she does not have to deal with the suicidal feelings.

A third set of difficulties involves using too many challenges or using challenges too harshly. Some helpers become too invested in having clients recognize their discrepancies. They might argue with clients to convince them of their observations. Or they become like detectives who present the evidence and want to force clients to admit their problems and confess that they are not being consistent. These helpers are like lawyers cross-examining witnesses in the courtroom; they seem eager to "catch" clients in their discrepancies. Some helpers use challenge as an opportunity to get back at clients they do not like or who upset them in some way. Needless to say, such challenges can make clients feel unsupported and confronted.

Finally, helpers often have trouble knowing how to respond when clients disagree with challenges and in effect challenge the helper in return. For example, the helper might say it seems like the client is coming across hostilely or seductively, and the client might deny it and say it is the helper's problem. Some helpers do not know whether to keep trying to get clients to see the evidence or whether to give up and try again later after they have more data to support the challenge. Helpers may even begin to distrust their perceptions when clients challenge them. At times, helpers might be wrong because they misperceived the situation due to their own issues or insufficient data. At other times, however, clients might be defensive, unwilling to examine themselves, or have a hard time acknowledging their behaviors. Having supervisors listen to tapes of sessions and provide feedback to the helper is useful for helpers to determine whether they were distorting because of their own needs or whether the challenge was accurate but presented in a nontherapeutic manner. Showing a videotape of the session to the client can also provide a powerful self-confrontation if the client is not aware of his or her behavior.

HELPFUL HINTS

- Be warm and empathic in challenging. Remember that you are offering your perception rather than providing the "truth."
- Use nonabrasive words and state the challenge as a hunch rather than an accusation.
- Don't make judgments or interpretations when you challenge.
- Be curious and collaborative in working with clients to become aware of their issues.
- Do not be aggressive or blaming with your challenge. Do not play a game of "Gotcha" or try to score points by pointing out the client's inconsistencies. Be careful not to come across as a trial lawyer trying to pin the blame on the client.
- Consider culture when giving challenges. If someone is from a different culture, be sensitive that the person might have different reactions than you to being challenged. Be alert to the client's reactions to challenges and talk about them.
- Use specific examples as evidence for the challenge (e.g., "When you said you were happy, you frowned") rather than being general or global in your statement (e.g., "You always seem so cheerful").

A specific behavioral example is easier to respond to than a global characterization.

■ It is better to give an example of something that just happened than to give a distant example that the client is not likely to remember.

■ Make sure the challenge is not for your needs (e.g., to appear insightful, to retaliate, or to elevate yourself in comparison with the client).

■ Do not apologize before delivering the challenge or minimize its value (e.g., "I'm sorry to do this, but . . .," "I'm not sure I'm doing this right, but . . . ," "Please don't get angry at me for saying this, but . . . "). When helpers couch what they say or apologize too much or too profusely, it can make the client doubt its value and dismiss it.

■ Watch carefully for the client's reactions to the challenge. Ask how he or she feels about the challenge. Keep the lines of communication open.

■ If the client is upset by the challenge or you feel you have blundered badly, apologize and ask how the client is feeling. Avoid apologizing too much or too often, however, because it gives an unprofessional appearance and takes the focus off the client.

■ Leave enough time after a challenge to talk about it and to help the client learn from it. It takes time to process the challenge.

■ Do not use too many challenges in any one session because they can create a negative, abrasive tone.

■ Follow challenges with reflections of feelings and open questions about feelings. When clients have come to a new awareness about their thoughts, behaviors, or feelings, you might go on to interpretation to investigate the reason for them.

PRACTICE EXERCISES

Read each of the following examples and write a challenge you might use if you were a helper with the client.

Statements

1. Client: "My family is really important to me. They mean more to me than anyone else in the world. I think about them a lot. I go home about once a year, and I call them every month or so when I'm running out of money."
    Helper response: You say _____ ,
    but you _____ .

2. Client: "I really want to go to graduate school, but I have lots of things going on right now, and I just want time for myself to travel and play. I don't think I want to study as much as I know I would have to in graduate school, but I do want to be able to get a good job as a psychologist so that I can do therapy with kids."
   Helper response: You say _____ ,
   but you _____ .

3. Client: "My parents are very religious. They tell me I have to go to church every Sunday as long as I'm living at home. I know I have to do it to please them, but I feel so confused about the whole topic. I don't know what I believe, and nothing makes sense. I feel like I'm going through the motions. I feel guilty even talking about this though, because they would be so upset that I don't agree with everything they say."
   Helper response: You say _____ ,
   but you _____ .

4. Client: "The guy I was going with said that he wants us to just be friends. He asked me to go to California with him on a big trip but just as friends. I don't know if I should go. I still like him a lot. Maybe if I went, he would start liking me again. I don't know what I did that made him quit liking me."
   Helper response: You say _____ ,
   but you _____ .

Possible Helper Responses

1. "You say your family is important to you, but you don't call them."
   "You told me your family is important to you, but you seem to talk to them only when you want money."

2. "You want the things that come from having a graduate degree, but you aren't so sure you want to do what it takes to get the degree."
   "You say you want to get a graduate degree, but your voice doesn't sound very enthusiastic as you talk."

3. "You want to please your parents, but you also really want to figure out for yourself what you believe."
   "You feel guilty that you might believe something that your parents don't, but perhaps you also feel angry that they don't allow you to have your own feelings."

4. "You want to go, but you're not sure if you should."
   "You are really upset that this guy doesn't want to be romantically involved anymore, but you think you can get him to change his mind."

WHAT DO YOU THINK?

- Are challenges necessary and helpful?
- Compare and contrast the effects of challenges and reflections of feelings.
- How can helpers maintain an attitude of curiosity and compassion for clients with their challenges rather than attacking them and getting invested in confronting clients?
- What types of helpers might be likely to use challenges inappropriately?
- Discuss cultural differences in using and reacting to challenges.

LAB 9

Challenge

Goals: For helpers to continue practicing exploration skills (reflection, restatement, and open questions) and then to challenge once they have established a supportive relationship and identified discrepancies.
In groups of four to six, one person will be the client and another the initial helper. The rest should be ready to take over as helper or give backup to the helper. Everyone will take turns being the client. Each group should have a designated lab leader (other than the helper) to organize and coordinate the session.

Helper's and Client's Tasks During the Helping Interchange

1. The client talks about something that he or she feels conflicted or confused about (e.g., future career choices, lifestyle issues). The client should plan on being at least moderately disclosing, although clients always have the right not to disclose when they are uncomfortable doing so.
2. The initial helper starts by using exploration skills to help the client explore. If one helper gets stuck, another helper can take over to facilitate a thorough exploration.
3. After several minutes of exploration, the group leader stops the helper and asks each person in the group to try a reflection of feelings (quite often students have forgotten to do reflections of feeling, and this is an excellent opportunity to affirm the importance of this intervention). The client should respond to each person.
4. The group leader then asks each person (except the client) to write down a challenge. Helpers can ask themselves whether they hear any "sour notes," discrepancies, or defenses. Once all helpers have written challenges, they take turns delivering their challenges to the client, who responds briefly to each challenge.

Processing the Helping Interchange

After everyone has had a turn and the client has responded, the client can talk about which challenges were most helpful and why. Clients should be as open and honest as possible so helpers can learn what they did well and what they did not do so well.

SWITCH ROLES SO THAT TWO TO THREE PEOPLE GET A CHANCE TO BE THE CLIENT

Personal Reflections

▪ What issues did using challenges raise for you?
▪ What are your strengths and weaknesses in terms of using challenges?
▪ How can you deliver challenges that clients can hear and absorb without being too aggressive or too passive?
▪ Describe what your intentions were for challenging and whether your clients reacted as you hoped.
▪ What role did your culture play in your giving or receiving challenges?

Interpretation 14

Men go abroad to wonder at the heights of mountains, at the
huge waves of the sea, at the long courses of the rivers, at the
vast compass of the ocean, at the circular motions of the
stars; and they pass by themselves without wondering.

—St. Augustine

J im told his helper that he was feeling depressed and aimless. He felt
that nothing made sense and that he had no purpose in life. He also
talked extensively about how his parents were anxious about him
taking risks since his older brother had died in a motorcycle accident.
With this and other information the helper had learned about Jim
through several sessions, the helper said, "I wonder whether your lack
of purpose in life is because you are still grieving the loss of your
brother and you haven't been able to make your own decisions and
figure out who you are as a person." This interpretation helped Jim
make sense of his depression and aimlessness. After continuing to talk
with the helper and trying to understand what was going on inside
himself, Jim was able to see his life in a new perspective and to think
about how he wanted to be.

Interpretations are interventions that go beyond what a client has
overtly stated or recognized and present a new meaning, reason, or explanation for behaviors, thoughts, or feelings so clients can see problems
in a new way (see Exhibit 14.1). Interpretations can

- Make connections between seemingly isolated statements or events
  (e.g., "Could your anger at your husband right now be connected
  to your grief over your mother's death?")
- Point out themes or patterns in a client's behaviors, thoughts, or
  feelings (e.g.,"It seems that you get fired from every job after about

Web Forms referred to in text can be found on the book's companion online guide described in the Preface.

245

EXHIBIT 14.1

Overview of Interpretation

Definition

An *interpretation* is a statement that goes beyond what the client has overtly stated or recognized and gives a new meaning, reason, or explanation for behaviors, thoughts, or feelings so the client can see problems in a new way. There are four types: (a) makes connections between seemingly isolated statements or events; (b) points out themes or patterns in a client's behaviors, thoughts, or feelings; (c) explicates defenses, resistances, or transferences; or (d) offers a new framework to understand behaviors, thoughts, feelings, or problems.

Examples

Client: "My mother keeps nagging me about keeping my room clean and doing my school work. I don't know why, but I just don't feel like doing either."
Helper: "Maybe you don't want to clean your room or do your work because you're angry with your mother."

Client: "Suzie killed herself a few days ago, but I haven't been thinking about it much. I have been really angry at my boss for making me work overtime. Plus my roommate is driving me crazy. My parents keep calling to find out how I'm doing. I feel so angry I could scream."
Helper: "Ever since your friend committed suicide, you have been on edge and having a hard time coping. I wonder if you feel responsible for her death?"

Client: "You act like you think you know everything about me, but you don't know anything."
Helper: "I wonder if I remind you of your father. You said he acts like he knows everything."

Client: "I just can't stand it anymore. My mother will never let up. She just doesn't trust me."
Helper: "Perhaps you're trying to get her to distrust you so you can get angry and leave. Otherwise it might be too hard to leave since she's alone."

Typical helper intentions

To promote insight, to identify and intensify feelings, to encourage self-control (see Web Form D)

Possible client reactions

Better self-understanding, new perspective, clear, relief, negative thoughts or feelings,

	responsibility, unstuck, scared, worse, stuck, lack of direction, confused, misunderstood (see Web Form G)
Desired client behaviors	Insight, cognitive–behavioral exploration, affective exploration (see Web Form H)
Potential difficulties	Not giving enough interpretations for fear of being wrong, premature, intruding on the client, or offending the client
	Need to appear insightful
	Thinking they know more than clients about the clients
	Not carefully observing client reactions
	Not working collaboratively with clients to construct the interpretations
	Delivering interpretations before clients are ready
	Providing interpretations that are too lengthy
	Providing too many interpretations in a single session

six months. I wonder if somehow your fear of success makes it difficult for you to keep a job longer.")

▪ Explicate defenses, resistance, or transference (e.g., "I wonder if you're expecting me to respond like your father does.")

▪ Offer a new framework to understand behaviors, thoughts, feelings, or problems (e.g., "You say you were spoiled as a child, but it seems to me that you often felt abandoned and anxious as a child and that leads you to cling to other people.").

Interpretations can be delivered through direct statements (e.g., "You are worried about whether you should get married, so you are diverting your anxiety about getting married into trying to make the wedding perfect"); done tentatively (e.g., "I wonder if your fear of failure could possibly be related to feeling that you are not sure you can please your mother"); or through questions (e.g., "Do you think you distrust men because of your bad relationship with your father?"). Although the last intervention is phrased as a question, it is clearly an interpretation because the content of the question assumes a relationship that the client had not articulated and provides an explanation for the behavior (see also Exhibit 14.1).

Why Give Interpretations?

One reason for using interpretations is that the empirical literature shows them to be valuable. A number of studies show that therapists used interpretations moderately often compared with other skills (ranging from 6% to 8% of all therapist statements; Barkham & Shapiro, 1986; Hill, Helms, Tichenor, et al., 1988). Furthermore, interpretations were rated as being very helpful, helped engage clients in therapeutic work, led to high levels of client experiencing, and led clients to free associate (Colby, 1961; Hill, Helms, Tichener, et al., 1988; Spence, Dahl, & Jones, 1993). However, research on transference interpretations (interpretations about the client's distortion of the therapist based on previous significant relationships; see chap. 12) has been more mixed (see review in Crits-Christoph & Gibbons, 2002), suggesting better results when therapists craft the interpretations to the beliefs and needs of the client and use them only with more well-adjusted clients.

Interpretations can provide clients with a conceptual framework that explains their problems and offers a rationale for overcoming their concerns. Frank and Frank (1991) noted that interpretations increase clients' sense of security, mastery, and self-efficacy by providing labels for experiences that seem confusing, haphazard, or inexplicable. Frank and Frank asserted that interpretations relieve distress in part by relabeling client emotions to make them more understandable. They noted that the inexplicable loses much of its power to terrify when it is put in words. For example, if a helper interprets that Pablo's vague uneasiness at work is anger at the boss, who is a stand-in for the client's father, Pablo's uneasiness loses its power. Pablo is no longer angry at his boss and instead can work on his feelings toward his father.

From a psychoanalytic perspective (e.g., Bibring, 1954; Blanck, 1966; Freud, 1914/1953b; Fromm-Reichmann, 1950), interpretations are the "pure gold" of therapy—the central technique for producing self-knowledge and change in clients. Psychoanalytic therapists create interpretations from client material that has been repressed and is unconscious. They postulate that interpretations are effective because they stimulate insight, which can lead to more reality-oriented feelings and behavior. Interpretations are thought to work by replacing unconscious processes with conscious ones, thus enabling clients to resolve unconscious conflicts. Although the exact mechanism by which insight works is vague and needs further explication, it is clear that insight plays a central role in the therapeutic change process.

In psychoanalytic theory, the role of early childhood is very important because it serves as the template for everything that comes afterwards. Hence, early childhood experiences are often the focus of interpretive behavior, although the childhood events that are focused on varies for different theorists. For Freudians (Freud, 1940/1949), the crucial early childhood event is the Electra–Oedipal conflict, in which the child seeks to have a romantic alliance with the parent of the opposite gender and to eliminate the parent of the same gender. Erikson (1963) postulated that the important early childhood events are interpersonal relationships. For Mahler (1968), the important early childhood event involves the symbiosis with the primary caregivers in very early years and the subsequent movement toward separation and individuation. Bowlby (1969, 1988) said that attachment to the caregiver is the crucial event in childhood.

Because psychoanalytic helpers believe that early childhood relationships form the foundation for all ensuing relationships, interpreting the transference (i.e., a distortion by the client of the helper based on early childhood relationships) is one of the most important types of interpretation. The assumption is that the client re-creates the problematic early relationship patterns with the helper either as a way to confirm or reject that the helper will act in the same way as the early caregiver (Weiss, Sampson, and the Mont Zion psychotherapy research group, 1986). The client might act as he or she did as a child (the passive victim) and expect the helper to play the complementary role (the dominant or oppressive dictator). Conversely, the client might take on the role that the parent played in the relationship (the dominant one) and expect the helper to act like the child (the passive victim). The helper's reaction to the client's behavior is crucial for confirming or disconfirming the client's expectations. For example, the helper might say to Amanda, "I wonder if you get so furious at me for seeing other clients because you always felt that your mother preferred your brother to you, and you don't like to have to share me with other clients."

Although psychoanalytic theory is the basis for our thinking about using interpretations, other theoretical orientations also use interpretations but postulate different mechanisms by which they work. From an information-processing perspective, L. H. Levy (1963) suggested that interpretations reveal discrepancies between the views of the therapist and client. In other words, an interpretation makes it clear that the helper has a different perspective than the client. The helper does not "buy" the client's view about the issue and postulates a different explanation. For example, a client might explain his depression as a chemical imbalance, whereas the helper asserts that the client's depression is due to unresolved feelings about his mother's suicide and subsequent abandonment by his father. Once there is a discrepancy in views, the client either has to change in the direction of the helper's viewpoint, try to change the helper's mind, or discredit the helper. If the client resolves the discrepancy in the direction of the helper's interpretation, the client is able to reconstrue how she or he views the issue. Clients are more likely to change in the direction of the helper's interpretation if they view the helper as expert, attractive, and trustworthy (Strong & Claiborn, 1982).

Cognitive psychologists (e.g., Glass & Holyoak, 1986; Medin & Ross, 1992) also construe the effectiveness of interpretations in different terms than do psychoanalytic theorists. Cognitive theorists believe that all thoughts, feelings, sensations, memories, and actions are stored in *schemas* (defined in chap. 3 as clusters of related thoughts, feelings, actions, and images). With interpretations, helpers attempt to change the way that schemas are structured. They bring back the memories and try to come to new understandings about them on the basis of more current and complete information. In effect, the schemas are changed and restructured.

The client has a new way of thinking, which must be reinforced or else it erodes. Hence, repeated interpretations with expansions to different areas of the client's life may be necessary for the connections to be made and retained. In addition, action and behavior change may be necessary to consolidate the changes in thinking. For example, Katerina may come to realize that she is lacking in self-esteem because she felt neglected as a child. However, she needs further interpretive work to understand the influences of the childhood experiences on her current life. In addition, making changes in her behaviors (e.g., getting a new job and leaving an abusive relationship) may help her begin to think more highly of herself and may also lead her to understand why she stayed in such a bad situation for so long.

To conclude this section, I should note that there is not enough evidence to support any one of these theories over the others. In fact, interpretations could work for all three reasons. Interpretations could work because the unconscious is made conscious and more under ego control, because discrepancies between perspectives propel clients to change in the direction of resolving the discrepancy, or because interpretations cause changes in schematic connections.

Sources of Data for Developing Interpretations

There are several sources of data that helpers can use for developing interpretations: verbal content of clients' speech, past experiences, defenses, developmental stages and culture, existential concerns and culture, and unconscious activities.

VERBAL CONTENT OF CLIENTS' SPEECH

A rich source of data for developing interpretations is in the content of what clients talk about. Given that people often compartmentalize things, listening carefully to what they say can reveal connections between relevant things that they had not put together. For example, if a client says she is having a hard time performing on her job and then goes on to talk about the seemingly unrelated topic of anxiety over her parents' health, the helper might connect the two if it seems probable that they are related (e.g., "Perhaps you're having a hard time concentrating because of anxiety about your parents").

PAST EXPERIENCES

In addition, helpers can speculate about how a client's behaviors might be related to how the client has interacted with significant others. When the client's responses to the helper seem distorted because of experiences with others in the past or present, helpers have material for making a transference interpretation. For example, Keisha responded with silence and tears every time her helper provided positive feedback. Silence and tears are not typical responses to positive feedback, so the helper made some guesses about what might be going on with Keisha. The helper knew about Keisha's history with her father and suggested that perhaps Keisha was afraid of what might follow positive feedback, given that her father often told her something good and then yelled at her for her mistakes. (More discussion of transference interpretations is available in several excellent texts: Basch, 1980; Freud, 1923/1961; Gelso & Carter, 1985, 1994; Greenson, 1967; Malan, 1976a, 1976b; Stadter, 1996; Strupp & Binder, 1984.)

A related way of examining transference is to look at the client's typical style of interacting and conceptualize what the client is trying to accomplish in interactions. Luborsky and Crits-Christoph (1990) described how helpers can look at these core conflictual ways of responding to others (including the helper) in terms of wishes or needs (what the client wants from others), expected responses from others, and the consequent response from the self. For example, Keisha might wish for affection and love but also to be in control. She might expect others to hurt and control her as her father did and hence feel anxious and disliked. Interpretations can thus be formulated about the development of a client's characteristic way of responding to others.

DEFENSES

Helpers can also provide interpretations based on observations of a client's defenses (e.g., "I wonder if your difficulty at work stems from your avoiding interactions with others, something you learned to do as a child to protect yourself from fears of abandonment). In the chapter on challenges, helpers were encouraged to point out defenses to raise the client's awareness of them. Now the helper can work with the client to understand the role the defenses play. People develop defenses early in life to help them cope with situations but then may fail to give up the defenses even though they are no longer needed. It is perhaps hardest to give up things that we believe protect us from harm, given that they protected us in the past. Through interpretive activity, helpers can help clients realize why they started using defenses and then make choices about the need to continue using them.

DEVELOPMENTAL STAGES AND CULTURE

An additional source of material for interpretations is the clients' life stages, within the context of their cultural referents. Are clients on or off course for mastering the developmental tasks that are important for them culturally (e.g., developing friendships, separating from parents, completing schooling, making decisions about life partners and children, developing a satisfying career, developing satisfying adult relationships, letting go of children and careers, adjusting to illnesses and dying)? Interpretations can be developed linking clients' current emotions and functioning to what they might be expected to be feeling or not feeling at this stage of life within their culture. For example, Ken, a 50-year-old White man, might feel depressed because he compares himself with other people his age who have accomplished more in their lives. He dropped out of high school to rebel against his parents, who were both physicians, and worked in construction his whole life; now he wonders if he made the right choices.

EXISTENTIAL ISSUES AND CULTURE

Helpers can also help clients understand themselves in terms of existential concerns. Yalom (1980) provided an excellent description of what he considered to be four universal existential concerns. First, he postulated that all people struggle with death anxiety. The fact that everyone dies at some point means we have to come to terms with the reality that we are not immortal. Particularly at times when one is ill or has been in an accident or attacked or a significant other is ill or has recently been hurt or died, people feel vulnerable and attuned to loss and death. A second existential issue is freedom, which refers to the lack of external structure and the need to take responsibility for one's destiny. The third issue is isolation, both from others and the world. Each of us enters and exits the world alone; therefore, we must come to terms with our isolation in contrast to our wish to be part of a larger whole, to be taken care of and protected. The fourth existential concern is the meaning of life. We must all construct our own life meanings, given that there is no predetermined path.

Note that culture plays a role in existential concerns, particularly in terms of religious beliefs. A person who believes in life after death experiences death anxiety differently than someone who does not believe in life after death. By listening carefully to what clients say and asking them about relevant cultural beliefs, helpers can often hear underlying existential concerns and then assist clients, via interpretation, to understand these critical issues.

UNCONSCIOUS SOURCES

Interpretations can be developed through indications of unconscious activities, most typically observable through dreams, fantasies, and slips of the tongue. Psychoanalytic theorists have long postulated that important unconscious material can be detected by looking at these manifestations. For more detail on how helpers can work with dreams, I refer readers to companion texts that also use the three-stage model (Hill, 1996, 2003).

Accuracy of Interpretations

For psychoanalytic theorists, the accuracy of the helper's interpretation is important. The client and helper are on an "archeological dig" to uncover what actually happened in the client's past and understand how these events affect the client's current behavior. Of course, psychoanalytic therapists emphasize that what they hear in therapy is the client's perceptions about the events rather than actual events; thus, accuracy can never be determined.

Reid and Finesinger (1952) suggested that insight must merely be believed or make sense to have a therapeutic effect. They thought that the psychological relevance of the interpretation to the client's problems is more important than the truth per se (i.e., does the interpretation help the client understand more about his or her problems). Similarly, Frank and Frank (1991) noted that interpretations do not have to be correct, only plausible. As an example, they cited a study by Mendel (1964) in which four clients responded with a drop in anxiety when they were offered the same series of six "all-purpose" interpretations (e.g., "You seem to live your life as though you are apologizing all the time"). I would not suggest that helpers ignore the "truth" and just have a set of standard interpretations to give clients. Quite the opposite: I believe that helpers should try as much as possible to develop interpretations that fit all of the data clients present. Helpers should remain humble, however, about how difficult it is to know all the data and to determine whether an interpretation is accurate.

Basch (1980), a psychoanalytic therapist, indicated that whether clients agree or disagree with interpretations is not a good indication of accuracy. Rather, he suggested, the criterion for accuracy should be whether clients bring up material in the next session that indicates they have gained insight into the problem. For example, if a helper interprets that Lao's fear of intimacy is based on feeling rejected by his father, the helper could conclude that the interpretation was accurate if Lao brings in additional memories of his father being distant and rejecting. I would disagree somewhat with Basch, however, because there is potential for clients to bring in (and even make up) memories to please helpers. Helpers can never really determine the accuracy of interpretations because we cannot observe what actually happened in the past. In addition, we know that events are not just facts, but also involve people's recall of them. We know that people perceive events idiosyncratically and then distort memories of events over time (Glass & Holyoak, 1986; Loftus, 1988). Research shows that people can "remember" events that never happened (Brainerd & Reyna, 1998), so helpers need to be careful not to try to persuade clients to have certain memories (e.g., repressed memories about childhood sexual abuse).

Frank and Frank (1991) noted that the client is the ultimate judge of the truth of the interpretation. They suggested that the helper's power to present an interpretation that is accepted by the client as valid depends on several factors:

- Whether the interpretation makes sense out of all the material the client has offered;
- The manner in which the interpretation is offered: Interpretations must be presented in ways that catch and hold the client's attention, such as with vivid imagery and metaphor, because clients need to be in a state of emotional arousal to be able to make use of interpretations;
- The client's confidence in the helper;
- The beneficial consequences for the client's ability to function and for the client's sense of well-being.

In sum, perceived helpfulness is a more important criterion for evaluating interpretations than is accuracy. I suggest the following criteria for determining whether interpretations are helpful for clients. First, when an interpretation is helpful, the client typically feels a sense of "aha," of learning something that "clicks," and has a feeling that things make sense in a new way. Second, clients typically have a feeling of energy and excitement about their new discoveries, particularly when they feel they have discovered the insight themselves. Third, clients present additional important information that confirms the insight. Fourth, the client starts thinking about what to do differently based on the insight. In short, the client has arrived at some personally relevant insight and can use it to talk more deeply about problems (emotional insight) and move to action.

How to Interpret

The major task is to engage in an interpretive process in such a way that the client and helper are working together to construct interpretations.

For the most part, helpers will ask clients for their interpretations and only occasionally offer their own ideas to stimulate further client insight. As with challenges, interpretations should be done carefully, gently, respectfully, thoughtfully, and empathically.

STEP 1. SET THE STAGE FOR INTERPRETATION

Helpers pave the way for interpretation through empathy, reflections of feelings, and challenges. There needs to be a good bond between the helper and the client to help the client feel it is safe to probe deep feelings and thoughts, without fear of judgment.

STEP 2. LOOK FOR MARKERS THAT CLIENTS ARE EAGER TO UNDERSTAND THEMSELVES AT A DEEPER LEVEL

Once the relationship is established, helpers watch for markers that clients are ready and eager for an interpretation. Possible markers of readiness are (a) a clear statement of a problem; (b) a statement of a lack of understanding; (c) an eagerness or willingness to understand; and (d) a high level of affective distress associated with the problem that is experienced as a pressure for resolution. For example, the client might say something like, "I just don't understand why I get so angry at my boyfriend. He usually does nothing wrong. I just suddenly get furious and I can't control my rage. I really wish I understood it because it is making me miserable and is about to destroy the best relationship I have ever had." On the other hand, if clients are telling a story, asking for advice, or blaming others for problems, they are probably not ready for an interpretation.

Some clients are psychologically minded and enjoy probing into their dynamics and motives. Others, however, are more concerned with logic, behavior change, or just feeling better rather than with understanding themselves and their motives. Helpers probably are more successful using interpretations with psychologically minded rather then non-psychologically-minded clients; although, it is important to stress that helpers should not assume from stereotypes that certain groups of clients (e.g., clients from a low socioeconomic class) are not suited for interpretations. Furthermore, some clients can be taught to be more introspective.

It is also important to be aware that some cultures may not value interpretive activity as much as the European American culture does. Some cultures (e.g., Asian, Hispanic) value action more than understanding. Because it is important to respect others' values, helpers should not force clients to work on insight if they are not amenable after being educated about it.

STEP 3. DETERMINE INTENTIONS

Helpers need to think about their intentions for providing an interpretation at a particular moment in the helping process. The most appropriate intentions are to promote insight, to identify and intensify feelings, and to promote self-control. Inappropriate intentions would be to make oneself look good at the expense of the client, to show off, or to punish clients for being frustrating. If helpers realize that they want to give an interpretation to meet their own needs, they can pause, think about themselves and the client, and try to figure out what is going on in the relationship.

STEP 4. ASK OPEN QUESTIONS TO STIMULATE CLIENTS' INSIGHT

Helpers should go into the interpretation process with an attitude of curiosity, of wondering what it is that makes clients act a certain way. They should also go into the process with a desire to help clients come to insight because insights that are discovered are typically better than those that are imposed. Another way of thinking about this is that helpers are teaching clients about the interpretive process so that they will be able to engage in it on their own after helping is completed.

An excellent idea is to begin by asking clients for their interpretation (e.g., "What do you make of your flunking out of school even though you are obviously very bright?" "How do you make sense of your reluctance to retire even though your wife keeps pressuring you to do so?"). Asking clients for their interpretations before providing them with the helper's thinking allows helpers to assess clients' current level of insight, stimulates clients to think about themselves, and gets helpers out of the position of being the ones who provide all the interpretations.

Another way to develop questions is to think about aspects of the narrative that do not quite fit. For example, in one session when the client was talking about her inexplicable and sudden bursts of anger at her boyfriend, the helper asked, "What is it about your boyfriend that allows you to blow up at him?" and "What might be some reasons that he doesn't deserve your respect?" These questions came directly from what the client was talking about and helped the client gain insight into her anger.

Note that I am suggesting that it is acceptable to ask "why" questions in this stage, although I advised against asking "why" questions in chapter 7. "Why" questions are more appropriate in the insight stage because the aim is for insight, but helpers must still be aware not to sound blaming, accusatory, or demanding. Again, the goal is for the helper and the client to work together to construct meanings, so helpers need to be respectful, gentle, and genuinely eager to help the client attain insight when asking "why" questions.

STEP 5. PROVIDE A TENTATIVE INTERPRETATION

If the client seems interested and engaged in the insight process, the helper might give a gentle, tentative interpretation to augment or extend the client's initial understanding. Helpers should view this initial interpretation as something like a working hypothesis of what might be going on for the client; this working hypothesis will be revised as the interpretive process ensues and more information is gathered. The purpose of the initial tentative interpretation is to help the client take the next step in the interpretive process, to stimulate the client's thinking about the reasons for his or her behavior.

Psychoanalytic theorists suggest that it is important to provide interpretations that are not too far beyond what clients already have recognized (e.g., Speisman, 1959). If interpretations are too deep, clients cannot understand what the helper is talking about; interpretations that are slightly beyond the client's awareness make more sense to the client and give the client a manageable stimulus for thinking. In the first session with a client who procrastinates, for example, the helper might not want to interpret the cause of the procrastination back to early childhood events because the client may not be ready to hear that interpretation. Instead, the helper might go just beyond what the client is aware of to push the client to slightly new levels of awareness (e.g., "Perhaps it's hard for you to study because you're afraid of succeeding"). Later, when the client is comfortable about thinking psychologically, the helper might push for deeper interpretations, such as the client's reluctance to supersede his or her parents.

Helpers can develop these gentle, tentative interpretations by paying attention to what the client is half saying, saying in a confused way, or saying implicitly. The client may have almost put it all together and may only need a little help to begin to integrate the pieces.

The phrasing of interpretations is crucial to their acceptance by clients. Phrasing the interpretation tentatively and without jargon makes it easier for clients to understand. For example, "I wonder if you might be afraid of what I say because I remind you of your mother, who was sometimes mean to you" is easier for a client to hear than "Your transference of your Oedipal rage onto me has caused you to distort my meaning." The latter interpretation is difficult for most clients to hear because it is stated too definitely and with too much jargon.

It is typically helpful for the interpretation process to be collaborative between the helper and client, with both working together to understand new reasons for the present situation. Helper and client work together to try to come to insights that the client can hear and assimilate. The process is a creative attempt to understand a puzzling phenomenon. Natterson (1993) stressed that when a helper who wants to exert power over a client offers a shocking interpretation of a dream, it usually has an antitherapeutic effect because it discourages the client from sharing dreams. Similarly, Reik (1935) emphasized the deep, collaborative nature of the therapeutic encounter. He suggested that insights that come to clients as a result of interpretations should come as a surprise to both the helper and the client, rather than because the helper forced a predetermined interpretation on the client. Basch (1980) likewise noted that any facile connections are usually trivial or wrong, whereas the important insights are those that come as a surprise to both client and helper.

STEP 6. CHECK OUT CLIENT REACTIONS

Helpers should carefully observe clients' reactions after any interpretations. They should remember, however, that clients do not always reveal their reactions, especially negative reactions. Hence, helpers should ask about clients' reactions to interpretations. Sometimes helpers move too quickly or too slowly or get too opinionated or too passive, so they need to hear from clients what is helpful for them.

After effective interpretations, a client may add new information or suggest alternate interpretations. This is wonderful and gives a clear indication that the client is responding well to the interpretative process. Helpers can respond by reflecting feelings or asking open questions to draw out the client's thoughts.

On the other hand, if a client rejects an interpretation, the helper needs to evaluate the situation. If the helper thinks the interpretation was right but the client was not yet ready to hear it, the helper can return to the interpretation at a later stage when she or he thinks the client is more able to tolerate insight (interpretations sometimes are painful to hear). If the helper is wrong (which is possible because helpers never have all the relevant information), the helper needs to return to using exploration skills to obtain more understanding of the client before attempting again to interpret. Alternatively, helpers can ask clients to provide an interpretation that fits for them.

STEP 7. OFFER A REVISED INTERPRETATION

After hearing more information, helpers might restate a reformulated interpretation. The new interpretation might lead the client to new material that confirms or denies the validity of the interpretation. Thus, rather than helpers having and delivering the "correct" interpretations to clients, the helper and client work together to create or construct interpretations. This collaborative process requires that helpers be invested in the interpretive process rather than in specific interpretations, so they can revise interpretations when clients offer new information, explanations, or ideas.

STEP 8: FOLLOW UP

Single interpretations rarely trigger new behaviors immediately. Clients typically require many reiterations of an interpretation before they begin to understand and use the insight. At first, interpretations may seem strange and foreign, but as clients hear them numerous times in different ways, they begin to understand them.

Helpers also need to extend the interpretations to a variety of situations to help clients reach greater understanding. For example, if the interpretation involves the client being unorganized and sloppy as a reaction to an overly neat and compulsive mother, the helper can extend this insight to how the client is messy in her apartment, unorganized in terms of her studying behavior, and late for appointments. By talking about all these different areas, the client is likely to begin to understand herself. Extending the interpretation to a number of situations also generalizes the learning, making it more likely that the client will begin to incorporate changes in thinking.

Helpers need to plan enough time in sessions to engage in working through and really understanding. They need to follow up on interpretations in subsequent sessions. Clients typically continue the interpretative process outside of sessions (which of course is the goal of helping), so following up on what the client thinks in between sessions can be very fruitful.

Examples of Interpretation

A wonderful example of the whole working through process comes from Hill, Thompson, and Mahalik (1989) in their examination of a single case of successful brief psychotherapy. The middle-aged client was the middle of 16 children. Her mother had married at a very young age; when her husband (the client's father) died, the mother abandoned the children. The client was divorced with three children and was depressed, blaming herself for being "spoiled." At the end of the therapy, the therapist and client both indicated that the most important interpretation was that the client's current difficulties were due to a difficult childhood and inadequate parenting. Interpretations occurred only in the last half of the 12-session therapy, were of moderate depth, seemed to be accurate, and were interspersed with approval–reassurance, questions, restatements, and reflections aimed at catharsis. The therapist repeated the interpretation many times and applied it to many situations, which she referred to in post-session interviews as "chipping away" at the client's defenses. The client not only accepted the interpretation but slowly began to incorporate it into her thinking (i.e., she changed from seeing herself as spoiled to seeing herself as neglected). The interpretation enabled her to disclose painful secrets (e.g., her father's attempted suicide and subsequent hospitalization in a mental institution). Finally, the therapist began to pair the interpretation with a directive that the client was a good parent to her children and thus could parent herself. The interpretation helped the client come to a greater self-understanding and, together with the direct guidance about parenting herself, enabled her to change in some fundamental ways (e.g., become a better parent, obtain a job, and begin an intimate relationship).

EXAMPLE OF INTERPREATION

Note that the helper explores the problem before interpreting.

Client: Lately, when I'm in church, I have been getting very anxious. I have been starting to panic when we have to hold hands to say a prayer. My palms get very sweaty, and I feel very embarrassed. I start worrying about it so much ahead of time that I cannot concentrate on the church service. I just don't understand why I should get so nervous. I wish I could understand it, though, because it is making my experience of going to church very unpleasant.

Helper: It sounds like you feel upset about it.

Client: I do. I feel foolish. I mean, who cares about my sweaty palms? I'm sure the other people are just interested in going to church and don't really care about me. I don't know the people very well though, because I just started going to this church when I moved here this fall.

Helper: Tell me a little bit about the role of the church in your life.

Client: I was hoping to have a community like we had in my hometown. I need something apart from the people I know at work. But it hasn't worked out. I haven't really met anyone there yet.

Helper: So you just moved here and have been hoping to make friends through the church.

Client: Church was always important in my family. I don't know how much I believe in the religion, but I do feel a need for the connection that you get in church.

Helper: So you want to make friends and find a community, but you also feel some ambivalence and you're not sure what you believe.

Client: Wow, that is really true. I do feel like I'm supposed to go to church, but I'm not sure I really want to. I feel like my parents expect me to go. But I don't quite know what I believe. I haven't taken the time to figure out what I believe separate from what my parents told me to believe.

Helper: *I wonder if worrying about your sweaty palms takes your mind off thinking about what you believe.*

Client: Yeah, that's a good point. I sure cannot listen to much of the sermon if I'm worried about the person next to me and what they will think of me.

Helper: *Perhaps going to this new church is difficult because it reminds you so much of your family* and *what you were supposed to do as a child.*

Client: You're right. I feel like I've been trying to establish myself as an independent person. I moved across country so I could be on my own and make my own decisions, but I miss my family and my community. I don't know how much I want to be here. I feel like I'm struggling with trying to figure out who I am and what I want out of life. (Client continues exploring.)

Effects of Interpretation

Helpers can watch tapes of their sessions and use the following three-point scale to determine the effects of their interpretations on clients:

1 = If an interpretation is inaccurate or too deep, or if the client is not ready to hear it, he or she might deny or ignore it. The client might feel confused, blamed, or misunderstood. Signs that indicate lack of involvement in the interpretive process are passive acceptance without deeper exploration ("yeah, you're right"), passive aggressiveness ("yes, but . . . "), or anger ("no, you're wrong").

2 = If interpretations are at least moderately helpful, clients might agree compliantly but not really absorb, hear, or understand the interpretations. Clients might be able to repeat the interpretations but not really grasp their significance intellectually or emotionally. Clients might agree and think about the intepretation superficially.

3 = If interpretations are very helpful and well timed, clients might have an "aha" reaction and become very excited about the new understanding, believing that it provides them with a way to make sense of their world. Clients might engage more deeply in the interpretive process and add to or contradict the helper's insight.

Potential Difficulties in Using Interpretation

Some helpers are hesitant to interpret because it feels intrusive to "poke around in clients' heads." They fear that they will be wrong, give interpretations prematurely, upset or anger clients, or destroy the therapeutic relationship. They err on the side of passivity and do not offer any of their own thoughts to the interpretive exchange.

Other helpers are too eager to give interpretations and err on the side of aggressiveness. The interpretation process brings out the worst in some helpers. They become invested in the intellectual challenge of figuring out clients and are eager to use their powers of insight. They lose sight of the need for empathy and a strong therapeutic relationship and charge into putting all the pieces of the puzzle together. I agree that people are infinitely intriguing, interesting, and fun to figure out, but helpers must temper such sentiments with a strong compassion for clients and a desire to help clients understand themselves.

I caution helpers in the use and potential abuse of interpretations because they can be powerful interventions. Helpers have the responsibility to appropriately use their power. I also caution helpers that clients may agree with interpretations because they want to please, but they may actually disagree with the interpretations and can feel wounded by them. Helpers need to be careful to encourage clients to become actively involved in collaborating on constructing interpretations. Helpers also need to be careful about timing, making sure clients are ready to hear the interpretations and can build on them in constructing their own understandings.

Another problem helpers have is giving too many interpretations in one session. Clients often need time to absorb and think about each interpretation, so helpers should gauge their pace on the basis of clients' reactions.

A final problem is that some helpers are not experienced enough with interpretation and feel unable to put all the pieces together to formulate interpretations. If helpers feel this way, they can practice on themselves trying to understand their own behavior, focus more on asking the client to come up with interpretations, have patience that more interpretive ability will come with practice, and read further in psychoanalytic theory.

HELPFUL HINTS

- Pave the way for interpretations with empathy, reflection of feelings, and challenges.
- Ask for clients' interpretations and encourage introspection. Be eager to help clients discover insights on their own.
- Wait until the problem has been explored thoroughly. Provide an interpretation only when you have an idea of what is going on for the client and you think the client is ready to hear an interpretation.
- Base interpretations on an understanding of clients' motives, defenses, needs, styles, and childhood experiences.
- Wait until you hear a marker that indicates that the client is ready for an interpretation. Possible markers of readiness are (a) a clear statement of a problem, (b) a statement of a lack of understanding, (c) an eagerness or willingness to understand, and (d) a high level of affective distress associated with the problem that is experienced as a pressure for resolution.
- Deliver interpretations tentatively and with empathy. Pose possible interpretations and ask clients for their perspectives.
- Collaborate with clients in trying to figure out the origins of the problem, their role in the problem, and why the problem continues. As with a puzzle, you want to work with clients to try to put the puzzle together—each of you picks up a piece of the puzzle and tries to see where it fits. If the interpretation fits, try to understand more about how it fits current aspects of the client's life. If the interpretation does not fit for any reason (lack of readiness, inaccuracy), recycle back to the exploration stage and try to understand the client's feelings.
- Interpretations should be at moderate depth and not far beyond what clients can readily understand and assimilate.
- Follow up on interpretations with open questions (e.g., "How did that feel?") and reflections of feelings (e.g., "I wonder if you feel scared right now"). Remember to return to the exploration skills because clients are at a new level of understanding and need time to explore feelings.
- Do not make judgments in interpretations. You are trying to understand rather than evaluate clients.
- Keep interpretations short. Going on and on takes the focus away from clients.

- Refrain from showing off in terms of understanding what is going on for the client. Work with the client to construct insights collaboratively.
- Do not provide too many interpretations in one session.
- Observe the client's reactions after interpretations.
- Leave enough time in sessions to discuss interpretations thoroughly.
- If the clients does not respond well to interpretations, reflect feelings and reconsider the usefulness of the interpretation and the readiness of the client. If you feel certain that the interpretation is accurate, rephrase the interpretation or use an example. Interpretations often have to be repeated several times over a number of sessions before clients are able to hear them.
- Let it go if the client does not accept the interpretation, but keep it in mind as a working hypothesis.

PRACTICE EXERCISES

For each of the following examples, write an interpretation.

Statements

1. Client: I'm not doing very well in school right now. I'm sure it's my study skills. I just don't seem to be able to concentrate—I keep gazing out the window instead of getting my work done. I try to make myself stay at my desk more and more, but I seem to be getting less done. I broke up with my boyfriend so I could have more time to study, but it just doesn't seem to be working.
    Helper response: _____

    _____

2. Client: I'm about ready to graduate and I need to decide what I'm going to do next with my life. I'm getting a lot of pressure from my parents, but I can't quite figure out what I want to do. I keep having this recurrent dream where I flunk out of a math class. I can never seem to get to class, and when I do get there, I don't understand any of the work. I never get to the tests on time, and I know I'm going to flunk out. I don't know why I keep having this dream. Math has always been difficult for me, but I got an A in my last math class.
    Helper response: _____

    _____

3. Client: I really love my boyfriend and I want to get married, I really do. But you know recently I have not wanted to see him much. Every time we're together, I find myself criticizing him.

You know, he does stupid things sometimes that just irritate me. I can just imagine him drinking beer and belching in front of my father. You know my parents still haven't met him. I don't know quite why, but I haven't wanted to take him home.

Helper response: _____

_____

Possible Helper Responses

1. "Perhaps you're not getting much work done because you regret breaking up with your boyfriend."
   "Perhaps your sadness at breaking up with your boyfriend is getting in the way of your schoolwork."
   "Maybe a fear of commitment keeps you from committing yourself to your schoolwork or a relationship."
2. "I wonder if your anxiety about your future is related to a fear of failing."
   "Could it be that you fear you will disappoint your parents if you don't succeed?"
3. "Perhaps you're worried that your parents won't like your boyfriend."
   "I wonder if you chose your boyfriend because he's different from your father."
   "Maybe your fear about taking your boyfriend to meet your parents is because you're unsure about your feelings for him."

WHAT DO YOU THINK?

- What role do you think culture plays in interpretations?
- Provide examples of situations in which you think it would be appropriate or inappropriate to offer interpretations.
- Do you agree about the necessity for developing a collaborative process of constructing interpretations with clients? Why or why not?
- Debate both sides of the idea that interpretations are a necessary prerequisite for change to occur (i.e., argue for and against the idea that interpretations are the "pure gold" of helping).
- Discuss whether clients can be taught to be more introspective.
- Debate whether interpretations should only be given after challenges.
- What are the dangers that helpers face in giving interpretations to clients?

- Debate how to determine the accuracy of interpretations.
- What theoretical approach do you prefer as a basis for developing interpretations?

LAB 10

Interpretation

Goals: For helpers to practice using the exploration skills (reflection, restatement, and open questions) and then learn to engage the client in the interpretive process.

In groups of four to six people, one person should be the client, one person should be the initial helper, and the rest can wait to take over as helper or give ideas to the helper. Each person should take a turn being the client. Each group should have a designated lab leader (other than the helper) to organize and coordinate the session.

Helper's and Client's Tasks During the Helping Interchange

1. The client talks about a problematic reaction to a specific situation that he or she would like to understand. In other words, the client should talk about an event to which he or she had a strong reaction but did not understand why; the reaction seemed out of proportion to the situation. For example, perhaps the client was driving along and someone swore at him and he got instantly rageful. Or perhaps the client was sitting in a classroom discussion and suddenly, for no obvious reason, felt like crying. The client should plan on being at least moderately disclosing, although of course clients always have the right to say that they do not want to disclose further.
2. The initial helper uses exploration skills (open questions, restatement, and reflection of feelings) for several minutes to help the client explore the problem. If the initial helper gets stuck, switch helpers to ensure a thorough exploration of the problem.
3. After several minutes of exploration, each group member should give a reflection of feelings, with the client responding to each reflection.
4. Each group member should ask an open question to stimulate insight (e.g., "What do you make of X?" "You mentioned Y, how does that fit with Z?")
5. The group leader asks everyone (except the client) to write down an interpretation. Helpers can ask themselves, "What do I hear the person saying underneath the words?" "What are the themes in what the client is saying?" "What might be the reason for the client's feeling?" "What things might be connected to this problem?"
6. Each group member delivers his or her interpretation and allows time for the client to respond.

Processing the Helping Interchange

After everyone has a turn and the client has responded, the client can talk about which interpretations were most helpful and why. The helper with the most helpful interpretation can talk about how he or she came up with it.

continues

LAB 10 (Continued)

Interpretation

SWITCH ROLES SO THAT TWO TO THREE PEOPLE GET A CHANCE TO BE THE CLIENT

Personal Reflections

- How did you feel giving interpretations?
- What were your intentions for using interpretations?
- Were you able to phrase the interpretations so the client could hear them? Describe any discrepancies between the reactions you expected from the client and the actual reactions that the client had.
- What are your strengths and weaknesses in engaging the client in the interpretive process?
- How did you feel about receiving an interpretation as a client? What factors about the delivery of an interpretation influenced your feelings?
- What role does your culture play in your ability to give and receive interpretations?

Self-Disclosure of Insight | 15

To know one's self is to know others, for heart can understand heart.

—Chinese proverb

O

lga was very emotional and upset when she revealed that her husband had left her for a younger woman. She felt abandoned and humiliated and did not want any of her friends to know he had left. She talked in her helping session about feeling very depressed, isolated, alone, and hopeless, and she said that she was too old to start over. The helper said, "You know, I got divorced several years ago, and I never thought I would recover. I came to realize that I had believed my worth was dependent on whether I had a man, rather than who I was. I wonder if that's true for you?" This disclosure helped Olga understand why she was so upset about her husband's leaving her. She did not really miss him; they had not been getting along well for many years. Instead, she missed the sense of security that being married gave her. Once she understood that about herself, she could begin to adjust to the divorce.

Self-disclosures of insight reveal something the helper has learned about him- or herself and are used to facilitate clients' understanding of their thoughts, feelings, behaviors, and issues. Instead of using challenges or interpretations, helpers share insights that they have learned about themselves in the hope of encouraging clients to think about themselves at a deeper level. Note that several types of self-disclosures are presented throughout the book. Disclosures of information, feelings, and similarities are presented in chapter 10; disclosures of immediate experiences in the therapeutic relationship are presented in chapter 16; and disclosures

---

Web Forms referred to in text can be found on the book's companion online guide described in the Preface.

of strategies are presented in chapter 20. In this chapter, I focus only on self-disclosures used to stimulate insight (see Exhibit 15.1).

Why Use Self-Disclosure of Insight?

A major reason for using self-disclosures is that they have been found to be helpful. Although therapists used them infrequently, clients rated them as very helpful and indicated that disclosures led them to gain insight, feel more normal, reassured them, and led to deeper therapeutic relationships (see review in Hill & Knox, 2002).

Helpers disclose their experiences to help clients attain realizations of which they had not been aware. This type of self-disclosure is useful when clients are stuck or are having a hard time achieving deep levels of self-understanding on their own. For example, if a client is talking about everything being just fine after leaving her abusive husband, but the helper suspects that the client needs insight, the helper might say, "I remember feeling like I wasn't sure if I made the right decision after I left my partner. It was real scary for me because my parents never allowed me to make my own decisions so I didn't trust myself. I wonder if something like that is true for you?" The helper hopes the client will understand more about herself by hearing about the helper's experience.

Another reason for using self-disclosure is to enable clients to hear things in a less threatening way than might happen with therapist challenges or interpretations. Hearing a disclosure such as "I also feel like a child when I go to visit my parents because I lose my identity and don't know who I am" or "I also have a hard time going to movies by myself because I feel like nobody loves me" provides an opportunity for clients to think about whether they have similar reasons for their behaviors. Rather than asserting an interpretation that may offend the client, helpers disclose personal insights and ask whether these insights might fit for the client, thus possibly facilitating new and deeper insight. By using self-disclosure, the helper admits that the insight may be a projection and allows the client to see if it fits. As with tentative interpretations, helpers are hoping that clients will feel more free to look for underlying reasons after they have heard helpers disclosing their insights. Thus, self-disclosures can have a modeling effect.

In addition, self-disclosures can alter the power balance of the helping relationship and lead to greater participation by the client. Rather than helpers being the experts with the answers and clients relying on helpers to solve their problems, helper self-disclosures make clear that

EXHIBIT 15.1

Overview of Self-Disclosure of Insight

Definition	*Self-disclosure of insight* refers to the helper's presentation of a personal experience (not in the immediate relationship) in which he or she gained some insight.
Examples	*Client:* "My roommate keeps wanting to know my grades. I feel awkward when she asks, so I just try to ignore her and change the topic." *Helper:* "In the past, I often did not want others to feel upset by my successes, so I would underplay anything I did well. I wonder if that happens for you?"
	Client: "I should quit procrastinating. I have not gotten anything done lately. I should get out more and meet people and volunteer so that I feel more productive. I'm just wasting time." *Helper:* "I indulge in some bad habits just like you. I know they're bad habits, just like you do, but I don't want to change them anymore. I've finally learned to accept these things about myself. Would that fit for you?"
Typical helper intentions	To promote insight, to deal with resistance, to challenge, to relieve the therapist's needs[a] (see Web Form D)
Possible client reactions	Understood, supported, hopeful, relief, negative thoughts or behaviors, better self-understanding, clear, feelings, unstuck, new perspective, educated, new ways to behave, scared, worse, confused, misunderstood (see Web Form G)
Desired client behaviors	Insight, affective exploration, cognitive–behavioral exploration (see Web Form H)
Potential difficulties	Disclosing to gratify own needs Projecting own issues onto client Not returning focus to client after self-disclosure Providing lengthy self-disclosures Disclosing more than the client is comfortable being aware of

Note. Self-disclosures are also discussed in the exploration stage (e.g., disclosing information, feelings, or similarities) and the action stage (e.g., disclosing strategies). Self-disclosures about the immediate therapeutic relationship are discussed in chapter 16.
[a]This intention is typically not therapeutic.

both are individuals who grapple with important human concerns. In addition, in dyads in which cultures differ, self-disclosures can be used to bridge the gap and make clients feel that their helpers can understand them.

I believe that self-disclosures can be very effective in enabling clients to gain insight when used properly. In this way, I am closer theoretically to the humanistic and cognitive–behavioral theorists than to psychoanalytic theorists. Because humanistic theorists (e.g., Bugental, 1965; Jourard, 1971; Robitschek & McCarthy, 1991; Rogers, 1957; Truax & Carkhuff, 1967) think helpers should be transparent, real, and genuine in the therapeutic relationship, they believe that helper self-disclosure can have a positive effect on treatment. In fact, humanists believe that a personal and transparent style of intervention benefits both the process and the outcome of therapy because it allows clients to see helpers as real people who also have problems. In addition, humanists believe that when helpers disclose, there is more of a balance of control in the relationship, in that clients are not the only ones who are vulnerable. Humanists also contend that disclosure enhances rapport because clients feel more friendly toward and trusting of helpers who disclose. It is interesting that humanists also think that self-disclosure can help to correct transference misconceptions as they occur because helpers are direct and honest with self-disclosures and, hence, challenge distortions as they arise. Additional benefits claimed by humanists for self-disclosures are that helpers are able to be more spontaneous and authentic and can model appropriate disclosure. Moreover, helpers' disclosures can facilitate client self-disclosure and work on the therapeutic relationship. In effect, humanists believe that helpers' self-disclosures encourage an atmosphere of honesty and understanding between helpers and clients that fosters stronger and more effective therapeutic relationships.

Similarly, cognitive–behavioral theorists believe that self-disclosure within the session, when used with appropriate boundaries, can strengthen the therapeutic bond and facilitate client change (Goldfried, Burckell, & Eubanks-Carter, 2003). Of particular interest for the insight stage, cognitive–behaviorists use self-disclosure to provide feedback on the interpersonal impact made by the client and model effective ways of interacting.

In contrast, traditional psychoanalytic theorists (e.g., Basescu, 1990; Greenson, 1967; Simon, 1988) view psychotherapy as focused on working through patients' projections and transferences. They believe helpers should be neutral or blank screens, so that clients can project onto them their feelings and reactions toward significant others. For example, a client's childhood experiences might prompt the client to transfer onto the helper a fear that the helper is going to be punitive. An analytic helper might sit behind the client to enable the client to focus inwardly rather than watching the helper's face for cues about his or her reactions. If helpers are in fact being neutral, they can assist clients in seeing that the belief that the helper will be punitive is a projection. If helpers deviate from neutrality, it is difficult to distinguish client projections from realistic reactions to what the helper is actually doing. For example, if a helper is consistently late, it would be difficult to determine whether the client's anger was a distortion based on previous experiences or legitimate anger at the helper's tardiness. Readers should not confuse neutrality with a lack of empathy, however, because competent analytic helpers are appropriately warm and empathic. It is not too surprising, given this emphasis on neutrality, that psychoanalytic helpers typically do not self-disclose. In fact, psychoanalysts propose an inverse relationship between the client's knowledge of the helper's personal life, thoughts, and feelings and the client's capacity to develop a transference to the helper (Freud, 1912/1959). They believe that helper revelations contaminate the transference process and deleteriously demystify the therapy, thereby reducing the helper's status (Andersen & Anderson, 1985). In addition, Cornett (1991) suggested that helper self-disclosure might represent unresolved countertransference difficulties on the part of the helper, which would seriously compromise the client's ability to profit from treatment. Furthermore, psychoanalysts argue that helper self-disclosure can expose helper weaknesses and vulnerabilities, thereby undermining client trust in the helper and adversely influencing outcome (Curtis, 1981, 1982). (I should note, however, that some current psychoanalytic theorists advocate the use of self-disclosure; see Geller, 2003.)

In sum, I believe that helpers can self-disclose beneficially for clients if they do it for the appropriate intentions, at the right moment. Disclosure for the helper's needs rather than for the client's, however, can be damaging to the relationship. Hence, if helpers disclose in a manner in which they maintain an objective stance, focus on the client, and observe client reactions, I believe that disclosures can be helpful. In fact, I think that sometimes they can be more helpful than other insight skills because the helper is not "putting something on" the client but is respectfully offering different possibilities to help the client gain insight.

How to Self-Disclose About Insight

When using self-disclosures of insight, helpers can follow the steps outlined in chapter 13 if the intent is to challenge and the steps in chapter 14 if the intent is to provide an interpretation. In addition, helpers need to consider the following specific guidelines for self-disclosures. Helpers need to think honestly about their intentions prior to disclosing. If they had an experience that could help clients understand more about themselves, it might be useful to disclose it for all the reasons noted above. Self-disclosures should not be used, however, to discuss or solve the helper's problems (e.g., "You think you've got it bad, let me tell you how bad it was for me"). Harm can result if helpers use self-disclosure because they have unresolved problems and are needy. In this case, the focus shifts from the client to the helper, perhaps resulting in the client taking care of the helper. Because self-disclosure should be used to help clients gain insight, helpers need to keep the focus on the clients.

To develop appropriate self-disclosures, helpers can think about what contributed to their behaviors when they were in situations similar to those of their clients. By focusing on insights they gained about themselves, helpers use their experiences to help clients attain insight. If helpers decide that self-disclosures are appropriate for the client at a particular moment, they should keep the focus of the disclosure on the insight rather than on recounting details of the experience (e.g., rather than talking about the details of how his father died, the helper might say, "When my father died, I didn't know what I was feeling so I relied on everyone to tell me what I should be feeling. In the process, I lost myself. I wonder if that's happening to you?").

It is important that when helpers disclose, they choose something that has occurred in the past, has been resolved, has resulted in a new perspective, can be helpful to the client, and does not make them feel vulnerable. In addition, disclosures that are short and immediately turn the focus back to the client tend to be most effective. Helpers should be honest about their experiences and should not make up things just to have a disclosure. If they have not had a similar experience that led to a new understanding, they should use a different intervention.

Once helpers have disclosed, they should return the focus to the client. Helpers can follow disclosures with open questions about whether the insight fits for the client (e.g., "I wonder how that fits for you?" or "I wonder if anything like that happens for you?").

A specific situation that requires a bit more attention is how to respond when clients ask for personal information. For example, a client might ask where the helper went for vacation or whether the helper is married or has children. A general rule would be to briefly provide information (if it feels comfortable) but also to be curious about what motivates the client's desire for this personal information. Helpers might ask clients about their thoughts, fantasies, or concerns about them to learn more about what motivated clients to ask for information. In addition to providing the personal information, helpers can thus use the situation as an opportunity to investigate why clients want the information. Processing these issues can provide insights about the client and strengthen the relationship.

If a self-disclosure does not work (e.g., the client denies or disavows having similar experiences or feels uncomfortable knowing information about the helper), it is probably best to refrain from making further self-disclosures. Several things could have happened. The helper could be right, but the client might not be ready to gain insight. Or, the helper could be projecting insight onto the client. In addition, the client could become upset about learning anything personal about the helper because it alters the distance between them. In such instances, the helper can collect more evidence to determine whether the helper's projection, the client's lack of readiness, or the client's need for distance is at issue. If lack of readiness is the problem, the helper can try other skills (e.g., reflection of feelings or challenge). If projection is the problem, the helper can seek supervision or therapy. If the client prefers not to know anything about the helper, the helper can change strategies and limit self-disclosures. Of course, any extreme reaction should be investigated further to assist in understanding and gaining insight into the client's underlying issues.

EXAMPLE OF SELF-DISCLOSURE

Client: I've been thinking a lot about death lately. I'm not thinking of suicide but more about the inevitability of death. There are so many senseless murders lately—the news is full of them. But I cannot quite grasp the idea of death—it doesn't make sense to me. It doesn't seem fair to be killed in the prime of life.

Helper: You sound scared about the idea of dying.

Client: Oh yeah, I really am. I really don't know what happens after death. Of course, my parents' religion talks about heaven and hell, but I can't quite buy all that. But if I don't believe what their religion says, I don't quite know what happens at death. And what is the meaning of life? I mean why are we here, and why does everyone rush around? What difference does it all make? I'm sure this all sounds very confusing, but I've been thinking about it a lot lately.

Helper: No, it makes a lot of sense. I think all of us need to grapple with the meaning of life and the fact that we are going to die. You know, though, let me make a guess about something. *When I have been most concerned about death and meaning in life is when I have been in moments of transition and trying to figure out what I want out of life.* I wonder if that's true for you now?

Client: Hmmm. That's interesting. I am about to turn 30, and it feels like a big turning point for me. I'm in a job I don't really like, and I haven't found the relationship that I always hoped I would find at this point. (Client continues talking productively about his personal concerns.)

Effects of Self-Disclosure of Insight

Helpers can listen to tapes of their session and use the following three-point scale to evaluate the effects of their self-disclosures on clients.

1 = After an inappropriate or unhelpful self-disclosure, the attention might shift from the client to the helper, with the client trying to soothe or attend to the helper. Other possible reactions include the client's becoming silent, talking about irrelevant material, or feeling contemptuous of the helper for self-disclosing.

2 = After neutral or moderately helpful self-disclosures, clients might acknowledge and even like the disclosure but not use it to gain insight.

3 = After very helpful self-disclosures, clients might recognize the similarity between themselves and their helpers, feel a sense of relief that someone else has felt or done the same thing, and gain new insight about themselves. Clients might say something like, "yeah, I've felt that" and go on to understanding themselves at greater depths. Clients might attain new awareness and insights. Some clients might feel a commonality with another human being and, thus, feel less alone and isolated. Alternatively, clients might gain insight through articulating how they are different from the helper.

Potential Difficulties in Disclosing Insight

One danger in using self-disclosure is that helpers might project their feelings and reactions onto clients. For example, if a client has been talking about getting bad grades and a helper states, "I feel panicked when I get bad grades because I am still afraid of my parents' anger," the helper might have projected his or her own insight onto the client. The client might confirm that this is a projection by responding, "No, I feel more like I deserved the bad grade because I didn't study." Helpers need to remember that they are separate from their clients, have different experiences, and that their personal insights might not apply to their clients.

Another problem is that some helpers use self-disclosure to satisfy their urge to reveal themselves, rather than using it intentionally to help clients gain insight. Similarly, some helpers mistake the notion of being open as an opportunity to say whatever is on their minds. Greenberg, Rice, and Elliott (1993) called such impulsive helper openness "promiscuous" self-disclosure. These types of self-disclosure may cause clients to feel uncomfortable and lose respect for the helper. For example, a client sought help to address her concerns about divorce. Unfortunately, her helper talked more about her own experiences with divorce than the client did. The client terminated and found a different helper who used self-disclosures more judiciously. Greenberg et al. suggested that self-disclosures need to be done with disciplined spontaneity on the basis of the helpers' accurate self-awareness of inner experience shared in a facilitative manner at a therapeutically appropriate moment. In other words, helpers need to be aware of themselves and of their intentions and deliver self-disclosures when they are most likely to help clients.

Beginning helpers tend to use too many self-disclosures. As with medical students seeing themselves in all the syndromes described in their medical texts, beginning helpers connect with many of their clients' struggles. They have a hard time setting aside personal issues to focus on their clients' problems. It is indeed difficult to shift from the mutual sharing that ideally occurs in friendships to the reduced amount of sharing that occurs in helping relationships. Paying attention to how a client's problems differ from the helper's can facilitate the helper to differentiate him- or herself from the client and use self-disclosures more judiciously.

Finally, some beginning helpers worry about making their self-disclosures perfect. They believe that disclosures could have negative effects if not done exactly right. They also worry about sounding patronizing, as if they have figured out everything for themselves whereas clients are still learning. They worry that they would feel too vulnerable and would lose any credibility they have as helpers if they disclose issues they are currently involved in and do not understand completely. Other helpers are concerned that they might not have an appropriate disclosure because they have not faced a similar situation or have not gained any insight into the situation—perhaps they are really in the same boat as the client. I recommend that helpers use other interventions if they feel uncomfortable or vulnerable using disclosures. I would also note that practice under close supervision helps greatly in terms of teaching beginning helpers the bounds of appropriate disclosures.

HELPFUL HINTS

- Think carefully about your intentions for providing a self-disclosure. Are you doing it for your benefit or to help the client?

If, on reflection, you realize that you want to give the self-disclosure for your own needs, do not disclose. If you believe that the disclosure will help the client gain insight, however, formulate the disclosure with the needs of the client in mind.

- Keep disclosures short and focus on the client.
- After you give a self-disclosure, turn the focus back to the client. For example, "When I was in your situation, I reacted with hostility because of my anxiety about being humiliated. I wonder what was going on for you."
- Follow self-disclosures with open questions (e.g., "What was your reaction to my disclosure?") and reflections of feelings ("You seem surprised that I had a similar experience"). Remember to return to the exploration skills because clients may need time to explore their feelings about their new discoveries.
- Observe and ask about the client's reaction after disclosures. If the client reacts negatively to the self-disclosure, use the occasion as an opportunity to learn more about the client.
- If clients react negatively to self-disclosures, use different interventions.
- Use self-disclosures infrequently. Remember that experienced therapists rarely disclose and disclosures may be effective and memorable because they are used infrequently.

PRACTICE EXERCISES

Read each of the following examples and write a self-disclosure you might use if you were the helper. Remember to use an open question or reflection after your self-disclosure to shift the focus back to the client.

Statements

1. Client: "I felt so weird when I had to get up and speak in front of the class last week. Everyone else seemed to feel so confident when they gave their speeches. I just felt like a total jerk, not knowing what to say. I feel so embarrassed that I can't speak as well as everyone else."
   Helper response: _____
   _____

2. Client: "Every time I go home, I feel like I'm 10 years old again. My parents treat me like a little child, and I actually get back into the same role I played as a little child. Even though I'm a grown-up, responsible person and never act this way anyplace else, some-

how I always revert to acting like a child when I visit my parents. I get so upset with myself."

Helper response: _____

3. Client: "I just feel like women can't do much careerwise. It really is true that men run the world. Look how much more money they make than women, and they have all the good jobs. Plus if you have a career, you can't do a very good job of raising children. It's probably not possible to have a family and a decent career."

Helper response: _____

_____

Possible Helper Responses

1. "I felt terrified when I gave speeches in class because I was always afraid people were going to laugh at me. Could that be true for you?"

"I feel embarrassed sometimes because my accent is different from other people and I fear that they will think I'm not adequate. I wonder if you feel that way?"

"Even though I've been giving speeches for over 20 years, I still feel nervous. I feel like I'm an imposter and have nothing to say that anyone would want to hear. For me, it's related to never being listened to in my family. I wonder if you can identify where your nervousness comes from?"

2. "Yes, I do that too. I notice that I have a tendency to regress to being dependent unless I am careful. I wonder if that's true for you?"

"I feel upset with regressing too when I visit my parents, but there's also a part of me that loves to sink back and be taken care of. My fear is that I'll never want to leave. I wonder if you have that fear?"

"I can relate to that because my parents don't want me to grow up and be different from them. What issues get raised for you when you visit your parents?"

3. "I've also struggled in thinking about my role as a professional woman and possibly having children. For me it's related to not being sure that I want both. I wonder if you experience any ambivalence about wanting both a career and a family?"

"I wonder if you're aware that I have a career and a family? I've had to figure out who I am and what I want out of life. I wonder if you've done that?"

WHAT DO YOU THINK?

- How are self-disclosures used differently in friendships than in helping relationships?
- Discuss when you would or would not want to use self-disclosure in a helping setting.
- What influence do you think theoretical orientation and culture play in helpers' preferences for using or not using insight disclosures?
- What role does culture play in clients' reactions to insight disclosures?
- Discuss the notion that self-disclosure reduces the power imbalance between helpers and clients. What are the advantages and disadvantages of having a power imbalance in a helping relationship?
- Discuss whether certain types of people feel more comfortable disclosing.
- Discuss the effects of self-disclosure on neutrality in the insight stage.
- Debate about the different effects of different types of self-disclosure (similarity, facts, feelings, insight, strategy).

LAB 11

Self-Disclosure of Insight

Goals: For helpers to practice using the exploration skills (reflection, restatement, and open questions) and then to learn to self-disclose.

Exercise 1

In groups of four to six people, one person should be the leader, one person the client, one person the initial helper, and the rest should be observers and ready to serve as helper. Each person should take a turn being the client. Each group should have a designated lab leader (other than the helper) to organize and coordinate the session.

Helper's and Client's Tasks During the Helping Interchange

1. The client talks about a common problematic experience (e.g., schoolwork, adjustment to college, or problems with friends).
2. The designated helper uses exploration skills (open question, restatement, and reflection of feelings) for 5 to 10 minutes to allow the client to explore. If one helper gets stuck, another can take over to ensure a thorough exploration.
3. The leader asks all the group members to go around and do a reflection of feelings to give the client a chance to explore more.
4. Everyone writes down a self-disclosure of insight. Helpers ask themselves, "When I was in a similar situation, what contributed to what I was doing? What did I learn about myself and my motivations that might be helpful to this client?"
5. Each helper in turn delivers a self-disclosure and gives the client a chance to respond.

After the Helping Interchange

The client can talk about which self-disclosures were most helpful and why. Helpers can talk about their intentions and their perceptions of the client reactions. Observers provide feedback about perceptions of which disclosures were helpful and why.

SWITCH ROLES

Exercise 2

Students should pair up, with one person as the helper and one as the client.

Helper's and Client's Tasks During the Helping Interchange

1. The client talks about a common problematic experience (e.g., schoolwork, adjustment to college, or problems with friends).

continues

LAB 11 (Continued)

Self-Disclosure of Insight

2. The helper uses exploration skills (open question, restatement, and reflection of feelings) for about 10 minutes, allowing the client to explore.
3. The helper spends about 10 minutes giving some insight skills (open questions about insight, challenge, interpretation, self-disclosures of insight), following up the insight skills with restatements and reflections of feelings.

After the Helping Interchange

The client can talk about his or her reactions to the insight skills. The helper can talk about his or her intentions and perceptions of the client reactions.

SWITCH ROLES

Personal Reflections

- Describe your reactions to giving and receiving disclosures in the helping setting.
- What is the role of your culture in your openness to giving and receiving disclosures?
- Describe your strengths and weaknesses as a helper in giving self-disclosures.

Immediacy 16

There are, in fact, no more important communications
between one human being and another than those expressed
emotionally, and no information more vital for constructing
and reconstructing working models of the self and other than
information about how each feels towards the other . . . it is
the emotional communications between a patient and his
therapist that play the crucial part.

—John Bowby (1988, pp. 156–157)

Evita constantly got angry at her helper, Angela, and criticized her for
everything she said. Angela began to feel inadequate and angry at
Evita and did not look forward to sessions. Angela consulted with her
supervisor, who reassured Angela that she was using the helping skills
appropriately and suggested that perhaps Evita's personal issues caused
her to denigrate Angela. The supervisor suggested that Angela use
immediacy in the next session to let Evita know how she was feeling.
So in the next session, when Evita criticized her for not saying the
right feeling word, Angela said, "You know, right now I'm feeling
badly because it feels like I cannot do anything right. I feel frustrated
because I don't know how to help you. I wonder how you feel about
our relationship?" Evita broke into tears and said that she seemed to
push everyone away. Angela was able to listen and eventually they
came to realize that Evita pushed people away because she feared
rejection. Using immediacy allowed Angela to help Evita understand
more about how she acted with others and strengthened the
therapeutic relationship.

Immediacy occurs when helpers disclose how they are feeling about
the client, themselves in relation to the client, or about the therapeutic
relationship. As Egan (1994) suggested, immediacy can focus on the overall
relationship (e.g., "It feels to me that we are getting along well now that
we have worked through our initial discomfort"), a specific event in the

---

Web Forms referred to in text can be found on the book's companion online guide described in the Preface.

session (e.g., "I was surprised when you said that you appreciated the sessions because I wasn't sure how you felt about our work"), or present-tense personal reactions to the client (e.g., "I am feeling hurt right now because you reject everything I say"). Further examples are provided in Exhibit 16.1.

Immediacy can be thought of as a type of self-disclosure because helpers are disclosing personal feelings, reactions, or experiences about the client or relationship (e.g., "I feel pleased that you remembered what I said"). Immediacy can sometimes be a type of challenge because it can be used to confront clients about issues in the relationship (e.g., "I feel annoyed that you avoid my questions"). In addition, immediacy can sometimes be a type of information if it is used to point out patterns in a client's behavior (e.g., "Whenever I go on vacation, you cancel the first two sessions after I return. I wonder if we could talk about this pattern?"). However, immediacy differs from feedback about the client (a type of information) because both people in the relationship are involved in immediacy interventions, whereas in feedback about the client the focus is only on the client (e.g., "You did a really good job when you spoke up to your mother"). Although immediacy overlaps with other skills, I highlight it as a separate skill because it can provide clients with powerful feedback about how they are perceived in interpersonal relationships.

Why Use Immediacy?

The helping relationship provides a microcosm of how clients relate in the real world. If clients are compliant with the helper, for example, they are often compliant with others in the outside world. If clients are arrogant and show off to impress the helper, chances are that they do similar things with other people. Therefore the client's general interpersonal style can be examined, at least in part, by an investigation of the relationship with the helper. Whereas helpers have to rely on clients' reports of how they act with other people, they have a firsthand experience of how clients behave with them. Of course, clients do not always act toward all other people as they act toward the helper—it may be that they only act that way to people in positions of authority or to people of that gender or some similar characteristic. But observing the behavior does provide firsthand evidence of how the client comes across in at least some relationships.

Resolving problems between the helper and client can provide clients with a model of how to resolve interpersonal problems in relationships. Clients learn that it is possible to talk about feelings and come to some

EXHIBIT 16.1

Overview of Immediacy

Definition	*Immediacy* refers to the helper disclosing immediate feelings about the client, her- or himself in relation to the client, or the therapeutic relationship
Examples	"Right now I'm feeling very tense because you seem to be angry at me." "I feel nervous too, but I'm pleased that you're sharing some very deep and personal feelings with me."
Typical helper intentions	To promote insight, to deal with the relationship, to challenge, to identify maladaptive behaviors, to identify and intensify feelings, to relieve therapist's needs[a] (see Web Form D)
Possible client reactions	Relief, negative thoughts or feelings, better self-understanding, clear, feelings, responsibility, unstuck, new perspective, challenged, scared, worse, stuck, confused, misunderstood (see Web Form G)
Desired client behaviors	Affective exploration, cognitive exploration, insight (see Web Form H)
Potential difficulties	Fears about intruding Uncertainty about feelings and perceptions of clients' Anxiety about dealing with interpersonal conflicts Removing focus from client

[a]This intention is typically not therapeutic.

resolution and perhaps develop closer relationships as a result of the discussion. Being able to resolve interpersonal problems can be a powerful experience, in that it can teach clients that it is possible, although not always easy, to deal openly with issues. Greenberg et al. (1993) suggested that encountering another real human being who both cares and is authentic helps clients grow.

In addition to addressing problems in relationships in general, immediacy can also be used to discuss issues of importance to the helping relationship. For example, a helper might want to process feelings with a client about their encounter at a party, or a helper could discuss with a client what has and has not worked well in the helping process, so adjustments can be made. Many issues present themselves in a helping relationship, so immediacy is a critical tool for working out inevitable interpersonal problems.

Another reason for using immediacy is to challenge clients to change maladaptive behaviors. When helpers are honest about their reactions, clients learn how they come across to other people and thus might change their problematic behaviors. Some examples of interpersonal behaviors that can cause problems for clients in helping relationships include being so talkative that the helper cannot speak at all, acting overbearing and arrogant and assuming that they are better than the helper, remaining passive and not saying anything without being asked, droning on and on in a monotone voice without maintaining eye contact, disagreeing with everything the helper says, constantly bringing gifts to the helper, or trying to be too helpful. In the world outside of helping, friends and acquaintances might not give honest feedback about how they perceive the person because it is too difficult, may hurt feelings, or could take too much time or effort. Because they do not receive feedback, however, clients often are not aware of how they come across to others. If individuals are oblivious to their own behaviors (which they often are because they are so used to them), they cannot change them, and there could be negative consequences (e.g., if a client is not aware that she speaks with a hostile tone, it could negatively affect her evaluations in the workplace). The helping relationship provides an opportunity for clients to become aware of how their behaviors affect another person.

Immediacy can also be used to make covert communication more direct. In some cases, clients talk covertly about the helping relationship because they are not sure how helpers will react if they say something directly. For example, a client might say that no one can help him. Because the helper is trying to help him, it is not a huge leap to guess that at least part of the communication is directed toward the helper. In any communication, helpers can ask themselves what clients are trying to communicate to them about the therapy relationship, although whether they use immediacy should be tempered by the clinical situation and the client's needs at the time.

Helpers who gently provide honest feedback may be giving their clients a special gift. Letting clients know how you perceive them in a caring way requires deep levels of empathy. Helpers take a huge risk in sharing these feelings, but it can be effective if helpers are empathic and sensitive. In effect, immediacy communicates that helpers are willing to take the time to let clients know about the effect of their behaviors so they can have an opportunity to increase awareness and change inappropriate behaviors.

It is also important to comment about cultural differences in terms of dealing immediately with relationship difficulties. In cultures in which typical communication is indirect, it can be considered rude to directly communicate about the relationship. Helpers can still use immediacy but may have to be very gentle and tentative in their manner of delivery.

Several theorists (e.g., Carkhuff, 1969; Cashdan, 1988; Ivey, 1994; Kiesler, 1988; Teyber, 2000) have written about immediacy. Kiesler stated that *metacommunication* (his term for immediacy) occurs when helpers disclose to clients their perceptions of and reactions to a client's actions. He distinguished metacommunication from other disclosures of personal factual or historical information about life experiences because they relate specifically to the helper's experience of the client. Kiesler indicated that metacommunication is one of the most powerful responses in the helper's repertoire because the helper responds to the client in a different manner than that to which the client is accustomed. Rather than ignoring obnoxious behavior, as is often the case in social interactions, for example, the helper confronts the client directly and describes the impact of the client's behavior on the helper. Similarly, Ivey called *immediacy* being "in the moment" with the client. He pointed out that most clients talk in the past tense about events but might profit from talking in the present tense about what is going on in the helping relationship.

How to Use Immediacy

Immediacy is a difficult and demanding skill. Helpers need to be aware of what is happening in the therapeutic relationship and have enough self-confidence and self-understanding not to react defensively to clients' open expression of feelings. Because they do not always openly deal with immediate feelings in nonhelping situations, helpers often feel frightened about doing so in helping situations. It takes courage, as well as skill, to be immediate with clients. Drawing liberally from other theorists who have written about immediacy (Carkhuff, 1969; Cashdan, 1988, Ivey, 1994; Kiesler, 1988, Teyber, 2000), the following steps are proposed to enable helpers to use immediacy in helping session.

STEP 1. BECOME HOOKED

Helpers first need to experience personally the impact of a client's behavior, which Kiesler (1988) and Cashdan (1988) called becoming "hooked." They noted that helpers are pushed into a constricted, narrow range of responses by the client's maladaptive behaviors. Helpers respond to clients unconsciously according to clients' demands (e.g., dominant clients elicit submissive behavior from helpers; hostile clients elicit hostile behavior from helpers). Thus, helpers experience firsthand how clients interact with at least some other people. If helpers attend carefully to their reactions, they can begin to understand how other people react to clients in interpersonal relationships.

Helpers need to allow themselves to have their feelings without judging themselves as "bad" or incompetent. Rather, helpers can view them-

selves as instruments and use their feelings to determine how they reso-
nate with or react to clients. Supervision can be very useful in facilitating
helpers in their struggle with experiencing negative feelings toward clients because supervisors can normalize such feelings. For example, the
supervisor might say, "If I were in this situation, I would feel sexually
attracted to this client. She is so beautiful that I would feel distracted in
sessions." When supervisors are able to admit to having "politically incorrect" feelings, helpers often are then able to acknowledge their feelings.
Thus, supervision is invaluable for enabling helpers to become aware of
their feelings and also for ensuring that helpers do not act impulsively on
their feelings.

STEP 2. BECOME AWARE OF AND PULL OUT OF BEING HOOKED

Helpers must become aware of and stop their automatic reactions by determining their inner feelings about clients. Typical markers are any
nontherapeutic feelings: boredom, sexual attraction, anger, feeling totally
stuck, feelings of greater incompetence than usual, feelings of great pride
or brilliance in one's interventions. Another typical marker for helpers is
feeling afraid and wanting to avoid certain topics with the client.

Sometimes this self-examination is difficult for helpers. Helpers typically like to think of themselves as being accepting and nurturing, but
they might instead find themselves feeling bored, sexually attracted, angry, entertained, incompetent, annoyed, adored, overidentified, sympathetic, or pitying and hence may act in a nontherapeutic manner. To get
into these potential feelings, helpers can ask themselves:

- "What am I feeling when I am with this client?"
- "What do I want to do or not do when I am with this client?"
- "What keeps me from using the skills that I know I should be using
  with this client?"

Rather than taking it personally and feeling badly that they had these
strong emotions, helpers can try to cultivate a sense of curiosity about
what contributes to clients' acting as they do, rather than blaming clients
for their behaviors. Often, clients have developed these behaviors as defenses. For example, if a client is very talkative and does not let anyone
else contribute to the discussion, the client could be defending against
letting anyone get close for fear of becoming engulfed. Thus, the constant
talking may serve a defensive function of keeping others at a safe distance. Helpers can aid clients in gaining insight about the reasons for their
behaviors.

By coming to an understanding of what clients are "pulling" from
them, helpers regain objectivity, which permits them to distance them-

selves from their reactions and begin to help the client. For example, by becoming aware that a client's whining pulls for the helper to be sadistic, the helper can stop trying to silence the client and shift to wondering what causes the client to whine. The helper can then think about how to provide the client with feedback about the effects of her or his whining.

STEP 3. DETERMINE INTENTIONS

Helpers need to determine their intentions for intervening with clients. The appropriate therapeutic intentions are to promote insight, deal with the therapeutic relationship, identify maladaptive behaviors, and identify and intensify feelings. It is inappropriate when helpers use immediacy for their own needs. Thus, helpers need to evaluate whether any of their own issues could be implicated in the feelings they have when they are with clients. Helpers must also be careful not to let countertransference reactions interfere with their reactions to clients. For example, a helper might be sensitive to a client's talkativeness and aggressiveness because the helper's mother is very dominant and talks incessantly. If helpers find they have similar feelings with several clients (e.g., being sexually attracted to several clients), this could be a clue that it is the helper's rather than the clients' problem.

STEP 4. ASSESS CLIENT READINESS

Helpers also need to determine whether they have enough information about the client's behaviors, whether the therapeutic relationship is strong enough to withstand direct communication, and whether clients can handle discussions of immediacy before they intervene. It is not a good idea to bring up the immediate relationship when clients are in crisis and very involved in working on some other problem. In contrast, a good time is when the client seems to be "circling," or talking about the same things over and over, the process is halted, or the client expresses curiosity about how he or she comes across in relationships.

STEP 5. USE IMMEDIACY TO TALK ABOUT THE RELATIONSHIP

When using immediacy, helpers talk directly to clients about their interactions. In other words, helpers and clients metacommunicate about their communication. Kiesler (1988) stressed that the success of the metacommunication depends on the extent to which helpers balance the challenge of the metacommunication with being supportive and protective of the client's self-esteem. Helpers need to present the metacommunication as a gentle examination of the process in which helpers communicate that they are committed to working with clients to understand their actions and the effects of their behaviors on relationships with other people.

Helpers should take appropriate responsibility for their feelings when using immediacy (e.g., "I feel uncomfortable that you keep praising me" or "I feel bad that I interrupted you"). "I" statements have a very different impact than "you" statements (e.g., "You shouldn't praise me" or "You talk too much"). Clients often have an easier time owning their responsibility (e.g., "I was probably talking too much") when helpers have candidly admitted their contribution to the interaction. Furthermore, it is only fair for helpers to admit their responsibility if they demand that clients acknowledge their part. When helpers acknowledge their role in relationship problems, an open exchange can occur about how both people feel. Problems can be resolved, the therapeutic relationship can be enhanced, and clients can be encouraged to become actively involved in problem solving. For example, at mid-semester, a helper discovered that her client (Maria) was in the same practicum class as the helper's partner. The helper repeatedly asked Maria to process this situation even though Maria indicated that she had worked through her feelings on her own at the beginning of the semester. The helper later apologized and indicated that she realized she had many feelings about the situation and had inadvertently projected them onto the client.

Of course some clients will be happy to lay all the blame on the helper and turn the tables to talk about the helper's problems. If this happens, the helper can use that as an immediacy intervention (e.g., "You know, I'm feeling a little attacked. I wonder if we both can look at our parts in this interaction?").

It is crucial that helpers not prescribe how clients should change, because "should" statements imply that the helper knows more about the client than the client does, which goes against the client-centered nature of this model. Instead, helpers merely point out how they react when clients act in a particular way and wonder why they act that way. It is also important that helpers are aware that their feedback about the client is based on their perceptions and reactions and that others might react differently to the client. Helpers might even suggest that clients gather feedback about how others react to the behaviors. An awareness of how they are perceived by others can enable clients to make choices about how to behave and decide whether they want to make changes.

STEP 6. PROCESS THE INTERACTION

After being immediate with clients, helpers need to ask clients about their reactions to the immediacy, so that the communication is two-sided. Hence, after the helper says something like, "I find myself having a hard time staying awake when you talk," the helper can ask the client, "How do you feel about what I said" or "You became awfully quiet when I said I had a hard time staying awake. What was going on inside you?" Thus, the helper tries to engage the client in a discussion of the interaction. Research shows that it is important for helpers to be open about exploring the interaction (Rhodes et al., 1994; Safran et al., 2002).

Because helpers have indicated that it is permissible to process the relationship, they need to be aware that clients may give them feedback about what they do not like about the helper's behaviors. After all, helping is a two-way interaction, and helpers may be doing things that are not optimal for clients. Some of this information may be accurate and valuable—clients are often wonderful sources of feedback because they are the recipients of what helpers do and know exactly how the interventions feel. In fact, I strongly urge helpers to obtain client feedback and reactions. However, helpers also must be aware that feedback is sometimes distorted (i.e., transference). For example, Yutta may say that the helper is mean, not because of what the helper has done, but because of unresolved feelings she has about her critical mother that she projects onto the helper. Helpers have to determine what feedback is genuinely related to their behavior and what is related to transference issues. I would suggest that there is at least a grain of truth in most client feedback, and helpers should investigate both their own behaviors and the client's contribution because both may be implicated.

EXAMPLE OF A HELPER USING STEPS 5 AND 6 OF IMMEDIACY

Client: I would really like to sleep with you. I think sex is very important and a natural way of relating to someone that you're close to. It's just a matter of time until you agree to sleep with me. I know you're attracted to me—I can see it in your eyes.

Helper: *It makes me uncomfortable when you talk about having sex with me. I wonder what your intentions are in talking with me about it?*

Client: Well, that's how men and women are supposed to relate. You say you're trying to help me. What I really need is for you to go to bed with me. That would give me some security that I am attractive.

Helper: So you have a hard time relating to me on a non-sexual basis.

Client: Yeah, I guess I do.

Helper: *I wonder if you have any ideas about what leads you to relate to me in a sexual way when it is not appropriate for what we are trying to do here?*

    Client: That's interesting. My mother was always very seduc-
            tive. I've always reacted to women on a sexual basis.
            Women are usually pretty eager to sleep with me.
    Helper: *I wonder how it feels to talk about our relationship?*
    Client: Well, I'm not used to it. I still can't see why you won't
            sleep with me.
    Helper: *I can understand more now that when you get anxious about*
            talking with me, you change the topic to talking about sex.
            Do you notice that?
    Client: Yeah, I guess I can see that. I am uncomfortable talk-
            ing. I'm more of an action-type person.

Effects of Immediacy

Helpers can watch tapes of their sessions and use the following three-point scale to determine the effects of their immediacy statements on clients.

1 = If the immediacy is not helpful or is poorly timed, clients could feel wounded, hurt, or abused. Some clients could become silent or wary. In addition, some clients might blame their helpers for making them feel bad or might not return for sessions because they felt so misunderstood.

2 = If the immediacy is moderately helpful, clients might listen to the feedback but not respond. They might be able to hear the feedback but be unwilling to share their thoughts or feelings.

3 = If the immediacy is very helpful, clients might engage in dialogue with the helper about the feedback, admit to their contribution to the interaction, and become interested in what might have led to them acting this way, thus gaining insight.

Difficulties Helpers Have in Using Immediacy

Beginning helpers often have fears about intruding and making clients angry if they use immediacy, even if they do it empathically. Indeed, clients do sometimes become angry when helpers point out their maladaptive behaviors. For example, a helper gently suggested that Olivia was acting helpless when she expected her helper to take responsibility for her behavior and failures. Olivia became angry and adamantly denied that her behaviors were similar to those of victims. Several sessions later, however, Olivia acknowledged that the immediacy intervention was accurate and helped her become motivated to take more control of her life. If the helper had withheld the immediacy intervention for fear of hurting Olivia's feelings, Olivia would not have learned a valuable lesson about herself. Although it is sometimes painful to hear, such feedback can be motivational and subsequently life changing.

Another problem is that some helpers do not trust their feelings (e.g., "Maybe it is all my fault that I'm bored—if I were a better helper, I wouldn't feel bored"). They might feel unsure about their reactions and hesitant about communicating their feelings to clients appropriately and empathically. Some helpers simply avoid immediacy because it is frightening to talk directly and honestly about the immediate relationship. They are not used to such open communication in their relationships, and they feel vulnerable when sharing immediate feelings. They might feel anxious about dealing openly with interpersonal conflicts because their families had strong rules against addressing conflicts openly. In fact, most helpers have an easier time being empathic with clients who are sad or depressed but are less skilled when it comes to talking directly with another person about negative reactions and working through interpersonal problems. Once again, personal therapy can be useful for providing an opportunity for helpers to come to understand their own issues. Supervision can also provide a reality check for helpers because they can learn how someone else reacts to the client.

Finally, helpers sometimes inappropriately (and often unconsciously) use immediacy to deal with their own needs. For example, a helper who had recently been divorced was feeling particularly vulnerable and needed affirmation that he was attractive, so he encouraged his client to talk about her attraction to him. Usually helpers are not aware that they are using immediacy to deal with their own needs. They might become aware that they are doing so, however, if their behaviors have negative consequences for their clients (e.g., a client quits after the helper gets angry at her for being too quiet). Hence, it is crucial that helpers are mindful of their needs so these needs do not intrude on the helping process.

It is often hard for beginning helpers to imagine using immediacy because most of their interactions with clients are very brief and require that helpers stay primarily in the exploration stage. However, beginning helpers can still practice this skill in role-plays and be aware of how it could be used in actual sessions with clients with whom they work for longer periods of time.

HELPFUL HINTS

- Use your inner reactions to the client as a guide. Allow yourself to be "hooked" but then step back and examine your reactions, become curious about what causes the client's behavior, think about your intentions and your contribution to the interaction, and assess the client's readiness before intervening.

- Be gentle and tentative (but not apologetic) in using immediacy. Remember that you are giving your opinion or perspective, not the "truth."

- Keep the immediacy statement short and keep the focus on the relationship.

- Be specific about a recent behavior rather than vague and general about things that occurred in the past.

- Be ready to talk about and process the feelings that arise after the immediacy intervention. Ask clients for their reactions to immediacy interventions.

- Take responsibility for your contribution to problems in the relationship. "Own" your feelings rather than blaming clients for "causing" you to feel a certain way.

- Implement this intervention first only under close supervision (i.e., being observed). Supervisors can work with you to ensure that your intentions are appropriate and to help you select the appropriate timing for intervening.

- I highly recommend that helpers read *Love's Executioner* by Yalom (1990). Yalom has written articulately and openly about his personal reactions to working with a variety of clients. He is refreshingly honest about his reactions and provides a model for how helpers can use their reactions to enhance the therapeutic process.

PRACTICE EXERCISES

For each of the following examples, write an immediacy statement. Compare your responses to the possible helper responses provided at the end of the section.

Statements

1. Client: "You know I thought about what you said last time, and I got really angry. I don't think you know what you're talking about when you suggest that I go to see my old boyfriend when I go into town to give a talk. He hasn't even tried to contact me for ten years, and I'm supposed to be focused on my work and giving a talk. I couldn't possibly concentrate if I knew I had to spend time going to see him and started worrying about what he would say."

Helper response: _____

_____

2. Client: "You sure haven't been very helpful today. You don't give me any good advice. I don't know why I bother coming here. It's a waste of time."
   Helper response: _____

   _____

3. Client: (silent for five minutes)
   Helper response: _____

   _____

4. (Client talks on and on without pausing for 15 minutes.)
   Helper response: _____

   _____

Possible Helper Responses

1. "I'm sorry I suggested that you contact your old boyfriend. It obviously was hurtful to you. Maybe we could spend some time talking about what was going on between us given that I don't usually tell you what to do."
   "I feel concerned that you are blaming me when my memory is that you were the one to suggest that you go to see him."
2. "I also am feeling frustrated that we don't seem to be getting anywhere."
   "I feel upset right now because I put a lot of time and energy into our relationship and yet it doesn't seem to be enough for you."
3. "You seem angry with me. Can you talk about what's going on?"
   "I am worried about you right now because you seem so distant."
4. "I'm feeling bored right now. I wonder if you're aware that you've been talking nonstop for 15 minutes? What do you suppose is going on inside you?"
   "I'm feeling a little irritated that we're not getting anywhere. You seem like you're more interested in telling stories than working today. How do you feel?"

WHAT DO YOU THINK?

▪ Discuss whether you think helpers can balance being direct with feedback and accepting clients for who they are.
▪ How might helpers respond when clients are angry at them?
▪ Discuss the idea that immediacy can be an enactment of a deep level of empathy.
▪ Discuss the advantages and disadvantages of using immediacy as compared with interpretations.

LAB 12

Immediacy

Exercise 1

Goal: For helpers to practice immediacy in the context of the other helping skills.

This lab is meant for advanced students who are seeing "real" clients. In this lab, I recommend forming groups of four to six people. I suggest that a helper who is currently seeing a client present a case. The helper plays the part of the client so the helper can portray how the client behaves (and also gain more empathy for the client by playing the client). A second group member plays the role of the helper. Other group members can provide ideas to the helper about other possible ways of intervening or take over the role of helper if the helper gets stuck. Each group should have a designated lab leader (other than the helper) to organize and coordinate the session.

Helper's and Client's Tasks During the Helping Interchange

1. The client (played by the actual helper) role-plays how the actual client presents him- or herself, trying to portray the client's behavior that makes it particularly difficult for the actual helper to respond therapeutically. The actual helper should not provide any introductory material or talk about the actual client or the history of the helping interaction prior to the role-play because the idea is for group members to respond naturally, without receiving potentially biasing information.
2. The helper should respond for several speaking turns using the exploration skills (open question, restatement, reflection) until she or he has formed some rapport and has experienced an inner reaction to the client.
3. When the interactional patterns are at least somewhat clear, the lab leader should ask the helper to pause for a moment.
4. Everyone (except the client) can write down an immediacy statement. Each helper can ask themselves, "What am I feeling right now?" "What is going on in the relationship?" "How much of this is due to my own personal issues?"
5. Each helper should give an immediacy statement and allow the client time to respond.

Observers' Tasks During the Helping Interchange

Everyone should observe all the interactions and note which ones seemed particularly helpful or unhelpful and why. How does the helper present the immediacy statement? Does the helper take responsibility for her or his feelings? How does the client respond to the immediacy statement? How does the relationship between the helper and client appear? How would you feel in each role?

After the Helping Interchange

The client can talk about reactions to hearing the immediacy intervention. The helper can talk about how it felt to use immediacy. Everyone can provide feedback about their observations and perceptions of the interaction.

SWITCH ROLES

Exercise 2

Goal: To integrate the exploration and insight skills.
Students should pair up. One person will be the helper and one the client.

Helper's and Client's Tasks During the Helping Interchange

1. Clients should talk about something that they do but they don't know why they do it, or about something that confuses or puzzles them.
2. Helpers should use exploration skills (open questions, restatement, and reflection of feelings) for five to ten minutes to help the client explore.
3. Once they have established some rapport, helpers should begin using insight skills (challenge, interpretation, self-disclosure, and immediacy) when appropriate, interspersed with exploration skills.

After the Helping Interchange

Clients can talk about their reactions. Helpers can talk about their intentions and their perceptions of the client reactions.

SWITCH ROLES

Personal Reflections

- How do you feel about dealing with interpersonal conflict?
- For the helpers who played the roles of their clients: What did you learn about your clients? How did your feelings change toward the clients? Describe any new ideas you learned for dealing with your clients.
- How would you respond to a client who wanted to give you feedback?

Integrating the Skills of the Insight Stage 17

He who has a *why* to live can bear with almost any *how*.

—Nietzsche

Benjamin, who has been unable to choose a career, comes to realize that he is afraid to compete with his father, a businessman who is an extremely successful but distant from his family. Yvonne comes to understand that her feelings of inadequacy are based on other children making fun of her for having a slight speech impediment. Nigel gains the insight that he avoids all risks because of his fear of dying at a young age as his father did. These are examples of new understandings that clients come to in the insight stage with the aid of helpers.

At the end of the insight stage, clients hopefully have some new understandings of themselves at a deep, emotional level. They see things in new ways or from different perspectives, are able to identify patterns or make connections, and have a deeper understanding of their inner dynamics. These insights usually have an "aha" quality to them, and clients feel relieved that they have new explanations for their behaviors and thoughts. Clients "own" their new understandings because they have been instrumental in helping to construct them.

Integrating the Insight Skills

In the insight stage, helpers assist clients in developing new perspectives about themselves, their feelings, and their behaviors. They maintain an

---

Web Forms referred to in text can be found on the book's companion online guide described in the Preface.

empathic connection with clients and continue using the exploration skills, but they are also willing to gently challenge clients and help them go to deeper levels of understanding. As Exhibit 17.1 illustrates, helpers use challenge, interpretation, self-disclosure, or immediacy, depending on what clients are presenting at the moment, what clients can tolerate, their intentions, and their overall plan for the session. They challenge clients' discrepancies, irrational ideas, or defenses to raise awareness. They use interpretations to facilitate new understandings of the underlying reasons or motivations for thoughts and behaviors. They self-disclose what they learned about themselves to suggest possible insights. They use immediacy to help clients attain insight about inappropriate behaviors or to deal with tensions or misunderstandings in the therapeutic relationship. These interventions help clients achieve greater depths of self-understanding and insight about who they are, how they got to be the way they are, and how they are perceived by others.

WHEN TO USE EXPLORATION SKILLS

In the insight stage, helpers still use exploration skills frequently. For example, when clients seem ready to gain some insight on their own with a little encouragement from the helper, the helper might only need to ask something like, "I wonder if you've thought of what might be going on to cause you to act in such an atypical manner?" Thus, rather than helpers giving insight, helpers can encourage clients to challenge themselves and think about what is going on inside. One advantage of encouraging clients to construct their own insights is that helpers are not always around to provide insights, so clients need to be able to think deeply about their own inner dynamics and be curious about their motives.

Exploration skills are also useful after helpers have challenged, interpreted, self-disclosed, or given an immediacy statement. Clients are now at a new point and need time to process (or "work through") the new information; using the exploration skills can help clients talk about their thoughts and feelings. For example, a statement such as "You sound surprised and pleased to realize that you might be reacting negatively to your boss because he is similar to your uncle, not because he is a bad guy" could help the client think further about the new insight.

WHEN TO USE CHALLENGES

Challenges are useful when clients are feeling ambivalent, contradictory, stuck, or unable to make a decision. Challenges can make clients more aware of what is going on inside them. For nonresistant clients, challenges are typically most helpful when done gently and tentatively, although they may need to be done more forcefully with resistant clients.

EXHIBIT 17. 1

A Guide for Which Helping Skills to Use During the Insight Stage

Marker in session	When helper intends to	Helper might try
At all points	Support	Attending and listening Approval and reassurance Open questions
Client is able to attain insight on own with a little encouragement	Promote insight	Open questions
After relationship is established and client is contradictory, ambivalent, unable to make a decision, or is stuck	Challenge, encourage self- control, deal with resistance	Challenge Open questions
After relationship is established and client seems receptive and lacks understanding about behaviors, thoughts, or feelings; seems to be acting from defenses, resistances, or transference	Promote insight, encourage self-control	Interpretation
After relationship is established and client feels shame about revealing things, has a hard time gaining insight, or feels blamed or isolated	Challenge, promote insight, encourage self-control	Self-disclosure Reflection of feelings Immediacy Approval and reassurance
If there is a problem in the relationship that impedes progress or if the client's behavior has negative effects on the helper (and probably others) and feedback would be helpful	Deal with relationship, encourage self-control, deal with resistance	Challenge Immediacy
If the client does not completely understand or expresses disagreement with insight interventions	Deal with relationship, encourage self-control, deal with resistance	Repeat intervention in a different way Wait until the client seems more receptive Immediacy Open questions about feeling Reflection of feelings
After a challenge, interpretation, self-disclosure, or immediacy has been used and the client is trying to understand it	Focus, clarify, encourage catharsis, identify maladaptive cognitions or behaviors, identify and intensify feelings	Open questions about feelings Reflection of feelings Restatement
If helper's countertransference feelings are interfering with the helping process	Not harm the client	Seek supervision or personal therapy

Helpers are identifying blind spots, problems, defenses, irrational ideas, or incongruencies of which the client might not have been aware or was trying to avoid, and so they must be sensitive to delivering challenges in ways that clients can hear them. Using humor can sometimes be an effective way to help clients see themselves in new ways.

WHEN TO USE INTERPRETATIONS

Interpretations can be useful when clients do not understand what motivates them to behave in maladaptive ways, are confused or curious about why they have certain thoughts or feelings, or seem to be acting from unconscious influences. Interpretations can be particularly useful to clarify the underlying reasons for current thoughts, behaviors, and feelings. The source of interpretations is often in childhood, the time when clients learned many of their maladaptive thoughts and behaviors. In a related vein, helpers can also develop interpretations on the basis of transference (distorted expectations about the helper based on early experiences) and defenses. Another source of interpretations is connecting seemingly disparate issues for clients to show that their behaviors make sense if one considers varied aspects of their lives. An additional source of interpretations is existential concerns, given that all of us struggle with issues about death, freedom and responsibility, isolation, and the meaning of life.

WHEN TO USE SELF-DISCLOSURES OF INSIGHT

Self-disclosures can be useful in bringing clients to insights that they might have felt too threatened to admit if suggested directly through other interventions. With self-disclosure, helpers reveal some aspect of their personal experience that they think might help clients gain greater self-understanding and think more deeply about themselves. Self-disclosure can be a powerful intervention, particularly when it allows clients to feel that they are not alone with their struggles. Empirical research shows that when experienced therapists used self-disclosure, clients perceived it as being very helpful, perhaps because it was used infrequently (Hill & Knox, 2002). It seems best if helpers disclose about past issues that have been resolved. Disclosure is often a difficult skill for beginning helpers to learn how to use well; they disclose too much because they overidentify with clients and are less skilled in keeping their unresolved issues from impinging on the helping process.

WHEN TO USE IMMEDIACY

Immediacy is a useful intervention when there are problems in the therapeutic relationship such that therapeutic progress is impeded, when the client's behavior in sessions is maladaptive and feedback would be helpful, or when the client is interested in learning more about how she or he comes across. Immediacy allows helpers to provide feedback to clients about how they are perceived in sessions and to gain some insight about why they act as they do. It is important that helpers admit their own feelings in addition to giving clients feedback about their behaviors. Discussing the relationship can provide a powerful learning experience because helpers are demonstrating to clients how to deal with interpersonal conflict in a respectful, yet assertive, manner. Thus, problems can be resolved, clients can gain some insight into the reasons for their behaviors, and clients can learn the skills to handle interpersonal conflicts better in relationships outside of the helping situation.

Caveats About Using Insight Skills

Several caveats apply to the use of insight interventions. First, the therapeutic relationship must be solid before insight skills are used. Clients must trust their helpers, and helpers must have a base of knowledge about clients from which to formulate insight interventions. A relationship can sometimes be established quickly, but at other times, a long period of testing is needed before the relationship can withstand insight interventions. In addition, helpers should always be attentive to client reactions to insight interventions. The most superb insight interventions are worthless if clients are not ready for them; relationships can be damaged by premature insight interventions.

It is best to encourage clients to come to their own insights, if possible, through probing open questions and adding just minimally from a different perspective. If clients are productively working on insight, helpers are mainly in the position of encouraging them and coaching them rather than telling them what to think. The process in the insight stage needs to be collaborative. Helpers and clients need to work together to construct understanding, rather than helpers articulating all the insights for the clients.

When used, insight interventions need to be delivered gently and tentatively, with caring and empathy, rather than with judgment or blame. They should be preceded by and interspersed with exploration skills (reflection of feelings, restatement, and open questions). As clients contemplate what they have learned from insight interventions, they are at a new level and need time and support to explore what they have discovered about themselves. Furthermore, helpers continually revise their insight interventions based on emerging information, treating them as working hypotheses rather than as fundamental truths.

In addition, insight interventions may need to be repeated many times, in diverse ways, over long periods of time, so clients can begin to incorporate them, use them to change their thinking, and apply them to different parts of their lives. Altering ingrained ways of thinking is difficult, and repetition often assists clients in being able to hear and use the new insights.

Many clients value insight and need to understand the reasons for their current troubles and ways of being to improve their functioning. However, it is important to recognize that not all clients are interested in or willing to search for insight. Thus, helpers will not want to pursue this deep understanding with all clients. Rather, helpers might move directly into action for clients who need an immediate sense of symptom relief, desperately need problem resolution, or have no interest in insight.

Finally, *countertransference* (defined and discussed in chaps. 3 and 12) can interfere with the helper's ability to deliver insight interventions effectively. For example, a client talking about abortion or divorce might stimulate unresolved feelings about these issues on the part of a helper; a helper who has problems dealing with anger might withdraw when a client becomes angry at her. Once again, I stress the value of therapy and supervision to ensure that personal issues do not negatively influence the helping relationship.

MULTICULTURAL CONSIDERATIONS

Given that helpers are relying more on their own reactions and thoughts in the insight stage, they have to be extraordinarily careful about imposing their own values on clients from other cultures. For example, a Western helper might challenge a 22-year-old Asian student about not being more independent and separate from her parents, but this might oppose the client's cultural value to be dependent on her parents until marriage. As another example, a helper might interpret a client's caring for an aging parent as self-defeating in terms of career advancement, whereas the client feels a cultural obligation to sacrifice self for others. Western values promote individualism and self-actualization, whereas Eastern cultures value collectivism and familial obligations (Kim, Atkinson, & Umemoto, 2001; Kim, Atkinson, & Yang, 1999); these differences in values can lead to cultural clashes in terms of understanding dynamics and psychological problems.

Another cultural consideration related to the insight stage is that some cultures teach people to think authority figures have the ultimate answers. Hence, interpretations may take on greater meaning to them as the "right" answer. In such instances, helpers have to be careful about what they say. In contrast, clients from non-Western cultures might benefit from judicious self-disclosure of insight as a way of building trust (Sue & Sue, 1999). Self-disclosure might provide a model for clients without dictating what the client should feel.

An additional consideration is that immediacy may seem quite rude and intrusive to people from cultures where open, here-and-now communication is not valued. Again, helpers should be very attentive to clients' reactions and ask about any discomfort.

Developing Hypotheses About Client Dynamics

To make decisions about how to intervene in the insight stage, helpers rely in part on their perceptions and intuitions. They use themselves as barometers of what is going on in the relationship. They allow themselves to have their inner reactions and then question how the client contributes to their interactions. Helpers can ask themselves the following questions to begin to assess client dynamics:

- Are there discrepancies or contradictions in feelings, actions, or thoughts expressed by the client?
- What might be causing the client to behave this way at this time?
- What contributes to keeping this client from changing at this time?
- What are the client defenses, resistances, and transferences operating in this situation?
- How am I feeling in the therapeutic relationship and could others react similarly to this client?

Teaching students about conceptualization skills can be built into the training program. After role-plays, the instructor can ask students to begin to think about client dynamics. For example, in one training session, Kunal (a student in class who was the volunteer client) talked about not having been accepted into graduate school and feeling unsure about what he wanted to do—did he really want to go to graduate school or do something else with his life? After one student acted as the helper going through the exploration stage, I stopped the interaction and initiated a discussion about emerging conceptualizations of this client. We wondered whether Kunal had problems with committment in other areas, and speculated about family pressures with regard to attending graduate school. (Note that I asked Kunal to sit quietly and listen but not respond.) These speculations were helpful in identifying issues for consideration in the insight stage. Similarly, it could be helpful for helpers to talk with supervisors about conceptualizations as a way to stimulate one's thinking.

Helpers can begin to develop intentions for interventions by hypothesizing about the client's problem, the reason the client is talking about the problem at this particular time, and what the helper can do to help. Conceptualization enables helpers to have a focus and intentions for interventions instead of just wandering around aimlessly in sessions.

Difficulties Helpers Experience in the Insight Stage

Becoming competent in the skills used during the insight stage is difficult; it often takes many years to master these skills. In addition, the skills cannot be applied in a rote, technical fashion to every client, which makes it challenging for instructors to teach and for students to learn these skills. Helpers have to use their intuition and rely on their reactions to clients, so there is more danger of countertransference interfering with the process. Helpers need to proceed slowly and observe clients' reactions to their insight interventions but should not avoid insight interventions because they might miss opportunities to help clients understand themselves at deeper levels.

MOVING PREMATURELY INTO THE INSIGHT STAGE

Helpers sometimes move into the insight stage before the therapeutic relationship has been firmly established, before the client has adequately explored the problems, or before the helper has a deep understanding of the problems. It is crucial that challenge, interpretation, self-disclosure of insight, and immediacy be used within the context of a strong therapeutic relationship and with a strong foundation of understanding. Otherwise, these techniques have the potential for damaging clients. For example, if a helper challenges before the client trusts the helper, the client might doubt the helper's motives and terminate the helping relationship.

TAKING TOO MUCH RESPONSIBILITY FOR DEVELOPING INSIGHTS

Some helpers feel that they have to be the ones to "put it all together" and connect all the client's past experiences with their present behaviors in a new way. The helper may be impatient because the client cannot see what is blatantly obvious to the helper. To this helper, figuring out clients is more important than helping clients figure out themselves. From my perspective, the more important task is for helpers to empathize with clients, determine what contributes to clients having difficulty putting it all together, ask them about their thoughts about insight, and work collaboratively with clients to construct insights.

GETTING STUCK ON ONE THEORETICAL PERSPECTIVE

One of the dangers in the insight stage is that helpers may try to apply psychoanalytic theory, even though the theory might not fit for an individual client. The psychoanalytic theories are incredibly cogent and thoughtful, and beginning helpers can easily become entranced by them, believing every word that Freud, Kohut, or someone else wrote. For example, a helper could be convinced that every client is suffering from an Oedipal–Electra complex because Freud said so, rather than attending to the data that the client presents. In fact, psychoanalytic theories are clinical theories developed by clinicians and have not for the most part been proven, so one must be judicious in applying them.

TAKING CLIENTS AT FACE VALUE AND NOT DIGGING DEEPER

Sometimes helpers are afraid of upsetting clients and being intrusive, so they neglect to search deeper to help clients. However, clients often value hearing another perspective about their problems because they feel stuck, so helpers need to be willing to help clients construct new understandings.

FORGETTING TO BE EMPATHIC

Some helpers get so excited about figuring out the puzzle of the client's problems that they forget to be empathic. They do not remember the importance of keeping clients involved in the therapeutic experience. It is crucial to be constantly aware of how clients are feeling and reacting and to work at maintaining the collaborative relationship.

CLIENTS NOT NEEDING OR WANTING INSIGHT

No matter how much we as helpers personally value insight, not all of our clients are equally enamored. Some clients (and even some helpers) do not want or need insight. They prefer support without challenge and insight, or they want immediate behavioral change without insight. They may want to feel better without understanding why they felt badly. Because this approach is essentially client-centered and values empathy above all, it is important not to impose insight on such clients but to respect their choice not to understand themselves. For such clients, I recommend making an assessment about whether they primarily need support, behavioral change, or something helpers cannot offer. If clients need support to make behavioral changes, helpers can provide that and reduce the emphasis on the insight stage. If clients need other things (e.g., medication, support groups, welfare), helpers can refer them to other sources.

Strategies for Overcoming Difficulties in Implementing the Insight Stage

USE EXPLORATION SKILLS

When in doubt or having problems, I recommend helpers use the basic skills of attending and listening, open questions, restatement, and reflection of feelings. In effect, helpers need to backtrack, rebuild trust, and make sure they hear the client's real problems. Helpers can keep exploring until an idea for a challenge or interpretation emerges naturally and the client is ready to hear it.

DEAL WITH PERSONAL FEELINGS

It is important for helpers to be as aware as possible of what they are feeling. They need to sort out how much is a reaction to the client and how much is related to their personal issues. I strongly recommend that helpers get personal therapy to deal with strong emotional reactions that arise when they are helpers. In addition, it is helpful to talk to supervisors about feelings that come up when working with clients.

DEAL WITH THE RELATIONSHIP

In one study (Rhodes et al., 1994), satisfied clients were asked what their helpers had done to resolve major misunderstandings that arose in relationships. The clients reported that their helpers asked them how they were feeling about what was going on in the therapeutic relationship. Helpers listened nondefensively to the clients and were willing to hear what they were doing wrong with clients. They apologized if they made a mistake or hurt the client's feelings. If helpers acknowledge their part in problems in the helping relationship, they serve as models for how to deal with mistakes and how to respond in a human way to another person. In addition, helpers can talk about their feelings about the relationship to let clients know how their behaviors influence others. Providing a place where clients can discuss both positive and negative feelings toward the helper and the sessions is both challenging and critically important. Finally, helpers can thank clients for sharing their feelings. It is often painful and difficult to process the therapeutic relationship, so clients need to be assured that they can bring up both positive and negative feelings.

AN EXAMPLE OF AN EXTENDED INTERACTION

In this example, the helper has established rapport and the client has explored her feelings about her relationship with her daughter. I start at the beginning of the insight stage:

Helper: So you said your daughter is not doing well in middle school and you're worried that she's going to flunk out of school. (The helper wants to tie together what the client has been talking about and so offers a summary statement.)

Client: Yeah, she just never does her homework. She watches television all the time, talks on the phone to her friends constantly, and eats. She's not even doing any extracurricular activities at school. I just can't get her to do anything. She just got her grades, which she wouldn't even let me see at first. I finally got them from her, and she's flunking two classes.

Helper: Have you considered getting her a tutor? (The helper jumps prematurely to the action stage here to offer suggestions for what to do about the problem.)

Client: We keep trying to get her to a tutor, but she doesn't want one. Last year we made her see a tutor, but it didn't help. She still flunked the course, and we wasted a lot of money.

Helper: You sound really frustrated. (The helper comes back to a focus on the client instead of on the client's daughter.)

Client: Yeah, I really am frustrated. I just don't know what to do. I feel so helpless. School was so important to me, and I feel that if she doesn't get a good education, she won't get anywhere in life. (The client really takes in the reflection and talks in more depth about her feelings about the problem with her daughter.)

Helper: You know, in my experience with my kids, it was really hard to separate myself from them. I wanted so much for them to be perfect to show that I was a perfect parent. (Helper uses self-disclosure to stimulate client insight.)

Client: Yeah, I get into that. I feel like I'm not a very good parent. Everyone else's kids are doing so well. They're all talking about their kids going to these expensive colleges. I want my kids to have all the things I didn't have and not feel as bad about themselves as adults as I do.

Helper: You really want the best for your children. (Helper shows support through a restatement.)

Client: Yeah. Education wasn't a big thing in my family. My parents pushed me on religion and health food. In fact, they were really pushy; well, at least my mother was pushy about wanting me to be a missionary. We had such incredible fights when I was a teenager. They didn't even notice that I did well in school. So it was something that I could do on my own.

Helper: Interesting—you wanted to be independent from your parents and make your own decisions in life, but you want your daughter to do what you tell her to do. (Helper challenges client with a contradiction of which the client seems to be unaware.)

Client: Wow, you're right! I can't believe that I would be doing the same thing to her that my parents did to me. I guess it seemed like such a different thing. I want her to do well in school, and my parents wanted to control me about religion. But I don't know how to be any different. I really try hard to be a good parent. It's so important to me.

Helper: I wonder if you think I'm judging you and maybe thinking you're bad for your parenting? (Helper picks up on the client's self-blaming and wants to see if she feels negatively toward her, so helper uses an immediacy statement.)

Client: Well, I don't know if you blame me. I blame myself. I just don't know how to quit doing what I'm doing with my daughter. I feel stuck. I don't know any other way to be a parent. I've tried as hard as I can.

Helper: You're feeling very discouraged. (Helper reflects feelings to support client.)

Client: When I was younger, I didn't want to be a parent because I thought I would be rotten at it. I thought people should have to pass tests before they could become parents. There are so many rotten parents out there. But I was in therapy for a lot of years, and I thought I had solved a lot of my problems. But I guess I didn't solve them all. You know it was so much easier when the kids were younger.

Helper: Perhaps you're having problems now that your kids are teenagers because that's when you had your problems with your parents. You didn't get much of a model on how to be a parent of teenagers. (Helper interprets client's current difficulties as related to past experiences.)

Client: Boy, that's really true. I sure didn't. You know, I still haven't forgiven my parents for some of the things they did. You wouldn't believe how controlling my mother was.

Helper: You still have some anger at them. I wonder if you can identify with your daughter's anger? (Helper reflects feelings and interprets a parallel of her feelings with her daughter's to help client get some empathy with daughter.)

Client: Yeah, I know she feels angry at me. And you know, I feel good that she can express it. I used to just withdraw and get depressed when I was a kid. She at least can express herself pretty well sometimes. You know she does have a lot of spirit. She's different from me in some ways, yet in some ways she's a lot like me. School really is difficult for her. It's not fun for her to sit down and read a book like it is for me. She's just not academically oriented. But I guess she has to find her own way. She's not five years old anymore. Maybe I just have to trust that she will find herself. I have to accept her as she is just as I have to accept myself as I am. Maybe what I need to do is go back and do some more work on myself to see why I'm so controlling.

Helper: You've done a really good job of focusing on yourself. You've gone from blaming your daughter to looking at your part in this whole situation. (Helper wants to reinforce client for all the work she's done.)

Client: Yeah, it's not easy though. It's so much easier to blame her.

Helper: How do you feel about the work we've done today in trying to understand your conflicts with your daughter? (Helper asks how the client is feeling about their interaction.)

Client: I think I have a new understanding of my issues with my daughter. I'm not sure yet that I'll be able to stop having the fights because they happen so quickly, but I do have a better idea what my part in the struggles is all about. I'll need to do a lot more thinking about what kind of relationship I want to have with my daughter.

WHAT DO YOU THINK?

▪ What would you have done differently as a helper in the previous example to help the client attain insight?

▪ Several students have noted how difficult it is to learn and use the insight interventions. They have said that the exploration skills seemed easy, whereas now all of a sudden the insight skills seem hard. What is your experience?

▪ Many students forget to use the exploration skills when trying to use challenge, interpretation, self-disclosure, and immediacy. They revert to using lots of closed questions. What is your experience? What can you do to remember to integrate the exploration skills into the insight stage?

▪ How do you think clients from different cultures react to the insight skills as compared to the exploration skills?

▪ Debate the advantages and disadvantages of the insight stage. Identify the benefits and possible problems with moving clients to deeper awareness.

▪ Check which of the following obstacles you are most likely to face in your development of insight skills:

_____ moving prematurely into the insight stage
_____ taking too much responsibility for developing insight
_____ applying psychoanalytic theory too rigidly
_____ forgetting to be empathic
_____ clients not wanting or needing insight from helper

▮ Which of the following strategies might help you cope with the potential obstacles you could face in the insight stage?

_____ rely on the exploration skills

_____ deal with personal feelings

_____ deal with the relationship

LAB 13

Integration of Exploration and Insight Skills

You are ready to integrate the exploration and insight skills. In this lab, you will meet with a volunteer client. You will first use exploration skills to help the client explore and use both exploration and insight skills to facilitate the client gaining insight.

Goal: For helpers to conduct a helping session using the exploration and insight skills.

Helper's and Client's Tasks During the Helping Interchange

1. Each helper will pair up with a volunteer client whom they do not know.
2. Helpers bring copies of the following forms to the session: The Session Review Form (Web Form A), the Helper Intentions List (Web Form D), and Client Reactions System (Web Form G). The observer brings the Supervisor Rating Form (Web Form B).
3. Helpers bring an audio- or videotape recorder (tested ahead of time to ensure that it works) and a tape. They turn the recorder on at the beginning of the session.
4. Helpers introduce themselves and remind clients that whatever they say is confidential (except if the client intends to harm self or others or if childhood abuse is revealed). Helpers also indicate exactly who will be observing or listening to the session (e.g., peer, supervisor).
5. Each helper conducts a 40-minute session with a client, being as helpful as possible. Use exploration skills to help the client explore for about 20 minutes, and then move to combining exploration and insight skills to help the client gain insight for about 20 minutes. Watch the client's reactions to each of your interventions and modify subsequent interventions when appropriate.
6. Watch the time carefully. About 5 minutes before the time is up, let the client know that you need to stop soon. Spend the remaining time asking the client about what they liked most and least about the session. When the time is up, say something like, "We need to stop now. Thank you for helping me practice my helping skills."

Supervisor's Tasks During Session

Supervisors use the Supervisor Rating Form to record their observations and evaluations.

Postsession

1. After the session, each helper goes over the tape with the client (review of a 40-minute session takes about 90 minutes. Alternatively, helpers might just review 10 minutes of each stage). Helpers stop the tape after each helper intervention (except minimal

acknowledgments such as "um-hmm," and "yeah") and write down the key words on the session review form so the exact spot on the tape can be located later for transcribing the session.
2. Helpers rate the helpfulness of the intervention and write down the numbers (from the Helper Intentions List; Web Form D) of up to three intentions that they had for the intervention, responding according to how they felt during the session rather than when listening to the tape of the session. Use the whole range of the Helpfulness Scale and as many categories as possible on the Helper Intentions List. Do not complete these ratings collaboratively with clients.
3. Clients rate the helpfulness of each intervention and write down the numbers of up to three reactions (from the Client Reactions System; Web Form G). Clients respond according to how they felt during the session rather than how they feel listening to the tape and use the whole range of the Helpfulness Scale and as many categories as possible on the Reactions System (helpers learn more from honest feedback than from "nice" statements that are not genuine). Clients should not collaborate with helpers in doing the ratings.
4. Helpers and clients write down the most and least helpful event in the session.
5. The supervisor gives feedback to the helper.
6. Helpers type a transcript of their 40-minute session (see Web Form C), skipping minimal utterances such as "okay," "you know," "er," "uh."
   a. Divide the helper speech into response units (see Web Form F).
   b. Using the Helping Skills System (Web Form E), determine which skill was used for each response unit (grammatical sentence) in your transcript.
   c. Indicate on the transcript what you would say differently for each intervention if you could do it again.
   d. Erase the tape. Make sure no identifying information is on the transcript.

Personal Reflections

▪ What did you learn about yourself as a helper from this experience?
▪ Some helpers feel intrusive using the insight skills. Was this true for you? If so, speculate about what makes it difficult for you to delve deeply into inner dynamics.
▪ Which skills are you most and least comfortable using? What might you do to increase your comfort with skills you were not comfortable using?
▪ Discuss how well you were able to select skills to match your intentions.
▪ Compare your performance of this session with your performance in earlier labs. What differences have you noticed? How do you account for the differences?
▪ Conceptualize the client's dynamics.

IV

Action Stage

Overview of the Action Stage | 18

It is movement, not just insight, that produces change.

—*Waters and Lawrence* (1993, p. 40)

onsuela sought help because she was feeling vaguely uninterested in life. Through exploration with her helper, she described her situation as being devoid of close friendships and feeling isolated. She also indicated that she had not been doing well in her job since she was promoted to a managerial position. She described her childhood as idyllic, with no major problems. After further exploration, Consuela revealed that her parents had been killed in a car accident a year ago. In the insight stage, the helper and Consuela began to piece together that Consuela had not had a chance to grieve the loss of her parents because she felt pressured to perform in her new job. She had moved to a new city to take the job right before her parents' deaths, and she had not made any friends who could have supported her in the aftermath. In addition, Consuela's childhood did not sound as idyllic as she had initially indicated, in that Consuela had gone through a rough adolescence with many fights with her parents. Through the helping process, she was able to understand that she felt angry at her parents because they had been so strict and had not allowed her to develop friendships outside the home. Although she still missed her parents and the support they provided, Consuela came to realize that she needed to move on. At this point, the helper felt that Consuela had some insight into her vague lack of interest in life and decided to move into the action stage. Consuela indicated that she had three areas in which she wanted to change: making new friends, dealing with the stress of her job, and resolving her anger toward her parents. They decided to work first on assertiveness training because that would help her make friends and deal with work issues. After several sessions, Consuela had gained confidence in dealing with friends and work and was ready to work on her anger and grief over her parents' deaths.

After clients have explored and gained insight, they are ready for the action stage, during which helpers collaborate with clients to explore options for change and help clients figure out how to make changes. These changes can be in thoughts (e.g., fewer self-defeating statements), feelings (e.g., less hostility), or behaviors (e.g., less overeating). The emphasis in this stage is on helping the client think about and make decisions about action rather than on dictating action to the client. The helper is a coach, not the expert dispensing advice.

Rationale for the Action Stage

Sometimes newly gained insights lead spontaneously to thinking about action. Clients begin to say things like, "I can see that I've been so angry at the world because it felt unfair that I am not as smart and good-looking as my brother. I don't need to feel so angry now, because I can accept who I am and see that I have other things to offer people. I am going to do the things that I want to do with my life," or "It makes sense that I had a hard time in my job if I kept treating my boss like my father. I don't need to do that anymore. I'm going to stand up to him and ask him for a raise." Hence, moving to action comes naturally to some clients as they begin to talk about how they might apply what they have learned about themselves in the insight stage.

DETERRENTS TO ACTION

At other times, however, insight does not always lead spontaneously to action, perhaps because clients might not have gained an adequate amount of insight. They might feel stuck, understand the situation incompletely or only at an intellectual level, or not take personal responsibility for their role in the maintenance of the problem. For example, Stefan might realize intellectually that he is upset about being fired, but he might not have allowed himself to feel the humiliation of the loss or anger at his boss. He also might not have understood that he set himself up in self-defeating ways. Expressing, understanding, and accepting his feelings and his role in creating the situation are important tasks before moving to action, so Stefan and his helper might need to spend more time in the insight stage.

Another reason that insight might not lead directly to action is that clients might not have the necessary skills. For example, even though a client understands why she is not assertive and wants to change her behavior, she might not know how to stand up for herself. Clients cannot behave more assertively if they do not have the skills associated with being assertive (e.g., maintaining eye contact, stating needs directly without blaming) in their repertoire. Hence, clients may need to be taught these skills and may need to practice and get feedback about their performance to develop the skills adequately.

An additional issue is that a person might not be aware of his or her behavior and how it interferes with interactions with others. For example, a person might not recognize that she behaves hostilely and puts others off. She might need feedback about her behavior so she can become aware of how she comes across before she can begin to change.

Even if clients understand themselves thoroughly and have the skills to change, they may lack the motivation to change. Clients might feel blocked from changing because old habits are hard to alter and they are afraid of trying anything new (e.g., a client learning to be more assertive might be reluctant to confront a friend for fear of losing the friendship). They may feel demoralized and not believe they can change. They may need encouragement to even begin thinking about change.

Finally, clients cannot always make all the changes they might want or need to make because of limited talents and resources. For example, if Andrew is not very bright and has earned poor grades in college, getting into a high-ranking graduate program is an unlikely proposition. Hence, the goal of this stage is to enable clients to learn to make changes within the limits of the possibilities and to expand these possibilities as much as possible. In the earlier example, Andrew's helper might help him explore advanced training in a related field so that he can pursue a career related to his goals. Although this view does not fit with the idealistic American notion that every person can do whatever he or she wants, it fits with the more realistic idea of realizing one's limits and maximizing one's potentials within those limits.

REASONS FOR ACTION

There are two important reasons for moving beyond insight to action. First, because most clients seek help to feel better or to change specific behaviors, thoughts, or feelings, it is important to help them attain their goals. They need to leave helping not only with insight, but also with some ideas about how to make changes in their lives. For example, Betty sought help because of problems with her roommate. She came to understand that she did not want to tell her roommate about her feelings because her family was very covert and indirect and never talked about feelings. The insight is important, but she also needs to translate the insight into action and change her behavior with her roommate.

Second, taking action is crucial for consolidating the new thinking patterns learned in the insight stage. Action makes abstract insights more understandable and practical. New understandings can be fleeting unless something is done to help the client consolidate the insights. Old thinking patterns and behaviors easily resurface unless new thinking and behaviors are practiced and incorporated into schemas. For example, Miguel's old thinking pattern might be that he is worthless unless he is perfect. When the helper challenges his thoughts, Miguel comes to realize that he does not have to be perfect to accept himself. Miguel might also come to understand that he acts needy and dependent because his parents never accepted him for who he is. His parents idealized his older, brilliant, and successful brother because they had never achieved much in their own lives. They had constantly put Miguel down for being only average in intelligence. He might come to realize that even though his parents do not accept him fully for who he is, he is still a worthy and lovable person. This insight is fragile and may erode, however, unless the helper helps Miguel understand on a deeper level and incorporate the learning into a new pattern of behavior and thinking. Thus, the helper works with Miguel to accept himself. They devise a list of things that Miguel wants to do (e.g., skydiving, rollerblading, going back to school) and figure out how he can pursue these activities. Beginning to do things he wants to do and at which he succeeds enables Miguel to feel better about himself. The helper also works with Miguel to help him develop friends who approve of what he does, so that he can receive social support. When he feels better about himself, Miguel can begin to question the things he has told himself about needing to be perfect. Hence, Miguel cycles back to insight after making changes.

WHAT IS ACTION?

In the action stage, the focus is on making changes in behaviors, thoughts, and feelings, but it also involves exploring feelings and examining values, priorities, barriers, and support in relation to change. Hence, helpers need to be just as empathic and supportive as they were in earlier stages. Mickelson and Stevic (1971) found that behaviorally oriented counselors who were warm, empathic, and genuine were more effective in generating information-seeking responses in their clients than were those who were low in these facilitative conditions.

This stage, then, is still client-centered, with helpers facilitating clients in thinking about change rather than imposing change on them. Helpers do not have to know the best action plans for clients. In fact, helpers rarely need to form an opinion about what clients "must" or "should" do. The goal for helpers in this stage is to provide a supportive environment and facilitate clients in resolving their problems and making their decisions. When clients decide for themselves what to do differently, they are more likely to take responsibility and ownership for their actions than if helpers tell them what to do. Helpers telling clients what to do, even if clients ask for advice, is not typically helpful because clients become dependent on the helpers, especially if the client has a similar pattern in other relationships (see Teyber, 2000). Helpers cannot always be there for clients, so they need to teach clients how to motivate themselves to change and how to implement changes in their lives. Thus, rather than solving clients' problems, helpers seek to enhance clients' problem-solving capacities. With better coping skills, clients can address the problems that led them to seek help and are better equipped to solve problems in the future.

As you can see, helpers need to be supportive of clients and not be invested in whether and how they change. Whether the client chooses to change is the client's choice and responsibility rather than a reflection on the helper's skills and personal qualities. The helper's skills are involved in helping the client explore and make a decision, not in which decision is made. Thus, the helper's goal is to encourage clients to explore whether they want to change, and if so, to assist them in making the changes they have identified as desirable. Although this objective stance is difficult to achieve, it is crucial that helpers not care which direction clients choose, while still caring for the client. Otherwise, it is too easy to replicate childhood patterns where clients act or do not act to get the attention of, please, or defy helpers as they did their parents. Instead, helpers collaborate with clients in making choices, serving as facilitators of the process rather than as experts who provide the answers and tell clients what to do.

Essentially, the action stage involves going through a number of steps beginning with identifying the specific problem and exploring whether the client really wants to change through implementing change in the session and outside of the session (see chap. 20). As in the previous two stages, helpers collaborate with clients.

Here is an example that illustrates the need for the action stage and shows how it is implemented. Casey acted silly (e.g., giggled uncontrollably) when she went to dances because she was extremely nervous. Because Casey felt so embarrassed and panicked when she acted silly, she would leave the dance early and then feel badly that she had missed all the fun. Through exploration and insight, she came to realize that her anxiety at dances was due to her fear of being with men. She was afraid no one would like her because her brothers had made fun of her when she was a child. Her brothers had told her that she was ugly and had taunted her about her face and hair. Insight was not enough, though. Casey needed something to help her deal with the anxiety in the situation. The helper taught her relaxation and then strategized with her about how to handle specific situations at dances. When she felt a "silly" attack coming on, she and the helper planned that she would take a time out in the bathroom, practice deep breathing, and watch what she was saying to herself. After practicing several times in sessions, Casey was able to attend a dance and enjoy it. She was even able to let a man touch her and allow herself to think that she was attractive. Being able to master the situation made Casey feel better about herself. She then began to reevaluate whether she was indeed ugly and wonder what had motivated her brothers to be so mean to her. Hence, insight led to action, which in turn led to more insight.

MARKERS FOR KNOWING WHEN TO MOVE TO ACTION

There are several indicators that tell helpers clients are ready to move on to action:

- The client has gained insight and starts spontaneously talking about action.
- The client is stuck at insight and is not making changes.
- The client is in crisis and needs to make some changes immediately.

With some clients, helpers need to move quickly to action, shortening the exploration and insight stages. Such clients need more direct interventions because they are in crisis, are not psychologically minded, or cannot articulate their concerns. Some clients just want something or someone to make them feel better, and it is important to meet clients where they are rather than imposing our values on them. For example, a person who has been kicked out of his house, has no job or food, and has delusions may need immediate help in terms of housing, food, and medication before he can focus on understanding. To rephrase Maslow's (1970) statement, "people cannot live on bread alone unless they have no bread." These clients, after they have received direct guidance about how to solve a pressing problem, might be willing to go back and understand what contributed to the problem or work on other problems.

ISSUES INVOLVED IN IMPLEMENTING THE ACTION STAGE

I suggest that helpers use the action stage in every session but use it somewhat differently, depending on which session it is. In initial sessions, the action stage is usually brief and focused on exploring the possibility of changing, helping clients think about whether and what they want to change, or if they want to return for another session. In later sessions, the focus of the action stage moves to discussing and choosing specific action plans, the positive and negative consequences of changes the client has tried to make, making modifications in action plans, and planning for termination of the helping relationship.

Action is often the most challenging of the three stages for beginning helpers. Beginning helpers tend either to avoid action in favor of being empathic and insightful or become overly directive and authoritarian while neglecting their empathic skills. Leaving enough time for action can also be difficult for beginning helpers who have trouble planning sessions.

Change is also difficult for most clients. Demoralization and hopelessness are major hurdles that must be overcome for clients before they can change (Frank & Frank, 1991). Clients often feel discouraged or defeated about their ability to change because of negative experiences with past attempts. Accordingly, helpers might need to encourage clients to take "baby steps" and explore the idea of change first, while recognizing how hard it is to change. Remembering how difficult it is to make changes in our own lives can assist helpers in being empathic with clients who are struggling with changing. Helpers also need to remember that clients developed their problems over many years and changing these ingrained patterns is difficult.

Although the action stage presents many challenges for both helpers and clients, helpers should not neglect helping clients make changes in their lives. They do, however, need to approach the action stage with appropriate caution, self-awareness, and empathy for their clients.

Theoretical Background: Behavioral and Cognitive Theories

Behavioral and cognitive theories lay the foundation for the action stage. In this section, I discuss the underlying assumptions of these theories, the principles of learning, and treatment strategies.

ASSUMPTIONS OF COGNITIVE AND BEHAVIORAL THEORIES

Cognitive and behavioral theories share several basic assumptions (Gelso & Fretz, 1992; Rimm & Masters, 1979):

- A focus on overt behaviors and cognitions rather than unconscious motivations
- A focus on what creates and maintains symptoms rather than on what caused them
- An assumption that behaviors and cognitions are learned
- An emphasis on the present as opposed to the past

- An emphasis on the importance of specific, clearly defined goals
- A valuing of an active, directive, and prescriptive role for helpers
- A belief that the helper–client relationship is important to establish rapport and gain client collaboration but is not enough to help clients change
- A focus on determining adaptive behaviors and cognitions for a situation rather than on personality change
- A reliance on empirical data and scientific methods

PRINCIPLES OF LEARNING

One of the defining characteristics of behavioral approaches is that behaviors, emotions, and cognitions (both adaptive and maladaptive) are learned (Gelso & Fretz, 1992); therefore, it is important to talk about how learning takes place. Four types of learning are covered: classical (also called respondent) conditioning, operant conditioning, modeling (also called observational learning), and cognitively mediated learning. Although the four types of learning are not as distinct as once thought, it is still useful to be aware of the different types.

Classical or Respondent Conditioning

Pavlov (1927) first identified classical or respondent conditioning in his work with dogs. He noted that before conditioning, only some stimuli elicit involuntary responses (e.g., food elicits salivation or noise elicits a startle response). In classical conditioning terms, the unconditioned stimulus (UCS) elicits an unconditioned response (UCR). However, when a stimulus that was previously neutral is paired several times with an unconditioned stimulus, the new stimulus takes on the conditioning properties of the original stimulus. Hence, if a bell is rung immediately before food for several trials, a dog salivates to the sound of the bell even when it is presented without the food. The bell is now a conditioned stimulus (CS), and the response of salivation to the bell is a conditioned response (CR). The previously neutral stimulus (bell) takes on the power to elicit the response. Here's how the steps would look if we diagrammed it out:

1. Food (UCS) → Salivation (UCR)
2. Bell presented before Food (UCS)→ Salivation (UCR)
3. Bell (CS) → Salivation (CR)

Furthermore, the organism (the dog) learns to discriminate which stimuli lead to reinforcement (bell) and which do not (trumpets or feathers). And, learning generalizes (transfers) from one conditioned stimulus to other similar ones (bells of different tones). However, the conditioned response (salivation in response to the bell) extinguishes (gradually lessens and disappears) if the conditioned stimulus (the bell) is presented repeatedly without at least an occasional pairing with the unconditioned stimulus (the food).

J. B. Watson and Rayner (1920) demonstrated that emotional responses also could be acquired through classical conditioning. They first observed that Albert, an 11-month-old boy, had a startle and fear reaction (an unconditioned response) to a loud noise (an unconditioned stimulus), although he had no fear when playing with a white rat. They then paired the rat with a loud noise. Whenever Albert reached out to touch the rat, the noise sounded and Albert was startled. After only seven pairings, Albert cried when the rat was presented without the noise. Hence, after conditioning, the conditioned stimulus (the rat) elicited the fear response. Furthermore, Albert's fear response generalized to other white furry things he had not been afraid of previously (a rabbit, a dog, and a Santa Claus mask). Hence, the development of anxieties and phobias may be at least partially due to classical conditioning.

Operant Conditioning

In operant conditioning, behaviors are controlled by their consequences (Kazdin, 2001; Rimm & Masters, 1979; Skinner, 1953). Reinforcement is anything that follows a behavior and increases the probability that the behavior will occur again. An event, behavior, privilege, or material object whose addition increases the likelihood of a behavior occurring again is called a *positive reinforcer*. Primary reinforcers (e.g., food, water, and sex) are biological necessities, whereas secondary reinforcers (e.g., praise or money) gain their reinforcing properties through association with primary reinforcers. An example of a positive reinforcer related to helping is an approval–reassurance given after a client talks about feelings. Note that reinforcers are not always reinforcing (e.g., food is typically reinforcing only if a person is hungry) and that reinforcers are not the same for all individuals (e.g., a long bath may be reinforcing for one person but not another). Whether something is a reinforcer can only be determined by looking at whether the target behavior occurs in response to the reinforcer being administered. Thus, a helper cannot determine if something is reinforcing until the client response is observed.

For a behavior to be reinforced, it must first be performed. Hence, helpers often have to engage in *shaping*, which refers to the gradual training of a complex response by reinforcing closer and closer approximations to the desired behavior. Goldfried and Davison (1994) give the example of training a developmentally disabled child to make his bed by first reinforcing him for fluffing up his pillow, then for pulling the top sheet forward, and so on. Each of these acts is a successive approximation to the final desired behavior. An example of shaping, related to learning exploration skills, is when helpers first practice listening empathically without saying anything and then repeat exactly what the client said, then say the main word, and then give restatements and reflections of feelings.

Negative reinforcement is when something is removed, and that removal increases the probability of the occurrence of the desired behavior. The removal can be by escape (e.g., leaving the room during a fight) or by avoidance (e.g., avoiding fights). Primary aversive stimuli are things that are inherently punitive (e.g., shock, noise, and pain), whereas secondary aversive stimuli (e.g., disapproval) are things that have gained their aversive quality from being paired with primary aversive agents. For example, if a child stops crying when the parent picks him or her up, the parent is more likely to pick up the child because picking up the child stopped the crying. Other examples include using an umbrella to avoid getting wet in the rain or putting on a seat belt to avoid the warning buzzer.

In contrast, *punishment* occurs after a behavior and reduces the probability that the behavior will occur again. Goldfried and Davison (1994) identified three punishment procedures: (a) presenting an aversive event (e.g., a frown when the client reports something undesirable), (b) removing a person from a situation where she or he would otherwise be able to earn reinforcers (e.g., a time-out in a room separate from the counselor who could provide positive reinforcement), and (c) reducing a person's collection of reinforcers (e.g., taking away candy). The purpose of punishment in clinical situations is to decrease the frequency of maladaptive behaviors.

To be effective, reinforcement or punishment must be contingent on, or linked directly to, the behavior (Rimm & Masters, 1979). An office worker who receives a raise every three months regardless of the quality of work is less likely to change his or her behavior than one whose raise is contingent on good performance. It is especially difficult to deliver punishment contingent with the behavior. Very often, what gets punished is being discovered rather than the behavior itself. Hence, when punishment is used as the primary mode of behavior management, people often figure out how to avoid getting caught rather than decrease the problematic behavior. For example, a child who steals cookies feels great when he gets the cookies because they taste good, but he feels lousy several hours later when he gets caught because it does not feel good to get caught and be punished. Because the punishment is contingent on getting caught rather than on eating the cookies, the child figures that he should not get caught again. If he is clever, he figures out a way to get the cookies without getting caught.

Another important behavioral concept is *generalization*, which involves the transfer of learning from one situation to similar situations. For example, if kicking and hitting are punished with time-outs and cooperative behavior is positively reinforced at school, one would expect a decrease in kicking and hitting and an increase in cooperative behavior in the home setting. Importantly, however, these behaviors are most likely to generalize if they are punished and reinforced in the same manner in the home setting as in the school setting. Another example of generalization is when a person acts frightened of a teacher or helper because she or he was punished by authority figures in the past (a concept similar to transference).

Extinction reduces the probability of a behavior occurring by withholding reinforcers after the behavior is established (Goldfried & Davison, 1994). For example, if a parent's attention is reinforcing fighting among siblings (when no other problems are apparent), a helper might instruct the parents to ignore the fighting and let the kids work out their problems on their own (unless one child is in danger of getting hurt) in the hopes that it will extinguish. Goldfried and Davison noted that extinction often is best facilitated by concurrently reinforcing an incompatible and more adaptive behavior. Thus, in the previous example, the parents might suggest that the siblings play separately and then praise them if they play quietly.

Although the concepts of operant conditioning sound relatively straightforward, helpers often have difficulty applying them due to the complexity of human nature and because helpers often have minimal control over the reinforcers and punishments in the environment. In fact, Goldfried and Davison (1994) noted that helpers typically do not reinforce the actual changes but rather reinforce the client's talking about making specific changes. Clients have to transfer the reinforcement from talking about changing to implementing the changes outside the session. Thus, helpers act more as consultants, whereas clients are the actual change agents.

Modeling

People sometimes learn things even though they have never been reinforced for performing them. The explanation for this learning is through modeling or observational learning, which occurs when a person observes another person (a model) perform a behavior and receive consequences (Bandura, 1977; Kazdin, 2001). For example, children learn how to be parents by watching their parents and experiencing the effects of their child-rearing practices. Students learn how to be teachers by observing effective and ineffective educators. Helpers learn how to help by observing the behaviors of effective and ineffective helpers.

To understand how modeling works, learning and performance must be distinguished. A person can observe a model and learn a behavior. Whether the person actually performs the learned behavior, however, depends on the consequences at the time of performance. Bandura (1965) demonstrated this distinction between learning and performance with his classic Bobo doll study. Children observed a film in which an adult hit or kicked a Bobo doll (a life-size, inflatable, plastic doll that is weighted so it pops upright after it is punched down). The adult's behavior was rewarded, punished, or met with no consequences. When the children were put in the room with the Bobo doll, those who had observed the aggression being punished were less aggressive than those who had observed the aggression being rewarded or ignored. When an incentive was given for performing the aggressive behavior, there were no differences among conditions, indicating that the children in all conditions learned the aggressive behaviors equally well. Bandura (1965) concluded that the learning occurred through observation but that the performance depended on whether the child perceived that the adult was rewarded or punished. Kazdin (2001) noted that imitation of models by observers is greater when models are similar to observers, more prestigious, higher in status and expertise than observers, and when several models perform the same behavior.

COGNITIVE THEORY

Early behaviorists believed in a stimulus–response (S-R) model, meaning that people respond directly to environmental cues (e.g., noise leads to a startle response). Cognitive theorists (e.g., Beck, 1976; Ellis, 1962; Meichenbaum & Turk, 1987) introduced a stimulus–organism–response (S-O-R) model, suggesting that the organism (i.e., person) processes the stimulus before determining how to respond. Thus, we respond not to stimuli, but to our interpretation of stimuli. For example, how we react to a noise heard in the middle of the night is dependent on whether we think it is a benign noise (the house "settling") or made by a burglar. Theorists such as Beck, Ellis, and Meichenbaum suggest that it is not so much events that cause us to become upset, but what we think about the events.

Cognitive processes are of utmost importance to the helping situation. As discussed in chapter 3, much of the helping process takes place at covert levels. Helpers' intentions for their interventions as well as their perceptions of clients' reactions influence their subsequent interventions. In addition, clients have reactions to helpers' interventions as well as intentions for how to influence helpers. Hence, a cognitively mediated model for understanding the helping process makes most sense.

Another cognitive process that is important for helping involves thoughts about one's abilities. Bandura (1986) defined self-efficacy as "people's judgments in their capabilities to organize and execute courses of action required to attain designated types of performance" (p. 361). According to Bandura (1986), self-efficacy relates to initiation of behaviors, persistence despite obstacles, and eventual success. For example, beginning helpers who lack self-efficacy in their helping skills might be very reluctant to role-play their helping skills in front of the instructor. They might use the slightest obstacle as an excuse to not attend class on the day students are practicing skills. Their lack of confidence would then manifest itself in poor skill development and ineffective helping relationships. Conversely, people can have unrealistically high self-efficacy; in other words, they can think that their abilities are better than they actually are. An example would be a person who thinks that her helping skills are terrific, when in fact, her skills are marginal. She would have a hard time believing that she needed helping skills training.

Obviously, self-efficacy also applies to the experiences of clients. Attention to the role of cognitions can enable helpers to understand a client's hesitance to try new behaviors. For example, a client who lacks confidence in public speaking might receive poor job evaluations for refusing to present his work in front of customers. Bandura (1986) would suggest that providing this client with small success experiences (e.g., having him present his work to his helper and to small groups of trusted friends) might enhance the client's self-efficacy and enable him to comply with the requirements of his job.

How Behavioral and Cognitive Theories Relate to the Three-Stage Model

Behavioral and cognitive theories fit well into the action stage of the helping model because they provide specific strategies for helping clients change. When clients have explored thoughts and feelings thoroughly and obtained insight about themselves, action allows them to determine how they would like to change their lives. Thus, helpers need to focus on action to help clients attain their goals. When used in an empathic and collaborative manner at the appropriate time, these treatments can be extremely helpful in facilitating change.

Goals of the Action Stage

The goals for the action stage are for helpers to encourage clients to explore possible new behaviors, assist clients in deciding on actions, facilitate the development of skills for action, provide feedback about attempted changes, assist clients in evaluating and modifying action plans, and encourage clients to process feelings about action. While in the action stage, helpers need to remember to be empathic and pace themselves according to clients' needs. A stance of exploring, rather than prescribing, action is typically most helpful.

Unlike the previous two stages where skills were relatively discrete and important in and of themselves, skills in this stage are more often combined into discrete steps. Hence, I discuss briefly the skills that are used primarily in the action stages (see chap. 19) and then discuss the steps that are used to facilitate the action stage in a separate chapter (see chap. 20). I focus more on the steps than on the skills.

Skills Used in the Action Stage

The skills used uniquely in the action stage are information, feedback about the client, process advisement, direct guidance, and disclosure of strategies. Information is important to educate clients about options for action. Feedback is important to shape clients' behavior. Direct guidance is useful to give some advice to clients about the best strategies. Disclosure of strategies is a minimally intrusive way to suggest action ideas.

Although not unique to it, the skills that are used most frequently in the action stage are the exploration skills, primarily open questions. Open questions are useful for obtaining information about what clients have tried before and how they felt about previous efforts. Helpers also use restatement and reflection of feelings to uncover feelings related to change, to demonstrate support, and to ensure that they accurately hear what clients are saying. When clients are stuck, insight skills such as challenge, interpretation, self-disclosure, and immediacy can be useful to probe for obstacles to action.

Steps of the Action Stage

In the exploration stage, the focus was not on specific sequencing of skills. There was more sequencing in the insight stage, with setting the stage for the insight skill and then following up on it. The sequencing idea is carried even further in the action stage by focusing on steps of action more than the individual skills. Helpers are urged to learn the individual skills but to focus most of their attention on putting these skills together into the steps to help clients move from identifying a specific problem to work on, to exploring the idea of action, to assessing the situation, to brainstorming options, to choosing an option, to working on action in sessions (using strategies such as assertiveness training), to assigning homework, and finally to checking on progress and modifying action plans. Typically, not all of these steps (especially the last) are carried out in a single session, and the steps will vary somewhat in sequence depending on the client and the presenting problem. These steps should give the beginning helper an idea about how to progress through the action stage.

Concluding Comments

Action is a natural outgrowth of exploration and insight. However, because of difficulties encountered in making changes, clients often need support and guidance to take action. Some helpers are nervous and uncomfortable with pursuing action, so they ignore the action stage. I encourage such helpers to look at their own attitudes about action and to struggle to implement this stage. If clients do not make changes in their lives outside of helping (in thoughts, behaviors, or feelings), helping has not been as successful as it could have been.

WHAT DO YOU THINK?

- Are clients naturally propelled toward action or do they need help to change?
- What is the role of helpers in assisting clients in changing?
- Brainstorm ideas for how helpers can make the transition from insight to action.
- Do you think a helper's manner of introducing action ideas influences the client's acceptance of the ideas?
- Is the helper or client responsible for client change?

Skills of the
Action Stage 19

Many seek advice, few profit from it

—Publius Syrus (42 B.C.)

T hrough working on a dream, Yelin came to realize that he allowed his mother to dominate him. When Yelin was 16, his father died after asking Yelin to take care of his mother. His mother, although only 45 years old and healthy, depended on Yelin to drive her everywhere and to be her companion. She refused to learn English, make friends, or work and clung to hopes of returning to her country of origin. Yelin felt like he would never be able to marry or have his own life. Consequently, he was beginning to drink several beers each night and isolate himself from his peers. After thorough exploration and insight that he was withdrawing from his mother and punishing her, Yelin was eager to make changes in his life. He asked for information about alcohol treatment, so the helper told Yelin about Alcoholics Anonymous and suggested he attend meetings. The helper also suggested that Yelin and his mother come in for a joint session, so they could work on their communication.

As in the insight stage, the most frequently used skill in the action stage is still open questions (refer to chap. 7 for an overview). In addition to open questions, helpers sometimes use the skills of giving information, feedback about client, process advisement, direct guidance, and disclosures about strategies in the action stage; these skills are the focus of this chapter. Chapter 20 focuses on putting all the skills together into the steps of the action stage.

Web Forms referred to in text can be found on the book's companion online guide described in the Preface.

Giving Information

Giving information can be defined as providing specific data, facts, re-sources, answers to questions, or opinions to clients (see Exhibit 19.1). There are several types of information:

- Explaining intentions and goals (e.g., "Let's explore what you've done in the past about this problem, brainstorm some ideas for what you could do differently, make some choices about what you want to do, try out your choices, and then evaluate how you feel about your choices.")
- Educating the client about various types of actions (e.g., "Role-playing involves practicing how you might respond differently when you talk to your mother." OR "Having a specific place to study allows students to concentrate better on their studies without distractions.")
- Providing information about activities or psychological tests (e.g., "The Strong Interest Inventory measures a person's interests and compares them with interests of people happily employed in a variety of occupations.")
- Educating the client about the world or psychological principles (e.g., "A moderate amount of stress is typically helpful to motivate a person, but too much or too little stress can be counterproductive." OR "Many women become depressed after giving birth. There's even a term for it—it's called postpartum depression.")

WHY GIVE INFORMATION?

In the action stage, helpers sometimes shift into a teacher's role to pro-vide information. Helpers thus act as educators, which is appropriate if the information is given in a caring manner when clients need informa-tion and are ready to listen. For example, a helper might educate a client about his mental condition or about what to expect in different situa-tions. Or, a helper might explain what happens during panic attacks as a way of teaching a client that the physical sensations she experiences (e.g., heart palpitations) are due to anxiety rather than a heart attack. Such information can lead to change when clients are open to learning.

Information is not always the most appropriate intervention in a situ-ation, however, even when the client has requested this type of assis-tance. Sometimes clients need to explore how they feel about situations without being told what is "normal" or expected. Other clients need to seek out information without having the investigative work done for them. Some clients need to be encouraged to think about why they do not al-

EXHIBIT 19.1

Overview of Information

Definition	*Giving information* refers to supplying data, opinions, facts, resources, answers to questions, or opinions
Example	"Both the career center and counseling center have information about careers."
Typical intentions	To give information, to promote change (see Web Form D)
Possible client reactions	Educated, new ways to behave, hopeful, no reaction (see Web Form G)
Desired client behaviors	Agreement, therapeutic changes (see Web Form H)
Difficulties helpers experience in giving information	Desiring to be viewed as the expert who has importance Needing to know all the relevant information Believing that helpers should provide a lot of information to be perceived as helpful Being judgmental when giving feedback Providing information before client has explored thoroughly Implying direct guidance (telling the client what to do)

Note. Another type of information (information about the helping process) was presented in chapter 10.

ready have the desired information or what motivates them to rely on others to give them information.

Finally, sometimes helpers do not have information to give. Rather than assume that one must know everything before becoming a helper (obviously an impossible task), helpers can be aware of some basic information (e.g., referral sources) but then focus on helping clients figure out how to get the needed information themselves.

HOW TO GIVE INFORMATION

Helpers should think carefully about their intentions before supplying information. What is motivating you to want to give information at this particular point? For whom (the client or you) is this information helpful? Do you want to stop exploration? Reduce client anxiety? Educate the client? Show the client how much you know? Normalize the experience? Explain what is happening in the session? Examination of intentions is critical to ensure that information is delivered appropriately. Providing too much information prematurely can create dependency rather than self-efficacy.

Before giving information, it is often useful for helpers to ask what information clients possess. Thus, rather than assuming clients need information, helpers can assess clients' knowledge base. They can also ask clients what strategies they have used to gather information.

If the issue is straightforward and not motivated by inappropriate needs and the helper has the requisite information, helpers can provide the information. We helpers sometimes do have valuable information and so can serve as resources for clients. When giving information, of course, helpers should be empathic, gentle, and sensitive to how clients are reacting. The goal of delivering information is not to lecture clients or act as an expert, but rather to educate clients when they are ready to learn and when it does not undermine clients' independence in searching out their own information.

If helpers determine that giving information is appropriate, they should not provide too much information at one time. In medical relationships, Meichenbaum and Turk (1987) found that patients remember very little of the information that doctors give them. Ironically, the more information given by doctors, the less patients remember. Similarly, when clients are anxious in helping situations, it is easy for them to forget information. Crucial information, such as referral numbers or homework assignments, should be put in writing to assist clients in accessing the information later.

As with disclosures, helpers turn the focus back to the client after providing information to see the client's reaction. For example, after describing his position on the use of prescription drugs for psychiatric illnesses, a helper asked the client about her thoughts and reactions to using prescription drugs.

If a client requests information, the helper needs to try to understand what is motivating the client to ask for information at this particular point in the therapeutic process. Awareness of a client's motives can help the helper decide how to respond. Is the client trying to make you feel needed or like an expert? Is the client trying to avoid exploration or insight? Is the client resorting to familiar defenses of being dependent on others? Does giving information foster further dependency in the client? Does the client expect you to be like a medical doctor who asks questions about the problem and then gives a diagnosis and course of treatment? Helpers might ask clients what is motivating them to ask for information, what they want to do with the information, or what they hope the helper will do for them (e.g., "I'd be happy to answer your question, but first let's talk about why you ask").

Once the helper knows the motives behind the request for information, he or she can address these motives directly. If the client expects the helper to make a diagnosis and dictate the course of treatment, the helper can either educate the client that she or he uses a different treatment strategy or refer the client to someone who is more likely to meet these expectations. If the client is requesting information as a ploy in the interpersonal interaction (e.g., for dependency needs or to make the helper feel needed), the helper can use immediacy skills to address this issue. It is better to find out what is beneath the request than to ignore it or engage in a power struggle over who controls the information. Helpers need to think carefully about how to handle these situations (and, as always, talking the situation over with supervisors can aid helpers in dealing with such situations in the future).

EXAMPLE OF GIVING INFORMATION

Client: So tell me all about your class. I think I want to take it next year.

Helper: It sounds like you would be interested in learning helping skills.

Client: Yeah, I've always had the idea that maybe I might want to be a social worker. But on the other hand, I'm not sure I would be very good at helping.

Helper: What concerns do you have about learning helping skills?

Client: I'm afraid of getting too involved with the clients. I feel so responsible for my friends when they talk about their problems. I feel like I have to solve all their problems and tell them exactly what to do.

Helper: So maybe you're worried that you won't be able to have any distance from clients in a helping setting.

Client: Yeah, do they talk about how to deal with that in the class?

Helper: Sounds like you really need some help with that.

Client: I do. I had a friend talk to me just yesterday, and I felt totally depressed when we were done because I felt like I had done nothing to help her. I'm afraid that she felt worse when we were done. It reminded me of my mother and father, who both want to talk to me ever since they divorced. Both want me to be on their side. Sometimes I feel split in half.

Helper: I can see why you'd be nervous about the helping situation after having to be a helper with your parents.

Client: Yeah. What was it like for you?

Helper: *I have had a good experience in the class. The professor has talked a lot about how we have to get personal issues dealt with in our own therapy or else it is difficult to help clients with their issues.* I wonder if you have ever explored the idea of getting into therapy?

Client: Not really. I don't know much about it.

Helper: *There's a counseling center on campus that offers 12 sessions of free therapy for students.*

Client: Really? I'll have to think about that. Maybe I'll check it out.

Feedback About the Client

Giving feedback can be defined as the helper giving information to the client about his or her behaviors or impact on others (see Exhibit 19.2). It is a type of information (see previous section) but it is confined to information about the client specifically. Examples of feedback about the client include the following:

- "You expressed yourself very clearly and concisely in the role-play."
- "You are smiling a lot and seem more open to making changes."
- "I noticed that you were tapping your foot during the relaxation exercise."

WHY GIVE FEEDBACK ABOUT CLIENT?

Brammer and MacDonald (1996) suggested that effective feedback can increase clients' self-awareness. Self-awareness can in turn lead to behavior change. For example, if the helper notes that Jennifer always ends her sentences with a question and thus sounds very tentative when she speaks, this might lead Jennifer to become aware of how she talks and try to change her behavior. When she begins to make definite statements, other people might begin to take her more seriously.

Research shows that clients prefer positive feedback and think it is more accurate (Claiborn et al., 2002). Positive feedback is good to use early on to establish the relationship and enhance credibility. In addition, if negative feedback must be given, it is best to precede it with positive feedback or to sandwich it between two pieces of positive feedback.

Feedback about the client is similar to immediacy. Both are feedback about the client, except that feedback about the client is only about the client (e.g., "you") individually, but immediacy is about the interaction between helper and client in the therapeutic relationship (e.g., "we" or "you and I"). In addition, whereas immediacy is used in the insight stage

EXHIBIT 19.2

Overview of Feedback About the Client

Definition	Giving information to the client about his or her behaviors or impact on others
Example	"You maintained good eye contact during the role-play, but your voice sounded hesitant when you told your partner that you were leaving the relationship."
Typical intentions	To give information, to promote change, to deal with the therapeutic relationship (see Web Form D)
Possible client reactions	New ways to behave, responsibility, misunderstood (see Web Form G)
Desired client behaviors	Cognitive–behavioral exploration, affective exploration, therapeutic changes (see Web Form H)
Difficulties helpers experience in giving feedback	Not giving difficult feedback (keeping mum) Feeling insecure about how to present feedback so as not to encounter resistance

to promote insight and deal with problems in the therapeutic relationship, feedback about the client is used in the action stage to assist clients in generating, implementing, and maintaining changes in thoughts, feelings, and behaviors.

It can be difficult for beginning helpers to provide feedback to clients because it is a very different behavior than one usually uses in social interactions and can be met with resistance. Beginning helpers often become victims of the *mum effect*, a tendency to withhold bad news even if it is in the best interest of others to hear it (Egan, 1994). In ancient times, bearers of bad news were killed, which not too surprisingly led to some reluctance to be the one to bear bad news or give negative feedback.

HOW TO GIVE FEEDBACK

Feedback about the client must be given cautiously, with the clear understanding that the helper is offering his or her personal observations about the client's behavior. Making the statements descriptive (e.g., "You spoke very softly") rather than evaluative (e.g., "You aren't taking this role-play very seriously") and emphasizing strengths (e.g., "You effectively articulated your feelings,") before weaknesses (e.g., "but you didn't sound like you really believed it") can make it easier for clients to hear the feedback. It is also important to give feedback (a) about things clients can change (e.g., nonverbal behaviors, actions) rather than about physical characteristics or life circumstances that cannot be changed (e.g., height, personality) and (b) as closely as possible to the behavior (e.g., "You spoke with more assurance that time") rather than waiting for a long time and then trying to re-create the situation (e.g., "A while back you looked away from me and wouldn't say anything").

As with the other action skills, feedback needs to be given with a lot of empathy and support. Negative feedback could damage the helping process if it is perceived as threatening or inaccurate, so helpers need to do it gently and tentatively after a good relationship is established.

EXAMPLE OF HOW TO GIVE FEEDBACK

Client: I tried the homework you suggested about trying to make more friends.

Helper: Fantastic. How did it go?

Client: Well, I smiled more often and tried to look people in the eye when I was crossing campus.

Helper: That's great. How did that feel?

Client: It was a little strange at first, but then it was nice to see people smiling back at me. No one came up to me, but it felt like a start.

Helper: You were also going to try to initiate a conversation with someone in class. How did that go?

Client: That didn't go so well. I picked Sally because she usually seems friendly. I sat near her as planned, but then I got scared at the last minute and didn't say anything to her.

Helper: Let's role-play that so I can see how you did it. Let's pretend that I'm Sally.

Client: I sat next to her but I didn't say anything, so there's nothing really to role-play.

Helper: Okay, let's try it where I play you and you play Sally and see if we can come up with some ideas about how to do it. Would that be okay?

Client: Sure, that would be great.

Helper: Hi Sally, how's it going?

Client: Oh hi, pretty good, except I'm stressed out about this test.

Helper: Me too. Would you be interested in studying together?

Client: Sure. Want to meet later for coffee and study?

Helper: How did that feel? Do you think you'd be able to do that?

Client: Yeah, I think I could. Let me try . . . Hi Sally. Umm, how's it going? Would you like to study for the exam together?

Helper: Great, you did it, you got it out, and you looked directly at me when you said it. That's a big improvement. Maybe next time you could just slow down a bit when you are talking. Let's practice again, because it can really help to practice until you feel comfortable here.

Process Advisement

With process advisement, helpers direct clients to do things within helping sessions (e.g., "Show me how you acted when your roommate asked to borrow your new dress" or "Play the part of the man in your fantasy"). Process advisement is a type of advice or direct guidance (see next section), but it is confined to directing what goes on in the session (see Exhibit 19.3).

WHY GIVE PROCESS ADVISEMENT?

Helpers are experts on how to facilitate the helping process and, hence, often have suggestions about what clients can do in sessions to facilitate the change process (see Step 6 in chap. 20). Clients, in contrast, are not experts in the helping process and consequently rely (within limits) on helpers for judgments about how to proceed in sessions. The primary use of process advisement in the action stage is through behavioral exercises such as behavioral rehearsal or role-playing (see chap. 20).

HOW TO GIVE PROCESS ADVISEMENT

Clients are generally agreeable to trying things that helpers deem appropriate if they are presented with a credible rationale for why the exercises are helpful (e.g., "Let's try this role-play to help you learn how to be more assertive. It may feel silly at first, but it can be helpful").

Helpers must be attentive to signs that clients do not want to follow process advisements. In cases when clients are reluctant, helpers often have not presented the task well. Helpers are sometimes apologetic (e.g., "I don't suppose you'd want to do this exercise that my supervisor suggested?") and defeat the possibility of gaining client cooperation. Or sometimes helpers are not clear about their suggestions or do not provide a rationale for them.

Some clients are resistant to suggestions, regardless of how skillfully they are presented. At all times, helpers need to respect the client's decision not to participate in an exercise or not to change (unless the decision involves harm to another person—in such a case, see chap. 4 for guide-

---

E X H I B I T   1 9 . 3

Overview of Process Advisement

Definition	*Process advisement* refers to helper directives for what the client should do within the session
Example	"Let's try a role-play to practice a new way of acting in that situation. You be yourself and I'll be your boss. Try to use the assertive behaviors we practiced earlier."
Typical intention	To promote change (see Web Form D)
Possible client reactions	Educated, unstuck, new ways to behave, hopeful, confused, misunderstood, no reaction (see Web Form G)
Desired client behaviors	Agreement, therapeutic changes (see Web Form H)
Difficulties helpers experience in using process advisement	Using it to meet the needs of the helper to feel expert and control Not collaborating with the client

---

lines about what to do). Perhaps the worst thing to do with reluctant or resistant clients is to get into a control struggle over which action clients should take. Control struggles tend to escalate, sometimes leading to disastrous consequences, with both people feeling that they lose "face" if they back down. I suggest that helpers use the basic listening skills to understand why clients are reluctant and perhaps resistant to change. Helpers can also work with clients to accept themselves for not changing. This example illustrates the need to be flexible in the action stage.

EXAMPLE OF PROCESS ADVISEMENT

Helper: I notice that you're vigorously swinging your foot. *Could you be your foot and tell me what you're feeling?*

Client: What? That sounds weird.

Helper: Perhaps your foot is trying to convey a message. *Tell me what your foot is trying to say.*

Client: Okay, this is hard, but if I am my foot—I'm feeling annoyed. It feels like we're not getting anywhere.

Helper: Good, you're getting into it. Say it louder this time— like you really believe it.

Client: I am annoyed. Actually, I am annoyed at myself. I meant to come in and talk about my feelings about my mother's death, and then I didn't. Can we talk about that now?

EXHIBIT 19.4

Overview of Direct Guidance

Definition	*Direct guidance* refers to helper suggestions, directives, or advice for the client
Example	"When you have the nightmare the next time, wake yourself up and imagine a new ending where you get angry at the intruder and chase him out of the house."
Typical intention	To promote change (see Web Form D)
Possible client reactions	Educated, unstuck, new ways to behave, hopeful, confused, misunderstood, no reaction (see Web Form G)
Desired client behaviors	Agreement, therapeutic changes (see Web Form H)
Difficulties helpers experience using direct guidance	Using it to meet the needs of the helper to feel expert and in control Using it before thorough exploration and insight Shifting the focus to the helper's experience Not collaborating with the client

Direct Guidance

Direct guidance can be defined as making suggestions, giving directives, or providing advice for what helpers think clients should do outside of helping sessions (see Exhibit 19.4). Examples include providing suggestions to parents who are exploring ways of dealing with bedtime for a young child, helping a client think of coping strategies after a hospitalization, or assisting a client in thinking of alternatives for dealing with an elderly parent with Alzheimer's disease.

It can be useful to contrast information giving and direct guidance because students often confuse the two. Giving information provides facts or data but does not suggest what clients should do; direct guidance directly indicates what a helper thinks a client should do. For example, contrast the effects of "The counseling center is in the Shoemaker Building" (information) versus "You should go to the counseling center" (direct guidance). Information often has an implied directive about what the client ought to do (e.g., "In my opinion, students earn better grades when they get a full night of sleep before taking a test"), but it does not state directly that the client should take a particular action (e.g., "I think you should make sure you get eight hours of sleep before taking the test").

One form of direct guidance is homework. Helpers often suggest that clients do homework (e.g., monitor exercise and eating behaviors, read a self-help book, seek information, practice being assertive, or record dreams). Homework gives clients the opportunity to practice what they are learning in helping, determine whether they can use it outside of the helping setting, and see what modifications are needed to fit their style and situation. Homework can be a particularly useful way to keep the client involved in the change process in between sessions. Homework can speed up the helping process because the client is actively involved in changing and bringing feedback about what happened back to the session. Homework can also encourage clients to act on their own without the helper's immediate monitoring.

Research suggests that clients are more likely to implement homework suggestions if therapists choose tasks that fit the problem, are not difficult to implement, and are based on clients' strengths (Conoley, Padula, Payton, & Daniels, 1994; Scheel, Seaman, Roach, Mullin, & Mahoney, 1999; Wonnell & Hill, 2002). Hence, helpers need to be attentive to how the homework is assigned.

WHY GIVE DIRECT GUIDANCE?

Dear Abby, Ann Landers, Dr. Laura, Dr. Joyce Brothers, Dr. Phil, and others give advice to millions of people. Many people (including me) read the newspaper columns and listen to the radio shows, which have become immensely popular because they are so entertaining. Providing advice is probably as old as human speech, but what are the consequences? Do people follow the advice, and if so, is it helpful or harmful? Unfortunately, no one has the answers to these concerns, except perhaps anecdotally. My main concern about direct guidance given in these entertainment formats is that the advice is not preceded by thorough exploration; the wrong problem might be addressed, and the recipient might think that it is not necessary to think about all the angles of the problem. Furthermore, some people begin to rely on others to make their decisions rather than coming to trust their own instincts. Moreover, some people seek guidance from many people and then either become confused or consider only the opinions they want to hear. It certainly can be valuable to gain input from many people, but hearing advice can make it difficult for clients to know what they want to do. In addition, people may follow direct guidance out of fear of hurting the feelings of the advice giver or out of fear of retribution.

Direct guidance can be useful in helping situations, especially when given by a trusted helper whose expert opinions are based on solid knowledge and experience and after extensive exploration and insight. Helpers can have good ideas about what might be helpful for clients to do. For example, Dorothy asked her helper for advice on negotiating her salary for her first job in an academic setting. Clearly, this was an area her helper knew something about: She had worked in an academic setting for some time, although she did not know the politics of the specific department with which Dorothy was negotiating. They talked about the information Dorothy had gathered about the salary range of other recent hires, what her values were, and what she wanted. They then discussed how Dorothy could navigate the negotiation process. The helper suggested that Dorothy not name a specific salary but say that she was dissatisfied with what had been offered. They talked about that possibility, and Dorothy modified it to fit her style. Note that the process was collaborative because the helper respected Dorothy's right and ability to make her own decisions. The helper was not invested in which strategy Dorothy chose but was interested in presenting alternatives for Dorothy to consider so she could develop a plan that worked for her. Although the strategy did not work as planned, Dorothy was able to modify it during the negotiation. She accepted the job at a competitive salary and started her new job soon afterward.

Most clients are able to make their own decisions, especially if they have input from others. However, an individual in a crisis situation may need more explicit guidance. When clients are suicidal, for example, they often have "tunnel vision" that prevents them from seeing options other than death. Helpers may need to intervene in such situations and try to ensure that clients do not harm themselves (see chap. 22 for more discussion on dealing with suicidal clients). It is important to emphasize that other than in extreme cases (e.g., child abuse or suicidal or homicidal risk), helpers typically do not take over and manage what clients do. Offering suggestions is quite different from demanding that clients do what you tell them to do.

HOW TO GIVE DIRECT GUIDANCE

Helpers should think about their intentions before using direct guidance. They should make sure they are using this intervention because clients are ready to change. As with information, helpers should not give direct guidance until they have assessed clients' motivation (as well as their own).

When clients ask (or sometimes even beg) for direct guidance, helpers have to be particularly careful to distinguish between the honest and direct request for direct guidance and the expression of dependent feelings. When in doubt, it is probably best to deal first with the feelings involved (e.g., "You seem pretty desperate to get some advice. I wonder what's going on for you?"). After such exploration, helpers have additional data to consider how to deal with the request. Helpers also have to assess their own motivation and ensure that their needs to take care of others do not interfere with allowing clients to make their own decisions.

Clients often have negative reactions if helpers ignore their requests for advice. Some clients want direct guidance and are angry when helpers refuse to tell them what to do. An example is a case presented in Hill (1989), where a woman wanted direct guidance about family issues in the early sessions, and the helper did not give it to her because she wanted to do insight-oriented helping. The client felt disregarded by the helper and became less invested in the therapy thereafter. In cases such as this, it might be better to give some advice, if the helper genuinely feels he or she has some, and then process with the client later about the origin of the desire for advice. In addition, openly addressing the client's feelings using immediacy skills may help repair breaches in relationships that occur when clients become angry at helpers for not providing any, enough, or the "right" direct guidance.

When giving direct guidance, helpers need to remember that it is easier for clients to make small, specific changes. Helpers should be very specific about which small steps could be done and when they could be done, and they should reinforce approximations toward the desired behaviors. For example, rather than suggesting that an inactive client try to lose five pounds in the next week (which is not under the client's control), the helper might suggest that the client walk for 15 minutes three times in the next week, reinforce herself by taking a hot bath after each walk, and allow herself to read a novel (assuming the client enjoys doing these things).

I also suggest that helpers write down homework assignments, so clients remember them. It is often difficult to remember everything that happened in sessions. Furthermore, clients are more likely to take written assignments seriously. Following up on homework assignments in subsequent sessions is also important, otherwise clients might feel that such assignments are frivolous and not to be taken seriously.

Helpers also need to be aware that they can offer help but cannot force clients to take it. Helpers are not taking over for clients, but are providing options for clients to consider. Clients have the right to decide for themselves what to do, even in the most desperate of circumstances. Furthermore, helpers have to know the limits of how much they can offer. Friedman (1990) recounts a fable about a rescuer who holds a rope over the rail of a bridge to save a drowning person. The drowning person grabs the rope but refuses to climb up. After a while, the rescuer holding the rope cannot hang on any longer because the person is so heavy. The rescuer has to make a decision about letting go or falling from the bridge himself, which clearly would not help either the drowning person or him- or herself.

Another problem with direct guidance is that it can foster dependency by shifting the responsibility for solutions from clients to helpers. Clients can become passive and helpless if helpers insinuate that they are not competent enough to solve their problems. When helpers rather than clients are responsible for the guidance, clients often blame the helpers when things do not go so well. In addition, when helpers use too much direct guidance, it can lead to tension, resistance, or rebellion if clients choose to ignore helpers who demand that clients pursue their advice. Hence, direct guidance can cause problems in therapeutic relationships if it is not done collaboratively, with helpers and clients together constructing the direct guidance.

EXAMPLE OF DIRECT GUIDANCE

Client: Our 3-year-old daughter has gotten into the habit of coming into our bedroom in the middle of the night and climbing in bed with us and wanting to stay until morning. At first it seemed okay because she seemed to need comforting, but it has gotten out of hand. We only have a double bed, and my husband takes up more than his half, so I end up being unable to sleep because I can't move. When I try to move her, she doesn't want to leave. So we've got to do something.

Helper: You sound frustrated.

Client: I am. We can't figure out what to do. I don't want to traumatize her if she needs comforting. She seems to really like sleeping with us.

Helper: What have you tried so far?

Client: Nothing really. It just started getting intolerable. So now I know we have to do something. Plus I think she's getting a little too old to be doing this.

Helper: What is your goal?

Client: When she wakes up and is upset, I'd like to comfort her and then have her go back to her bed. I don't want her to get into our bed. Once she gets in, it's too hard to get her out.

Helper: What are your usual strategies for dealing with problems with kids?

Client: We talk things out ahead of time so the kids are prepared and are in on it.

Helper: *Maybe that would work here if you talked with her ahead of time about what you are planning to do.* How would you do it?

Client: Before bedtime, I could tell her that during the night when she wakes up, she can't come into our bed anymore. But I'm afraid there's nothing positive to replace it with.

Helper: That's a good point. *What if you were to lay down next to her on her bed until she went back to sleep. Then you could go back to your own bed.*

Client: That sounds like a good idea. So when she comes into our room, I would just take her back to her room, lay down with her for awhile until she's asleep, and then go back to my bed. I think that would work, especially if I tell her about it ahead of time. I might miss some sleep but not as much as I am now.

Helper: Sounds good. Do you see any problems?

Client: Well, I might fall asleep on her bed, but probably not for long because it would be uncomfortable there too. I might also be groggy in the middle of the night and just let her in out of habit.

Helper: *Well, it probably would only take three to five nights, so you could tell yourself that if you can just do it for that long, the habit will be broken.*

Client: Good point. I'm going to do it. It fits with the way I like to do things, so I know it will work.

Disclosure of Strategies

Helpers can make suggestions through disclosing strategies that they personally have tried in the past (another form of self-disclosure). In effect, rather than telling clients what to do, helpers provide suggestions through disclosing what has worked for them previously (see Exhibit 19.5). They then turn the focus back to the clients and ask if that strategy might work for them (e.g., "When I feel angry, I take a deep breath and count to ten. I wonder if that would work for you?").

WHY DISCLOSE STRATEGIES?

Hearing what another person has done can provide specific ideas for new behaviors (e.g., "I brush my teeth as soon as I have finished eating so I don't forget to do it or am too tired to do it") and can also encourage clients to think of novel action plans (e.g., "I treat myself to a cruise each year as a reward for working hard all year. I wonder what you could do?"). Disclosing what has worked for the helper is also somewhat disarming—rather than telling clients what to do, helpers communicate that

E X H I B I T   1 9 . 5

Overview of Disclosure of Strategies

Definition	*Disclosure of strategies* refers to the helper's presentation of actions that he or she has used in the past to cope with problems.
Example	"When I have been in similar situations with my mother, I call her and ask to talk. I try to be as honest as possible and let her know that I messed up. Usually she is pretty understanding."
Typical intention	To promote change (see Web Form D)
Typical client reactions	Educated, unstuck, new ways to behave, hopeful, confused, misunderstood, no reaction (see Web Form G)
Desired client behaviors	Agreement, therapeutic changes (see Web Form H)
Difficulties helpers experience in disclosing strategies	Disclosing to meet own needs Not shifting focus back to client Trying to influence client too much

Note. Other types of self-disclosures were presented in chapter 10 (disclosures about similarities, information, and feelings) and chapter 15 (disclosures of insight).

they do not have the answers but are willing to share what has worked for them. By disclosing strategies, helpers are able to provide ideas for clients without imposing the type of demands that may result from directives. Disclosing strategies is a more tentative way of giving information or direct guidance.

HOW TO DISCLOSE STRATEGIES

As with self-disclosures of insight, helpers need to give the disclosure but then turn the focus back to the client. For example,

> When I'm reading a book, I make myself read a chapter and then I reward myself by doing something I like—I might get a soda, make a phone call, or play a video game, although I limit any of those activities to ten minutes. Would that work for you?

Helpers should be aware, however, that clients might be unduly influenced by the helper's disclosure to adopt a similar action plan. Helpers can provide the option tentatively, indicate that it might or might not work for the client, and then turn the focus back to the client for their reaction. In addition, helpers need to be careful not to slip into disclosures to relieve their own feelings because then the focus shifts from the client to the helper (e.g., "Let me tell you all about what I did because it's so fascinating and interesting").

EXAMPLE OF HOW TO DISCLOSE STRATEGIES

Client: I know that I need to exercise but I just can never seem to find anything I like to do.

Helper: *One thing that works for me is to go for a half-hour walk every morning with my husband. I get exercise and get to spend some time with my husband at the beginning of the day.* I wonder if something like that would work for you?

Client: Well, that kind of appeals to me, but I'm really out of shape.

Helper: *I started out walking ten minutes a day and worked my way up over several years. Now I hate to miss my morning walk.* Would ten minutes be easier for you?

Client: Yeah, but how would I get my husband involved?

Helper: What thoughts do you have about that?

WHAT DO YOU THINK?

▪ Clients often ask for information. How would you decide when to give clients the requested information and when to probe them for their ideas?

▪ How can you determine whether clients really want or need direct guidance?

▪ Argue for or against the opinion that direct guidance should generally be given tentatively and only after thorough exploration and insight.

▪ Describe what it might be like for you to tell clients that you do not know the answer to their questions. How might not knowing an answer influence the client's perception of the helper?

▪ How do you feel about receiving information from other people? What feelings do you have when you seek information or when people ask you for information?

▪ Debate the pros and cons related to radio talk show psychologists giving direct guidance after having spoken only briefly with callers.

The Steps of the Action Stage 20

Vision without action is a daydream.
Action without vision is a nightmare.

—Japanese proverb

helper at a homeless shelter listened to Debi talk about her rage, feelings of powerlessness, and sense of humiliation at being evicted from her home. The helper challenged Debi's irrational thoughts that she was worthless and a social outcast. The helper self-disclosed about her own experiences with poverty and losing her job and how she had been forced to figure out what she wanted to do with her life. Debi felt better after expressing her feelings and gaining insights about how she had gotten to this situation, but she also wanted to learn skills so she would never be homeless again. The helper asked for more details about how she had come to lose her job and home. Debi said that she had been fired because of downsizing and had become discouraged about getting another job after being turned down by 15 employers. The helper gave Debi some tests to figure out her interests, helped her write a resume, and then did role-playing with her about how to do a job interview. Debi applied for several jobs while living at the shelter and was offered one that she liked.

The action skills come together in a series of steps on how to proceed through the action stage. Helpers serve as coaches or guides during these steps to help clients move toward implementing changes in their lives. Helpers can start with these steps and modify them in creative ways according to the needs of particular clients (e.g., some clients might be ready to start changing and will not need to spend as much time exploring action; other clients might not have tried to change their behavior in the past, so the step about assessing past change attempts can be skipped). When clients have strong reactions to any of the steps, helpers will need to step back and help clients process their reactions and possibly alter their strategies. In each step, I discuss the helping skills used to implement the step. See Exhibit 20.1 for a summary of the steps and skills.

Step 1. Identify a Specific Problem

The specific problem might be very clear after going through the exploration and insight stages (e.g., increasing study time, increasing exercise, eliminating nail biting, becoming more assertive, communication problems). It could be a behavior (e.g., wanting to be more assertive), a thought (e.g., not wanting to think that everyone should love me), or a decision (e.g., whether to go to graduate school).

Helpers should focus on one problem at a time because dealing with several problems simultaneously can be confusing and diffuse any change efforts. If the client has multiple problems, the helper could work with the client to list all the problems and then order them. It is better to focus initially on easier (but still meaningful) problems, so clients can gain a sense of accomplishment when they change. Furthermore, accomplishing small changes can provide clients with the confidence to pursue additional challenges.

If a clear, specific problem was not identified earlier, the helper can now work with the client to choose one. For clients whose concerns are more global or vague (e.g., general feelings of dissatisfaction), helpers will need to help clarify and construct an explicit problem. This often requires helping the client explore the problem, think about his or her values, and develop more understanding and motivation for change (in other words, going back to do more exploration and insight about the problem and the client's life situation).

To help the client identify a specific problem to focus on in the action stage, the helper can ask open questions such as the following:

- "What is the first thing that you would like to be different?"
- "What do you specifically want to change in your life?"
- "Describe your dreams for the future. What would you need to change to make those dreams become a reality?"

The helper might also want to use approval–reassurance to support the client:

- "That sounds like a good problem to start with given what we have talked about."

EXHIBIT 20.1

Steps of the Action Stage

Step	Possible Skills to Use	Intervention
1. Identify a specific problem	Open question Approval–reassurance	
2. Explore action	Open question Restatement Reflection of feeling Process advisement	
3. Assess previous attempts	Open question Restatement Reflection of feeling Approval–reassurance	
4. Make a commitment to change	Closed question	
5. Brainstorm options	Open question Direct guidance Disclosure of strategies	
6. Choose action option	Open questions Information Direct guidance	
7. In-session interventions	Process advisement	Relaxation Feedback about behaviors Operant methods Behavioral rehearsal Cognitive restructuring Decision making Testing referral Communication training Crisis management
8. Choose tasks for outside the session	Open question Direct guidance Disclose strategies	
9. Check in and modify assignments	Open question Direct guidance Feedback about progress	

If the client has identified a specific problem (e.g., becoming violently angry), the helper might ask for a specific example (along with details) of when the behavior last occurred:

■ "Tell me about the last time you got angry. Describe the situation to me as fully as possible."

By the end of this step, the helper should know a well-articulated, specific problem that the client wants to address. If the issue is behavioral, the helper should also know details of what happened during a specific instance (e.g., details of the last argument with a partner), because it is easier to do the action stage with a specific event rather than a vague description.

Step 2. Explore the Idea of Action on This Problem

Rather than assume clients are eager to change, it is important to allow them to explore the idea of changing. Most of us are ambivalent about changing. Although we might be unhappy with the way things are, we are often scared by what things might be like if we change.

Not every client is ready to change. In chapter 3, I listed six stages of clients' readiness for change: precontemplation, contemplation, preparation, action, maintenance, and termination (Prochaska et al., 1992). Assessing the stage is important before proceeding in the action stage. In the precontemplation and contemplation stages, clients typically require much time to explore their feelings and develop insights before making a commitment to change; clients in the preparation and action stages often are more ready to move directly to action. Clients in the maintenance and termination stages probably are more interested in stabilizing the changes they already have made.

Other clients might want to change inappropriate things. Oscar Wilde said that "the only thing worse than not getting what you want is getting what you want" (from *Lady Windemere's Fan*, Act 3; Murray, 1989). Rather than rushing to change, clients need an opportunity to explore the pros and cons of changing and make good choices about whether to change.

If helpers plunge too quickly into action with clients who are not ready, they typically hear "Yes, but. . . . " These clients will have all kinds of reasons why action is not possible. Alternatively, some clients might simply withdraw and act compliant but have no intention of following through on the action. Helpers need to respect clients' choices about whether to change.

Helpers should not be invested in whether or not clients choose to change. Rather than perceiving that their success as a helper is based on clients' making radical changes, helpers need to view their success as based on helping clients decide what is best for them. The key is to provide a good enough climate so clients feel comfortable talking about and then making decisions about changing. Helpers might find it helpful to cycle back to the exploration and insight stages to assist clients in exploring feelings about change and to understand what contributes to clients' ambivalence.

The goal is to encourage clients to express their thoughts and feelings about action and examine the benefits and drawbacks of changing or not changing, rather than forcing clients to make changes. Helpers can maintain an attitude of curiosity and ask open questions to assess client readiness to change and encourage client exploration of feelings:

- "What are the benefits of changing?
- "What are the benefits of not changing?
- "How would changing make you feel?"
- "What keeps you from changing?"
- "What goes through your mind as we talk about changing?"
- "What feelings are you having when you contemplate making changes in your life?"
- "How would others react to your changing?"

The helper also can support clients and facilitate exploration of change through restatements and reflection of feelings, such as,

- "You haven't thought much about whether you want to change."
- "It's exciting for you to think about doing something new."

Hence, the primary skills used in this step are open questions and reflection of feelings. Open questions are useful to begin the discussion, which helpers can then facilitate by reflecting feelings and drawing clients into a discussion of values, needs, and problems related to change.

If the client is clearly conflicted about changing, it might be helpful to use a two-chair technique (see Greenberg et al., 1993) to allow the client to experience and express both sides of the conflict. Resolution of the conflict is typically easier after both sides of the conflict are brought into awareness. For this technique, the helper uses process advisement.

EXAMPLE OF TWO-CHAIR TECHNIQUE

Helper: Be the side of you that says you should quit biting your fingernails. You can pretend that you're talking to that chair over there.

Client: [to empty chair] It's disgusting when you do that. Look how awful you look. Just stop it.

Helper: Can you say it a little louder, like your father might have said it to you when you were 12 years old?

Client: [to empty chair] Yeah. (louder) Just stop it. You look ugly when you're chewing your fingernails. What's wrong with you anyway? Stop it right now.

Helper: Now go over to the other chair and be the 12-year-old side of you who wants to chew her fingernails. What would you have wanted to say back to your father?

Client: [from other chair to empty chair] I'll chew my fingernails if I want. You can't stop me. I don't care what

> you think. All you want is for me to be perfect, so I'll look good for you.
>
> *Helper:* How did that feel to you going through that? Did you learn something new about why you might chew your fingernails?
>
> *Client:* I sure did. I can see that I wanted to get back at my father. It was a small way that I could have some control over my life.
>
> *Helper:* When you think about it that way, what do you think about being ready to change your fingernail biting now?
>
> *Client:* I think I'm ready to change biting my fingernails. I'm pretty disgusted by it too at this point. But I want to come back after that to try to understand more about my relationship with my father.
>
> *Helper:* Okay then. Let's spend some time working on the fingernails first and then go back to the issue with your father.

After weighing all the options, some clients might choose not to change. They might decide that the costs of changing are not worth the benefits. Sometimes change is too painful, and sometimes clients discover that their current life is not so bad. Choosing not to change can be just as valid a choice as deciding to change. For example, after having tried for years to be assertive with her boss, only to be punished and ridiculed in front of her coworkers, Sandra decided not to fight back any longer against her boss' inappropriate behaviors. The helper (who was initially overly invested in the client being assertive) had to respect this decision and assist the client in developing coping skills to help manage her reactions at work.

By the end of this step, the client should have made some commitment about changing. Note that clients are rarely one hundred percent in favor of change, but the advantages should clearly outweigh the disadvantages, or else it is not a good idea to go forward with the next steps.

Step 3. Assess Previous Change Attempts and Social Support

When helpers have established that clients want to change, they can assess what attempts, if any, clients have already made. Finding out about previous attempts can avoid encouraging actions that have not worked in the past, indicate that the helper respects the client's change efforts, and let the client know the helper is aware that the client has been attempting to solve problems. After all, clients have usually had lengthy experiences with their problems and have undoubtedly tried, and have many feelings about, various alternatives. Helpers act as consultants with clients, collaboratively working to learn what they have tried and how these strategies have worked.

The following are examples of open questions helpers can use to assess previous efforts:

▪ "What have you tried before?"
▪ "Describe the strategies you have used in trying to change."

In this step, helpers also need to assess what worked and what didn't work in the previous attempts. In effect, the helper is assessing the forces facilitating change as well as the forces inhibiting change. Helpers can focus on both internal (e.g., motivation, anxiety, insecurity, and self-confidence) and external factors (resources that clients have available in their environment to support them when they make changes, obstacles such as discrimination and social injustice). It is better to know as much as possible about the factors influencing the change process from the outset so the same problems are not repeated. It is important to realize that clients may not be aware of all the influencing factors, but it is good to get as many as possible out in the open.

Helpers use open questions to assess the facilitating and restraining influences:

▪ "What parts of what you tried worked?"
▪ "What parts didn't work?"
▪ "What problems did you encounter that made it difficult the last time?"
▪ "When you tried the last time, what things made it easier for you?"
▪ "What was going on in your environment when you tried last time?"
▪ "What thoughts and feelings were you having?"

It is important for helpers to remember to support client exploration because it can sometimes be quite threatening to disclose. Using restatements and reflections of feelings can demonstrate to clients that helpers are listening.

▪ "Sounds like you've tried lots of things to help you overcome your depression."
▪ "You sound frustrated that after all your efforts, nothing happened."

Using approval–reassurance can let clients know that helpers are aware of their hard work in exploring and that helpers value what clients are saying.

■ "You've done a great job working so hard to get information about services available in the community. You've been very resourceful."

Finally, helpers might want to assess social support, given that research indicates social support is very important in terms of change efforts (Sarason, Sarason, & Pierce, 1990). Breier and Strauss (1984) noted that the benefits of a social support system include a forum for ventilation, reality testing, support and approval, integration into the community, problem solving, and constancy. Positive support can provide encouragement and reinforcement (e.g., having a supportive, nonjudgmental partner can enable one to stick to a diet). In contrast, negative support can undermine the person's resolve (e.g., if a person decides to go on a diet and the partner says that she was more attractive before or can't stay on a diet, it will be very difficult for that person to continue the diet). In addition, helpers can discuss with clients how change will influence their social network.

■ "How much can you rely on other people to help you with this problem?"
■ "How do others respond to you about this problem?"
■ "How would others react if you change?"

By the end of this step, the helper should have a fairly good idea of what the client has tried before and how much social support the client has in his or her environment. In addition, the helper should have some ideas of what has worked and what has not worked in terms of previous change attempts. The helper puts this information together with data gathered during the exploration and insight stage to begin to conceptualize what types of strengths and problems the client will have in terms of making changes (e.g., resistance to an authority figure telling him or her to change).

Step 4. Help Client Decide About Making a Commitment to Change

During this step, the helper can work to determine if the client really wants to change. If the answer is affirmative, they can go onto the next steps. If negative, they can return to earlier stages of the model:

■ "At this point, are you ready to commit yourself to changing?"

Step 5. Brainstorm Options

One of the biggest benefits for clients of working with helpers is that they can brainstorm options together. Through collaboration, more ideas can usually be produced than can be generated by one person alone or two people working independently. The idea in this step is to generate as many ideas as possible, without judgment, to enable clients to see that there are many alternatives. Reality can come later when deciding among the possibilities, but the ideas must first be generated. One useful strategy is to set a specific time limit, such as two minutes, for the brainstorming process. It is important for clients to lift restrictions on themselves while brainstorming and to suspend judgment about what is possible so they do not censor any possibilities. Although I do not usually recommend that helpers take notes, it can be helpful during this step for helpers to write down the ideas so they can refer back to them in the next step.

To aid brainstorming, helpers can use open questions to ask clients to think of whatever action comes to mind, no matter how unlikely or silly it might initially sound.

- "If money or time were not an issue, how would you try to change this problem behavior?"
- "What would you suggest to someone else in this situation?"

Helpers can add ideas of their own using direct guidance. It is fine for helpers to make suggestions here because it can open clients up to new ideas they might not have considered. Of course, it is important for helpers not to get invested in their ideas but just to offer possibilities to give clients more options.

- "What about talking to your boss?"
- "Maybe you could. . . . "

Helpers can also self-disclose about strategies they have tried in similar situations. By disclosing, helpers not only admit that they too have had problems but also make clear that this option worked for them but might not work for the client.

- "When I have trouble remembering all the things I have to do, I make a list."
- "I try to keep a routine and brush my teeth right after my shower."

By the end of this step, the helper should have a list of a number of possibilities of what the client might try. No order of preferences are necessarily known at this point, but hopefully a lot of ideas have been generated.

Step 6. Choose
Action Options

Now that brainstorming has generated a number of options, the task for the helper is to help the client think through the options systematically and choose which ideas to try. Clients need to select ideas that are specific, realistic, within the realm of possibility, and consistent with their values. Helpers can ask which options seem appealing and why. Helpers can also ask about client's values to determine whether any of the options violate the client's values. For example, even though a quick way to obtain money might be to rob a bank, clients (one hopes) have values against theft.

The following are examples of open questions that helpers might use to help a client choose the best idea:

- "Which options seem most appealing?"
- "Which options seem least appealing?"
- "What are your values about the different alternatives that you might try?"
- "What options go against your values or beliefs?"

Helpers might want to use information to educate clients about the various possibilities, for example,

- "One way to work with anxiety is by doing relaxation exercises to help you learn how to cope with the anxiety. In relaxation training, we go through the various muscles and teach you to tense them and then relax them. We go through the training in the session and then you practice it on your own several times. After practicing several times, most people are able to relax by just thinking about relaxing. Then you can do deep breathing to get you right into a state of relaxation."

If clients have a hard time thinking through the options, helpers can ask them to list the advantages and disadvantages of each option (with helpers adding opinions if appropriate). If the disadvantages of the option outweigh the advantages, it is unlikely that the client will want to implement the option.

- What are the advantages of practicing relaxation each night?"
- "What are the disadvantages of practicing relaxation each night?"

Helpers can offer their own opinion about the best options for clients to pursue, as long as they offer their opinions in a collaborative manner and allow clients to make their own decisions about what to do. It is especially appropriate for helpers to offer advice when they have expertise about what might work.

■ "I suggest that we teach you relaxation to help you deal with the anxiety, and then we can do role-playing to teach you ways to interact. How does that sound?"

By the end of this step, the helper should have an idea of the rankings of the client's preference for options. They can then proceed to the next step. Step 6 might be quite short if the client immediately jumps into the problem solving that takes place in subsequent steps. Or, the client might be quite reluctant, which can alert the helper to problems in the relationship that must be addressed by cycling back to the insight stage. Finally, for some clients, they might have gotten enough out of action at this stage and not need to go further (e.g., the client might have made a decision and needs to go home and see how it feels).

Step 7. Implement In-Session Interventions

There are many behavioral and cognitive interventions that helpers can use in sessions to help clients change. Helpers need to be aware of and skilled in using the different interventions, so they can choose among them to help the individual client. Several interventions are reviewed briefly, but readers are encouraged to seek out other texts for more detail about these and other interventions (e.g., Goldfried & Davison, 1994; Kazdin, 2001; Watson & Tharp, 2002).

RELAXATION

An extensive amount of data shows that relaxing one's muscles reduces anxiety (Jacobson, 1929; Lang, Melamed, & Hart, 1970; Paul, 1969) and that it is useful to teach certain (particularly anxious) clients to relax (Bernstein & Borkovec, 1973; Goldfried & Trier, 1974). When people are relaxed, they are more open and able to handle information, so relaxation is a good thing to do prior to other behavioral interventions. Although many methods of relaxation training exist (e.g., meditation, deep muscle relaxation), Benson's (1975) extensive research has found two main components: (a) the repetition of any word, sound, prayer, thought, phrase, or muscular activity and (b) the passive return to repeating when other thoughts intrude. Following Benson's suggestions, helpers can teach clients to relax in the session by going through the following steps, using a calm, slow voice:

1. "Get as comfortable as possible in your seat. Remove everything from your lap and put your feet firmly on the floor. Close your eyes."
2. "Relax your body starting from your toes up through your head. Shrug your shoulders and release the tension. Breathe deeply."
3. "Pick a word (e.g., *one, peace*), sound (e.g., om), prayer (e.g., the Lord's Prayer), thought or phrase (e.g., the river runs through it). Pick something that fits with your beliefs and feels comfortable to you. Repeat that phrase each time you breathe out."
4. "Let all your other thoughts go. When you find yourself thinking about something else, don't worry, just passively let it go and return to repeating."
5. "Do this for three to five minutes and then sit quietly for a minute."

Because doing a relaxation exercise during a session could be threatening to some clients, helpers might want to ask clients about thoughts and feelings before, during, and after the exercise. They might also want to check with them about how much they liked doing the relaxation. If clients feel that it would be useful, helpers can suggest that they practice relaxing 10 to 20 minutes, twice a day (e.g., in morning before breakfast and in the late afternoon) in a quiet place where they will not be distracted. If clients like relaxation and have a tendency to become panicked in sessions, helpers can also suggest that they use it within sessions.

OPERANT METHODS FOR BEHAVIOR CHANGE

As described in chapter 18, operant methods are based on the assumption that behaviors are controlled by their consequences. Hence, the first step in using operant methods for behavior change is to carefully assess the problem in terms of the ABCs of it (i.e., the antecedents, behaviors, and consequences). The assessment might involve first interviewing the client about the conditions under which the target behavior occurs. Then a helper typically would instruct a client to monitor his or her behavior over the course of one to two weeks to gather specific information about the antecedents, behaviors, and consequences. For example, a client who wants to reduce his overeating might be asked to write down all the food he eats, where he eats it, who he is with when he eats, and how he feels before and after eating. Clients often learn that their behavior differs dramatically from what they reported earlier to helpers. For example, an overweight man who claims that he never snacks might learn that he consistently nibbles on something while watching television in the evenings. A person who feels lonely might discover that she never looks people in the eye and never says hello when passing others.

When helpers have an idea of the baseline (typical) behavior, they can help clients determine realistic goals for change. For example, if an overweight person wants to lose 50 pounds in one month, the helper can work with the client to recognize that this goal is unrealistic. Often the goals have to be modified to be more attainable. For example, instead of encouraging the overweight client to begin a severely restricted diet of 800 calories per day, the helper might encourage the client to walk 20 minutes a day in addition to eating more moderately (e.g., 1,500 calories per day) to facilitate gradual weight loss (which is most likely to be maintained).

Helpers also work with clients to identify reinforcers. For example, one client might find it reinforcing to look forward to going on a vacation to a Caribbean island if she can get all As on her report card. Another client might need the more immediate reinforcement of being able to call a friend after he studies for one hour.

When the target behavior is identified, baseline information has been gathered, realistic goals set, and reinforcers identified, the helper works with the client to figure out how to modify the behavior. It is preferable to look for ways to increase positive behavior than to decrease negative behaviors because it is easier to change in the positive direction. For example, for a problem with social anxiety, the helper might identify that the client needs to make more overtures to others. The chosen behaviors must be observable, behavioral, and specific (e.g., smiling at strangers) rather than broad and vague (e.g., becoming more friendly) because specific behaviors are easier to work on and monitor for changes. In addition, helpers target specific behaviors to change (e.g., a certain amount of homework) rather than trying to change the outcome (e.g., the final grade) because the specific behaviors are within one's control, whereas the outcome is not (e.g., one never knows how instructors will curve the grades). The principle of "baby steps" is also important here. Rather than expecting the client to make huge changes immediately, small changes are more likely to be attainable.

BEHAVIORAL REHEARSAL OR ROLE-PLAYING

Behavioral rehearsal or role-playing is used to help clients learn new ways of responding to specific life situations (Goldfried & Davison, 1994). Rather than talking about behavioral changes in the helping setting, new behaviors are taught through acting out situations in which the behaviors could be used. Because assertiveness is the most common problem focused on for behavioral rehearsal, I illustrate interventions designed to increase assertive behaviors.

According to Alberti and Emmons (2001), the goal of assertiveness training is to teach clients to stand up for their rights without infringing on the rights of others. Unassertive people let others walk all over them, whereas aggressive people walk all over other people. Both unassertive and aggressive people can be taught to express both positive and negative feelings more appropriately, although one cannot guarantee that clients get their way when they assert themselves. In fact, aggressive people who are used to getting their way are not likely to respond favorably to a previously unassertive person acting assertively. Hence, helpers also have to assist clients in thinking not only of how to present an initial, empathic, assertive statement but also then how to respond to escalated aggressiveness.

The first step in assertiveness training is to assess the actual behavior. Helpers might ask clients to describe a typical scene and then role-play exactly how they usually behave (with the helper playing the role of the other person). For example, a client might present with extreme awkwardness and unassertiveness in interactions with interesting men. The helper can role-play a situation where the client meets an attractive man at a party. The helper should observe the client's behavior (e.g., eye contact, voice volume, statement of needs, and attitude), although the helper should not comment on these behaviors at this point. Helpers can ask clients for self-evaluations of how assertive they were and how they felt in the situation.

Helpers then work with clients to determine specific goals of how they would like to behave differently (e.g., make one comment during class discussion). Clients are much more likely to make changes when they have specific, clear goals than if they have vague goals. To construct goals, helpers and clients can brainstorm different possible behaviors and determine which behaviors would feel comfortable to clients. I should note that there is no "right" way to be assertive, so this step is crucial in devising goals that clients can embrace. For example, one female client may want to learn how to ask an interesting man for a date, whereas another would not find this action desirable.

When the target behavior is determined, helpers can reverse roles with clients and provide a model of how clients could implement the new behaviors (e.g., the helper could show how she would ask an instructor for an extension of a deadline because of a documented illness). Helpers then can ask clients to try the chosen behavior in a role-play, again observing the client's behavior carefully.

After the role-play, helpers should provide honest positive feedback. Even if the positive feedback is about something minor, clients need to feel that they are doing something well and making some progress. Helpers then can give corrective feedback about one or two things, remembering the behavioral principle of working on small, manageable steps. Helpers might also provide some coaching about what clients could try differently in the next role-play (e.g., "Okay, say it louder and with more conviction this time"). Using videotape feedback can be invaluable be-cause clients may be unaware of how they are perceived. Role-plays can be continued until the client feels confident that she or he can perform the desired behaviors. During the role-plays, helpers might also discover that they need to do relaxation training or cognitive restructuring with clients to overcome obstacles to change.

Helpers should start with relatively easy behaviors first (e.g., ques-tioning a clerk in a store) rather than major behaviors (e.g., asking for a raise) to maximize the possibility of success. In the previous example, the client might first work on initiating a conversation with a man in class and work up to asking him out on a date.

COGNITIVE RESTRUCTURING

Cognitive theorists have suggested that irrational thinking keeps people from coping effectively and makes them unhappy. Ellis (1962, 1995) sug-gested that people say irrational things to themselves, such as "I must be loved by everyone," "I must be completely competent and perfect to be worthwhile," "It is awful if things are not the way I want them to be," "There should be someone stronger than me who will take care of me," and "There is a perfect solution to human problems, and it is terrible if I don't find it."

The main goal of cognitive restructuring is to help clients recognize their faulty thinking and change it. To enable clients to recognize their maladaptive thoughts, helpers such as Ellis (1962, 1995) use persuasion and challenges. They attack the irrational thoughts ("What are you tell-ing yourself now?" "You are telling yourself that it would be awful if you did not succeed at being a physicist, but what would be the worst thing that would happen?" "What would be so horrible about that?" "You say you can't stand it, but is that true, would you fall apart?" "It might not be pleasant, but would it actually be catastrophic?"). It is important, how-ever, that helpers attack the beliefs, not the person.

Ellis's approach is didactic, in that he teaches clients an ABC model, where A is the activating event, B is the irrational beliefs, and C is the consequent negative emotional reactions or behaviors. Whereas clients make the assumption that events (A) cause emotions (C), Ellis believes that it is the irrational beliefs (B) that lead to negative emotions (C). For example, if Sam gets a C on an exam (A), he might think that the failure make him feel bad (C); in fact, it is what he tells himself about getting a C (e.g., "I'm a failure as a person; I should be perfect"). Hence, if we replace the irrational beliefs (B) with more rational cognitions (D), clients have more positive emotions (E). In this example, Sam might be taught a more rational thought such as, "It's too bad that I got a C on the exam but that doesn't make me a bad person. It just means that I have to study harder next time, instead of going out drinking the night before." Ellis would also give clients homework to test the validity of irrational beliefs. He might suggest that Sam study more before the next exam to see if that improves his grade. He would also encourage Sam to record his irrational thoughts and combat them with more rational thoughts.

A. T. Beck and his colleagues (A. T. Beck, 1976; A. T. Beck & Emery, 1985; A. T. Beck & Freeman, 1990; A. T. Beck, Rush, Shaw, & Emery, 1979; A. T. Beck & Weishaar, 1995; J. S. Beck, 1995) developed a cognitive theory that is slightly different from Ellis's theory. They postulated that automatic thoughts and dysfunctional interpretations are the major source of problems for clients, and that clients misconstrue events on the basis of faulty logic and beliefs in the cognitive triad of the self, world, and future. Hence, clients often view themselves as defective, inadequate, or unlovable; the world as unmanageable, uncontrollable, or overwhelming; and the future as bleak and hopeless.

A. T. Beck's gentle therapeutic approach is quite different from Ellis's direct confrontational style. He recommended that helpers work collaboratively with clients as scientists to uncover faulty logic and examine its impact. Helpers ask a series of questions to help clients arrive at logical conclusions ("What happens when you say X to yourself?"). Helpers also actively point out cognitive themes and underlying assumptions that work against clients. A. T. Beck suggested that people often draw conclusions without having adequate evidence (e.g., a person might conclude that he is unlovable just because he has no one with whom to eat lunch one day). People also take details out of context (e.g., focus on one negative comment about a presentation in class and ignore several positive ones), develop general rules out of a few instances (e.g., because she made a mistake one time, a person generalizes that she cannot handle any responsibility), and make something more or less important than it is (e.g., perceive a person not saying "hello" as meaning that he is angry; minimizing the importance of failing a course). In addition, people attribute blame to themselves without any evidence (e.g., a secretary believing that a company's going out of business is due to her not coming into work one day), and engage in rigid, either–or thinking (e.g., a man may think that women are either goddesses or whores). (For those who want to learn more about cognitive therapy, I recommend the widely used self-help book by Burns, 1999.)

DECISION MAKING

Clients often have major life decisions to make: which job to take, whether to go to graduate school, whether it is best to buy a house or rent an apartment, or whether to get married. In decision making, helpers work with clients to help them articulate their options, explore their values, and evaluate the options according to their values (Carkhuff, 1973).

The helper first asks the client to articulate the various options. As an example, let us consider that the helper is working with a middle-aged teacher, Bess, who is trying to plan her future. Bess states that she has several options she has been considering: she and her husband could retire at 55, sell their house, and travel around the country in a recreational vehicle; she could wait to retire until 65 and then get involved in volunteer activities; she could keep teaching indefinitely since there is no mandatory retirement age in her job. As the woman is talking, the helper makes a grid and records the options along the top (see example in Exhibit 20.2). Note that sometimes it takes a fair amount of exploration for all these options to emerge (and clients sometimes add options or modify the options as they go through the process).

Next, the helper asks about relevant values, desires, or needs. Through considerable exploration, Bess says that the important considerations for her are that she wants to travel, she likes to be intellectually stimulated, she wants to spend time with her husband, she wants more time to be with friends, she wants to have enough money to be comfortable, she wants to feel that she is doing something meaningful with her life, and she wants to be near her children, especially when they have grandchildren. The helper then asks the client to weight the importance of each consideration (1 = not important, 10 = extremely important). Bess might put intellectual stimulation as her most important value and give it a weight of 9, whereas she might rank having time to spend with friends at the bottom of her list and give it a weight of 2.

Using a scale of –3 to +3 (–3, –2, –1, 0, +1, +2, +3), the helper can then ask the client to rate the various options on each of the values and also to discuss the reasons for the ratings. For example, Bess might say that retiring at 55 would get a +3 on travel because they would be touring the country but would be rated a –3 on intellectual stimulation because she would not be teaching any longer and might not be doing as much reading.

The next step is to multiply the rating for the option by the weight for the value and then add up the scores for each option. For our client, the options of retiring at 65 and working indefinitely both received the highest total scores, indicating that Bess preferred these two options to the other option.

Her helper can then ask Bess how she feels about these results. When clients see the total scores for each option, they sometimes realize that the scores are not reflective of what they truly want, so they have to go back through and reweight their values or change their ratings of each option. This exploration process of putting numbers on feelings can be valuable because it makes the decision-making process very concrete.

EXHIBIT 20.2

Example of a Decision-Making Chart

Considerations	Options Retire at 55 and tour country		Retire at 65 and volunteer		Stay at same job indefinitely	
Travel (5)	+3	(15)	+1	(5)	−2	(−10)
Intellectual stimulation (9)	−3	(−27)	+1	(9)	+3	(27)
Time with spouse (7)	2	(14)	+1	(7)	−2	(−14)
Friends (2)	+1	(2)	+1	(2)	−1	(−2)
Money (5)	−3	(−15)	+1	(5)	+3	(15)
Being near children (1)	−2	(−20)	+2	(20)	+2	(20)
Meaning of life (8)	0	(0)	+1	(8)	+2	(16)
Total	−29		54		52	

Note. The number in parentheses after each of the considerations is the weighting of that consideration (range is 1 to 10, where 10 = the greatest weighting). The number in the columns are the ratings of each option on the particular consideration (range from −3 to +3, where +3 = the highest rating). The number in the parentheses after the rating for each option is the multiplicative value of the rating by the weighting of the value (e.g., $+3 \times 5$ for the option of retiring at 55 for the value of traveling).

I should note that some clients really like this systematic method of decision making, whereas others get annoyed by all the numbers and prefer a more intuitive approach. Obviously, helpers will want to use it only if clients seem attracted to the method.

EDUCATIONAL, PERSONALITY, AND APTITUDE TESTING

There are many times when helpers might benefit from knowledge about their clients that can be obtained through standardized tests. For example, if a helper needs to know more about the extent of a client's pathology to make better decisions about treatment, the helper might want the client to take the MMPI or Rorschach tests. Other clients might need testing to determine whether they have learning disabilities. Still other clients might need testing to determine career interests and options. Psychologists have many good tests for all of these areas, so it makes sense to take advantage of this type of information.

Crucial, however, to test taking is proper preparation before the test and then proper interpretation of the results after the test is administered and scored. In terms of preparation, it is imperative for helpers to provide adequate information to clients about the benefits of the testing and the procedures involved. It is also important for clients to be motivated to learn about themselves through the test. In terms of test interpretation, it appears to be better for helpers to engage the client in a collaborative process of trying to understand the results rather than acting as the expert who just tells the client the results (see Finn & Tonsager, 2002; Hanson, Claiborn, & Kerr, 1997).

FINAL THOUGHTS

By the end of this step, helpers should have gotten a pretty good sense of the client's willingness to try different tasks in the session. If the client is eager and cooperative and seems to enjoy doing the behavioral work, the helper can proceed to assigning homework and can come back to additional in-session behavioral work in subsequent sessions. If the client has not gotten engaged in this step, the helper could work with the client to understand the resistance, whether it relates to issues in the therapeutic relationship (e.g., not liking the helper telling the client what to do) or whether it relates more to dynamic issues within the client (e.g., not being ready to give up anger at a parent).

Step 8. Choose Tasks for Outside the Session

Helpers often want clients to make changes in their lives outside of the helping setting, so they assign tasks for outside the session. Such tasks can be particularly effective in providing additional opportunities for clients to practice newfound skills in other settings. For example, after practicing assertiveness in sessions, a helper might suggest that a client try being more assertive the next time she is at a store. (Note that it is typically better to practice new skills in a safe or insignificant setting before trying them out in a more difficult setting.) Or after discussing study skills, a helper might make a contract with a client to study at least 30 minutes a night at his desk, after which he can reinforce himself by getting a soda and calling his girlfriend.

In choosing tasks, helpers need to be attentive to choosing tasks that (Conoley et al., 1994; Scheel et al., 1997; Wonnell & Hill, 2002)

▪ fit the problem
▪ are not difficult to implement
▪ are based on the client's strengths

In a study on homework, Conoley et al. (1994) gave an example in which a client was depressed and angry. During the session, the client said that he wished he had written down instances when he felt badly the previous week so that he could remember them to talk about in the sessions. For homework, the helper asked the client to write down instances when he felt badly, recording what he was thinking, doing, and feeling and what the situation was so they could discuss the problem more specifically in the next session. The client responded favorably, saying he liked to write and that writing had helped him in the past. Thus, the recommendation was judged as not being difficult because it required only a small amount of time, was not anxiety producing, and was clear. In addition, it was based on the client's strengths, given that the client had indicated that he liked to write. Furthermore, it matched his problem because it facilitated the client in remembering situations in which he was depressed and angry. During the next session, the client indicated that he had implemented the recommendation.

Helpers might also warn clients to "go slow" to prevent too much enthusiastic initial behavior that often results in not being able to sustain the change. Many people enthusiastically say they will make an extreme change (e.g., exercise three hours a day) but then get discouraged when they discover how difficult it is to carry out this change. It is better to take too small a step but do it than to overestimate what one can do.

To assign tasks, helpers use direct guidance or disclosure of strategies:

- "Based on what we've talked about in the session, I'd like to suggest a couple of things. First, keep a journal for the next week. When you catch yourself chewing your nails, write down what you are feeling so we can try to figure out what's going on there. Also, put a quarter in a jar for each time you're able to stop biting your fingernails and save up for something special that you'd like. What do you think of those two suggestions?"
- "What worked for me when I used to bite my nails was to keep a nail clipper and file close by. When I felt those ragged edges and felt the compulsion to chew, I immediately smoothed the edges. Then I rewarded myself with a quarter. I wonder how that would be with you to try those two things next week?"

In addition to being aware of the types of tasks assigned, it is important that helpers are aware of not being too "bossy." Several studies have shown that clients become resistant and uncooperative if helpers become too directive (Bischoff & Tracey, 1995; Gillespie, 1951; Mahalik, 1994; Patterson & Forgatch, 1985), so helpers need to remember to be collaborative in developing homework assignments with clients. One way to do this is to follow up direct guidance with open questions to see how the client responds.

- "What I'd like you to try over the next week is to say hello to one new person each day when you're walking on campus. How would that be for you?"
- "How about doing some more thinking over the week about what you really want to do in the future. You could keep a journal and write in it at least five minutes a night. Would that work for you?"

Helpers also need to work with clients to identify potential facilitating and restraining forces in implementing the tasks to avoid failure to complete the assignment. For example, a man thinking about beginning an exercise program where he walks for 15 minutes each day might identify the restraining forces as the time commitment and weather and the facilitating forces as eventual weight loss and increased self-efficacy. Furthermore, if the person does not discuss social support, it is a good idea to ask specifically about this. To assess the facilitating and restraining forces, the helper can ask open questions.

■ "What things would help you in doing the homework?"
■ "What things would prevent you from doing the homework?"
■ What kind of social support do you have to help you do the homework?

An example of how this step might be implemented involves Charlene, a 30-year-old homemaker, who was depressed, overweight, and out of shape. Through the exploration and insight stages, the helper discovered that Charlene was frustrated about staying home but felt that it was her duty to take care of the children full-time. She came to the insight that she thought she should be a stay-at-home mom because she believed that was the only way her husband would love her. She recounted memories of her parents having an awful relationship and her dad resenting her mom for having a successful career. Through helping, she came to understand that she could achieve in her own career without destroying her husband. At this point, however, she realized that she had been unemployed outside the home for so long that she did not know how to cope with the world of work. The helper used operant methods in the session to devise a plan to get her back in shape physically to gain some confidence. Her homework for the first week was to take a 30-minute walk at least three times with her husband (to lose weight and have some private time with her husband) and to monitor her caloric intake.

By the end of this step, the helper should have helped the client choose some tasks, so the client can continue practicing newfound skills outside the session. Of course, clients might not need outside tasks, either because it is not appropriate for their problems or because they are not ready to take this step.

Step 9. Check on Progress and Modify Assignments

Problems can arise when clients try to implement actions outside sessions on their own. Changing is often more difficult than anticipated and may include obstacles that were not anticipated. On the basis of experiences clients have had trying out action plans in the real world, helpers can work with clients in subsequent sessions to modify homework assignments.

Helpers need to determine what did and did not work in trying to implement the tasks, without judging clients for their efforts, so modifications can be made to the tasks. If helpers can think of themselves as uninvested observers or scientists, they can help clients modify the plans to make them more effective. Helpers can use open questions to ask about progress.

▌ "How did it go last week when you tried to talk to your mother? Tell me exactly what happened."

Developing effective homework is a process of trial and error because the helper has to figure out what does and does not work for the individual client. Rather than becoming angry with clients for not implementing the homework perfectly, helpers should view modifications as a natural part of the process. Often clients are not aware of all the barriers in their environment until they try to change, so helpers might want to modify previous suggestions.

▌ "Last week we suggested that you study 30 minutes before you took a break, but that seemed like it was too long. What would you think about trying to study for 15 minutes and stopping as soon as you have a hard time concentrating?"

Clients can become discouraged with relapses. Brownell, Marlatt, Lichenstein, and Wilson (1986) noted that a slip or lapse need not lead to a relapse. Helpers can work with clients to help them adopt an attitude of forgiving themselves for lapses and learning from them. For example, when Frank drinks too much at a party after having been sober for six months, he might learn that he cannot drink, even in moderation. This learning might lead him to take steps to determine how to handle parties in the future. In contrast, if Frank beats himself up too much for the relapse, he might feel even worse about himself and will not be able to cope productively with the problem, which might lead him right back to the problematic drinking.

Throughout this step, helpers can also give clients feedback about their progress. Clients need to know how well they are performing and they need reinforcement for what they are doing well. All feedback should be given in a caring manner, be brief and to the point, focus on client behavior rather than personality characteristics, be given in moderate doses so as not to overwhelm the client, and have a balance between positive and negative feedback (Egan, 1994).

▌ "You did a really good job recording how many times you yell at your daughter and what provokes you to do it. Now you can start to try to figure out other ways to behave when you get angry."

▪ "Congratulations on being able to keep organized this week."
▪ "It seems that you had some trouble keeping up your end of the bargain about getting home before curfew several times this week."

By the end of this step, the client should have some success implementing the change process for one particular problem. The helper and client will then have to decide if helping is over or if they want to go back and tackle another problem. In either event, it is a good time for the helper and client to evaluate how they feel about what has gone on so far.

Example of Action Stage Steps

An example is presented below to illustrate the steps of the action stage. In this example, the helper has already explored with Sam his feelings about his recent diagnosis of terminal cancer. They have come to the insight that his depression over the diagnosis is due to feelings that he has not yet lived fully. They have traced his passivity back to his having controlling parents who told him how to live his life. He now recognizes that no matter what his childhood was like, he is the one responsible for the rest of his life and he cannot blame anyone else.

Readers should note that this example is meant to illustrate how the steps can work. Of course, each situation is different, and it will not always go so smoothly for each helper who tries this out. In addition, sometimes there is not enough time to go through all the steps in one session, so this process gets divided into several sessions.

Helper: So what specifically would you like to work on changing? (Step 1: identifying problem; skill: open questions)

Client: I want to change my lifestyle but I am not certain how to do that.

Helper: What do you mean by that? (Step 1: identifying problem; skill: open questions)

Client: I want to change my priorities in terms of how I spend my time.

Helper: You've been talking about how you want the remainder of your life to be different. What would it mean for you to make changes at this time? (Step 2: exploring action; skills: restatement, open questions)

Client: It would be scary because I've been resistant and angry and blaming my parents for so long, but I want to try.

Helper: You sound sure about wanting to change. (Step 2: exploring action; skill: reflection of feelings)

Client: Yeah, I am, even though I know it's going to be difficult. Maybe if I take it slowly, it will be easier. But I don't have much time left, so I want to get started.

Helper: Okay, well, let's take the issues one at a time. First, you indicated that you want to have more meaningful relationships. What have you tried in the past? (Step 3: assessing previous attempts; skills: information, restatement, open questions)

Client: Well, I'm pretty shy. It's not easy for me to make friends. I never joined groups or clubs or anything. I guess I hoped that people would come to me. My parents always pushed people on me, so I never took an active role in making friends. I don't need a lot of friends. I would be more interested in having two or three close friends—people I could really count on.

Helper: You sould like you know yourself pretty well.

Client: Yeah, I've thought a lot about myself and these issues.

Helper: So you're ready to make some changes? (Step 4: getting a commitment to change; skills: closed question)

Client: I'm a little scared and not sure what to expect, but I'm willing to give it a try.

Helper: Okay, let's brainstorm how you might go about making some new friends. What ideas do you have? (Step 5: brainstorming options; skills: process advisement, open questions)

Client: I thought about joining a cancer support group. There would be people there who are going through the same thing I am and would understand me. Also, my neighbor suggested that there's a poker game starting with a bunch of guys in the building. It's only once a month, but I like playing poker. I always wanted to do something like that, but I thought I should be working. Oh, I just remembered that a person who I used to be friends with in college moved back to town. Maybe I could get together with him.

Helper: Those sound like terrific ideas. Which ones are most appealing? (Step 6: choosing options; skills: approval–reassurance, open questions)

Client: Actually, I think I could easily do all of them. The cancer support group is once a week, and it's not far away. The poker game is only once a month. And I've been meaning to call my friend anyway. So that doesn't seem like too much at all. I definitely want to do those things. But it still leaves one empty spot. I would like to have a good relationship with a woman before I die. I wonder, you know, I've been thinking a lot about my ex-wife lately. I think that a lot of the problems in our marriage were due to my passivity and never having resolved things with my parents. Now that I have some understanding of my relationship with my parents, I think I could be different with my ex-wife. I realize now that she is not my mother. She does have some quirks, but I do still care for her.

Helper: How would you feel about checking whether she's still available and interested? (Step 6: choosing options; skill: open questions)

Client: I know that she's not with anybody because of what my daughter says. If I got back together with my ex-wife, I could also spend more time with my daughter, which is something I really want to do.

Helper: It sounds like that might work. But I need to caution you that things might not be so smooth given all the past history that you and she had. You were very passive and might still have a tendency to fall into those behaviors. I think we need to work on some assertiveness training for you to be able to stand up to her better and say what's on your mind. (Step 6: choosing options; skills: information, direct guidance)

Client: That would be helpful. Could we begin today?

Helper: Sure, give me an example of a recent situation with your ex-wife in which you were passive and you wished that you had behaved differently. (Step 7: in-session interventions; skill: open questions)

Client: She might say something like she thinks I ought to be spending more time with our daughter. She gets mad that I don't take more responsibility. She has her ideas of exactly what I should be doing and doesn't mince words. Yesterday she called and wanted to know exactly what I planned to do about the babysitting situation. I just said I didn't know, I hadn't really thought about it, and I was really busy right then. I felt irritated that she was bringing it up and was so bossy that I shut down and wouldn't give her any satisfaction.

Helper: Okay, let's role-play that so I get a clear idea of what happened. I'll be your ex-wife, and you be you. I want you first to role-play exactly what you did in the situation. (Step 7: in-session intervention; skill: process advisement)

Helper: Okay, I'm your ex-wife. Mark, I want you to take more responsibility for our daughter. I just can't handle it all. I'm supposed to be working full-time, and I can't be the one to take off for everything. I'm going to lose my job if I keep having to take off every time she gets sick or needs to go to the doctor. You know that the day care center won't let her come if she has even the slightest sniffle. Plus, she needs to see her father more. She needs to have you around. (Step 7: in-session interventions; skill: process advisement)

Client: (whines) Well, I just can't do more right now. I'm so busy at school.

Helper: Okay, let's stop there. What are you aware of feeling? (Step 7: in-session interventions; skills: process advisement, open question)

Client: I felt resentful. She's bossing me around again, and I don't like it. She's right, of course, that I ought to spend more time taking my share of the burden, but as soon as she starts up, I just don't want to do anything. I hear my mother's voice nagging me, and I shut down.

Helper: That's great, you can really identify what's going on inside you. And did you notice your tone of voice? (Step 7: in-session interventions; skills: approval–reassurance, feedback about behavior)

Client: Not really. I didn't notice anything.

Helper: You sounded totally different from before. You actually started whining. Before, in talking with me, you were talking like an adult, but as soon as you role-played talking with your ex-wife, you sounded like a whiny child (illustrates). (Step 7: in-session interventions; skill: feedback about behavior)

Client: Wow, that's incredible. That's exactly what I do with my mother. I can't believe that it came out so quickly without my awareness. And you played it exactly the way my ex-wife does—so bossy and controlling. I hate it when we get into these power struggles. Neither of us wins. But I can see how she feels that she has no choice but to get bossy and controlling when I get so passive and withdrawn.

Helper: Now what would you like to say to her instead? (Step 7: in-session interventions; skill: process advisement)

Client: I would like to say that she's right and that we need to work out a schedule because I really want to do my part. I want to spend more time with my daughter— that's really not a chore. But I wish she wouldn't treat me like a child. Perhaps if we could work on this like two equal adults, we could resolve this problem. I recognize my side of it, but she's got to see what she's doing too.

Helper: Wow! That sounds great the way you said that. It sounded firm but not nasty. You weren't whiny. You sounded more in control of the situation, and I believed that you wanted to work it out with her. I think if I were your ex-wife, I would be willing to talk with you rationally. Do you think that you could say that to her? (Step 7: in-session interventions; skills: approval–reassurance, feedback about behavior)

Client: I think I could. I would have to overcome a lot of past experiences with her. But I think I could do that. I want to because I want things to change.

Helper: Well, you were able to do it here, so I have confidence that you could be assertive with her. One thing that might help is if you took a deep breath before you say anything to her. Think about what you want to say, what you want to accomplish. Remind yourself that you are an adult and that she's not your mother. (Step 7: in-session interventions; skills: approval–reassurance, direct guidance)

Client: Yeah, I think that would work. If I told her ahead of time what I was trying to do, she would be very understanding. She often has said that we get tangled up in these situations that we can't seem to resolve. I think she knows that she gets bossy and doesn't want to but just feels really frustrated with the situation.

Helper: Let's role-play it one more time to make sure you have it down. Again, I'm your ex-wife (pause). Mark, I want you to take more responsibility for our daughter. I want you to spend more time with her and help me out more when she needs to go to the doctor. I can't keep taking off work every time she needs to be taken out of day care (pause). Now remember to take a deep breath, Mark, and think about what you want to say to her. (Step 7: in-session interventions; skills: process advisement, direct guidance)

Client: You know, you're absolutely right to be angry at me. I haven't done my share in the past, and I want to start doing my share now. But we need to step back and talk about how you and I are going to handle this situation. I want to quit acting like the bad child and forcing you to play the nagging mother to increase my involvement with our daughter. I'd like us to work on this like equal adults because I want to have a better relationship with you.

Helper: That's great. You didn't have any whine in your voice. You assertively told her what you would like to happen rather than blaming her. (Step 7: in-session interventions; skills: approval–reassurance, feedback about behavior)

Client: Thanks, it felt good. I might have to practice it a couple more times, but I liked how it felt. I think it would work with her too.

Helper: Unfortunately, we are almost out of time for today. But I wanted to check in with you about how you felt about the ideas we came up with for you to make some changes. (Step 8: homework; skills: information, open questions)

Client: I am really excited because I think this is something I can try. I feel hopeful about being able to have a better relationship with her.

Helper: So you think you'll be able to try this out with your wife? (Step 8: homework; skill: open questions)

Client: "Yes, I definitely will.

Helper: Great. Try it out and let's talk next week about how it went. We can see if we need to make any changes in the plan then after we see how it goes. (Step 9: check in; skills: approval–reassurance, direct guidance, information)

WHAT DO YOU THINK?

■ How do the action steps fit for you?

■ How do you know when to move from one action step to another? How do you know when you have spent enough time in each of the steps?

■ How should helpers decide which action possibilities to pursue in a given situation?

■ What do you think is going on when clients say "Yes, but . . . " frequently?

■ How can you tell the difference between client resistance to change and helper lack of competence in progressing through the action steps?

■ In what instances and with what clients do you think specific interventions (e.g., relaxation training, systematic desensitization) would be useful?

LAB 14

Steps of the Action Stage

Goal: To teach helpers about how to do the steps of the action stage.

Divide into groups of four to six people, with one person taking the role of the client. The other people will alternate in the role of helper. A lab leader should direct the flow of the session. Helpers are encouraged to bring in a sheet outlining the steps (perhaps Exhibit 20.1), so that they remember what to do in each step.

Helper's and Client's Tasks During the Helping Interchange

1. Clients should talk about something that they understand at least somewhat and which they want to change (e.g., increasing amount of study or exercise).
2. Helper 1 should ask the client to explore (using primarily open questions, restatements, and reflections of feelings) for about five to ten minutes.
3. Helper 2 should then take over and do the insight stage for five to ten minutes. The helper should intersperse challenges, interpretations, self-disclosures, and immediacy with open questions, restatements, and reflections of feelings (thinking carefully first about his or her intentions).
4. When the client has gained some insight, Helper 3 should take over and do Step 1 (identifying the problem) with the client.
5. Helper 4 should do Step 2 (exploring action) with the client.
6. Helper 5 should do Step 3 (assessing situation) with the client.
7. Helper 6 should do Step 4 (getting a commitment to change) with the client.
8. Helper 7 should do Step 5 (brainstorming options) with the client.
9. Helper 8 should do Step 6 (choosing an option) with the client. Remember to explore values related to the different options and to examine the restraining and facilitating forces for each action.
10. Helper 9 should do Step 7 (in-session change strategies) with the client. When helpers have trouble with this step, the lab leader can prompt them about what to do or another helper can take over.

Processing the Helping Interchange

The "client" can talk about what the experience was like and which steps were most helpful. The helpers can talk about how they felt trying to do the different steps. The lab leader can give specific behavioral feedback about the helpers' skills during the different steps.

Personal Reflections

- What are your strengths and areas that need improvement in terms of doing the action steps?
- Were you able to maintain empathy with the client while going through the steps?
- How comfortable are you with implementing the various behavioral and cognitive interventions (e.g., relaxation training, assertiveness training)?
- How could you apply the behavioral principles to improve your skills as a helper?

Integrating the Skills of the Action Stage

21

Whatever you do or dream you can do—begin it. Boldness
has genius and power and magic in it.

—Johann Wolfgang von Goethe

Tako understood that he worked too much because of cultural demands
about providing for his family and achieving. However, he did not feel
happy and felt life was too short to be working all the time. Working
with his helper, he explored his desire to change his lifestyle and they
brainstormed several ways that he could make changes.

Integrating the Action Skills

It is difficult to make changes, so clients have continued need for empathy, support, and encouragement throughout the entire action stage, even
if they decide not to change or have only accomplished one small step
toward their goals. Making changes can be difficult, and clients can be
supported by feeling that helpers are on their side. Clients appreciate knowing that their helpers are benevolent coaches or guides rather than harsh
parents or dictators.

NEED FOR FLEXIBILITY

In addition, flexibility and creativity are critical in the action stage. The
steps are presented in a clear-cut linear manner so students can learn
them easily, but in practice, they are not always implemented in such a
straightforward manner. Helpers need to learn them and then be able to
modify them to fit the needs of the client.

If one intervention does not work, helpers need to try something else. If several interventions are unsuccessful or the client continually says, "Yes, but . . ." in response to interventions, helpers should explore how clients feel about the therapeutic relationship or the process of change. Helpers also can use insight skills to help clients understand their resistance to change.

MULTICULTURAL CONSIDERATIONS

Some clients want and expect a lot of action and direction from their helpers, whom they perceive as authorities or wise people (Pedersen et al., 2002). If helpers do not focus on action, these clients might lose respect for the helper and the helping process. Such clients may get frustrated if helpers do not tell them what to do, so helpers may need to educate these clients about this model of helping.

Another consideration is that helpers may need to incorporate spirituality into the action stage (e.g., using prayer as an action strategy) for clients for whom spirituality and religion are important issues (Fukuyama & Sevig, 2002). If helpers are not responsive to such needs, clients may feel disrespected and may devalue the helping process.

Finally, helpers need to be aware of barriers to action facing clients from other cultures. For example, impoverished clients may not have transportation, child care, or access to public services. Refugee clients may face discrimination and language problems. Older clients may not be able to leave their houses. Asian clients may not want to go outside the family for help or may not know how to change in a way that respects and incorporates the family's needs. Helpers need to be aware of such cultural considerations, ask clients about possible barriers, and be sensitive to different needs.

Difficulties Helpers Experience in the Action Stage

MOVING TOO QUICKLY TO ACTION

Some helpers rush to action before they have established a firm enough foundation of exploration and insight. They might feel impatient with the long process of exploration and insight; they might feel that they "know" what the client should do; they might feel compelled to "do" something for the client. Unfortunately, when helpers move too quickly to action, clients often are "resistant," not attuned with the helper, unable to take responsibility for their changes, or unmotivated to make changes. Helpers need to remember to spend the majority of their time in exploration to establish the foundation for insight and action.

If information or advice is provided before clients are ready for it, clients might not be able to use it. For example, some volunteers in battered women's shelters immediately provide information to women when they come in about how to make it on their own. At this point, clients more often need to explore their feelings about being in an abusive relationship. They are not ready yet to use information, no matter how helpful or well intentioned it is.

Some helpers move to action before they know enough about the client's situation. They might jump quickly to a solution before exploring the complexity of the situation—and most problems are quite complex when the client's feelings and values are examined. Furthermore, it can appear disparaging to clients for helpers to jump to quick solutions and imply that they were inept for not knowing how to solve such simple problems. If problems were so simple, clients would have solved them on their own.

NEEDING TO BE THE EXPERT

Providing information and giving advice gratify some helpers' needs to be viewed as the expert. Some helpers like being perceived as "knowing it all" and enjoy having clients admire them. I caution these helpers that they might be looking like the expert at the expense of encouraging clients to seek out their own information and make their own decisions. Other helpers might embrace the role of expert because they want to assist clients and they believe that helpers should provide all the answers and give lots of helpful information to clients. Both types of helpers do a disservice in neglecting the client's role in the information-generating process. I agree that helpers might know more about helping than their clients, but they do not know more than clients about clients' inner experiences or what actions clients should implement.

TOO MUCH INVESTMENT IN CLIENT'S CHANGES

Some helpers become so invested and feel so responsible for developing action plans that they try to make decisions for the client. They feel that things would be much easier if clients just did what helpers told them to do. However, taking over for clients is typically counterproductive (except in extreme cases of suicidal or homicidal ideation or intent) because clients become dependent and do not develop the skills needed to make changes in the future. In addition, what might work for the helper might not work for the client. Furthermore, if helpers become too invested in what they think clients should do, it is difficult for them to listen supportively and objectively to clients. Hence, helpers generally need to be uninvested in what action the client chooses (or does not choose) to pursue. Helpers must allow clients to make their own decisions, and should serve as guides and supporters rather as than bosses.

IMPOSING ONE'S VALUES ON CLIENTS

Sometimes helpers lose sight of trying to help clients uncover their values and instead impose their own beliefs and values on clients. It can be difficult for helpers to accept that clients have different values, especially when the values differ significantly from the helper's cherished beliefs. For example, a client dying of a terminal illness might want to talk about the possibility of suicide. If helpers are rigid about the value of life, they might not allow clients to explore the possibility of suicide, thus limiting the client's ability to contemplate all the options thoroughly and make an informed decision. In another example, a helper might tell a client to smile more because he wants all women to appear happy. Helpers always need to be attentive to their own issues and needs and try to minimize their effect on clients.

NOT ENCOURAGING CLIENTS ENOUGH TO MAKE CHANGES

Helpers may not challenge clients enough to make changes. Some helpers are worried about intruding on their clients and, thus, do not encourage them to change. They believe it is not their place to challenge. I agree that clients need to be the ones who choose to change, but helpers can encourage and challenge clients when they are stuck and struggling. In addition, helpers are sometimes nervous about challenging clients because they are not sure what to do to help clients. In this case, I suggest that these helpers study the action skills carefully and practice more.

NOT BEING SUPPORTIVE

Sometimes helpers become so involved in developing the action plan during this stage that they forget to be supportive. Encouragement and reinforcement are crucial both for actual change and for efforts to change. I suspect that when helpers remember aspects of their lives that are difficult to change, they are more sympathetic to clients who have difficulty changing.

GETTING STUCK ON ONE ACTION IDEA

Helpers often remain committed to action ideas that they have developed, even when it is clear that they are inappropriate and clients cannot or will not follow them. Perhaps these helpers have spent a lot of time thinking about what their clients should do and have become very invested in the action plans. However, helpers need to realize that helping requires flexibility, and that action ideas often require adjustment because helpers and clients are not aware of all the problems that can arise. They need to select and keep the parts that work and revise the parts that do not.

FEELING A NEED TO RIGIDLY ADHERE TO THE STEPS

Helpers who follow these action steps precisely will probably feel frustrated because the exact sequence of steps will not apply to working with every client. I want to emphasize that these steps are provided so that students can see a structure of how to proceed through the action stage. But because every client and every problem are slightly different, helpers will rarely proceed through the steps in such a clear-cut manner. I suggest that helpers learn and practice the steps as presented but then use their creativity and flexibility to modify the procedures for themselves and the individual client. This stage allows for incredible flexibility as helpers try to creatively work with individual clients to help them.

Strategies for Overcoming the Difficulties

SELF-REFLECTION

When helpers get trapped in any of the pitfalls (moving too quickly to action, becoming too invested in clients' changing, imposing their values on clients, not being challenging enough, not being supportive enough, or getting stuck on one plan), they might spend some time reflecting and hypothesizing about what caused them to lose objectivity in this situation. If helpers discover that they get overly invested and too directive across several clients, they really need to look inward to understand themselves so they do not harm clients. Consulting with peers, seeking personal therapy, and receiving supervision are all helpful methods for learning more about oneself. In addition, helpers can go back and use the management strategies suggested in chapter 5 for dealing with anxiety (e.g., relaxation, imagery, positive self-talk, focus on the client).

RETURN TO THE EXPLORATION SKILLS

After an impasse or problem has arisen in the helping process, it is often helpful to return to using the exploration skills (open questions, restatement, and reflection). The helper needs to try to understand what is going on with the client at this particular time. When clients feel misunderstood, helpers also need to rebuild trust and reassure clients that helpers can listen to and collaborate with them.

DEAL WITH PROBLEMS IN THE THERAPEUTIC RELATIONSHIP

Helpers can ask clients how they are feeling about what is going on in the helping relationship, particularly when they have reached an *impasse* (defined by Elkind, 1992, as a deadlock or stalemate that causes helping to become so difficult that progress is not possible). Using immediacy to deal with the relationship and resolve problems is particularly crucial (see Hill et al., 1996, 2003; Rhodes et al., 1994; Safran et al., 2002). Helpers need to listen for feedback and be willing to hear how they can improve their work with their clients. If appropriate for the helping situation, helpers can talk about their own immediate feelings (without burdening clients with their personal problems). Acknowledging their part in the problems in helping relationships (e.g., apologizing if they have made a mistake) can be therapeutically beneficial. Helpers also can thank clients for sharing their feelings and working hard to make positive changes in their lives.

Example of an Extended Interaction

An example is presented to illustrate working through all three stages. For ease of presentation, this example presents all three stages in a single session, although working through all three stages for a given problem often requires more than a single session.

The example involves a session with a young woman, Maria, who sought assistance because she could not decide on a major. Career concerns are common issues that many people struggle with throughout the life cycle (Brown & Brooks, 1991; Zunker, 1994). However, career difficulties are not as simplistic as psychologists once thought. It is not simply a matter of deciding on one's talents, interests, and skills. Our career identities are intertwined with our personal lives (Blustein, 1987; Brown, 1985; Hackett, 1993; Herr, 1989; Richardson, 1993; Savickas, 1994; Spokane, 1989), and hence both must be addressed in the helping process.

EXPLORATION STAGE

Helper: Tell me a little about yourself and why you came for helping today. (The helper uses an open-ended question to start the interaction and to allow Maria to communicate her most pressing concerns.)

Client: I'm a junior at the university. I should have declared a major already, but I just cannot decide what I want to do. I feel stuck, and they're trying to force me to declare something in the next couple of weeks. I don't want to just put something down and then have to shift after a semester or two. But I just don't have anything that I'm particularly good at. You know, in high school when everyone else was in plays or orchestra or dancing or sports, I wasn't really doing anything. I just don't have any major talents. I seem to be mediocre in everything.

Helper: You sound anxious about having to declare a major so quickly. (The helper wants to focus Maria on her feelings about the urgency of the situation.)

Client: I am really anxious. You wouldn't believe how anxious I am. I haven't been able to sleep at night. I just keep trying to figure out what I want to do with my life. I guess I have never had any major ambitions.

Helper: I wonder if you have feelings about trying to figure out who you are? (The helper wants to determine how much of Maria's life is influenced by this issue.)

Client: I have been feeling out of sorts. But I guess it's really hard to tell how much of it is because of trying to choose a major and not knowing who I am or where I'm going, and how much of it is due to feeling badly that I have never had a boyfriend and also feeling under stress that my parents are going through a divorce.

Helper: Wow! Sounds like you have a lot of difficult things going on right now. (The helper wants to support Maria.)

Client: Yeah, it's been a rough semester. I just found out my parents were going to get a divorce over the holidays. They said that they stayed together until my younger sister went to college. I'm not sure that their staying together was actually so good for us because they were always fighting. Each of my parents has always talked to me about how horrible the other one was. I feel like I've always been the mediator, trying to help each of them understand the other.

Helper: How was it for you being the one in the middle? (The helper wants to allow Maria to explore her feelings more deeply.)

Client: Part of me liked it because they both needed me. But it was also pretty bad because I felt like they both depended on me too much and I couldn't live my own life. I was glad to get away to college, but then I felt guilty about leaving. I go home a lot. I also feel like I have to take care of my little sister and shield her from the pain. I don't want her to end up feeling as badly about herself as I do about myself.

Helper: It sounds like you feel pretty overwhelmed right now. (The helper wants to help Maria become aware of her feelings.)

Client: I do. I feel about 20 years older than the other kids here. They are always talking about parties and drinking. It all seems so trivial.

Helper: You mentioned that you have to choose a major soon. You also said that there's nothing you're particularly good in. Tell me more about that. (The helper wants to guide Maria back to exploring her problem in choosing a major.)

Client: Well, I think I'm an average student. I get Bs in most of my courses. I probably don't put as much time in as I could, but I just can't get into studying.

Helper: Tell me something about the courses that you have enjoyed. (The helper wants to help Maria explore specific interests.)

Client: Well, I'm rotten at math and science. I almost flunked biology last semester. I guess the classes I have enjoyed most are my psychology courses. I like trying to figure people out. You know, I'm always the person whom people talk to about their problems. I'm taking this class in helping skills and am excited about it. I think I'm pretty good at helping. At least I enjoy being a helper.

INSIGHT STAGE

Helper: What do you think got you so excited about learning helping skills? (The helper wants to assist Maria in thinking about her motives.)

Client: Everyone has always come to me with their problems, and I feel like I'm good at listening. And I was able to help my sister when she got so upset.

Helper: I wonder if operating as a helper in your family helped you become interested in the helping field? (The helper tries an interpretation to see whether Maria can engage in the interpretive process.)

Client: You know, you may be right. Maybe helping my sister and mediating my parents' arguments helped me develop effective helping skills. It's funny that I've never really thought about majoring in psychology before. I guess my parents have always looked down on psychology. They would never go to a therapist because they have always said people should solve their own problems. Well, they didn't do too good a job on their own. But I don't know, what do you think I should do? Why did you choose psychology?

Helper: I really liked to help other people with their problems. I also found that all my friends turned to me to talk about their problems. (The helper uses self-disclosure to reassure Maria that her feelings are normal.)

Client: That's interesting. Do you like the field?

Helper: Yes, I like it a lot. Tell me more about your thoughts about psychology. (The helper wants to turn the focus back to Maria.)

Client: Well, I think I might like to do it, but I don't know if I'm smart enough for it. I've heard an awful lot about how you have to be really smart to get into graduate school in psychology. I might not be able to make it.

Helper: You know, you say you're not really smart, but I haven't heard much evidence for that. (The helper challenges Maria about her lack of self-efficacy.)

Client: Well, I haven't gotten very good grades in college. I did get pretty good grades in high school though, and

Helper: my SAT scores were pretty high. In fact, I was close to the top of my class.

Helper: So something has happened during college to make you lose your confidence and not do as well in your classes. What might have contributed to your inability to study? (The helper wants to facilitate Maria to think about insight and so restates and then asks an open question.)

Client: Well, I'm not sure. Perhaps it has to do with my family, but I'm not sure how.

Helper: Perhaps your concern about your parents and leaving home has distracted you from your ability to study. (The helper works with Maria to stimulate insight. Maria had a glimmer that her difficulties were related to her family, so the helper gives an interpretation that goes just beyond what Maria has stated.)

Client: Hmm, I had never thought about that, but you're probably right. I've been so concerned about everyone else that I haven't had time to take care of myself. It's not really fair that my parents messed up my life just because they cannot get their act together.

Helper: Yeah, you seem angry at them. (Maria has responded well to the interpretation, so the helper wants to help her explore her feelings about her discoveries.)

Client: I am. I have been so worried about leaving my sister at home and not being able to calm my parents during their horrible arguments. These are supposed to be the best years of my life. And all I'm concerned about is them. When do I get my chance?

Helper: I wonder if your parents really need you as much as you think they do? (The helper challenges Maria about her assumed need to be in the middle.)

Client: Maybe they don't. In fact, maybe if I quit interfering, they would be able to make a decision about what they need to do. And you know my sister is not a kid anymore. She's 18 years old. I mean, I love them, but maybe I've just been doing too much, going home all the time.

ACTION STAGE

Helper: So what would you like to do differently? (The helper wants to move Maria into thinking about how to make changes in her life.)

Client: Well, I think I'm going to tell my parents that I am going to stop listening to each of their problems. I am going to suggest that they go to a therapist. It's been so helpful talking to you. That's what I think they need to do. If they don't do it, that's their problem, but I've got to get out from the middle.

Helper: What feelings might come up for you in telling your parents your decision not to be in the middle? (The helper wants to have Maria explore her feelings about this change.)

Client: I'm pretty fed up right now, so I think I could do it. The difficult part will come when my mom calls late at night crying and says I'm the only one who really understands her. You wouldn't believe how many times she's done that right before a major exam.

Helper: What could you do when that happens? (The helper wants to guide Maria into problem solving what to do in the specific situation.)

Client: Well, I could go to the library to study when I really need to focus on my work. Then my mom couldn't reach me. I really study better at the library anyway because the residence hall is so noisy.

Helper: That's a great idea. (The helper reinforces Maria's feelings.)

Client: Yeah, I don't know why I didn't think of that sooner. I guess I was just stuck in thinking I was the only one who could help my mom. You know, maybe I even kept her from going to a therapist because she could always talk to me. In fact, maybe I wanted her to talk to me because it made me feel so important and helpful.

Helper: Yeah, that might be hard to give up. You feel pretty special when you believe that you're the one who can make everyone feel better. (The helper wants to warn Maria that it might be hard to change.)

Client: Yeah, it could be hard. But I think it's time to start living my own life instead of living in their world.

Helper: What could you do to make the transition easier? (Again, the helper wants to prepare Maria for the difficulties involved in changing.)

Client: Well, I would like to continue to talk with you. Would that be possible? I think if I had your support, it would be easier to change.

Helper: Sure, we could arrange for eight sessions. That's the limit of the number of sessions I can offer to you through the counseling center. (The helper wants to let Maria know the limits of her availability.)

Client: That would be great. Thanks.

Helper: Now back to the major. What are your thoughts about what you would like to do about that at this point? (The helper wants to bring some closure to the topic about the major since that was Maria's presenting concern.)

Client: I'm leaning toward psychology. I get excited about some of the psychology courses I've had, particularly the ones that involve personality and helping people. But I'm also interested in English. I've always liked to write. I've kept a journal for years. I have a fantasy of some day writing a novel or working on a newspaper.

Helper: Perhaps you can do some more thinking about your likes and dislikes before the next session. It would also be a good idea to gather some information about majors and careers. There's some excellent information in the career center on campus. Perhaps you could go there before our next session. I'd also like you to take some vocational interest tests so we can determine more about your interests. What do you think? (The helper wants to give Maria specific guidance about how to proceed with this issue, but does not want to be seen as being too pushy.)

Client: Terrific. Sounds like a great idea. Where do I take the tests?

Helper: I'll take you down and show you where to sign up after the session. How are you feeling about what we've done today? (The helper wants to give Maria specific information about how to find the tests and also wants to assess how Maria felt about the session.)

Client: I feel better than I've felt for so long. I actually have energy. I can't wait to take the tests. I can't wait to talk to my parents. I think they are going to understand that I need to do this for myself. They've been worried about me. It's not like me to be as upset as I've been. I can see some light at the end of the tunnel. It's very exciting.

Helper: Good for you. So let's plan on meeting next week at the same time?

WHAT DO YOU THINK?

- Which of the following obstacles do you anticipate that you are most likely to experience in using the action skills?

  ____ moving too quickly to action

  ____ needing to be the expert

  ____ being too invested in clients' changes

  ____ imposing one's values on clients

  ____ not encouraging enough change

  ____ not being supportive

  ____ getting stuck on one action idea

- Which strategies would work to help you cope with the obstacles in the action stage?

  ____ self-reflection

  ____ address issues related to the therapeutic relationship

  ____ consultation with supervisors, peers, or teachers

  ____ return to exploration skills

Integration of Exploration, Insight, and Action Skills

You are ready to integrate the skills that you have learned so far. In this lab, you meet with a client and first use exploration skills to help the client explore. Next, you use exploration and insight skills to facilitate the client gaining insight. Then you use exploration and action skills to assist the client in deciding what type of action to take.

Goal: For helpers to participate in a 50-minute helping session using all of the helping skills.

Helper's and Client's Tasks During the Helping Interchange

1. Each helper should be paired with a volunteer client whom they do not know.
2. Helpers should bring the following forms with them to the session: the Session Review Form (Web Form A), Helper Intentions List (Web Form D), Client Reactions System (Web Form G), Session Process and Outcome Measures (Web Form I), and Self-Awareness and Management Strategies Scales (Web Form J). Supervisors bring the Supervisor Rating Form (Web Form B).
3. Helpers should bring an audio- or videotape recorder (tested ahead of time to ensure that it works) and a tape. They should turn the recorder on at the beginning of the session.
4. Helpers should introduce themselves and remind clients that everything they say will be kept confidential. Helpers should indicate exactly who will be listening to the session (e.g., peer, supervisor).
5. Each helper should conduct a 50-minute session (about 20 minutes of exploration, 15 minutes of insight, 15 minutes of action) with the client. Be as helpful to your client as possible. Watch for the client's reactions to each of your interventions and modify subsequent interventions when appropriate.
6. Watch your time carefully. About two minues before the end of the session, let the client know you need to stop soon (e.g., "We need to stop soon. Did you have any reactions to the session?")

Supervisor's Tasks During Session

Supervisors should use the Supervisor Rating Form to record their observations and evaluations.

Postsession

1. Both helper and client complete the Session Process and Outcome Measures; helper also completes the Self-Awareness and Management Strategies Scales.
2. After the session, each helper should review the tape with his or her client (review of a 50-minute session takes about 90–120 minutes); alternatively, helpers might just review ten minutes of each stage. Helpers should stop the tape after each helper intervention (except minimal acknowledgments such as "um-hmm," and "yeah"). Helpers

should write down the key words on the Session Review Form (to enable locating the exact spot on the tape later).

3. Helpers should rate the helpfulness of each intervention and write down the numbers of up to three intentions for that intervention (responding according to how they felt during the session rather than when listening to the tape of the session). Use the whole range of the Helpfulness Scale and as many intentions as possible. Do not complete these ratings collaboratively with clients.

4. Clients should rate the helpfulness of each intervention and write down the numbers of up to three reactions, circling any reactions that they hid from helpers during the session. Clients should respond according to how they felt during session rather than how they feel listening to the tape of the session. Clients should use the whole range of the Helpfulness Scale and as many categories as possible on the reactions system. Clients should not collaborate with helpers in doing the ratings.

5. Helpers and clients write down the most and least helpful event.

6. Supervisors give feedback to helpers based on the Supervisor Rating Form.

7. Helpers should type a transcript of their session. Skip minimal utterances such as "okay," "you know," "er," and "uh."
   a. Divide the helper speech into response units
   b. Using the Helping Skills System determine which skill was used for each response unit in your transcript.
   c. Indicate what you would say if you could do each intervention again.
   d. Erase the tape. Make sure the transcript has no identifying information.

Personal Reflections

■ What did you learn about yourself in this session as compared with the other sessions you did during the course?
■ What problems did you have getting the client to think about action?
■ Were you able to move smoothly from exploration to insight to action?
■ Which action skills did you and the client find most helpful?
■ How did you feel about giving information and direct guidance?

V

Final Thoughts

Integrating the Three Stages 22

Ideal teachers are those who use themselves as bridges over
which they invite their students to cross, then having
facilitated their crossing, joyfully collapse, encouraging them
to create bridges of their own.

—Leo Buscaglia

Josh was an honors student in psychology and had volunteered at a
hotline before taking a therapy skills course. He thought he knew how
to be a helper when he started, but he quickly became discouraged
after the first few labs when he had difficulty doing and integrating the
skills. He considered giving up on his dream of being a therapist
because the helping skills were more complicated and challenging to
implement than he had ever imagined. After his first session with a
client, however, Josh received positive feedback from his peers and lab
leaders and began to feel that he was understanding what being a
helper is all about. By the end of the course, Josh felt confident that if
he continued to practice, he could become a good therapist.

Congratulations! You have learned the skills of each of the three stages,
although of course you still need to keep practicing to maintain and enhance these skills. The next step is to integrate the therapy skills for use in
therapy sessions with actual clients.

In this chapter, I cover several issues related to using the skills across
the therapy process and dealing with difficult clinical situations. This chapter is *not* meant as a complete guide on how to do therapy, nor is it meant
to suggest that beginning students are ready to do therapy with real clients (indeed they are not ready without further training and supervision). However, the chapter is intended as a primer for how therapy might
work using the three-stage model for those students who are continuing

---

Web Forms referred to in text can be found on the book's companion online guide described in the Preface.

in a training program with close supervision. It is also intended for students who do not plan to continue to give them some idea of how the skills are integrated in an actual therapy setting. This chapter is meant to be more explicitly related to therapy, so I use the terms *therapy* and *therapist* rather than *helping sessions* and *helper*, which were used in earlier portions of the book.

Using the Skills in Therapy

THE FIRST SESSION

A lot takes place in the first session of therapy. The therapist has to impart information about the therapy process, begin to establish a relationship with the client, assess whether he or she can help the client, and begin to establish goals for the work.

Beginning the Session

Therapists need to do several things at the beginning of the first session: introduce themselves, explain the structure of the therapy process, discuss limits to confidentiality, and then ask the client what he or she wishes to talk about in the session. For further discussion of these tasks, refer to chapter 11.

Developing Appropriate Boundaries

Therapists need to manage the boundaries of therapy (the ground rules and limits of the therapeutic relationship). Boundaries can be about the structure of therapy (e.g., length, fees, policies about touching and violence, confidentiality) or about the interpersonal nature of the interaction (no sexual intimacies, friendships or other types of relationships with clients outside of therapy). Research about the practices of experienced therapists (Borys & Pope, 1989; Conte, Plutchik, Picard, & Karasu, 1989; Epstein, Simon, & Kay, 1992; Holroyd & Brodsky, 1977) and the ethical considerations discussed in chapter 4 provide some ideas about the most important boundaries.

Initially, therapists need to clarify the rules about confidentiality, the length of the therapy, and any fees involved. Therapists typically choose to avoid involvement in social activities with clients outside of sessions, because such activities may make it difficult for therapists to be objective and for clients to feel comfortable disclosing in the therapy setting. I encourage beginning therapists to provide the phone number at a work setting so clients can reach them for emergencies, but I suggest they not give a home phone number unless clients are actively suicidal. The reason to not give out home phone numbers is that some clients take advantage of beginning therapists, who have difficulty setting limits about not talking on the phone at any hour for any reason. I vividly recall my very first client in a practicum in graduate school. She called for several nights at midnight because I had not clarified that calling was not appropriate. When I finally let the client know after several nights that she could not keep calling every night, she felt hurt, and the therapeutic relationship was damaged. It would have been better if I had discussed this limit with her initially, so the rules and the appropriate behaviors for the therapy relationship were clear.

Developing appropriate boundaries is often quite difficult. Beginning therapists should start out being overly cautious and then relax their boundaries as they gain experience. Consultation with supervisors can be helpful when therapists are in doubt about which boundaries are appropriate and how to set them. Furthermore, exploring one's own countertransference issues is important when thinking about establishing boundaries in general; it is even more important for therapists to examine their own issues when they want to violate or adjust boundaries with a particular client.

Establishing Goals and Clarifiying Expectations

An important task of the first session is to determine why the client sought out a therapy experience at this particular time and what the client's goals are for counseling. It is helpful to know what motivated the client to seek help at the particular time because this tells about what is going on with the client. Many people have experienced distress for a long period, but something tips them over the edge to seek help.

In addition, it is important to learn about what the client expects and wants from the therapy experience. If expectations are unrealistic, the therapist can clarify what therapy can realistically provide. If the number of sessions is limited, therapists and clients need to have realistic expectations for what can be accomplished. If there are only a few sessions, therapists can help clients explore problems and perhaps work on symptom relief or specific behavioral changes, such as study skills. With more sessions, therapists can help clients with more deeply rooted personality problems (e.g., working through childhood sexual abuse, engrained interpersonal deficits, or personality change). The therapist and the client must agree that the goals are reasonable and possible to attain in the therapy process.

Throughout this process of establishing goals, the therapist may come to the realization that the client is not ready for therapy or that he or she is not the best therapist for this client (e.g., the client needs medication and the therapist cannot prescribe; the clients wants cognitive–behavioral therapy and the therapist does not specialize in that; the therapist has strong negative countertransference reactions). The most ethical thing to do if the client is not ready for therapy is to talk with the client about what therapy is all about and suggest that the client wait until he or she is ready. In the situation where the therapist is not the best provider for the client, the therapist can refer the client to a more qualified service provider.

Developing a Focus

A crucial task of the first (and every) session is developing a focus for that particular session. It is best for therapists to focus on one problem at a time; otherwise, there is a danger of becoming so diffuse that nothing gets accomplished. A clear focus typically involves a specific incident or behavior such as a fight with a roommate, procrastination over completing assignments, or concern over how to communicate with a partner. The focus should be neither too vague nor too diffuse. To develop a focus, therapists typically ask clients what is troubling them now. It may take a few minutes to determine what the most pressing issue is, because clients often start with one concern whereas another issue is actually more critical. For example, Michael initially said that he was concerned about his grandmother's imminent death. After talking for a few minutes, it emerged that Michael was far more concerned about the end of a relationship with a woman whom he had been dating for four years. The therapist focused on his feelings about the breakup for the rest of the session. If it is not possible to get the client to focus, the lack of focus in itself becomes the important issue for the session that the therapist needs to talk about with the client.

Therapists must respect client decisions about the focus of the sessions. For example, Judy wanted to work on existential issues such as the meaning of life, whereas the therapist was much more concerned with the high likelihood that she was about to flunk out of school and lose her job. Although the therapist needs to keep the holistic picture of the client in mind (and perhaps later challenge the client about the discrepancies), it is important that the therapist not impose his or her wishes on the client.

Applying the Three Stages in the First Session

The exploration stage may well take the whole first session, particularly because the therapist spends a lot of time helping the client explore the depth of the presenting problem from the client's perspective. The therapist's goal is to understand the client's experience of this concern. Although the focus stays on the problem, therapists also facilitate client exploration of how the concern is affected by, and influences, other parts of the person's past, current, and future life.

If there is time after the client has explored, the therapist might begin tentatively using the insight stage to see how the client responds. The therapist might try to help the client develop insight into how the problem developed and what contributes to the maintenance of the problem.

There might be times when the therapist goes on to the action stage in the first session, particularly if the client comes in with a well-defined problem and wants immediate relief, or if the client is in crisis. In such situations, it is often useful for the therapist to assign homework to help clients cope during the interval before the next session.

Possible Referral for Psychological or Educational Assessment

Therapists might want to ask the client to take some psychological tests before the second session to aid in conceptualizing the client and planning treatment. Psychologists have a number of tests they have been trained to administer that can be helpful for assessing intelligence, educational disabilities, personality, and vocational interests.

Assessment can also be useful for clients who need additional information about their interests or abilities before they can proceed with change efforts. For example, a client who has come in because he has not been able to choose a major might profit from taking the Strong Interest Inventory to figure out his preferences. Other examples might include an elderly client who wants her husband tested to determine if he is getting Alzheimer's disease, or parents who want their children tested to determine if they have attention-deficit disorder. In addition, a person might benefit from understanding more about his or her personality and how personality helps or hinders him or her in interactions with others. Although I will not address further how assessment can be used therapeutically, I refer readers to the excellent work of Finn and Tonsager (2002).

Ending Sessions

Therapists need to be aware of the time in sessions. Five to ten minutes before the end of the session, therapists might advise clients that the session is almost over. Mentioning the approaching end of the session gives clients time to prepare themselves for leaving the session and to reflect on what they have accomplished in the session. Some clients wait until a couple of minutes before the end of session to bring up important feelings. They could be anxious about the therapist's reaction, ambivalent about discussing the topic, or trying to manipulate the therapist into extending the session. Therapists should try to understand why their clients wait to bring up important topics.

As a way to start to close the session, therapists might ask clients how they felt about the session and the work that was done. This processing of sessions is important so that therapists can become aware of how clients reacted to various interventions. As discussed in chapter 3, clients often do not reveal their feelings about the therapist and the therapy process unless asked explicitly. For therapists to be able to plan the next sessions, they need to know what worked and what was not effective. Therapists should not, however, ask only for clients' reactions to elicit platitudes about their skills. In fact, they should be suspicious if clients repeatedly talk about how wonderful therapists were. Instead, they should be genuinely interested in hearing both positive and negative reactions.

Therapists might also want to reinforce clients for what they have accomplished in sessions and encourage them to think about carrying these changes over to their lives outside sessions. Finally, it can be helpful to ask clients to summarize what they learned in the session to reinforce what was covered.

In closing, therapists sometimes shake hands or engage in a small amount of social pleasantries (e.g., "Have a good week," "Enjoy the holiday"). These rituals can serve as a transition for clients in returning to their everyday life.

BETWEEN SESSIONS

Therapists need to think about their clients between sessions to try to conceptualize their problems. Specifically, they need to think about origins of clients' problems, the underlying themes in the problems, and appropriate interventions to help clients.

One way to facilitate this conceptualization process is for therapists to listen to the audiotapes or, even better, to watch the videotapes of their sessions. Observing sessions enables therapists to re-create what they were thinking and feeling and to observe clients' reactions to their interventions. It also can provide a powerful self-confrontation about one's use of attending and helping skills.

Therapists can then make extensive process notes after each session to facilitate their recall of the salient issues that were covered during the session. In the process notes (see Web Form F), which are best done as soon as possible after sessions and observing the session, therapists can use their experience and perceptions to write about the following areas (Mary Ann Hoffman, personal communication, January 9, 1998): (a) manifest content (what the client talked about); (b) underlying content (unspoken meanings in what the client said); (c) defenses and barriers to change (how the client avoids anxiety); (d) client distortions (ways in which the client responds to you as she or he has to other significant persons in her or his life, i.e., transference); (e) countertransference (ways in which your emotional, attitudinal, and behavioral responses may have been stimulated by the process); and (f) personal assessment (your evaluation of your interventions; what would you do differently and why). Therapists should look for underlying themes and recurring patterns across all the problems that clients raise. For example, is the client always the passive victim in every encounter, does the client idealize everyone, or is the client always angry? These themes provide important clues for the underlying personality problems that need attention in therapy.

Ideally, beginning therapists should meet with supervisors after each session for assistance in conceptualizing clients. Supervisors can aid therapists in thinking about various hypotheses about what caused and maintained problems as well as possible interventions to help clients. They can also provide a different perspective to aid therapists when they become stuck in their perceptions and countertransferences.

Therapists also need to educate themselves about theories and research to obtain a framework with which to understand client dynamics (i.e., what causes and maintains problems). Therapists need to select a theoretical framework and read current research so they can think carefully about their interventions with clients. Furthermore, if clients are from a different culture or have a problem with which the therapist is not familiar, the therapist should read about the issue and consult with supervisors between sessions to ensure that she or he can give the best available services to the client.

SUBSEQUENT SESSIONS

Beginning the Session

At the beginning of subsequent sessions, therapists might sit quietly and wait for clients to talk about what is on their minds (if they have educated clients to expect this); they might summarize what took place in the former session; they might start by asking how the client felt about the previous session; or they might simply ask what the client would like to talk about during the session. All are appropriate, but which one should therapists use? It depends on the client and the therapist. The therapist might personally like more or less structure or assess that the client needs more or less structure.

Establishing a Focus

As with the first session, therapists need to establish a focus for the discussion in each session. Therapists cannot assume that clients will continue talking about what they discussed the previous session or that clients have the same feelings that they had during the previous session. Many beginning therapists spend a great deal of time debriefing after sessions and approach subsequent sessions with an agenda about what to do to help clients with problems raised in the previous session. Therapists are often surprised, however, when clients are not concerned with or interested in talking about the same issues. When clients leave the therapy setting, many things happen that change the way that clients feel. They may have spent time thinking about the issues and resolved them, or other issues might have become more salient in the interim that clients are concerned about and want to discuss. Thus, therapists have to be prepared to respond to clients in the moment. Being prepared, yet flexible, is one of the biggest challenges for beginning therapists.

Using the Skills of the Three Stages

Toward the beginning of therapy, therapists spend more time in exploration, whereas they spend more time in insight and action as therapy progresses. Furthermore, with each new problem, therapists first start with exploration and then move gradually to insight and action. For example, the client might first focus on academic concerns, which requires the therapist to go through all three stages. Then the client might decide to work on interpersonal concerns, at which point the therapist has to go through all three stages for this new problem. Of course, the therapist remembers and uses the material from the exploration of the first problem and looks for patterns and themes in the client's responding, particularly in the insight stage. Once again, I remind readers that the stages are not implemented as simplistically and rigidly as this structure implies, but the three-stage model is a useful structure that therapists can use to think about where they are in the therapy process.

TERMINATION

Because therapy sessions do not continue forever (even in long-term psychoanalytic therapy), separation is inevitable. After therapists and clients have accomplished as much as they can within the confines of their contracted relationship, the time comes to terminate the therapy relationship. The therapist and client might have gone through several cycles of exploration–insight–action, dealing with several different problems, with the client gradually taking more responsibility until he or she feels ready to manage his or her life independently. One goal of therapy is to prepare clients to leave therapy and become self-reliant. Just as parents raise children to grow up, leave home, and function on their own, therapists teach and encourage clients to cope on their own.

When to Terminate

How can therapists determine when to terminate the therapy relationship? Sometimes the end is imposed by external time limits (e.g., beginning therapists often are only allowed to provide one to three sessions with volunteer clients; some counseling centers on university campuses allow only six to twelve sessions). In such cases, therapists may have to be ready to refer clients (to be covered shortly) if they still need help.

In contrast, in open-ended, long-term therapy, therapists and clients decide when they are ready to terminate the relationship. Rarely is there such a thing as a "cure," because cure implies a static state rather than the continual changes and challenges involved in living. Most often, clients decide they are tired, have reached a plateau and are ready for a break, or have accomplished as much as they can with a particular therapist. Often clients signal to therapists that they are ready to terminate; at other times, therapists have to tell clients that they think they are ready to terminate. According to the ethical standards for psychologists (American Psychological Association, 2002), therapists should terminate with clients when they feel they are no longer working productively. Sometimes therapy goes on interminably because neither therapist nor client knows when and how to end it. Therapists need to be very mindful of continuing therapy sessions only when clients are benefiting and making changes.

Budman and Gurman (1988) proposed that therapists adopt a model like that of family doctors. Just as one would never expect that antibiotics would inoculate patients for the rest of their lives against the flu, they argued that we should not assume that one therapy experience could cure a client for life. They suggested that it makes more sense to see clients on an intermittent basis, such that therapists see clients for a few sessions until the current issues or crises are resolved and then see them again when other crises or life transitions arise. With such a model, termination is not typically as difficult because clients know that they can return to their therapists when they need further help (if that therapist is still available).

How to Terminate

Mann (1973) considered termination of therapy to be an important task because loss is an existential fact of life; everyone must cope with loss. He recommended that therapists spend considerable time in planning and preparing for termination in both short- and long-term therapy. He suggested that therapists discuss termination in every session to remind clients where they are in the process (e.g., "This is our eighth session; we have four more sessions. How do you feel about being almost through with therapy?").

Clients sometimes think that therapists are exaggerating the concerns about termination because they cannot anticipate how they will feel when they leave the therapy relationship. Once they have terminated, they have an understanding of the feelings involved, but then it is too late for therapists to process the feelings of abandonment and loss with clients. Hence, before termination, therapists must assess whether clients might have strong feelings about ending the relationship, so these feelings can be addressed adequately.

There are three main steps to effective termination of therapy relationships: (a) looking back, (b) looking forward, and (c) saying goodbye (Dewald, 1971; Marx & Gelso, 1987; Ward, 1984). In looking back, therapists review with clients what they have learned and how they have changed. Clients also can provide feedback about the most helpful and least helpful aspects of the therapy process. Reviewing the process can help clients consolidate their changes and feel a sense of accomplishment. In looking forward, therapists and clients set an ending date, discuss future plans, and consider the need for possible additional counseling. Therapists review with clients the issues they still want to address. No therapy process is ever complete. We keep changing (for better or worse) for the rest of our lives. The task for therapists is to assist clients in identifying the ongoing issues, determining how they will address these issues, and clarifying how they can find support in their lives for making changes. If such plans are not realistic, therapists need to confront clients so they do not set themselves up for failure. Finally, in saying goodbye, clients express their thanks to therapists and both share their feelings about ending and say their farewells.

Termination is often challenging for both therapists and clients. Once two people have spoken about many deep and personal issues, it is often difficult for them to think about not seeing each other again. Termination thus often brings up issues of loss for both therapists and clients. Some evidence shows that therapists and clients who have the most trouble with termination are those who have a history of painful losses (Boyer & Hoffman, 1993; Marx & Gelso, 1987). If loss has been painful in the past, it is difficult to go through another loss. Other clients may not experience intense sadness but may struggle with how to thank the therapist and show appreciation for the therapist's role in their process of change. Other clients may be disappointed about not having received the "magic cure" and feel upset that they still have unresolved problems. Therapists need to talk openly about the client's feelings about the separation. Furthermore, they need to anticipate the separation well ahead of time, so they have time to deal with the client's feelings that arise from ending the relationship (and deal with their own loss issues in therapy or supervision).

Making Referrals

Clients' needs are sometimes beyond what therapists are qualified to address or capable of delivering. For example, a client might have an eating disorder, substance abuse problem, or serious mental illness, and the therapist might lack expertise in that area. Sometimes the therapist and client have accomplished as much as they can together, but the client needs a different kind of help. For example, a referral may be needed because a client needs marital or family therapy, but the therapist is trained only in individual therapy (note that family treatment is typically more beneficial than individual treatment if clients are having difficulties with family members; Haley, 1987; Minuchin, 1974; Nichols & Schwartz, 1991; Satir, 1988). In addition, clients might need referrals for medication, long-term therapy, assessment of learning disabilities, financial assistance, housing information, spiritual guidance, or legal advice.

The therapist needs to be careful to explain the reason for the referral to the client. Otherwise, clients could easily feel that they are hopeless, need endless treatment, or are "bad clients." If therapists do a thorough job of the three steps of termination discussed above, clients are less likely to have negative feelings about being referred.

Dealing With Difficult Clinical Situations

Many clients are eager and ready to work on their problems when they come to therapy. Some clients, however, are not ready to work or are difficult to interact with. Sometimes the very reason they are clients is because they have interpersonal problems. Rather than getting angry at the client for having these problems, therapists need to be curious about why the client has the problem, empathize with the underlying pain, and try different strategies to connect with and help the client. In this section, I discuss just a few of the many difficult clinical situations that beginning therapists might face: reluctant and resistant clients, overly talkative clients, suicidal clients, feeling sexual attraction toward clients, and dealing with hostile, angry clients.

RELUCTANT AND RESISTANT CLIENTS

Most clients have at least some reluctance to change. Egan (1994) suggested that the roots of reluctance are fear of intensity, lack of trust, fear of falling apart, shame, and fear of change. For many clients, it is easier to stick with known misery than to face the unknown possibilities of changing. Signs of reluctance are varied and often covert. Reluctant clients might talk only about safe subjects, seem unsure of what they want from therapy, act overly cooperative, set unrealistic goals and then give up on them, not work very hard at changing, or blame others for their problems.

Whereas reluctance is typically passive, resistance (i.e., feeling coerced and wanting to fight back) is often active (Egan, 1994). Resistant clients often present themselves as not needing help and as feeling misused. They show minimal willingness to form a relationship and often try to manipulate the therapist. They might be resentful, try to sabotage the therapy process, terminate as quickly as possible, and act abusively or belligerently to the therapist. Clients who come to therapy because they are mandated to do so (e.g., are court ordered) are often resistant. For example, one male client who was ordered by a judge to participate in 12 therapy sessions because he had urinated on public property was resistant about being there and got very little out of the experience (he even asked the therapist for a date!). Egan suggested that resistance can come from seeing no reason for therapy, resenting being referred for help, feeling awkward about participating in therapy, or having a history of rebelliousness. Other reasons for resistance are having values or expectations that are inconsistent with the help being offered, having negative attitudes about therapy, feeling that going for therapy is admitting weakness and inadequacy, feeling a lack of trust, or disliking the therapist.

When faced with clients who are reluctant or resistant, therapists often become confused, panicked, angry, guilty, or depressed (Egan, 1994). They might try to placate the client, become impatient or hostile to the client, become passive, or lower their expectations and do a halfhearted job. Alternatively, therapists might become warmer and more accepting to win over the client, engage in a power struggle with the client, allow themselves to be abused or bullied by the client, or try to terminate the therapy process. The source of the stress is not only the client's behavior but also the therapist's self-defeating attitudes and assumptions. Therapists might be saying things to themselves like, "All clients should be committed to change," "Every client must like and trust me," "Every client can be helped," "No unwilling client can be helped," "I am responsible for what happens to the client," "I must succeed with every client," "I am a rotten therapist if I cannot help this client." Therapists need to become aware of these self-defeating attitudes and assumptions to reduce their influence on the therapy process.

Therapists should not avoid dealing with reluctance and resistance, but they also should avoid reinforcing these processes in clients (Egan, 1994). Goldfried and Davison (1994) suggested that the role of the therapist is to make the reluctant–resistant client ready for change; hence, the challenge for therapists is to find creative ways to deal with reluctance and resistance. Here are several suggestions for dealing with reluctance and resistance (see also Egan, 1994).

- Learn to see reluctance and resistance as normal.
- Recognize that reluctance and resistance are sometimes a form of avoidance and are not necessarily due to ill will toward the therapist.
- Explore your own reluctance and resistance to changing problematic aspects of your life. Once therapists figure out how they cope with their own reluctance and resistance, they probably are more able to help clients with theirs. An awareness of their own foibles can make therapists more empathic and less impatient.
- Examine the quality of your interventions. Therapists might be provoking resistance by being too directive or too passive or by disliking the client.
- Be empathic; try to understand what it is like to be the client.
- Work directly with the client's reluctance and resistance rather than ignoring it, being intimidated by it, or being angry at the clients for his or her behaviors.
- Help the client explore feelings about the reluctance or resistance to therapy.
- Be realistic about what you can accomplish with a client.
- Establish a relationship on the basis of mutual trust and shared planning rather than trying to assume all the power.
- Work with the client to search for incentives for changing.

OVERLY TALKATIVE CLIENTS

Some clients talk nonstop about things that are not related to therapeutic goals (although therapists have to be careful about making judgments about what is worth discussing in therapy). In the Client Behavior System (see chap. 3 and Web Form H), this type of talking is considered recounting rather than affective or cognitive–behavioral exploration. Talkativeness is often a defense on the part of clients, in that it is an attempt to keep others at a distance. In situations in which the client's talking is not productive, the therapist needs to intervene cautiously after several minutes and interrupt the talking. The therapist can say something like, "Sorry to interrupt, but I'm not going to be able to help you unless I can add a few things here and there. Let me see if I understand what you're saying right now. . . . " Subsequently, therapists could even hold up a hand and say, "Excuse me again, but I want to make sure I am hearing you correctly." Thus, therapists let clients know that they are interrupting to assist (not because of boredom or irritation).

Interruptions done in a hostile manner ("Whoa, hold on there, you're talking too much") could hinder the therapeutic relationship and make the client feel that she or he had done something bad. If done appropriately, gently, and respectfully, however, clients could feel relieved that their therapists interrupted them to help them overcome their defenses and learn how to interact more appropriately.

Rather than getting angry at clients for monopolizing the conversation, therapists can empathize with the client's difficulty in communicating. The therapist can also hypothesize about why the client uses talking as a defense, recognizing that it keeps the client from forming close relationships. Such conceptualization can lead to the development of better interventions.

Therapists can also use their immediacy skills with overly talkative clients if therapists judge that the client can handle the interpersonal challenge. Therapists can talk about how they feel when clients do let them have a chance to talk and ask about clients' experiences when talking.

SUICIDAL CLIENTS

When a therapist thinks that a client might be at risk for suicide, he or she needs to actively and directly assess the seriousness of the risk rather than ignoring or minimizing it. Although the choice about suicide is ultimately up to the client, therapists can assume clients are asking for help when they bring up the topic of suicide.

There are a series of steps that therapists can follow with suicidal clients. First, a general assessment of suicidal risk usually involves asking directly about suicidal potential. Therapists might ask the following questions:

- "Are you thinking about suicide?"
- "Do you have a plan for attempting suicide?"
- "Do you have the means to carry out the plan?"
- "Have you attempted suicide in the past?"
- "Do you use (or plan on using) alcohol or drugs?"
- "Have you been withdrawn and isolated lately?"
- "Have you been focused on death (e.g., giving away prized possessions or planning your funeral)?"
- "Are you feeling helpless or worthless?"
- "Do you have plans for the future?"
- "Who knows about your suicidal feelings?"
- "How would others feel if they knew you committed suicide?"

If a client indicates a clear intent to commit suicide and has a clear viable plan and the means to do it (e.g., a client plans on killing him- or herself tonight and has purchased the pills and alcohol necessary to accomplish this plan), the therapist needs to take steps to ensure the client's safety. The beginning therapist should first consult with a colleague or supervisor to determine the best steps to take (the client should not be left alone during the consultation because he or she might leave to carry out the plan or implement the plan in the therapist's office).

In some cases, therapists (in consultation with supervisors) might decide that suicidal clients should be hospitalized to protect themselves from self-injury. In some cases clients realize the danger and agree to be hospitalized to receive intensive psychiatric and psychological treatment. In other cases, therapists may have to admit clients to the hospital against their will. In yet other cases, therapists may ascertain that hospitalization is not necessary and instead can develop a contract with the client that involves the client agreeing not to hurt him- or herself and promising to contact the therapist or a crisis line for assistance if thoughts of suicide occur. In these cases, it may be useful for therapists to notify the client's family, close friends, or significant others about the client's suicidal ideation. Note that when clients threaten to harm themselves, confidentiality no longer applies. Hence, therapists can perform the necessary steps to ensure the safety of suicidal clients (still, of course, being empathic rather than authoritarian and demanding). For legal purposes, therapists should document in writing the procedures they followed to assess and assist suicidal clients, including the questions that were asked, consultations that occurred, and interventions that were made.

In some cases, a therapist may decide that although a client is not actively suicidal, a contract would he helpful to ensure that the client has access to assistance if needed. Therapists can provide the numbers of 24-hour crisis lines and assist the client in identifying a support system. Additional sessions can be suggested or the therapist can offer to call the client between sessions to provide extra support.

As therapists who have provided crisis counseling know, dealing with someone who is contemplating suicide can be very challenging. Beginning therapists often fear that asking about suicidal feelings encourages clients to think about or commit suicide. In fact, the opposite is typically true—by talking about suicidal feelings, clients can bring their worst fears into the open. Clients often appreciate that therapists view their problems as serious. If therapists are not willing to discuss suicidal feelings, clients often feel even more alone, ashamed, strange, or "crazy." Perhaps the worst thing to do is to diminish or negate the feelings (e.g., "You'll feel better tomorrow"), point out positive aspects of their lives (e.g., "You have so much to live for"), or give false reassurance (e.g., "Everything will be okay"). These responses often result in clients not only feeling depressed and suicidal, but also feeling desperate because they cannot get help, hopeless that they are beyond help, misunderstood, and worried that their suicidal feelings are unacceptable or too frightening to others.

One of the most difficult issues any mental health professional can face is dealing with the aftermath of a client who committed suicide. Many therapists agonize, feel guilty, and spend a lot of time second-guessing whether there was something else they could have done to prevent the suicide. A certain amount of introspection is important and may enable therapists to handle similar situations better in the future, but therapists should not unnecessarily take on too much responsibility. It is often wise for therapists to seek supervision and therapy after such a difficult situation to help them cope and understand their feelings.

SEXUAL ATTRACTION

Therapist sexual attraction toward clients is a common occurrence in therapy relationships. Approximately 87% of surveyed therapists reported that they have been sexually attracted to clients at some point in their careers; many felt guilty, anxious, and confused about the attraction (Pope, Keith-Spiegel, & Tabachnick, 1986; Pope & Tabachnick, 1993). Feeling attracted is not unethical, but acting on the attraction (e.g., socializing with the client, having a sexual relationship) can harm clients and is considered unethical.

As a beginning therapist, you may find yourself sexually attracted to someone you are trying to help. Although discussing this attraction with a supervisor could be uncomfortable (some therapists might feel ashamed or guilty for having these feelings), a supervisor can assist you in working through these feelings in a healthy, rather than a destructive, manner (Ladany et al., 1997; Pope et al., 1993). For example, a therapist found herself attracted to a client who communicated admiration, respect, and even awe for the assistance she provided for him. Although the therapist had a good relationship with her partner, she enjoyed the positive feedback from the client and began thinking about him in a romantic way. Fortunately, she talked with her supervisor, who assisted her in sorting out her feelings related to the attraction and in understanding how sexual involvement might harm the client. The therapist benefited from coming to understand how these feelings developed and how they could negatively influence the therapy process. The supervisor also normalized the therapist's feelings by letting her know that many therapists become attracted to clients during their career.

ANGRY CLIENTS

For most therapists, it is extremely stressful when clients are directly and hostilely angry at them (Deutsch, 1984; Farber, 1983; Hill, Kellems, et al., 2003; Matsakis, 1998; Plutchik, Conte, & Karasu, 1994). In fact, in one study, more than 80% of therapists said that they felt afraid or angry when clients were verbally abusive toward them (Pope & Tabachnick, 1993). Matsakis (1998) noted that client anger often disrupts the therapy process, especially when therapists feel angry, confused, hurt, guilty, anxious, or incompetent, instead of being able to remain empathic and objective and talk about the client anger.

To avert the negative consequences associated with inappropriately managing client anger, several authors have suggested that therapists respond to client anger as they would to any other emotion (Adler, 1984; Burns & Auerbach, 1996; Cahill, 1981; Hill, Kellums, et al., 2003; Joines, 1995; Kaplan, Brooks, McComb, Shapiro, & Sodano, 1983; Lynch, 1975; Matsakis, 1998; Newman, 1997; Ormont, 1984). These authors also recommended that therapists work with clients to help them uncover underlying feelings, express anger verbally instead of acting it out physically, and decide what to do about the anger. To achieve these goals, they suggested that therapists need to listen when clients are angry and try to understand the anger. Furthermore, if clients are justified in their anger at the therapists, they stressed that therapists need to alter their behaviors.

Concluding Comments

I hope this book has provided you with the essential tools to begin your journey toward becoming a therapist. I would encourage you to complete the Counselor Self-Efficacy Measure (Web Form K), so you can make a self-assessment of your therapy skills, your skills in managing sessions, and your skills in terms of handling difficult clinical situations. You can complete the measure for how you feel right now, as well as retrospectively for how you think you were before reading this book and practicing the skills. This assessment might give you some ideas about what you have learned as well as about areas that still need work.

As a result of learning about therapy skills, many of you may have decided that you would like to pursue a career that involves extensive use of therapy skills; others may have decided not to pursue such a career. Regardless of the career you have chosen, these therapy skills can be used to enhance your personal and professional functioning. I encourage each of you to set specific goals on how to continue to develop these skills, given that this text and these practice exercises provide only a foundation on which your skills can be cultivated. Many sites are available for advanced training in therapy skills (e.g., graduate programs in counseling and clinical psychology, social work, counseling, psychiatry, psychiatric nursing). Volunteering at nonprofit agencies also provides a useful setting for obtaining additional practice for your skills while assisting people with pressing concerns. Whatever your path, I hope that it involves continued exploration of your feelings, increased self-awareness and insight, and positive changes that enable you to fulfill your potential and succeed in your interpersonal relationships and in your career.

I would appreciate any feedback (on the form at the end of the book) that you might have about this text. I will continue to revise this book to make it responsive to student needs.

WHAT DO YOU THINK?

▮ Discuss other possible ways that therapists could manage sessions (e.g., begin sessions, develop a focus, end sessions).

▮ Who should decide that it is an appropriate time to terminate, and what marker should help them decide that termination is appropriate?

▮ What do you think the ideal length of a therapy relationship is?

▮ Debate whether clients should ever be forced to go for therapy.

▮ Describe the personality characteristics a therapist could have that might influence her or his ability to respond effectively to reluctant or resistant clients, overly talkative clients, suicidal clients, or angry clients.

▮ What would you do if you felt sexual attraction for a client?

▮ Identify what steps you might take if you were a therapist dealing with the following suicidal clients:

> A. Ilya is a 23-year-old man who mentions that he feels really depressed because his girlfriend broke up with him last week. He states that he does not think he can live without her. He does not have a plan and has never attempted suicide before. He drinks occasionally and recently has been drinking more.
>
> B. Jackie is a 45-year-old woman who recently lost her job as a manager for a public relations firm. She was divorced five years ago, and her husband has custody of their two children. At the time of the divorce, she attempted suicide by ingesting 50 aspirins. She was hospitalized at that time. She recently returned to counseling because of a general dissatisfaction with her life. She plans on taking 100 aspirins and has a bottle in her purse. She has written notes to both of her children.
>
> C. Omar is a 17-year-old boy who was suspended from school for fighting with another student. His parents are angry with him and have insisted that he attend counseling. He states that maybe he should try to hurt himself because then they would really think he had a problem. He does not have a plan and has never attempted suicide before. He says, "I'd never really hurt myself. I want to go to college and get away from my parents and have fun."

▮ What theoretical orientation is emerging for you? Describe your goals for learning more about this theoretical orientation.

▮ What goals do you have for the continued development of your therapy skills?

LAB 16

Conceptualizing Clients

Goals: To teach therapists about how to conceptualize clients and to think more about the timing of interventions.

Tasks

This lab is meant for advanced students who are seeing "real" clients. Within a classroom setting of five to ten students, one student should role-play a client that he or she is seeing. The student who is doing the role-playing should provide a very brief description of the client (age, gender, occupation, involvement in relationship with significant other, presenting problem); the rest will be learned through the role-play. Another student should begin taking the role of the therapist doing the exploration stage. Other students can take over the role of therapist whenever necessary to continue the exploration.

When the leader determines that enough exploration has occurred (about 10–15 minutes), he or she can stop the process and ask the students to conceptualize the client's problems. They can talk about what they have learned so far about the client and what they do not know.

All the students can take turns being therapists and try using challenge, interpretation, self-disclosure, or immediacy. Each therapist can interact with the client for two or three exchanges to see how the interaction works. The "client" should stay in the role and refrain from talking about interventions that he or she used with the real client or providing more information about the real client.

When the leader determines that an adequate amount of time has been spent in the insight stage, she or he can stop the process and ask the students to conceptualize the client's problems again. Therapists can discuss what they have learned through the insight stage. Therapists can talk about the theories that they think best explain how the client developed and maintains his or her problems. Furthermore, the leader can ask therapists to share what feelings and reactions were evoked in them by the client (e.g., boredom, anger, irritation, sexual attraction, deep empathy). Therapists can then turn their attention to discussing the action stage. Do they think the client is ready for action? If not, why not? What else needs to be done? If yes, what actions might be appropriate? How could the therapist implement the desired interventions?

Again, one therapist can begin the action stage with the "client," going through the first seven steps outlined in chapter 21 (explore action, assess what clients have tried before, set specific goals, brainstorm possible ways to reach goals, explore the different options, decide on an action, and implement the action). Other therapists can take over when one therapist needs assistance.

Processing the Therapy Interchange

The "client" can talk about what the experience was like and about what he or she learned that will help in working with the real client.

continues

LAB 16 (Continued)

Conceptualizing Clients

Personal Reflections

▪ What are your strengths and weaknesses in terms of conceptualizing clients?
▪ What specific issues tend to "hook" you most and make it difficult for you to respond objectively to clients (e.g., hostility, sexuality, passivity, dependency)?

References

Adler, G. (1984). Special problems for the therapist. *International Journal of Psychiatry in Medicine, 14*, 91–98.

Ainsworth, M. D. S. (1989). Attachments beyond infancy. *American Psychologist, 44*, 709–716.

Ainsworth, M. D. S., Blehar, M. C., Waters, E., & Wall, S. (1978). *Patterns of attachment: A psychological study of the Strange Situation.* Hillsdale, NJ: Erlbaum.

Alberti, R. E., & Emmons, M. L. (2001). *Your perfect right: Assertiveness and equality in your life and relationships* (8th ed.). Atascadero, CA: Impact.

American Association for Marriage and Family Therapy. (2002). *AAMFT code of ethics.* Washington, DC: Author.

American Counseling Association. (1995). *Code of ethics and standards of practice.* Alexandria, VA: Author.

American Psychological Association. (2002). Ethical principles of psychologists and code of conduct. *American Psychologist, 57*, 1060–1073.

American Psychological Association. (2003). Guidelines for multicultural education, training, research, practice, and organizational change for psychologists. *American Psychologist, 58*, 377–402.

American School Counselor Association. (1998). *Ethical standards for school counselors.* Alexandria, VA: Author.

Andersen, B., & Anderson, W. (1985). Client perceptions of counselors using positive and negative self-involving statements. *Journal of Counseling Psychology, 32*, 462–465.

Archer, D., & Akert, R. M. (1977). Words and everything else: Verbal and nonverbal cues in social interpretation. *Journal of Personality and Social Psychology, 35*, 443–449.

Arlow, J. A. (1995). Psychoanalysis. In R. J. Corsini & D. Wedding (Eds.), *Current psychotherapies* (5th ed., pp. 15–50). Itasca, IL: F. E. Peacock.

Arredondo, P., Toporek, R., Brown, S. P., Jones, J., Locke, D. C., Sanchez, J., & Stadler, H. (1996). Operationalization of the multicultural competencies. *Journal of Multicultural Counseling and Development, 24*, 42–78.

Atkinson, D. R., & Hackett, G. (1998). *Counseling diverse populations* (2nd ed.). Boston: McGraw-Hill.

Atkinson, D. R., Morten, G., & Sue, D. W. (Eds.). (1993). *Counseling American minorities* (4th ed.). Madison, WI: Brown & Benchmark.

Atkinson, D. R., Morten, G., & Sue, D. W. (1998). *Counseling American minorities: A cross-cultural perspective* (5th ed.). Boston: McGraw-Hill.

Axelson, J. A. (1999). *Counseling and development in a multicultural society* (3rd ed.). Pacific Grove, CA: Brooks/Cole.

Bachelor, A. (1995). Clients' perception of the therapeutic alliance: A qualitative analysis. *Journal of Counseling Psychology, 42*, 323–327.

Bandura, A. (1965). Influence of models' reinforcement contingencies on the acquisition of imitative responses. *Journal of Personality and Social Psychology, 1*, 589–595.

Bandura, A. (1969). *Principles of behavior modification*. New York: Holt, Rinehart & Winston.

Bandura, A. (1977). *Social learning theory*. Englewood Cliffs, NJ: Prentice Hall.

Bandura, A. (1986). *Social foundations of thought and action: A social cognitive theory*. Englewood Cliffs, NJ: Prentice Hall.

Barkham, M., & Shapiro, D. A. (1986). Counselor verbal response modes and experienced empathy. *Journal of Counseling Psychology, 33*, 3–10.

Basch, M. F. (1980). *Doing psychotherapy*. New York: Basic Books.

Basescu, S. (1990). Tools of the trade: The use of self in psychotherapy. *Group, 14*, 157–165.

Beauchamp, T. L., & Childress, J. F. (1994). *Principles of biomedical ethics* (4th ed.). New York: Oxford University Press.

Beck, A. T. (1976). *Cognitive therapy and the emotional disorders*. New York: International Universities Press.

Beck, A. T., & Emery, G. (1985). *Anxiety disorders and phobias: A cognitive perspective*. New York: Basic Books.

Beck, A. T., & Freeman, A. (1990). *Cognitive therapy of the personality disorders*. New York: Guilford.

Beck, A. T., Rush, A. J., Shaw, B. F., & Emery, G. (1979). *Cognitive therapy of depression*. New York: Guilford.

Beck, A. T., & Weishaar, M. (1995). Cognitive therapy. In R. Corsini & D. Wedding (Eds.), *Current psychotherapies* (5th ed., pp. 229–261). Itasca, IL: F. E. Peacock.

Beck, J. S. (1995). Cognitive therapy: Basics and beyond. New York: Guilford.

Benson, H. (1975). *The relaxation response*. New York: Morrow.

Bernstein, D. A., & Borkovec, T. D. (1973). *Progressive relaxation training*. Champaign, IL: Research Press.

Beutler, L. E., & Bergan, J. (1991). Value change in counseling and psychotherapy: A search for scientific credibility. *Journal of Counseling Psychology, 38*, 16–24.

Bibring, E. (1954). Psychoanalysis and the dynamic psychotherapies. *Journal of the American Psychoanalytic Association, 2*, 745–770.

Bischoff, M. M., & Tracey, T. J. G. (1995). Client resistance as predicted by therapist behavior: A study of sequential dependence. *Journal of Counseling Psychology, 42*, 487–495.

Blanck, G. (1966). Some technical implications of ego psychology. *International Journal of Psychoanalysis, 47*, 6–13.

Blustein, D. L. (1987). Integrating career counseling and psychotherapy: A comprehensive treatment strategy. *Psychotherapy, 24*, 794–799.

Bohart, A. C., Elliott, R., Greenberg, L. S., & Watson, J. C. (2002). Empathy. In J. C. Norcross (Ed.), *Psychotherapy relationships that work: Therapist contributions and responsiveness to patients* (pp. 89–108). New York: Oxford University Press.

Bohart, A. C., & Tallman, K. (1999). *How clients make therapy work: The process of active self-healing*. Washington, DC: American Psychological Association.

Bordin, E. S. (1979). The generalizability of the psychoanalytic concept of the working alliance. *Psychotherapy: Theory, Research, and Practice, 16*, 252–260.

Borys, D. S., & Pope, K. S. (1989). Dual relationships between therapist and client: A national survey of psychologists, psychiatrists, and social workers. *Professional Psychology: Research and Practice, 20*, 283–293.

Bowlby, J. (1969). *Attachment and loss: Vol. 1. Attachment*. New York: Basic Books.

Bowlby, J. (1988). *A secure base*. New York: Basic Books.

Boyer, S. P., & Hoffman, M. A. (1993). Counselor affective reactions to termination: Impact of counselor loss history and perceived client sensitivity to loss. *Journal of Counseling Psychology, 40*, 271–277.

Brainerd, C. J., & Reyna, V. F. (1998). When things that never happened are easier to "remember" than things that did. *Psychological Science, 9*, 484–489.

Brammer, L. M., & MacDonald, G. (1996). *The helping relationship: Process and skills* (6th ed.). Boston: Allyn & Bacon.

Breier, A., & Strauss, J. S. (1984). The role of social relationships in the recovery from psychotic disorders. *American Journal of Psychiatry, 141*, 949–955.

Brown, D. (1985). Career counseling: Before, after, or instead of personal counseling. *Vocational Guidance Quarterly, 33*, 197–201.

Brown, D., & Brooks, L. (1991). *Career counseling techniques*. Boston: Allyn & Bacon.

Brownell, K. D., Marlatt, G. A., Lichenstein, E., & Wilson, G. T. (1986). Understanding and preventing relapse. *American Psychologist, 41*, 765–782.

Budman, S. H., & Gurman, A. S. (1988). *Theory and practice of brief therapy*. New York: Guilford.

Bugental, J. T. (1965). *The search for authenticity*. New York: Holt, Rinehart & Winston.

Burns, D. D. (1999). *The feeling good handbook* (Rev. ed.). New York: Plume/Penguin Books.

Burns, D. D., & Auerbach, A. (1996). Therapeutic empathy in cognitive–behavioral therapy: Does it really make a difference? In P. M. Salkovskis (Ed.), *Frontiers of cognitive therapy* (pp. 135–164). New York: Guilford.

Burton, M. V., Parker, R. W., & Wollner, J. M. (1991). The psychotherapeutic value of a "chat": A verbal response modes study of a placebo attention control with breast cancer patients. *Psychotherapy Research, 1*, 39–61.

Cahill, A. J. (1981). Aggression revisited: The value of anger in therapy and other close relationships. *Adolescent Psychiatry, 9*, 539–549.

Carkhuff, R. R. (1969). *Human and helping relations* (Vols. 1 & 2). New York: Holt, Rinehart & Winston.

Carkhuff, R. R. (1973). *The art of problem-solving.* Amherst, MA: Human Resource Development.

Carkhuff, R. R., & Anthony, W. A. (1979). *The skills of helping: An introduction to counseling skills.* Amherst, MA: Human Resources Development.

Carkhuff, R. R., & Berenson, B. G. (1967). *Beyond counseling and psychotherapy.* New York: Holt, Rinehart & Winston.

Carroll, L. (1962). *Alice's adventures in wonderland.* Harmondsworth, Middlesex, England: Penguin Books. (Original work published 1865)

Cashdan, S. (1988). *Object relations therapy.* New York: Norton.

Cassidy, J. & Shaver, P. R. (Eds.) (1999). *Handbook of attachment: Theory, research, and clinical application.* New York: Guilford.

Claiborn, C. D., Goodyear, R. K., & Horner, P. A. (2002). Feedback. In J. C. Norcross (Ed.), *Psychotherapy relationships that work: Therapist contributions and responsiveness to patients.* New York: Oxford University Press.

Colby, K. M. (1961). On the greater amplifying power of causal–correlative over interrogative inputs on free association in an experimental psychoanalytic situation. *Behavioral Science, 10*, 233–239.

Conoley, C. W., Padula, M. A., Payton, D. S., & Daniels, J. A. (1994). Predictors of client implementation of counselor recommendations: Match with problem, difficulty level, and building on client strengths. *Journal of Counseling Psychology, 41*, 3–7.

Conte, H. R., Plutchik, R., Picard, S., & Karasu, T. B. (1989). Ethics in the practice of psychotherapy: A survey. *American Journal of Psychotherapy, 43*, 32–42.

Cornett, C. (1991). The "risky" intervention: Twinship self–object impasses and therapist self-disclosure in psychodynamic psychotherapy. *Clinical Social Work Journal, 19*, 49–61.

Cournoyer, R. J., & Mahalik, J. R. (1995). Cross-sectional study of gender role conflict examining college-aged and middle-aged men. *Journal of Counseling Psychology, 42*, 11–19.

Crits-Christoph, P., Barber, J. P., & Kurcias, J. S. (1991). Introduction and historical background. In P. Crits-Christoph & J. P. Barber (Eds.), *Handbook of short-term dynamic psychotherapy* (pp. 1–16). New York: Basic Books.

Crits-Christoph, P., Cooper, A., & Luborsky, L. (1988). The accuracy of therapists' interpretations and the outcome of dynamic psychotherapy. *Journal of Consulting and Clinical Psychology, 56*, 490–495.

Crits-Christoph, P., & Gibbons, B. B. C. (2002). Relational interpretations. In J. C. Norcross (Ed.), *Psychotherapy relationships that work: Therapist contributions and responsiveness to patients* (pp. 285–300). New York: Oxford University Press.

Curtis, J. M. (1981). Indications and contraindications in the use of therapist's self-disclosure. *Psychological Reports, 49*, 499–507.

Curtis, J. M. (1982). Principles and techniques of non-disclosure by the therapist during psychotherapy. *Psychological Reports, 51*, 907–914.

Darwin, C. R. (1872). *The expression of the emotions in man and animals* (1st ed.). London: John Murray.

Delaney, D. J., & Heimann, R. A. (1966). Effectiveness of sensitivity training on the perception of non-verbal communications. *Journal of Counseling Psychology, 4*, 436–440.

Deutsch, C. J. (1984). Self-reported sources of stress among psychotherapists. *Professional Psychology: Research and Practice, 15*, 833–845.

Dewald, P. A. (1971). *Psychotherapy: A dynamic approach.* New York: Basic Books.

Duan, C., & Hill, C. E. (1996). Theoretical confusions in the construct of empathy: A review of the literature. *Journal of Counseling Psychology, 43*, 261–274.

Egan, G. (1994). *The skilled helper* (5th ed.). Monterey, CA: Brooks/Cole.

Eibl-Eibesfeldt, I. (1971). *Love and hate: The natural history of behavior patterns.* New York: Holt, Rinehart & Winston.

Ekman, P. (1993). Facial expression and emotion. *American Psychologist, 48,* 384–392.

Ekman, P., & Friesen, W. V. (1969). Non-verbal leakage and clues to deception. *Psychiatry, 32,* 88–106.

Ekman, P., & Friesen, W. V. (1984). *Unmasking the face* (Reprint ed.). Palo Alto, CA: Consulting Psychologists Press.

Elkind, S. N. (1992). *Resolving impasses in therapeutic relationships.* New York: Guilford.

Elliott, R. (1985). Helpful and nonhelpful events in brief counseling interviews: An empirical taxonomy. *Journal of Counseling Psychology, 32,* 307–322.

Elliott, R., Barker, C. B., Caskey, N., & Pistrang, N. (1982). Differential helpfulness of counselor verbal response modes. *Journal of Counseling Psychology, 29,* 354–361.

Elliott, R., Hill, C. E., Stiles, W. B., Friedlander, M. L., Mahrer, A. R., & Margison, F. R. (1987). Primary therapist response modes: Comparison of six rating systems. *Journal of Consulting and Clinical Psychology, 55,* 218–223.

Elliott, R., Shapiro, D. A., Firth-Cozens, J., Stiles, W. B., Hardy, G. E., Llewelyn, S. P., & Margison, F. R. (1994). Comprehensive process analysis of insight events in cognitive–behavioral and psychodynamic–interpersonal psychotherapies. *Journal of Counseling Psychology, 41,* 449–463.

Ellis, A. (1962). *Reason and emotion in psychotherapy.* New York: Lyle Stuart.

Ellis, A. (1995). Rational emotive behavior therapy. In R. Corsini & D. Wedding (Eds.), *Current psychotherapies* (5th ed., pp. 161–196). Itasca, IL: F. E. Peacock.

Epstein, R. S., Simon, R. I., & Kay, G. G. (1992). Assessing boundary violations in psychotherapy: Survey results with the exploitation index. *Bulletin of the Menninger Clinic, 54,* 150–166.

Erikson, E. H. (1963). *Childhood and society* (2nd ed.). New York: Norton.

Eysenck, H. J. (1952). The effects of psychotherapy: An evaluation. *Journal of Consulting Psychology, 16,* 319–324.

Falk, D., & Hill, C. E. (1992). Counselor interventions preceding client laughter in brief therapy. *Journal of Counseling Psychology, 39,* 39–45.

Farber, B. A. (1983). Psychotherapists' perceptions of stressful patient behavior. *Professional Psychology: Research and Practice, 14,* 697–705.

Farber, B. A., & Geller, J. D. (1994). Gender and representation in psychotherapy. *Psychotherapy, 31,* 318–326.

Farber, B. A., & Lane, J. S. (2002). Positive regard. In J. C. Norcross (Ed.), *Psychotherapy relationships that work: Therapist contributions and responsiveness to patients* (pp. 175–194). New York: Oxford University Press.

Ferenczi, S., & Rank, O. (1956). *The development of psycho-analysis* (C. Newton, Trans.). New York: Dover. (Original work published 1925)

Finn, S. E., & Tonsager, M. E. (2002). How therapeutic assessment became humanistic. *Humanistic Psychologist, 30,* 10–22.

Fitzpatrick, M. R., Stalikas, A., & Iwakabe, S. (2001). Examining counselor interventions and client progress in the context of the therapeutic alliance. *Psychotherapy: Theory, Research, Practice, and Training, 38,* 160–170.

Fouad, N. A., & Brown, M. T. (2000). Role of race and social class in development: Implications for counseling psychology. In S. D. Brown & R. W. Lent (Eds.), *Handbook of counseling psychology* (3rd ed., pp. 379–408). New York: Wiley.

Frank, J. D., & Frank, J. B. (1991). *Persuasion and healing: A comparative study of psychotherapy* (3rd ed.). Baltimore: Johns Hopkins University Press.

Frankl, V. (1959). *Man's search for meaning.* New York: Simon & Schuster.

Freud, S. (1933). *New introductory lectures on psychoanalysis* (J. H. Sprott, Trans.). New York: Norton.

Freud, S. (1943). *A general introduction to psychoanalysis* (J. Riviere, Trans.). New York: Garden City. (Original work published 1920)

Freud, S. (1949). *An outline of psychoanalysis* (J. Strachey, Trans.). New York: Norton. (Original work published 1940)

Freud, S. (1953a). Fragment of an analysis of a case of hysteria. In J. Strachey (Ed.), *Standard edition of the complete psychological works of Sigmund Freud* (Vol. 7, pp. 15–122). London: Hogarth. (Original work published 1905)

Freud, S. (1953b). Remembering, repeating, and working through. In J. Strachey (Ed.), *Standard edition of the complete psychological works of Sigmund Freud* (Vol. 12, pp. 147–156).

London: Hogarth. (Original work published 1914)

Freud, S. (1959). The dynamics of transference. In E. Jones (Ed.) & J. Riviere (Trans.), *Collected papers* (pp. 312–322). New York: Basic Books. (Original work published 1912)

Freud, S. (1961). The ego and the id. In J. Strachey (Ed. & Trans.), *The standard edition of the complete psychological works of Sigmund Freud* (Vol. 19, pp. 3–66). London: Hogarth. (Original work published 1923)

Freud, S. (1963). *Character and culture.* Oxford: Crowell-Collier. (Original work published 1923)

Friedman, E. H. (1990). *Friedman's fables.* New York: Guilford.

Fromm-Reichmann, F. (1950). *Principles of intensive psychotherapy.* Chicago: University of Chicago Press.

Fukuyama, M. A., & Sevig, T. D. (2002). Spirituality in counseling across cultures: Many rivers to the sea. In P. B. Pedersen, J. G. Draguns, W. J. Lonner, & J. E. Trimble (Eds.), *Counseling across cultures* (5th ed., pp. 273–296). Thousand Oaks, CA: Sage.

Fuller, F., & Hill, C. E. (1985). Counselor and helpee perceptions of counselor intentions in relationship to outcome in a single counseling session. *Journal of Counseling Psychology, 32,* 329–338.

Geller, J. D. (2003). Self-disclosure in psychoanalytic and existential therapy. *Journal of Clinical Psychology, 59,* 541–554.

Geller, J. D., Cooley, R. S., & Hartley, D. (1981). Images of the psychotherapist: A theoretical and methodological perspective. *Imagination, Cognition, and Personality, 1,* 123–146.

Geller, J. D., & Farber, B. A. (1993). Factors influencing the process of internalization in psychotherapy. *Psychotherapy Research, 3,* 166–180.

Gelso, C. J., & Carter, J. A. (1985). The relationship in counseling and psychotherapy. *Counseling Psychologist, 13,* 155–243.

Gelso, C. J., & Carter, J. A. (1994). Components of the psychotherapy relationship: Their interaction and unfolding during treatment. *Journal of Counseling Psychology, 41,* 296–306.

Gelso, C. J., & Fretz, B. R. (1992). *Counseling psychology.* Orlando, FL: Holt, Rinehart & Winston.

Gelso, C. J., & Fretz, B. R. (2001). *Counseling psychology* (2nd ed.). Belmont, CA: Thomson-Wadsworth.

Gelso, C. J., & Hayes, J. (1998). *The psychotherapy relationship: Theory, research, and practice.* New York: Wiley.

Gelso, C. J., Hill, C. E., Mohr, J., Rochlen, A., & Zack, J. (1999). Describing the face of transference: Psychodynamic therapists' recollections about transference in cases of successful long-term therapy. *Journal of Counseling Psychology, 46,* 257–267.

Gendlin, E. T. (1978). *Focusing.* New York: Everest House.

Gillespie, J. F., Jr. (1951). Verbal signs of resistance in client-centered therapy. *Dissertation Abstracts International, 5* (01), 454B. (University Microfilms No. AAI000305)

Glass, A. L., & Holyoak, L. J. (1986). *Cognition* (2nd ed.). New York: Random House.

Goldfried, M. R., Burckell, L. A., & Eubanks-Carter, C. (2003). Therapist self-disclosure in cognitive–behavior therapy. *Journal of Clinical Psychology, 59,* 555–568.

Goldfried, M. R., & Davison, G. C. (1994). *Clinical behavior therapy* (2nd ed.). New York: Wiley.

Goldfried, M. R., & Trier, C. S. (1974). Effectiveness of relaxation as an active coping skill. *Journal of Abnormal Psychology, 83,* 348–355.

Good, G. E., Robertson, J. M., O'Neil, J. M., Fitzgerald, L. F., Stevens, M., DeBrod, K. A., et al. (1995). Male gender role conflict: Psychometric issues and relations to psychological distress. *Journal of Counseling Psychology, 42,* 3–10.

Gourash, N. (1978). Help-seeking: A review of the literature. *American Journal of Community Psychology, 6,* 413–423.

Grace, M., Kivlighan, D. M., & Kunce, J. (1995). The effect of nonverbal skills training on counselor trainee nonverbal sensitivity and responsiveness and on session impact and working alliance ratings. *Journal of Counseling and Development, 73,* 547–552.

Greenberg, L. S. (2002). *Emotion-focused therapy.* New York: Guilford.

Greenberg, L. S., Rice, L. N., & Elliott, R. (1993). *Facilitating emotional change.* New York: Guilford.

Greenson, R. R. (1967). *The technique and practice of psychoanalysis* (Vol. 1). Madison, CT: International Universities Press.

Grissom, G. R., Lyons, J. S., & Lutz, W. (2002). Standing on the shoulders of a giant: Development of an outcome management system based on the dose model and phase model of psychotherapy. *Psychotherapy Research, 12,* 397–412.

Gross, A. E., & McMullen, P. A. (1983). Models of the help-seeking process. In B. DePaulo, A. Nadler, & D. Fisher (Eds.), *New directions in helping* (Vol. 2, pp. 45–70). New York: Academic Press.

Haase, R. F., & Tepper, D. T., Jr. (1972). Nonverbal components of empathic communication. *Journal of Counseling Psychology, 19,* 417–426.

Hackett, G. (1993). Career counseling and psychotherapy: False dichotomies and recommended remedies. *Journal of Career Assessment, 1,* 105–117.

Haldeman, D. C. (2002). Gay rights, patient rights: The implications of sexual orientation conversion therapy. *Professional Psychology: Research and Practice, 33,* 260–264.

Haley, J. (1987). *Problem-solving therapy.* San Francisco: Jossey-Bass.

Hall, E. T. (1963). A system for the notation of proxemic behavior. *American Anthropologist, 63,* 1003–1026.

Hall, E. T. (1968). Proxemics. *Current Anthropology, 9,* 83–108.

Hall, J. A., Rosenthal, R., Archer, D., DiMatteo, M. R., & Rogers, P. L. (1978). Profile of nonverbal sensitivity. In P. McReynolds (Ed.), *Advances in psychological assessment* (Vol. 4, pp. 179–221). San Francisco: Jossey-Bass.

Hanna, F. J., & Ritchie, M. H. (1995). Seeking the active ingredients of psychotherapeutic change: Within and outside the context of therapy. *Professional Psychology: Research and Practice, 26,* 176–183.

Hanson, W. E., Claiborn, C. D., & Kerr, B. (1997). Differential effects of two test interpretation styles in counseling: A field study. *Journal of Counseling Psychology, 44,* 400–405.

Harper, R. G., Wiens, A. N., & Matarazzo, J. D. (1978). *Nonverbal communication: The state of the art.* New York: Wiley.

Hayes, J. A., McCracken, J. E., McClanahan, M. K., Hill, C. E., Harp, J. S., & Carozzoni, P. (1998). Therapist perspectives on countertransference: Qualitative data in search of a theory. *Journal of Counseling Psychology, 45,* 468–482.

Helms, J. E. (1990). *Black and White racial identity: Theory, research, and practice.* Westport, CT: Greenwood.

Helms, J. E., & Cook, D. A. (1999). *Using race and culture in counseling and psychotherapy: Theory and practice.* Needham, MA: Allyn & Bacon.

Herr, E. L. (1989). Career development and mental health. *Journal of Career Development, 16,* 5–18.

Highlen, P. S., & Hill, C. E. (1984). Factors affecting client change in individual counseling: Current status and theoretical speculations. In S. D. Brown & R. W. Lent (Eds.), *Handbook of counseling psychology* (pp. 334–398). New York: Wiley.

Hill, C. E. (1978). Development of a counselor verbal response category system. *Journal of Counseling Psychology, 25,* 461–468.

Hill, C. E. (1989). *Therapist techniques and client outcomes: Eight cases of brief psychotherapy.* Newbury Park, CA: Sage.

Hill, C. E. (1992). An overview of four measures developed to test the Hill process model: Therapist intentions, therapist response modes, client reactions, and client behaviors. *Journal of Counseling and Development, 70,* 729–737.

Hill, C. E. (Ed.) (2001). *Helping skills: The empirical foundation.* Washington, DC: American Psychological Association.

Hill, C. E., Carter, J. A., & O'Farrell, M. K. (1983). A case study of the process and outcome of time-limited counseling. *Journal of Counseling Psychology, 30,* 3–18.

Hill, C. E., Helms, J. E., Spiegel, S. B., & Tichenor, V. (1988). Development of a system for categorizing client reactions to therapist interventions. *Journal of Counseling Psychology, 35,* 27–36.

Hill, C. E., Helms, J. E., Tichenor, V., Spiegel, S. B., O'Grady, K. E., & Perry, E. S. (1988). The effects of therapist response modes in brief psychotherapy. *Journal of Counseling Psychology, 35,* 222–233.

Hill, C. E., & Kellems, I. S. (2002). Development and use of the Helping Skills Measure to assess client perception of the effects of training and of helping skills in sessions. *Journal of Counseling Psychology, 49,* 264–272.

Hill, C. E., Kellems, I. S., Kolchakian, M. R., Wonnell, T. L., Davis, T. L., & Nakayama, E. Y. (2003). The therapist experience of being the target of hostile versus suspected-unasserted client anger: Factors associated with resolution. *Psychotherapy Research, 13,* 475–491

Hill, C. E., & Knox, S. (2002). Therapist self-disclosure. In J. C. Norcross (Ed.), *Psychotherapy relationships that work: Therapist contributions and responsiveness to patients.* Oxford, England: Oxford University Press.

Hill, C. E., & Lambert, M. J. (2003). Methodological issues in studying psychotherapy process and outcomes. In M. J. Lambert (Ed.), *Bergin and Garfield's handbook of psycho-*

therapy and behavior change (5th ed., pp. 84–135). New York: Wiley.

Hill, C. E., Nutt-Williams, E., Heaton, K. J., Thompson, B. J., & Rhodes, R. H. (1996). Therapist retrospective recall of impasses in long-term psychotherapy: A qualitative analysis. *Journal of Counseling Psychology, 43,* 207–217.

Hill, C. E., & O'Grady, K. E. (1985). List of therapist intentions illustrated in a case study and with therapists of varying theoretical orientations. *Journal of Counseling Psychology, 32,* 3–22.

Hill, C. E., Siegelman, L., Gronsky, B., Sturniolo, F., & Fretz, B. R. (1981). Nonverbal communication and counseling outcome. *Journal of Counseling Psychology, 28,* 203–212.

Hill, C. E., & Stephany, A. (1990). The relationship of nonverbal behaviors to client reactions. *Journal of Counseling Psychology, 37,* 22–26.

Hill, C. E., Thames, T. B., & Rardin, D. (1979). A comparison of Rogers, Perls, and Ellis on the Hill counselor verbal response category system. *Journal of Counseling Psychology, 26,* 198–203.

Hill, C. E., Thompson, B. J., Cogar, M. M., & Denman, D. W., III. (1993). Beneath the surface of long-term therapy: Client and therapist report of their own and each other's covert processes. *Journal of Counseling Psychology, 40,* 278–288.

Hill, C. E., Thompson, B. J., & Corbett, M. M. (1992). The impact of therapist ability to perceive displayed and hidden client reactions on immediate outcome in first sessions of brief therapy. *Psychotherapy Research, 2,* 143–155.

Hill, C. E., Thompson, B. J., & Ladany, N. (2003). Therapist use of silence in therapy: A survey. *Journal of Clinical Psychology, 59,* 513–524.

Hill, C. E., Thompson, B. J., & Mahalik, J. R. (1989). Therapist interpretation. In C. E. Hill (Ed.), *Therapist techniques and client outcomes: Eight cases of brief psychotherapy* (pp. 284–310). Newbury Park, CA: Sage.

Hill, C. E., & Williams, E. N. (2000). The process of individual therapy. In R. W. Lent & S. D. Brown (Eds.), *Handbook of counseling psychology* (pp. 670–710). New York: Wiley.

Holroyd, J. C., & Brodsky, A. (1977). Psychologists' attitudes and practices regarding erotic and nonerotic physical contact with patients. *American Psychologist, 32,* 843–849.

Horvath, A. O., & Bedi, R. P. (2002). The alliance. In J. C. Norcross (Ed.), *Psychotherapy relationships that work: Therapist contributions and responsiveness to patients* (pp. 37–70). New York: Oxford University Press.

Howard, K. I., Lueger, R. J., Maling, M. S., & Martinovich, Z. (1993). A phase model of psychotherapy outcome: Causal mediation of change. *Journal of Consulting and Clinical Psychology, 59,* 12–19.

Hunter, M., & Struve, J. (1998). *The ethical use of touch in psychotherapy.* Thousand Oaks, CA: Sage.

Ivey, A. E. (1994). *Intentional interviewing and counseling: Facilitating client development in a multicultural society* (3rd ed.). Pacific Grove, CA: Brooks/Cole.

Izard, C. E. (1977). *Human emotions.* New York: Plenum.

Izard, C. E. (1994). Innate and universal facial expressions evidence from developmental and cross-cultural research. *Psychological Bulletin, 115,* 288–299.

Jacobson, E. (1929). *Progressive relaxation.* Chicago: University of Chicago Press.

Joines, V. S. (1995). A developmental approach to anger. *Transactional Analysis Journal, 25,* 112–118.

Jourard, S. M. (1971). *The transparent self.* New York: Van Nostrand Reinhold.

Jung, C. G. (1984). *Dream analysis.* Princeton, NJ: Princeton University Press.

Kaplan, A., Brooks, B., McComb, A. L., Shapiro, E. R., & Sodano, A. (1983). Women and anger in psychotherapy. *Women and therapy, 2,* 29–40.

Kazdin, A. E. (2001). *Behavior modification in applied settings* (6th ed.). Pacific Grove, CA: Brooks/Cole.

Kelly, A. E. (1998). Clients' secret keeping in outpatient therapy. *Journal of Counseling Psychology, 45,* 50–57.

Kendon, A. (1967). Some functions of gaze-direction in social interaction. *Acta Psychologica, 26,* 22–63.

Kestenbaum, R. (1992). Feeling happy versus feeling good: The processing of discrete and global categories of emotional expressions by children and adults. *Developmental Psychology, 28,* 1132–1142.

Kiesler, D. J. (1988). *Therapeutic metacommunication: Therapist impact disclosure as feedback in psychotherapy.* Palo Alto, CA: Consulting Psychologists Press.

Kim, B. S. K., & Abreu, J. M. (2001). Acculturation measurement: Theory, current instruments, and future directions. In J. G. Ponterotto, J. M. Casas, L. A. Suzuki, & C. M. Alexander, (Eds.), *Handbook of multicultural counseling* (2nd ed., pp.394–424). Thousand Oaks, CA: Sage.

Kim, B. S. K., Atkinson, D. R., & Umemoto, D. (2001). Asian cultural values and the counseling process: Current knowledge and directions for future research. *Counseling Psychologist, 29,* 570–603.

Kim, B. S. K., Atkinson, D. R., & Yang, P. H. (1999). The Asian Values Scale: Development, factor analysis, validation, and reliability. *Journal of Counseling Psychology, 46,* 342–352.

Kitchener, K. S. (1984). Intuition, critical evaluation and ethical principles: The foundation for ethical decisions for counseling psychology. *The Counseling Psychologist, 12,* 43–55.

Klein, M. H., Kolden, G. G., Michels, J. L., & Chisholm-Stockard, S. (2002). Congruence. In J. C. Norcross (Ed.), *Psychotherapy relationships that work: Therapist contributions and responsiveness to patients.* New York: Oxford University Press.

Kleinke, C. L. (1986). Gaze and eye contact: A research review. *Psychological Bulletin, 100,* 78–100.

Knox, S., Goldberg, J. L., Woodhouse, S., & Hill, C. E. (1999). Clients' internal representations of their therapists. *Journal of Counseling Psychology, 46,* 244–256.

Kohut, H. (1971). *The analysis of the self.* New York: International Universities Press.

Kohut, H. (1977). *The restoration of the self.* New York: International Universities Press.

Kohut, H. (1984). *How does analysis cure?* Chicago: University of Chicago Press.

Kopta, S. M., Howard, K. I., Lowry, J. L., & Beutler, L. E. (1994). Patterns of symptomatic recovery in psychotherapy. *Journal of Consulting and Clinical Psychology, 62,* 1009–1016.

Ladany, N., O'Brien, K. M., Hill, C. E., Melincoff, D. S., Knox, S., & Petersen, D. A. (1997). Sexual attraction toward clients, use of supervision, and prior training: A qualitative study of psychotherapy predoctoral interns. *Journal of Counseling Psychology, 44,* 413–424.

LaFrance, M., & Mayo, C. (1976). Racial differences in gaze behavior during conversations: Two systematic observational studies. *Journal of Personality and Social Psychology, 33,* 547–552.

Laing, R. D., & Esterson, A. (1970). *Sanity, madness, and the family.* Middlesex, England: Penguin.

Lambert, M. J., & Hill, C. E. (1994). Assessing psychotherapy outcomes and processes. In A. E. Bergin & S. L. Garfield (Eds.), *Handbook of psychotherapy and behavior change* (4th ed., pp. 72–113). New York: Wiley.

Lang, P. J., Melamed, B. G., & Hart, J. (1970). A psychophysiological analysis of fear modification using an automated desensitization procedure. *Journal of Abnormal Psychology, 76,* 220–234.

Lauver, P., & Harvey, D. R. (1997). *The practical counselor: Elements of effective helping.* Pacific Grove, CA: Brooks/Cole.

Lent, R. W., Hill, C. E., & Hoffman, M. A. (2003). Development and validation of the Counselor Activity Self-Efficacy Scales. *Journal of Counseling Psychology, 50,* 97–108.

Levy, A. (1989). Social support and the media: Analysis of responses by radio psychology talk show hosts. *Professional Psychology: Research and Practice, 20,* 73–78.

Levy, L. H. (1963). *Psychological interpretation.* New York: Holt, Rinehart & Winston.

Lin, M., Kelly, K. R., & Nelson, R. C. (1996). A comparative analysis of the interpersonal process in school-based counseling and consultation. *Journal of Counseling Psychology, 43,* 389–393.

Loftus, E. (1988). *Memory.* New York: Ardsley House.

Luborsky, L., & Crits-Christoph, P. (1990). *Understanding transference: The CCRT method.* New York: Basic Books.

Lynch, C. (1975). The freedom to get mad: Impediments to expressing anger and how to deal with them. *Family Therapy, 2,* 101–122.

Mahalik, J. R. (1994). Development of the Client Resistance Scale. *Journal of Counseling Psychology, 41,* 58–68.

Mahler, M. S. (1968). *On human symbiosis of the vicissitudes of individuation.* New York: International Universities Press.

Mahrer, A. R., Sterner, I., Lawson, K. C., & Dessaulles, A. (1986). Microstrategies: Distinctively patterned sequences of therapist statements. *Psychotherapy, 23,* 50–56.

Maki, M. T., & Kitano, H. H. L. (2002). Counseling Asian Americans. In P. B. Pedersen, J. G. Draguns, W. J. Lonner, & J. E. Trimble (Eds.), *Counseling across cultures* (5th ed., pp. 109–131)

Malan, D. H. (1976a). *The frontier of brief psychotherapy.* New York: Plenum.

Malan, D. H. (1976b). *Toward a validation of dynamic psychotherapy: A replication.* New York: Plenum.

Mallinckrodt, B., Gantt, D. L., & Coble, H. M. (1995). Attachment patterns in the psychotherapy relationship: Development of the

Client Attachment to Therapist Scale. *Journal of Counseling Psychology, 42,* 307–317.

Mann, J. (1973). *Time-limited psychotherapy.* Cambridge, MA: Harvard University Press.

Markus, H., & Kitayama, S. (1991). Culture and the self: Implications for cognition, emotion, and motivation. *Psychological Review, 98,* 224–253.

Martin, J., Martin, W., & Slemon, A. G. (1989). Cognitive–mediational models of action–act sequences in counseling. *Journal of Counseling Psychology, 36,* 8–16.

Marx, J. A., & Gelso, C. J. (1987). Termination of individual counseling in a university counseling center. *Journal of Counseling Psychology, 34,* 3–9.

Maslow, A. (1970). *Motivation and personality* (Rev. ed.). New York: Harper & Row.

Matarazzo, R. G., Phillips, J. S., Wiens, A. N., & Saslow, G. (1965). Learning the art of interviewing: A study of what beginning students do and their pattern of change. *Psychotherapy: Theory, Research, and Practice, 2,* 49–60.

Matsakis, A. (1998). *Managing client anger: What to do when a client is angry at you.* Oakland, CA: New Harbinger Publications.

Matsumoto, D., Kudoh, T., Sherer, K., & Wallbott, H. (1988). Antecedents of and reactions to emotions in the United States and Japan. *Journal of Cross-Cultural Psychology, 19,* 267–286.

McGoldrick, M. (Ed.). (1998). *Re-visioning family therapy: Race, culture, and gender in clinical practice.* New York: Guilford.

McGoldrick, M., Giordano, J., & Pearce, J. K. (Eds.) (1996). *Ethnicity and family therapy.* New York: Guilford.

McWhirter, E. H. (1994). *Counseling for empowerment.* Alexandria, VA: American Counseling Association.

Meador, B. D., & Rogers, C. R. (1973). Client-centered therapy. In R. Corsini (Ed.), *Current psychotherapies* (pp. 119–166). Itasca, IL: F. E. Peacock.

Meara, N. M., Schmidt, L. D., & Day, J. D. (1996). Principles and virtues: A foundation for ethical decisions, policies, and character. *The Counseling Psychologist, 24,* 4–77.

Medin, D. L., & Ross, B. H. (1992). *Cognitive psychology.* New York: Harcourt Brace Jovanovich.

Meichenbaum, D., & Turk, D. C. (1987). *Facilitating treatment adherence: A practitioner's handbook.* New York: Plenum.

Mendel, W. M. (1964). The phenomenon of interpretation. *American Journal of Psychoanalysis. 24,* 184–189.

Meyer, B., & Pilkonis, P. A. (2002). Attachment style. In J. C. Norcross (Ed.), *Psychotherapy relationships that work: Therapist contributions and responsiveness to patients* (pp. 367–382). Oxford, England: Oxford University Press.

Mickelson, D., & Stevic, R. (1971). Differential effects of facilitative and nonfacilitative behavioral counselors. *Journal of Counseling Psychology, 18,* 314–319.

Miller, J. B. (1976). *Toward a new psychology of women.* Boston: Beacon.

Miller, W. R., Benefield, R. G., & Tonigan, J. S. (1993). Enhancing motivation for change in problem drinking: A controlled comparison of two therapist styles. *Journal of Consulting and Clinical Psychology, 61,* 455–461.

Minuchin, S. (1974). *Families and family therapy.* Cambridge, MA: Harvard University Press.

Mitchell, S. A. (1993). *Hope and dread in psychoanalysis.* New York: Basic Books.

Montagu, A. (Ed.). (1971). *Touching: The significance of the human skin.* New York: Columbia University Press.

Murray, I. (Ed.). (1989). *Oscar Wilde.* Oxford, England: Oxford University Press.

Nagel, D. P., Hoffman, M. A., & Hill, C. E. (1995). A comparison of verbal response modes by master's-level career counselor and other helpers. *Journal of Counseling and Development, 74,* 101–104.

National Association for Social Workers. (1996). *NASW code of ethics.* Washington, DC: Author.

Natterson, J. M. (1993). Dreams: The gateway to consciousness. In G. Delaney (Ed.), *New directions in dream interpretation* (pp. 41–76). Albany: State University of New York Press.

Newman, C. F. (1997). Maintaining professionalism in the face of emotional abuse from clients. *Cognitive and Behavioral Practice, 4,* 1–29.

Nichols, M., & Schwartz, R. (1991). *Family therapy: Concepts and methods* (2nd ed.). Boston: Allyn & Bacon.

Nisbett, R. E., & Wilson, T. D. (1977). Telling more than we can know. *Psychological Review, 83,* 231–259.

Nutt-Williams, E., & Hill, C. E. (1996). The relationship between self-talk and therapy process variables for novice therapists. *Journal of Counseling Psychology, 43,* 170–177.

O'Farrell, M. K., Hill, C. E., & Patton, S. (1986). Comparison to two cases of counseling with the same counselor. *Journal of Counseling and Development, 65,* 141–145.

Olson, D. H., & Claiborn, C. D. (1990). Interpretation and arousal in the counseling process. *Journal of Counseling Psychology, 37,* 131–137.

O'Neil, J. M. (1981). Male sex-role conflicts, sexism, and masculinity: Psychological implications for men, women, and the counseling psychologist. *The Counseling Psychologist, 9,* 61–81.

Orlinsky, D. E., & Geller, J. D. (1993). Patients' representations of their therapists and therapy: New measures. In N. E. Miller, L. Luborsky, J. P. Barber, & J. P. Docherty (Eds.), *Psychodynamic treatment research: A handbook for psychodynamic research* (pp. 423–466). New York: Basic Books.

Orlinsky, D. E., Grawe, K., & Parks, B. K. (1994). Process and outcome in psychotherapy— Noch einmal. In A. E. Bergin & S. L. Garfield (Eds.), *Handbook of psychotherapy and behavior change* (4th ed., pp. 270–376). New York: Wiley.

Ormont, L. R. (1984). The leader's role in dealing with aggression in groups. *International Journal of Group Psychotherapy, 34,* 553–572.

Patterson, G. R., & Forgatch, M. S. (1985). Therapist behavior as a determinant for client noncompliance: A paradox for the behavior modifier. *Journal of Consulting and Clinical Psychology, 53,* 846–851.

Patton, M. J., & Meara, N. M. (1992). *Psychoanalytic counseling.* New York: Wiley.

Paul, G. L. (1969). Outcome of systematic desensitization: II. Controlled investigations of individual treatment, technique variations, and current status. In C. M. Franks (Ed.), *Behavior therapy: Appraisal and status* (pp. 105–159). New York: McGraw-Hill.

Pavlov, I. P. (1927). *Conditioned reflex: An investigation of the physiological activity of the cerebral cortex* (G. V. Anrep, Trans.). London: Oxford University Press.

Pedersen, P. B. (1991). Multiculturalism as a generic approach to counseling. *Journal of Counseling and Development, 70,* 6–12.

Pedersen, P. B. (1997). *Culture-centered counseling interventions: Striving for accuracy.* Thousand Oaks, CA: Sage.

Pedersen, P. B., Draguns, J. G., Lonner, W. J., & Trimble, J. E. (Eds.) (2002). *Counseling across cultures* (5th ed.). Thousand Oaks, CA: Sage.

Pedersen, P. B., & Ivey, A. (1993). *Culture-centered counseling and interviewing skills: A practical guide.* Westport, CT: Praeger.

Plutchik, R., Conte, H. R., & Karasu, T. B. (1994). Critical incidents in psychotherapy. *American Journal of Psychotherapy, 48,* 75–84.

Ponterotto, J. G., Casas, J. M., Suzuki, L. A., & Alexander, C. M. (Eds.). (2001). *Handbook of multicultural counseling* (2nd ed.). Thousand Oaks, CA: Sage.

Poortinga, Y. H. (1990). Toward a conceptualization of culture for psychology. *Cross-Cultural Psychology Bulletin, 24,* 2–10.

Pope, K. S. (1994). *Sexual involvement with therapists: Patient assessment, subsequent therapy, forensics.* Washington, DC: American Psychological Association.

Pope, K. S., Keith-Spiegel, P., & Tabachnick, B. (1986). Sexual attraction to clients: The human therapist and the (sometimes) inhuman training system. *American Psychologist, 41,* 147–158.

Pope, K. S., Sonne, J. L., & Holyroyd, J. (1993). *Sexual feelings in psychotherapy: Explorations for therapists and therapists-in-training.* Washington, DC: American Psychological Association.

Pope, K. S., & Tabachnick, B. (1993). Therapists' anger, hate, fear, and sexual feelings: National survey of therapists' responses, client characteristics, critical events, formal complaints, and training. *Professional Psychology: Research and practice, 24,* 142–152.

Prochaska, J. O., DiClemente, C. C., & Norcross, J. C. (1992). In search of how people change: Applications to addictive behavior. *American Psychologist, 47,* 1102–1114.

Prochaska, J. O., Norcross, J. C., & DiClemente, C. C. (1994). *Changing for good.* New York: Guilford.

Regan, A. M., & Hill, C. E. (1992). Investigation of what clients and counselors do not say in brief therapy. *Journal of Counseling Psychology, 39,* 168–174.

Reid, J. R., & Finesinger, J. E. (1952). The role of insight in psychotherapy. *American Journal of Psychiatry, 108,* 726–734.

Reik, T. (1935). *Surprise and the psychoanalyst.* London: Routledge.

Reik, T. (1948). *Listening with the third ear.* New York: Grove.

Rennie, D. L. (1994). Clients' deference in psychotherapy. *Journal of Counseling Psychology, 41,* 427–437.

Rhodes, R. H., Hill, C. E., Thompson, B. J., & Elliott, R. (1994). Client retrospective recall of resolved and unresolved misunderstanding events. *Journal of Counseling Psychology, 41,* 473–483.

Richardson, M. S. (1993). Work in people's lives: A location for counseling psychologists. *Journal of Counseling Psychology, 40,* 425–433.

Rimm, D. C., & Masters, J. C. (1979). *Behavior therapy: Techniques and empirical findings.* New York: Academic.

Robitschek, C. G., & McCarthy, P. R. (1991). Prevalence of counselor self-reference in the therapeutic dyad. *Journal of Counseling and Development, 69,* 218–221.

Rogers, C. R. (1942). *Counseling and psychotherapy.* Boston: Houghton Mifflin.

Rogers, C. R. (1951). *Client-centered therapy: Its current practice, implications, and theory.* Boston: Houghton Mifflin.

Rogers, C. R. (1957). The necessary and sufficient conditions of therapeutic personality change. *Journal of Consulting Psychology, 21,* 95–103.

Rogers, C. R. (1959). A theory of therapy, personality, and interpersonal relationships, as developed in the client-centered framework. In S. Koch (Ed.), *Psychology: A study of a science: Vol. 3. Formulations of the person and the social context* (pp. 184–256). New York: McGraw-Hill.

Rogers, C. R. (Ed.). (1967). *The therapeutic relationship and its impact: A study of psychotherapy with schizophrenics.* Madison: University of Wisconsin Press.

Rogers, C. R. (1980). *A way of being.* Boston: Houghton Mifflin.

Rogers, C. R., & Dymond, R. (1954). *Psychotherapy and personality change.* Chicago: University of Chicago Press.

Rosenthal, R., Hall, J. A., DiMatteo, M. R., Rogers, P. L., & Archer, D. (1979). *Sensitivity to nonverbal communication: The PONS Test.* Baltimore: Johns Hopkins University Press.

Safran, J. D., Muran, J. C., Samstag, L. W., & Stevens, C. (2002). Repairing alliance ruptures. In J. C. Norcross (Ed.), *Psychotherapy relationships that work: Therapist contributions and responsiveness to patients* (pp. 235–254). Oxford, England: Oxford University Press.

Salerno, M., Farber, B. A., McCullough, L., Winston, A., & Trujillo, M. (1992). The effects of confrontation and clarification on patient affective and defensive responding. *Psychotherapy Research, 2,* 181–192.

Sarason, I. G., Sarason, B. R., & Pierce, G. R. (1990). Social support: The search for theory. *Journal of Social and Clinical Psychology, 9,* 133–147.

Satir, V. M. (1988). *The new peoplemaking.* Palo Alto, CA: Science and Behavior Books.

Savickas, M. L. (1994). Vocational psychology in the postmodern era: Comment on Richardson (1993). *Journal of Counseling Psychology, 41,* 105–107.

Scheel, M. J., Seaman, S., Roach, K., Mullin, T., & Mahoney, K. B. (1999). Client implementation of therapist recommendations predicted by client perception of fit, difficulty of implementation, and therapist influence. *Journal of Counseling Psychology, 46,* 308–316.

Segall, M. H. (1979). *Cross-cultural psychology.* Monterey, CA: Brooks-Cole.

Shakespeare, W. (1980). *Macbeth* [Play]. New York: Bantam. (Original work published 1603)

Shapiro, E. G. (1984). Help-seeking: Why people don't. *Research in the Sociology of Organizations, 3,* 213–236.

Sileo, F. J., & Kopala, M. (1993). An A–B–C–D–E worksheet for promoting beneficence when considering ethical values. *Counseling and Values, 37,* 89–95.

Simon, J. C. (1988). Criteria for therapist self-disclosure. *American Journal of Psychotherapy, 42,* 404–415.

Singer, E. (1970). *New concepts in psychotherapy.* New York: Basic Books.

Skinner, B. F. (1953). *Science and human behavior.* New York: Macmillan.

Skovholt, T. M., & Rivers, D. A. (2003). *Skills and procedures of helping.* Denver, CO: Love.

Smith, M. L., Glass, G. V., & Miller, T. J. (1980). *The benefits of psychotherapy.* Baltimore: Johns Hopkins University Press.

Sommers-Flanagan, R. & Sommers-Flanagan, J. (1999). *Clinical interviewing* (2nd ed.). New York: Wiley.

Speisman, J. C. (1959). Depth of interpretation and verbal resistance in psychotherapy. *Journal of Consulting Psychology, 23,* 93–99.

Spence, D. P., Dahl, H., & Jones, E. E. (1993). Impact of interpretation on associative freedom. *Journal of Consulting and Clinical Psychology, 61,* 395–402.

Spokane, A. R. (1989). Are there psychological and mental health consequences of difficult career decisions? *Journal of Career Development, 16,* 19–23.

Stadter, M. (1996). *Object relations brief therapy: The therapeutic relationship in short-term work.* Northvale, NJ: Jason Aronson.

Stiles, W. B. (1979). Verbal response modes and psychotherapeutic technique. *Psychiatry, 42,* 49–62.

Stiles, W. B., Shapiro, D. A., & Firth-Cozens, J. (1988). Verbal response mode use in contrasting psychotherapies: A within-subjects comparison. *Journal of Consulting and Clinical Psychology, 56,* 727–733.

Strong, S. R., & Claiborn, C. D. (1982). *Change through interaction: Social psychological processes of counseling and psychotherapy.* New York: Wiley.

Strupp, H. H. (1955). An objective comparison of Rogerian and psychoanalytic techniques. *Journal of Consulting Psychology, 19*, 1–7.

Strupp, H. H. (1957). A multidimensional analysis of therapist activity in analytic and client-centered therapy. *Journal of Consulting Psychology, 21*, 301–308.

Strupp, H. H. (1996). The tripartite model and the *Consumer Reports* study. *American Psychologist, 51*, 1017–1024.

Strupp, H. H., & Binder, J. L. (1984). *Psychotherapy in a new key: A guide to time-limited dynamic psychotherapy*. New York: Basic Books.

Strupp, H. H., & Hadley, S. W. (1977). A tripartite model of mental health and therapeutic outcomes: With special reference to negative effects in psychotherapy. *American Psychologist, 32*, 187–196.

Sue, D. W., & Sue, D. (1999). *Counseling the culturally different: Theory and practice* (3rd ed.). New York: Wiley.

Sue, D., Sue, D. W., & Sue, S. (1994). *Understanding abnormal behavior* (4th ed.). Princeton, NJ: Houghton Mifflin.

Suinn, R. M. (1988). Imagery rehearsal applications to performance enhancement. *Behavior Therapist, 8*, 155–159.

Teyber, E. (2000). *Interpersonal process in psychotherapy: A relational approach* (4th ed.). Pacific Grove, CA: Brooks/Cole.

Thompson, B. J., & Hill, C. E. (1991). Therapist perceptions of client reactions. *Journal of Counseling and Development, 69*, 261–265.

Tinsley, H. E. A., de St. Aubin, T. M., & Brown, M. T. (1982). College students' help-seeking preferences. *Journal of Counseling Psychology, 29*, 523–533.

Toro, P. A. (1986). A comparison of natural and professional help. *American Journal of Community Psychology, 14*, 147–159.

Truax, C. B., & Carkhuff, R. R. (1967). *Toward effective counseling and psychotherapy*. Chicago: Aldine.

Wampold, B. E. (2001). *The great psychotherapy debate: Models, methods, and findings*. Mahwah, NJ: Erlbaum.

Wampold, B. E., Mondin, G. W., Moody, M., Stich, F., Benson, K., & Ahn, H. (1997). A meta-analysis of outcome studies comparing bona fide psychotherapies: Empirically "all must have prizes." *Psychological Bulletin, 122*, 203–215.

Ward, D. E. (1984). Termination of individual counseling: Concepts and strategies. *Journal of Counseling and Development, 63*, 21–25.

Waters, D. B., & Lawrence, E. C. (1993). *Competence, courage, and change: An approach to family therapy*. New York: Norton.

Watson, D. L., & Tharp, R. G. (2002). *Self-directed behavior: Self-modification for personal adjustment* (8th ed.). Belmont, CA: Wadsworth-Thomson.

Watson, J. B., & Rayner, R. (1920). Conditioned emotional reactions. *Journal of Experimental Psychology, 3*, 1–14.

Watzlawick, P., Weakland, J. H., & Fisch, R. (1974). *Change: Principles of problem formation and problem resolution*. New York: Norton.

Webster, D. W., & Fretz, B. R. (1978). Asian-American, Black and White college students' preference for help-giving sources. *Journal of Counseling Psychology, 25*, 124–130.

Weiss, J., Sampson, H., and the Mount Zion psychotherapy research group. (1986). *The psychoanalytic process: Theory, clinical observations, and empirical research*. New York: Guilford.

Williams, E. N., Hurley, K., O'Brien, K., & DeGregorio, A. (2003). Development and validation of the Self-Awareness and Management Stratgies (SAMS) Scales for therapists. *Psychotherapy, 40*, 278–288.

Williams, E., Judge, A., Hill, C. E., & Hoffman, M. A. (1997). Experiences of novice therapists in prepracticum: Trainees', clients', and supervisees' perceptions of therapists' personal reactions and management strategies. *Journal of Counseling Psychology, 44*, 390–399.

Wonnell, T. L., & Hill, C. E. (2002, June). *The action stage and predictors of action in dream interpretation*. Paper presented at the annual meeting of the society for psychotherapy research, Santa Barbara, CA.

Yalom, I. D. (1980). *Existential psychotherapy*. New York: Basic Books.

Yalom, I. D. (1990). *Love's executioner*. New York: Basic Books.

Yalom, I. D. (1995). *Theory and practice of group psychotherapy* (4th ed.). New York: Basic Books.

Zunker, V. G. (1994). *Career counseling: Applied concepts and life planning* (4th ed.). Pacific Grove, CA: Brooks/Cole.

Author Index

Subject Index

Olga (case example, self-disclosure of insight), 269
Omar (case example, suicide), 418
Open questions, 117–119, 189
    in action stage, 332, 335, 355, 372
    in career-concerns interaction 389
    on changing, 357
    clients' own insights from, 303
    difficulties in delivering of, 119, 123–124
    effects of, 123
    in examples of extended interaction, 196, 197, 392
    examples of proper use of, 122
    excessive use of, 124
    following clients' responses to, 190
    guidelines for, 120–123, 124–125, 301
    helpfulness of, 49–50
    in insight stage, 224–225
    lab exercise on, 127–128
    practice exercises on, 125–126
    and reflection of feelings, 189
    after self-disclosures, 278
    timing of (exploration stage), 187
    See also Exploration skills
Open stance, toward clients, 102, 104–105, 188
Operant conditioning, 327–329
Operant methods for behavior change, 364–365
Organismic valuing process (OVP), 83, 84, 85, 87, 88, 90
Overly talkative clients, 413–414
OVP (Organismic valuing process), 83, 84, 85, 87, 88, 90

Panicking, by helpers, 202
Parroting, by helper, 130, 135–136, 161
Past experiences, as source for interpretations, 251
Pause
    following client statement, 107, 152, 162, 181
    at start of session, 188
Peers, consulting with, 387
Perceptions of outcome of helping process, differences in among parties involved, 58
Perceptual distortion, 86
Performance, vs. learning, 329–330
Personal assessment, in process notes, 407
Personal experience, and lab sessions, 16–17
Personal feelings
    helpers' awareness of, 308
    See also Feelings
Personal information, client's asking for, 179–180, 274
Personality, 27
    early development as foundation of, 31
Personality development, theories of

client-centered (Rogerian), 29, 82–86, 96
    (*see also* Client-centered theory)
    psychoanalytic, 215–217 (*see also* Psychoanalytic theory and therapists)
Personality testing, 370
    referral for, 405
Personal relationships
    and helping skills, 21–22
    and immediacy, 284
    and insight stage, 31, 223
Personal space, 104
Perspective
    of helper, 223–224, 225
    of helper vs. client, 109
    See also Empathy
Phone numbers, of therapists, 402–403
Phrasing
    of interpretations, 257
    See also Grammatical style and pace of speech
Positive reinforcer, 327
Positive self-talk, 204
Posture, body, 104–105
    sitting back with legs apart, 105, 112
Powerlessness, 6
Power struggles, 339
    in example, 378
    with reluctant or resistant clients, 412
    See also Control struggles
Practice, as anxiety management, 205
Practice exercises, 15–16
Precontemplation stage (of readiness for change), 42, 43, 233, 356
Prejudice
    confronting of, 72
    understanding of, 71
Preparation stage (of readiness for change), 42, 43, 356
Preparatory strategies, 204–205
Presenting problems, 43–44
Primary reinforcers, 327
Principles of ethics, 62–64, 72
Principles of learning. *See* Learning principles
Probes, 117–119
    difficulties in delivering of, 123–124
    effects of, 123
    guidelines for using, 120–123, 124–125
    lab exrcise on, 127–128
    See also Open questions
Problematic aspects of helping, 7–8
Problems
    complexity of, 385
    identification of, 354–356
    presenting, 43–44
Problem-solving approach, xix
Problem-solving capacities, enhancement of, 323
Process advisement, 335, 343–344, 355

About the Author

Clara E. Hill earned her PhD at Southern Illinois University in 1974. She started her career as assistant professor in and is currently professor and codirector of the Counseling Psychology Program at the Department of Psychology, University of Maryland. She has been the president of the Society for Psychotherapy Research, the editor of the *Journal of Counseling Psychology*, and the winner of the Leona Tyler Award from Division 17 (Society of Counseling Psychology) and the Distinguished Psychologist Award from Division 29 (Psychotherapy) of the American Psychological Association. She is North American editor-elect of *Psychotherapy Research*, the journal of the Society for Psychotherapy Research. Her major research interests are dream work, the psychotherapy process, and training therapists in helping skills. She has published more than 120 journal articles; 20 chapters in books; and 6 books, including *Therapist Techniques and Client Outcomes: Eight Cases of Brief Psychotherapy, Working With Dreams in Psychotherapy, Helping Skills: Facilitating Exploration, Insight, and Action* (1st ed.; American Psychological Association, 1999), *Helping skills: The Empirical Foundation* (American Psychological Association, 2001), and *Dream Work in Therapy: Facilitating Exploration, Insight, and Action* (American Psychological Association, 2004).

Feedback Form

To the reader of this book:

I hope that *Helping Skills: Facilitating Exploration, Insight, and Action, Second Edition* has been useful to you in learning the helping skills. We would like to hear your feedback, so that we can improve future editions of the book. Please complete this sheet and send it to us. Thank you for your help.

Name (optional): _____

School and address: _____

_____

Department: _____

Instructor's name: _____

Name of course for which this book was used: _____

_____

1. What did you like most about this book?

2. What did you like least about this book?

3. In the space below or on a separate sheet of paper, please write specific suggestions for improving this book and anything else that you would like to write about your experience using this book and trying to learn the helping skills.

4. What is the most important or surprising thing you learned about helping skills?

Please return this form to APA Books, 750 First Street NE, Washington, DC 20002-4242.